DATE DUE FOR RETURN

~~21 JUN 1983~~	~~05 OCT 87~~	17. JUN 91
~~24 JUN 1983~~	24. JUN 1988	27 JUL 92
	24. JUL 1989	14 FEB 94
~~2 NOV 198~~	**30.** NOV 87	17 JUN 1994
21 JUN 198	**17.** DEC 87	**2 0 JAN 1995**
30-9-'85	24. JUN 1989	**27 JAN 1995**
20 JUN 1986	**25** APR 89	**0 8 MAR 1996**
12. JAN **87.**	22. JUN 1990	**2 MAR 2000**
26. JUN 1987	1981 JUN	**3 0 SEP 2005**
27. APR 87.	22. APR 91.	**1 8 FEB 2008**
27. APR **87.**	03. JUN 91.	

INTERNATIONAL ECONOMIC POLICY

International Economic Policy

Theory and Evidence

EDITED BY

Rudiger Dornbusch

AND

Jacob A. Frenkel

THE JOHNS HOPKINS UNIVERSITY PRESS

BALTIMORE AND LONDON

198150

HF141

The Johns Hopkins University Press, Baltimore, Maryland 21218
The Johns Hopkins Press Ltd., London

Library of Congress Catalog Number 78–8423
ISBN 0–8018–2132–0 (hardcover)
ISBN 0–8018–2133–9 (paperback)
Library of Congress Cataloging in Publication data will be found on the last printed
page of this book.

The chapters comprising this book were prepared for the Wingspread III Conference
on International Economic Policy: An Assessment of Theory and Evidence, Racine,
Wisconsin, July 27–30, 1977, with subsequent revisions for publication.

CONTRIBUTORS

Robert E. Baldwin, Department of Economics, University of Wisconsin

Jagdish N. Bhagwati, Department of Economics, Massachusetts Institute of Technology

John F. O. Bilson, Graduate School of Business, University of Chicago

Michael Bruno, Department of Economics, Hebrew University, Israel

Richard E. Caves, Department of Economics, Harvard University

Richard N. Cooper, Under Secretary for Economic Affairs, United States Department of State

Alan V. Deardorff, Department of Economics, University of Michigan

Wilfred Ethier, Department of Economics, University of Pennsylvania

Ray C. Fair, Department of Economics, Yale University

Koichi Hamada, Department of Economics, University of Tokyo, Japan

Ronald W. Jones, Department of Economics, University of Rochester

Richard M. Levich, Graduate School of Business, New York University

Rachel McCulloch, Department of Economics, Harvard University

Ronald I. McKinnon, Department of Economics, Stanford University

Franco Modigliani, Alfred P. Sloan School of Management and Department of Economics, Massachusetts Institute of Technology

Robert A. Mundell, Department of Economics, Columbia University

Michael Mussa, Graduate School of Business, University of Chicago

John Pomery, Department of Economics, Rice University

J. David Richardson, Department of Economics, University of Wisconsin

T. N. Srinivasan, Special Adviser, Development Research Center, The World Bank

Alexander K. Swoboda, The Graduate Institute of International Studies, Switzerland

Henry C. Wallich, Member, Board of Governors, Federal Reserve System

THIS BOOK IS DEDICATED
TO THE MEMORY OF
HARRY G. JOHNSON

Contents

Preface

This book brings together a collection of essays in the field of international economics. The essays share the common objective of assessing where trade and payments theory and policy stand after a proliferation of writing in recent years. Beyond that broad objective there are, of course, common themes. They include the special problems in trade and payments relations of developing countries, the implications for stabilization policy of world capital market integration, questions of exchange rate regimes, and the issues posed by monetary integration. While there is thus a considerable interdependence between the various contributions to this book, we have not tried to achieve an artificial coordination that would eliminate any overlap or force a synchronization of views or perspectives. On the contrary, each of the essays stands as a reasonably independent statement of a problem area and represents a scholar's critical assessment of where the field has come and where the frontiers of research lie.

In the first chapter, Jagdish N. Bhagwati and T. N. Srinivasan review some of the major issues that international trade poses for economic development. Their essay concentrates mainly on two sets of analyses that have been the focus of recent policy discussions, both theoretical and empirical. The first deals with the question of optimal trade and developing strategy for a less-developed economy that plans to accelerate its rate of economic growth. The second deals with the complementary subject of how to define the various trade opportunities. Thus, rather than being an exhaustive guide to the literature on the subject of trade and development, Bhagwati and Srinivasan provide a selective review of the major policy issues associated with the topic of international trade and development policy.

The traditional analytical framework of international trade theory relies on the assumption of pure competition. Yet, frequently, imperfect competition is called to our attention in the context of international economic policy. In the second chapter, Richard E. Caves reviews the major issues that arise when industrial organization departs from pure competition. The chapter summarizes the theory and empirical evidence relevant to governments' policy choices as exploiters of monopoly power and as enforcers of competition. Caves analyses in detail the economic considerations and the empirical evidence relevant to the creation and maintenance of international cartels. This essay also deals with the question of economic policies toward monopolies.

The third chapter, by Rachel McCulloch, is an essay on international trade and direct investment. The author identifies areas in which policy problems posed by trade and investment, or the solutions to these questions offered by international economists, have changed significantly in recent years. With this perspective, McCulloch deals with the relationships between domestic policies and international economic policy, tariffs and the distribution of income, as well as with various barriers to trade. The review of the major problems relating to direct investment deals with taxes and capital flows, with the transfer of technology, as well as with the effects of direct investment on employment and wages.

The fourth chapter, by John Pomery, is an essay on uncertainty and international trade. Pomery assesses some recent developments in the literature and integrates them into a unified conceptual framework. He classifies models according to the timing of production and trade decisions relative to the realization of random variables and according to the market structure of trade in commodities and in assets.

The essays by Bhagwati and Srinivasan, Caves, McCulloch, and Pomery cover topics that are usually classified as dealing with the "real" side of international trade. The following chapters deal with theoretical and empirical aspects of topics that deal with financial and macroeconomic issues of the open economy.

Michael Mussa, in chapter 5, reviews the theory of the transmission of macroeconomic disturbances under alternative exchange rate regimes. Mussa analyzes the extent to which monetary and fiscal policies adopted in one country generate disturbances in the rest of the world. He also examines the extent to which flexible exchange rates insulate an economy from disturbances in the rest of the world. Special attention is paid to the implications of the international mobility of capital for the transmission of disturbances and for the conduct of policy. Mussa reviews and interprets in his analysis recent developments in the field. These include exchange rate theory, the monetary approach to the balance of payments, the relationship between inflation and aggregate supply, and, finally, the special role that expectations play in the transmission of disturbances between national economics.

Side by side with the developments of the theory of interdependent economies, there has been progress in the econometric modeling of these linkages. In the sixth chapter, Ray C. Fair reviews and assesses the literature on econometric modeling. He provides a comparison of the quantitative properties of seven multicountry econometric models and presents a "quasi-empirical" two-country model. That model is constructed by linking Fair's econometric model of the United States to a second economy with assumed identical structure. One of the major limitations of the existing econometric models remains the treatment of capital flows and exchange rates that by and large are taken to be exogenous. Fair concludes his review by suggesting some econometric modeling improvements for a small, multicountry model.

The seventh chapter, by Richard M. Levich, is a review of the theory and empirical evidence on the efficiency of the markets for foreign exchange. Levich outlines the essential elements of the efficient market hypothesis and highlights some of the difficulties in the empirical testing of the hypothesis. His analysis covers both the spot and forward markets for foreign exchange.

Much of the theoretical and empirical literature on macroeconomics of the open economy deals with industrial developed economies. Some of the policy prescriptions that are appropriate for such countries, however, may be inappropriate when applied to a developing semi-industrialized economy. The eighth chapter, by Michael Bruno, contains a review of the major policy issues that are relevant for the analysis of stabilization policies for semi-industrialized economies. Among the major characteristics of such economies are low income per head, small economic size, high dependence on imports of machinery, large structural trade deficits, a fiscal base that is dominated by indirect taxation, and an underdeveloped system of financial intermediation. Bruno's analysis highlights the constraints imposed on various macroeconomic adjustment policies by their possible side effects on inflation and unemployment, and he demonstrates that the existence of a segmented credit market imposes a severe limitation on monetary management.

The increased degree of interdependence raises the important question of harmonization and coordination of macroeconomic policies among the various interdependent economies. In the ninth chapter, Koichi Hamada reviews and assesses the theoretical literature and the empirical evidence concerning the nature of international interdependence, the rationale for policy coordination, the various methods for coordination and policy interaction under fixed and flexible exchange rate regimes. Hamada concludes the chapter by extending the analytical framework to a regime of managed floating.

The various essays are followed by comments that extend, criticize, or complement the analysis. The last chapter contains statements by Richard N. Cooper, Ronald I. McKinnon, Franco Modigliani, Robert A. Mundell, and Henry C. Wallich, on Problems and Prospects for the World Economy.

In concluding, we have the pleasant task of thanking those who have made this book possible. We are indebted to the Johnson Foundation, our generous host at Wingspread, not only for an unrivaled atmosphere for the conference at which the papers were first presented but also for financial support. The Norman Wait Harris Foundation at the University of Chicago and the Center for International Economics at the Graduate School of Business of the University of Chicago provided generous grants that are gratefully acknowledged. We owe a special debt to Robert Z. Aliber and Bert Hoselitz of the University of Chicago and to Henry Halsted, Kay Mauer, and Leslie Paffrath of the Johnson Foundation for their interest in this project and their help in making it possible. Our final thanks go to Nancy Middleton Gallienne of the Johns Hopkins University Press and Melanie Lau for their help in the preparation of the book.

Cambridge, Mass. and Chicago, Ill.
RUDIGER DORNBUSCH
JACOB A. FRENKEL

INTERNATIONAL ECONOMIC POLICY

CHAPTER ONE

Trade Policy and Development

JAGDISH N. BHAGWATI
T. N. SRINIVASAN

The interaction between international trade and development is a subject of such complexity and importance that it has rarely ceased to attract the attention of economic theorists, analysts of the world economy, and designers of the international economic system. Inevitably, therefore, it has drawn into its fold and its many controversies some of the best minds of each generation of economists: dating from Adam Smith, David Ricardo, and John Stuart Mill, down to Alfred Marshall and, in our own times, to Dennis Robertson, Ragnar Nurkse, Jacob Viner, Gottfried Haberler, and Arthur Lewis.[1]

There are far too many questions that the topic raises: witness, for example, the elegant recent review by Carlos Diaz-Alejandro.[2] We propose rather to concentrate on two sets of analyses that have currently been the focal point of theoretical, empirical, and policy discussions.

In Section I, we review the evidence that is currently available on the question that Nurkse had raised in the early 1950s regarding the optimal trade and developmental strategy for a postwar LDC (less developed country) planning to accelerate its economic growth. Arguing that the nineteenth-century mechanism of trade as "an engine of growth" (in Dennis Robertson's catching phrase) was not available to present-day LDCs for a number of reasons, he noted that a policy of "balanced growth," reflecting essentially domestic demands, was inevitable. Remarkably, he did contrast this, what we would today describe as an IS (import substitution) strategy, with the policy alternative of promoting new, manufactured exports, *à la* what we would today call the EP (export promoting) strategy:

[1] Cf., in particular, Jacob Viner (1953), Ragnar Nurkse (1959), Gottfried Haberler (1959), and W. Arthur Lewis (1969).

[2] Carlos Diaz-Alejandro (1975).

The views expressed in this paper are personal and do not reflect those of the institutions to which the authors are affiliated. Thanks are due to the National Science Foundation (Grant No. SOC77-07188) for partially supporting the research underlying this paper. Section I draws on earlier work for UNCTAD.

1

but felt that the latter offered little promise, as it was likely to run into DC market disruption-related trade restraints, as with textiles. As it happens, the postwar period did witness both sets of policies, starting in the early 1960s, and we have the evidence of two major projects on these issues so that we can, with hindsight, see which strategy was the more successful ex post. Our analysis will not merely review these empirical results, it will also indicate the unsettled questions on which only future research can generate persuasive evidence.

Therefore, while Section I focuses principally on the trade policies of LDCs, in regard to the optimal methods of utilizing the available trade opportunities, we turn in Section II to the complementary subject of how those trade opportunities ought to be defined. In particular, we will consider two subjects of recent policy interest, namely, (i) the theoretical and policy issues raised by the problem of market disruption-related threats of trade restrictions on imports of manufactures by DCs; and (ii) the recent demands by LDCs, as part of the New International Economic Order (NIEO), for commodity agreements.

The reader should be forewarned that this chapter is therefore a selective review of the major trade-and-developmental policy issues; it is certainly not intended to be an exhaustive guide to the voluminous literature on the subject.[3]

I. PROTECTION, INDUSTRIALIZATION, EXPORT PERFORMANCE, AND ECONOMIC DEVELOPMENT

We turn now to the "foreign trade strategy" issues that were admirably, and with much prescience, raised by Ragnar Nurkse.[4] Cairncross, in an insightful review of Nurkse and Haberler, having reviewed the general argumentation couched in terms of trends in world trade and whether these justified elasticity pessimism or optimism and whether these in turn required balanced growth or not, summed up as follows:[5]

At the end of it all, the reader may still feel that neither Nurkse nor Haberler has settled the primary issue: how far a shortage of foreign exchange (contrasted with capital, skilled labour, land, etc.) is a limiting factor in economic development. The majority of the under-developed countries are monocultures, dependent for their earnings of foreign exchange on a single commodity (or at most two or three). These earnings are highly inelastic except when exports of the principal commodity form a small fraction of the world's consumption. At the same time, nearly all the plant and machinery that they require has to be imported, so that the scale of industrial investment is limited by the foreign

[3] The many distinguished researchers whose contributions are not noted explicitly should equally take note of this fact!
[4] This section draws heavily on J. Bhagwati (1976).
[5] Cf. A. K. Cairncross (1960, chap. 12, p. 208).

exchange available to pay for it. In those circumstances, what should be the policy of a country seeking to accelerate its development? We know what most countries have done; it would be interesting if we could be told, by an economist of the standing or Nurkse or Haberler, what the results have been and what they should have done.

Modesty should prevent us from laying claim to the "standing of Nurkse or Haberler." However, we are certainly now in a position to respond to Cairncross's query, thanks principally (though not exclusively) to two major projects on foreign trade regimes and their effects on economic development: the OECD project, directed by Ian Little, Tibor Scitovsky, and Maurice Scott, whose results have been known since the early 1970s; and the NBER project, directed by Jagdish Bhagwati and Anne Krueger, whose results have now become generally available.[6]

In particular, we now have statistical evidence and economic argumentation on the following, related issues: (i) The degree and structure of protection that have been practiced in the developing countries; (ii) The analytical rationale for relating this to the pattern of industrialization and export performance of these developing countries via the effect on the relative incentives for import substitution and export promotion; (iii) The statistical evidence for the argument that such incentives affect the pattern of industrialization and export performance in the developing countries; and (iv) The question whether, and if so why, better export performance is related to better economic performance.

A. The degree and structure of protection: Concepts

In analyzing protection, one needs to distinguish among three sets of concepts: (i) Trade policy protection versus domestic policy protection:

[6] The Organization for Economic Cooperation and Development (OECD) project (organized by the OECD Development Center) covered Brazil, India, Mexico, Pakistan, the Philippines, and Taiwan; whereas the NBER project covered ten countries: Brazil, Chile, Colombia, Egypt, Ghana, India, Israel, the Philippines, South Korea, and Turkey. The NBER project (National Bureau of Economic Research [1975, 1976]) essentially takes off from the OECD project, in extending the analysis to much more systematic attention to the exchange-control aspects of the foreign trade regimes in the developing countries; it also considers dynamic aspects of the trade regimes and the problems of trade liberalization. The OECD studies (Organization for Economic Cooperation and Development [1970]) have been published in five country volumes and one overall volume: (1) Little, Scitovsky, and Scott (1970), overall; (2) Bergsman (1970), Brazil; (3) Bhagwati and Desai (1970), India; (4) Lewis (1970), Pakistan; (5) Hsing, Power, and Sicat (1970), Taiwan and the Philippines; and (6) King (1970), Mexico. The NBER studies are being published in ten-country volumes and two synthesis volumes; the following are already published: (1) Krueger (1970), Turkey; (2) Michaely (1975), Israel; (3) Baldwin (1975), the Philippines; (4) Leith (1975), Ghana; (5) Frank, Westphal, and Kim (1975), South Korea; (6) Bhagwati and Srinivasan (1975), India; (7) Hansen and Nashashibi (1975), Egypt; (8) Diaz-Alejandro (1976), Colombia; and (9) Behrman (1976), Chile. Bhagwati (1978) and Krueger (1978) have written two separate synthesis volumes, focusing on different parts of the project results.

an activity may be protected through tariffs and quotas (QRs), on the one hand, or through domestic subsidies, etc., on the other hand;[7] (ii) Tariffs versus quota protection, or alternatively, explicit versus implicit protection: within trade policy, we can distinguish between protection furnished by tariffs or by QRs; in turn, QRs may be specifically designed for protecting the activity in question or they may be a result of an overvalued exchange rate that results in the use of QRs as a technique for balancing international accounts; and (iii) nominal versus effective protection: the protection may be measured in the conventional way as on goods and services (i.e., as nominal rates) or on value added (i.e., as effective rates).

It is clear from these conceptual distinctions that, in examining protection, the international economist aims at comparing the total structure of incentives (to import-competing and other activities) as contrasted with those that would be provided under a regime of *laissez faire*, or what has been more aptly described as a regime of unified exchange rates.[8] Thus, the incentives for domestic import substitutes that would follow from over-valued exchange rates, and the attendant implicit tariffs implied by QRs, must be allowed for; and so must the use of domestic subsidies, in several forms, to domestic production. The early studies of protection in the LDCs allowed for neither the use of QRs nor the presence of domestic taxes and subsidies.[9] However, the well known IBRD (International Bank for Reconstruction and Development) studies,[10] as also the NBER studies, typically attempt to allow for implicit tariffs (i.e., QRs) and, occasionally and partially, for indirect taxes insofar as they affect domestic prices of inputs or differently affect import substitutes and imports.

The use of implicit tariffs involves, typically, the conversion of import premium data or, alternatively, data on differentials between domestic and c.i.f. prices of comparable items into equivalent tariffs. This procedure is subject to both empirical and conceptual difficulties, a few of which may be mentioned here:[11] (i) quality differences exist between imports and import substitutes, which imply that some of the differential in prices, when used for estimation, is attributable to this factor; (ii) frequently the QR regime may be so restrictive that imports are prohibited and there is, in consequence, often no easy and reliable way to get comparable c.i.f. prices;

---

[7] The choice between these alternative instruments of protection has, of course, been the subject matter of contributions by Meade, Bhagwati, Ramaswami, Srinivasan, Corden, Johnson, and other theorists of trade policy. We do not discuss these issues here.

[8] This phrasing was used in Bhagwati (1968).

[9] This was true of the early estimates for Pakistan, for example, by Soligo and Stern (1965).

[10] Cf. Balassa and Associates (1971).

[11] Cf. the treatment in Balassa (1971, chap. 3); also consult Bhagwati (1978, chap. 5) for a more detailed discussion.

(iii) if perfect competition in quota allocation and use, and in foreign and domestic supply and demand, cannot be assumed, the import premium cannot be meaningfully converted in general into an equivalent implicit tariff; (iv) where domestic licensing contributes to the generation of monopoly profits, the import premium will reflect this factor as well and hence is not interpretable as protection from the viewpoint of inferring resource allocational shifts; (v) in the nature of the case, QRs will be, and are, associated with fluctuating premiums, so that it is extremely difficult to arrive at one set of premiums to convert into implicit tariffs, and totally misleading to use one such set to indicate the tariff structure (which is to be taken, in turn, to indicate the structure of price incentives to domestic protection).

Given these, and other, serious shortcomings, it is best to treat the resulting estimates of the implicit tariff structure as descriptions, in varying degrees of loose approximation, of the pattern of incentives that may be appearing in the developing countries in question, thanks to QRs.[12]

Similarly, the description of the tariff structure in effective tariff, as distinct from nominal tariff, terms raises both conceptual and empirical questions.[13] In particular, it is not possible to utilize the computed effective tariff rates to indicate in an unambiguous fashion the direction of change in resource allocation that is resulting from the set of nominal tariffs that we use to compute the effective tariffs.[14]

In light of these problems, it is best perhaps to regard the effective tariff structures that have been estimated in the OECD, NBER, and IBRD studies, among many others, as also essentially descriptions that, in a very loose way, indicate the differential nature of incentives that the combination of tariffs, QRs and (in some instances) domestic subsidies and taxes seem to throw up in the economy being studied.

While the tariff structures are defined and estimated in the manner indicated above, and must be interpreted with great caution, the concept of

---

[12] In some of the studies, the protection granted is broken down into that resulting from explicit tariffs and the additional element due to QRs, when the implicit tariffs exceed the explicit tariffs. Cf. the Bhagwati–Desai–Panchamukhi estimates in the OECD India volume (1970), and the Leith estimates in the NBER Ghana volume (1975).

[13] For a detailed consideration of the empirical questions, see Balassa (1971, chaps. 3 and 4); for conceptual problems, see in particular the contributions by Bruno (1973) and Bhagwati and Srinivasan (1973), to the "Journal of International Economics Symposium on the Theory of Effective Protection in General Equilibrium" (1973).

[14] This point has been established, and sufficient conditions under which the direction of change in resource allocation may nonetheless be inferred, investigated, by international trade theorists recently. A good starting point for reading this literature is in the "Journal of International Economics Symposium on the Theory of Effective Protection in General Equilibrium" (1973). The statistical evidence on this question, discussed in the text above, also corroborates this theoretical skepticism, while indicating a few of the reasons for it. For fuller discussion, see Bhagwati (1978, chap. 5).

the degree of protection reflects essentially a weighted average of such tariffs.[15] In addition to such averages, some economists have also attempted to adjust the average degree of protection downward by arguing that the removal of the tariffs would generally generate a balance-of-payments deficit that would have to be eliminated by devaluing the exchange rate. The devaluation, in turn, would imply that the domestic price of the imported commodities would fall by less than the tariff removal would imply.[16] While this is a theoretically correct thing to do, if one is interested in what happens (net) to the nominal domestic price of importables as a result of the tariff imposition,[17] the practical estimation of this adjustment factor, as attempted in several of the IBRD studies, relies on procedures that can be defended only by making highly restrictive assumptions.[18]

Finally, in anticipation of the analysis in Subsection D on the interaction between protection and export performance, it may be noted that the degree of protection is often taken as a reasonable explanatory variable for export performance. Additionally, three other concepts are used frequently as explanatory variables in analyzing export performance, two relating in some fashion to protection in the broad sense defined above. First, the ratio of the effective exchange rate on exports (EER_x) to that on imports (EER_m) is taken as an index of how far the average exports are profitable relative to average import-competing production.[19] Second,

[15] The nominal tariffs may be weighted by shares in imports or in domestic production; effective tariffs may be weighted by shares in nominal value added of the activities in question.

[16] Thus a removal of an average tariff of 50 percent, resulting in a devaluation of 20 percent, would imply a net, adjusted average tariff of 30 percent; the domestic, nominal price of the imported items would fall only by 30 percent when the tariffs were removed and the balance-of-payments position left unchanged.

[17] Note that it would require, even in theory, special restrictions to infer from such a (net) effect on the average domestic (nominal) price of importables that, for example, the share of trade in national income is reduced by such a tariff.

[18] Cf. Balassa (1971, Appendix 3) for the specification of the procedures used, and an excellent theoretical survey of them in Dornbusch (1974). Aside from the theoretical objections, spelled out by Dornbusch, one might note also the general inconsistency between using less than infinitely elastic foreign elasticities of demand for exports to compute exchange rate change and constant international prices for computing effective protection (as required by the fact that the general equilibrium analyses of effective protection in the available literature universally make the assumption of constant international prices).

[19] The effective exchange rate on exports is defined as the units of domestic currency that can be obtained for a dollar's worth of exports, taking into account export duties, subsidies and surcharges, special exchange rates, input subsidies related to exports, etc. The effective exchange rate on imports (EER_m) is correspondingly defined as the units of domestic currency that would be paid for a dollar's worth of imports, taking into account tariffs, surcharges, interest on advance deposits, etc. In principle, the EER_m should include premia on import licenses; however, in the NBER studies, the EER_m was defined exclusive of them, for the simple reason that for many countries no reliable data on import premia could be obtained either directly or via suitable surveys of c.i.f. and retail prices. As stated later, the ratio EER_x/EER_m as an index of export bias dates back to before even the OECD project studies and was used, without detailed quantification, in Bhagwati (1968).

for any one activity, the effective tariff rate as applicable to production for domestic sales may be compared with the effective tariff rate as applicable to exports and the ratio thereof, when exceeding unity, would be described as the "export bias" characterizing that activity.[20] But, if the EER_x and EER_m are defined (as they were traditionally in the 1960s in India) as including the incentives and disincentives on outputs as also those related to inputs,[21] then the definition of export bias as the ratio of effective tariffs in export and domestic markets is identical with the better-known and earlier definition of export bias in terms of the ratio EER_x/EER_m.[22] Third, we may note the concept of real effective exchange rates, or what the NBER project calls the price-level deflated effective exchange rates (*PLDEER*s). In contrast to the EER_x/EER_m ratio, the $PLDEER_x$ would show the relative price of the exportables to home goods (as distinct from importables) and hence capture a different element of the total picture regarding incentives to produce for exports. Furthermore, the NBER project utilized, in some studies, the concept of purchasing-power parity effective exchange rates, *PPPEER*s, which adjust also for changes in the foreign price level.

We shall return to these concepts when we examine the relationship of protection with export performance. For the present, it is important to distinguish broadly between two basic implications of any observed tariff structure: (i) the import-competing activities are being, broadly speaking, encouraged relative to what the absence of protection would imply: this is what might be called the "degree of import substitution" aspect of the protective structure; and (ii) there are (usually) differential tariffs on, and therefore differential incentives to, different activities within the import-competing sectors: this is what could be called the "pattern of import substitution" aspect of the protective structure.[23] In an approximate fashion, we can then argue that the degree-of-protection concept corresponds to

[20] This concept was used in the International Bank for Reconstruction and Development (IBRD) studies and is used in the South Korean study of the NBER project; it was not used in the OECD project at all. However, as noted below, it reduces in effect to the (properly defined) ratio of EER_x/EER_m in any case.

[21] Thus, for example, exporters in India typically receive imported materials at international prices, so that EER_x is defined as inclusive of the implied subsidy from this scheme. See Bhagwati and Srinivasan (1975), for example.

[22] This is seen readily by stating that, for the usual notation, export bias under the former concept amounts to:

$$\frac{t_j{}^x - \Sigma_{aij}{}^x}{t_j{}^d - \Sigma_{aij}} < 1$$

where the superscripts x and d relate to export and domestic markets respectively, and the latter amounts to:

$$1 + (t_j{}^x - t_j{}^d) + \Sigma_{aij}(t_i{}^d - t_i{}^x) < 1.$$

[23] The terminology of degree and pattern of import substitution was introduced in Bhagwati (1972).

the degree of import-substitution aspect, and the structure-of-protection concept corresponds to the pattern of import-substitution aspect, of the process of economic expansion and, in effect, of industrialization in the LDCs.

In the rest of this section we will essentially deal with both these aspects: Subsection C will consider the pattern of import substitution; whereas Subsection D, in considering export performance, will simultaneously imply consideration of the question of the degree of import substitution. Prior to these analyses, however, a brief review of the empirical studies on the degree and structure of protection is presented in the next Subsection B.

B. The degree and structure of protection: Evidence

Although both the OECD and NBER projects contain, within their more ambitious and wide-ranging framework, estimates of the protective structure, the best-known and standardized estimates for a set of developing countries are to be found in the six IBRD studies for Brazil, Chile, Malaya, Mexico, Pakistan, and the Philippines.[24]

Essentially, these estimates relate to specific dates, typically deploy the effective tariff concept, and utilize implicit tariff estimates (based largely on estimated differentials between foreign and domestic prices of imports). Net protection estimates (adjusting for exchange rate change) are also included. The studies also proceed to present effective protection by export and domestic markets, so that export bias, so defined, is also typically estimated by the authors.

The IBRD studies indicated that the manufacturing sector was protected, relative to the primary sector in nearly all the countries in question and, in the case of Chile and Philippines, the average tariff rate for manufacturing was fairly sizable.

The OECD synthesis volume by Little, Scitovsky, and Scott also contained estimates of average tariff levels for manufactures that indicated again that the degree of protection used for manufactures by developing countries was extremely high: protection being defined as nominal, explicit

[24] The OECD and NBER studies offered much more comprehensive and detailed analyses of the countries being studied than the IBRD study. In particular, most of the NBER volumes examined export performance in depth, systematically analyzed the evolution of the exchange-control regime over time, examined fully the conditions determining the outcomes of liberalization attempts (including political factors plus the role of foreign aid, etc.) and attempted (in some cases) more systematic examination of dynamic arguments relating to investment, innovation, savings formation, etc. and their interaction with the foreign trade regime. In all these respects, the NBER studies were, for the most part, more comprehensive and ambitious than other efforts, such as, for example, the IBRD project, though the latter did touch marginally on some of the issues (e.g., Balassa's brief treatment of "dynamic" effects in his introductory essays, relating however mainly to static, scale economies and competition aspects). The relationship between the NBER and the OECD projects, which were both ambitious, has been spelled out above.

tariffs alone. By contrast, they argued that most of the present DCs had used substantially lower tariffs in the course of their development.[25] This contrast was sustained by examination of the effective tariffs as well.

While the OECD project did note the "variability of protection" to different manufacturing activities, the main focus of the NBER studies has been precisely on this aspect of the overall foreign trade regime. Thus, while stressing the many difficulties in interpreting the structure of protection, the estimates were used to underline the differential-incentives-generating nature of the regime, while stressing equally the administrative-cum-allocational procedures that led to automaticity of protection, fluctuating incentives through varying import premia reflecting changing allocations and rules, and numerous other facets without whose adequate understanding the analyst of the effects of tariff structures would be making, at best, misleading inferences.[26] While using the estimated tariffs on several manufacturing activities (and, in the case of Egypt, for agricultural crops as well)[27] to show the wide dispersion in the implied incentives, the NBER project also utilized concepts and measures such as domestic resource costs (DRCs) to indicate rather the varying social rates of return to production in alternative manufacturing activities.[28]

The major conclusion of the NBER studies is that the protective structure, when inclusive of the implicit tariffs (implied by QRs) under exchange controls, is characterized by considerable dispersion and unpredictability, and that the effects are to create resource misallocation whose incidence is indicated by the DRC-dispersion observed in the empirical studies.[29]

C. Protection and pattern of industrialization

The effect of the structure of protection on the pattern of industrialization may first be noted, before proceeding to consider the effect of the degree and pattern of such protection on export performance.

[25] Cf. Little, Scitovsky, and Scott (1970, chap. 5). It should be added, however, that an unpublished NBER project-commissioned examination of Japanese tariff protection during the period of early industrialization, by Ippei Yamazawa, suggests a substantially greater role of tariffs, and other forms of protection, than the Little–Scitovsky–Scott figure indicates for Japan.

[26] For details, see Bhagwati (1978, chap. 5).

[27] Cf. Hansen and Nashashibi (1975) on Egypt.

[28] Of course, if shadow prices for domestic factors, and marginal revenues for commodities facing declining prices as exports increase, are not used to calculate DRCs, they can be reduced by a simple transformation to effective rates of protection.

[29] The stress on dispersion of incentives is to be found particularly in Leith's NBER Ghana volume (1975) and in Bhagwati and Srinivasan's NBER India volume (1975), and is spelled out overall in Bhagwati's NBER synthesis volume (1978, chap. 5). Balassa (1971) also stresses the variability of incentives in the tariff structure but needs to pay the same degree of attention to interpreting it in light of the unpredictability, built-in automaticity of future protection, and other integral aspects of QR regimes that define the context, and hence the true meaning, of these tariff estimates. More is said on this in the next subsection.

While it is true in reality that protection of the manufacturing sector, *in toto*, is supportive of industrialization in the LDCs, it should be noted that it does not follow that the pattern of manufacturing production, or import substitution, also is explainable by the pattern of protection that is being measured for the LDCs. Thus, it is tempting to argue that industries when arrayed in ascending order by their (effective or nominal) protective rates should also be ranked in ascending order by their growth rates, or their import-substitution ratios. But there is neither analytical, nor clear empirical, support for such a hypothesis; and, in fact, it is encouraging that where theory suggests there should be no such correlation, there is mixed evidence to be found in practice as well.

Among the favorable results for the hypothesis stated is that for Colombia. Thus, in the NBER study of Colombia, Carlos Diaz-Alejandro cites the earlier work of Hutcheson on Colombian protection that regresses growth rates successfully on effective protective rates.[30]

Similarly, Frank et al., in the NBER study on South Korea, report on rank correlation coefficients between various measures of effective protection, and of effective incentives (defined so as to include the effects of tax rebates, credit preferences, and such incentives) and resource-allocational indices such as import-substitution ratios (or export shares for export industries) and growth contribution.[31] Their results, however, are generally poor on the import side: the correlation between import ratios and effective incentives is significant and positive, suggesting that import substitution had progressed the least [rather than the most] in those sectors that had a high level of effective incentives on domestic sales, and the correlations between effective incentives to domestic sales and growth contributions are not significant, though they are negative.[32]

Additional cross-sectional analysis of this variety was also conducted by Jere Behrman in his NBER study of Chile, to determine whether the price structures created by the international economic regimes were associated with growth across sectors.[33] He found a positive relation between growth in value-added and in horsepower capacity between 1961 and 1967 and the implicit tariff rates (ITRs) for 1967 and also for the incremental ITRs between 1961 and 1967. But this relationship has little plausibility, as Behrman notes, and may be rationalized only by argument, such as that the ITRs "perhaps . . . served as signals, however, of the

---

[30] The Hutcheson estimates of effective protection use the early Balassa method for treating nontraded goods as enjoying zero protection rather than as value added *à la* Corden. Note, however, that in the case of Chile, at least, the distinction between the two measures is not empirically important. Cf. Behrman (1976) on Chile.

[31] Frank, Westphal, and Kim (1975, chap. 10) on South Korea.

[32] Ibid. (1975, chap. 10, p. 36).

[33] Cf. Behrman (1976, chap. 12) on Chile, for full details of this analysis.

government's intentions to favor particular sub-sectors."[34] Interestingly, Behrman found no evidence for a link between effective rates of protection and growth: in fact, the only significant nonzero correlation coefficient, using alternative estimates, was a negative one between effective rates and growth in production from 1953 to 1961.[35]

Going beyond the NBER studies, furthermore, we may note two successful sets of regressions: for Pakistan by Guisinger[36] and for Nigeria by Oyejide.[37] The Pakistani analysis was unsuccessful for import-substitution ratios, but successful for growth rates for a 23-industry study. The Nigerian analysis, for 42 industries, resulted in successful regressions of import-substitution ratios on effective rates of protection and changes therein.

While, therefore, the results for the different countries are fairly mixed, we also need to note that the construction of a theoretical rationale for a successful regression of import-substitution ratios or growth rates in cross-section analysis is difficult, and one may reasonably expect to find no relationships of the kinds postulated. It should be useful to spell out why this is so, taking the import-substitution ratio as the dependent variable and effective tariffs as the independent variable.

i) To begin with, effective tariffs being the independent variable, a basic difficulty arises. The effect on the import-substitution (production-to-total-supply) ratio is not uniquely determined by the effective tariff: for the same effective tariff is compatible with different combinations of nominal tariffs on output and inputs and hence with different effects on production and consumption of the output. Therefore, even if the partial-equilibrium, supply-and-demand curves were identical across the industries, the relationship postulated would not follow unless the input-output structure and the structure of nominal tariffs on each industry's outputs and inputs were identical.

ii) Once we go beyond partial into general-equilibrium analysis, furthermore, the hypothesis refuses to hold up for the further reason that the theory of general equilibrium tells us unhappily that, in an n-output $(n>2)$ economy, if more than one price changes, the direction of individual output changes cannot be predicted from this fact alone: one really has to work out the full general-equilibrium solution.[38] This nihilistic conclusion carries

[34] Ibid. (1975, chap. 12).

[35] Nor, for that matter, did Behrman manage to find any significant association between DRCs and growth indicates.

[36] Guisinger (1971).

[37] T. A. Oyejide (1971).

[38] One may further be tempted to infer (as we did in the Conference paper) that, if there are n (>2) different tariffs, resulting in n prices changing, there is no theoretical presumption at all for asserting that the changes in the n activities' outputs will be *correlated* with the n tariffs. However, as noted by Alan Deardorff in his *Comment*, this would be an invalid inference.

over, of course, to a general equilibrium model with imported inputs as well.[39]

iii) Finally, while the analytical points made above relate to the effects of the tariffs vis-à-vis the free trade situation, with given resources, the exercises testing the postulated hypothesis relate often to a situation of growing resources. But, in this event, there is even less presumption theoretically in support of the hypothesis.[40]

Thus, even within the confines of conventional economic theory, one would have serious difficulties with the hypothesis that higher effective tariffs lead to higher import-substitution ratios on a cross-sectional basis. In the context of actual developing countries, these difficulties are accentuated indeed. For example, the growth of industries is likely to reflect industrial licensing and targeting; and, as noted below in the context of QRs, anticipation of tariff protection, as distinct from initial protection, once the industry has built up to size leading to an effective political pressure group,[41] may be quite important in determining growth incentives.

In fact, we must recognize many additional difficulties, specific to exchange control regimes, (where QRs typically may dominate tariffs), with the notion that observed protective structures will tell the analyst anything terribly conclusive about growth incentives. In particular, an important

---

[39] In fact, for predicting output changes (as one must be, if one's interest is in the import substitution ratio), as distinct from "value-added" changes, in models with imported inputs, the effective protection measures run into trouble even if we confine ourselves to *two* goods. This problem was first raised by V. K. Ramaswami and T. N. Srinivasan (1971) and is extensively analyzed in the contributions of Bruno (1973) and Bhagwati and Srinivasan (1973) to the "Journal of International Economics Symposium" (1973).

[40] Thus, take a simple two-sector example, using the standard two-by-two model of trade theory. We know from Rybczynski's theorem that the supply curves of the two commodities will shift differentially rather than identically, so that even if the supply curves were identical in the initial situation across activities, they would cease to be so with economic expansion (unless all factors expanded uniformly). And hence any effect of the tariff structure on the import-substitution ratio would be "muddied" by this additional growth effect. This is clearly a pertinent point when one is relating the import ratios for 1967, for example, to effective protection in 1962 (as in the Nigerian exercise reported above): a period over which the capital stock may have increased by nearly 30 percent (assuming a capital-output ratio of 3:1 and an average savings rate of 15 percent of GNP), and hence certainly in excess of the labor force.

[41] Thus, the causal relationship may well run from the growth and size of an industry to the magnitude of its tariff protection. In fact, it is only recently that economists have begun to concern themselves with the question of why tariff structures are what they are, as distinct from what they should be. At an institutional-analytical level, the work of Padma Desai on the criteria used by the Indian Tariff Commission in granting tariff protection represents one approach of interest and importance (cf. Desai 1970). At a statistical-econometric level, the work of Basevi (1966) on examining the factor intensity of protected industries in the United States represents a different, and equally useful, approach; for an interesting analysis of the relationship between the labor force characteristics of an industry and the degree of exemption secured by it from the across-the-board 50 percent tariff cut in the Kennedy Round, see Cheh (1974).

fact is that many developing countries have operated with rules of "automaticity" in protection: QRs were used to grant protection as soon as domestic production was started. Once this "institutional" feature of the system is taken into account, it is easy to see that any observed (implicit) tariff structure fails to incorporate the incentive effects of guaranteed, "potential" tariff protection, which is clearly a significant factor on the scene. More precisely, we should not expect the resource-allocational effects of n prespecified tariffs to be identical with the effects of a process of tariff-imposition that is characterized by automatic protection to any potential activity, the degree of protection, in turn, being expected by potential investors with uncertainty regarding its precise extent (this, in turn, being dependent largely on the restrictiveness of the foreign exchange situation), and which process winds up with the n observed tariffs in place.

It is for this set of reasons that the notion of relating tariffs, effective or nominal, to the pattern of industrial expansion—no matter how measured—seems to be lacking in sufficient rationale, especially for countries with restrictive exchange-control regimes: as, indeed, several developing countries have been for the bulk of the postwar period. This may well account for the mixed nature of the statistical results reported in this section.

On balance, therefore, we should be content to take the view, admittedly less ambitious, that the differential tariff structure among different activities merely indicates, very broadly indeed, the differential nature of the incentives that exchange-control regimes in developing countries tend to generate: a conclusion that, in itself, is sufficiently interesting and important.

Next, we may note, in this context, that the differential nature of the incentives, as indicated by the differential rates of protection to different manufacturing activities, can be shown rather to result simultaneously in differential social returns from the allocation of resources in producing these alternative items. This can be done qualitatively by showing how the actual allocational criteria used for making production and investment decisions, whether through the use of QRs or through the use of domestic licensing or via both sets of instruments (as in India and Pakistan), can hardly be expected to yield anything like an economically rational allocation of resources.[42] Quantitatively, it can be done by doing sophisticated cost-benefit analysis on a number of different activities, thereby showing the differential social returns resulting from different activities encouraged (or enabled to exist) by the entire framework of protection. It can also be done by using somewhat rough-and-ready calculations, such as those implied by DRC estimates, of the kind deployed in the NBER studies, which essentially use "illustrative" shadow prices and arrive at notions of

[42] This, in fact, was done in the India study of the OECD (Bhagwati and Desai 1970) and was also the reason for the analytical focus on methods of exchange control in the NBER studies.

differential returns produced by different activities by estimating the foreign exchange that the same value of domestic, primary factors is producing in alternative activities. Primarily using the DRC method therefore as a rough device for estimating social returns, the NBER project does show the wide variations that obtain in the restrictive foreign trade regimes that have been deployed in the LDCs studied under the project.[43]

Finally, note that the NBER studies explicitly extend the analysis of the economic consequences of protection, as generated by restrictive foreign trade regimes, to issues such as underutilization of capacity, excessive inventory holdings, etc., with findings generally adverse to the case of those who favor the use of restrictive trade regimes. They also investigate the dynamic aspects of foreign trade regimes quite explicitly, examining the effects on domestic savings formation, foreign capital inflows and efficiency thereof, quality of entrepreneurship, technical change and innovation, etc. The general conclusion from such analyses is that there is little empirical support for those who would argue that restrictive regimes generate dynamic gains that offset the static inefficiencies that are documented in the NBER studies and that, in fact, were spelled out also in the earlier OECD studies at some length.[44]

D. Protection and export performance

We turn now to the issue of the degree of import substitution that corresponds, as noted earlier, to the question of the degree of protection. Two points need to be noted at the outset. First, recalling that protection is defined here, as in the NBER studies, as inclusive of the effects of the exchange control regime via import premia etc., the analysis in this subsection will extend to the issue of whether restrictive foreign trade regimes, associated with high import premia, lead to deteriorating or inferior export performance, whereas liberalized foreign trade regimes tend to have improved export performance. Second, we should also note that the common distinction drawn between import-substituting strategy and export-promoting strategy may be made, in sharper analytical terms, by observing that the former group essentially works with a degree of protection that implies that the ratio of EERs for exports is less than unity, whereas the latter group of countries essentially has this ratio closer to unity (as export

---

[43] For detailed analytical and empirical discussion, see Bhagwati (1978, chap. 5).

[44] Many of these dynamic questions were dealt with explicitly for India in Bhagwati–Srinivasan (1975), in particular; they have been considered more generally, with an eye on the entire set of countries in the NBER project, in Bhagwati (1978, chaps. 6–8). Note equally that, contrary to the enthusiasm of many proponents of liberalized regimes, there is no systematic evidence on their side either of dynamic efficiencies. The facts, and for that matter, the theoretical arguments, in these dynamic areas go in both directions and no general conclusions seem warranted. Cf. Bhagwati (1978).

subsidies of various types bring the *EER* for exports much closer to that for imports).[45]

There are several different types of evidence available in the NBER studies, to suggest that restrictive foreign trade regimes, with high explicit or implicit tariffs and lower-than-unity EER_x/EER_m ratios, are associated with lower export performance and that changing the overall foreign trade regime successfully in the direction of reduced reliance on exchange control and increased liberalization pays handsome dividends in terms of higher exports.

First, there is the usual type of evidence that, after successful liberalization (normally accompanied by devaluation), exports having generally declined tend to show responsiveness. This phenomenon, known in the literature on devaluation as the *J*-curve behavior (with initial decline and later rise), has been documented for several (though by no means all) of the liberalization episodes that the NBER countries experienced and that have been studied in depth. Thus, for example, the June 1966 Indian devaluation and liberalization policy package, once adjustment was made for the exogenous decline in exports brought about by two serious agricultural droughts, showed this type of pattern of export behavior.[46] Occasionally, attention has been focused on the short-run export response, so that the medium and long-run response, which was more favorable, has been missed by earlier analysts.[47]

Second, there is a considerable amount of statistical analysis, in the NBER studies, of the responsiveness of minor exports in particular and manufactured exports in general, which (on the basis of regression analysis using mainly time series estimates) suggests strongly that the exports of these developing countries are, in general, responsive to price changes. This evidence is at the microlevel for specific commodities (including sometimes even primary products) and also for broad aggregates by sectors.[48] It should be noted that the studies do deploy different indices for their price variable; and there is, indeed, here some of the tendency

---

[45] In practice, the export-promoting countries do not seem to make the export *EER* identical to that for imports; but they do make it substantially closer. In theory, one should want to define export-promoting strategy as making the EER_x/EER_m ratio exceed unity, so that there is a net incentive to export rather than serve the domestic market! These issues are discussed in Bhagwati (1978, chap. 8).

[46] For a full discussion of the cross-country evidence, see Krueger (1978).

[47] For a notable exception, see Cooper (1971).

[48] This evidence would suggest that while the 2×2 trade-theoretic model, where both goods are traded, is unrealistic, the augmentation of this model with a preassigned nontraded good is also incapable of capturing reality adequately. What one needs is a model where, depending on the policy equilibrium, a good may be traded or may cease to be traded. Such a model, on Ricardian lines, was considered by Samuelson (1964) many years ago and has been recently explored by him in a joint study: Dornbusch, Fischer, and Samuelson (1977), and independently in Samuelson (1979).

among econometricians to keep shifting among alternative price variables until something works. But, with this customary *caveat* in mind, we should note that the evidence broadly supports those who contend that prices do matter.

Third, Krueger's cross-sectional analysis of the ten NBER countries in her synthesis volume also seems to underline the significance of prices in improving or inhibiting the growth of exports. In her regressions, she uses dummies to represent Phases I, II, IV, and V: these refer to different degrees of restrictiveness of the trade regime (as spelled out in the NBER studies), where Phase I primarily initiates in a simple way the QR regime, Phase II represents proliferation of QRs and increased restrictiveness, Phase III is attempted liberalization, Phase IV represents successful movement toward liberalization, and Phase V is a full shift to a liberal-payments regime.[49] The Krueger regressions indicate that *PLDEER*s on exports seem to affect both traditional and nontraditional (otherwise described as minor in many of the studies) export values, and that Phases IV and V do seem to affect export performance favorably.[50]

In this regard, note furthermore that there seems to be a general case, underlined by the detailed analysis in the NBER studies, for arguing that it is really a shift to successful liberalization and therefore continuing liberalization that is critical to improved export performance on a sustained basis: i.e., a shift to Phase IV from Phase II will show such an improved performance, but not really occasional jabs at liberalization, each resulting in eventual relapse into Phase II (from Phase III liberalization attempts). Thus, it is the sustained transition during the 1960s and later from Phase II to Phase IV by South Korea, Taiwan, and Brazil that has been attended by high rates of export growth.[51]

Additionally, it is also worth noting that it is not just the price aspects of the restrictive Phase II regimes that inhibit export performance. As has been documented in the Indian case, for example, and by contrast in the South Korean case, in the NBER studies, the whole framework of exchange controls in a Phase II situation militates against export performance. Thus, for example, the ability to expand production to fill export orders requires access to import licenses for raw materials and capacity expansion requires import (and industrial) licenses: in each case, red tape and uncertainty cloud the scene.[52]

Fourth, statistical analysis of the usual decomposition variety, where the

---

[49] For more systematic and careful definitions of the Phases, see any of the NBER volumes; for convenience, they are stated fully in the Appendix.

[50] Cf. Krueger (1978). *PLDEER* stands for price-level deflated *EERs*.

[51] The role of expectations ensuring that export incentives are seen to have been made favorable over continued periods is obviously critical to this result, for that is when entrepreneurs will wish to make investments in export markets.

[52] Again, this is the kind of effect on exports that only Phase-change analysis can pick up statistically, if at all.

export performance of several LDCs is decomposed into that attributable to overall growth of demand, regional composition, commodity composition, and a residual "competitive" factor effect, contrasting the 1950s when most LDCs were in Phase II and the 1960s when some had successfully shifted to Phase IV, shows that the latter group of Phase IV countries had dramatically improved export performance and that a sizable share of it could be assigned to the residual, "competitive" factor.[53] Such analysis of the "competitive" factor is not generally considered to be as persuasive as the time-series analysis deployed in many of the NBER studies. However, it has considerable suggestive value and is corroborative of the conclusions arrived at through use of other analytical approaches.

E. Protection and economic performance

We may finally address the central question of whether LDCs with superior export performance also have superior economic performance and, if so, why?

There is little doubt that, in the NBER studies for example, the countries that have managed to shift to improved export performance by reducing export bias have also managed to register acceleration in their growth rates, whereas countries that have not done so (and have remained in Phase II regimes) have had poorer growth rates. The contrast between the success of South Korea and the failure of India, in this regard, is cross-sectionally the most telling.

A recent statistical analysis of Irving Kravis also supports this conclusion.[54] Using decomposition analysis to differentiate LDCs with high export performance based on domestic policies, and taking a 39-country sample, Kravis has noted a 0.51 Spearman coefficient between ranks with respect to the index of such export performance and ranks regarding the growth rate of real national product.

That the superior-export-performance countries do better compared to both their own earlier growth performance under restrictive trade regimes and other countries with inferior export performance seems therefore to be, generally speaking, a valid assertion. The interesting question is: why? Here, we have a few answers and many questions.

1. First, it would appear that the pattern of incentives, and hence of export promotion, is less skewed in practice than the chaotic pattern of import-substituting incentives under the restrictive trade regimes. The statistical quantifications of EER_xs for several activities in South Korea, for the mid-1960s, for example, suggest that the variability (including the extremes) of incentives is significantly lower than the EER_ms for several

[53] Cf. Askari and Corbo (1975). This statistical study also distinguishes between "minor" and other exports, defining the "minor" as all those exports that were below 10 percent of the total value in the initial year.

[54] Cf. Kravis (1970; pp. 868–69, in particular).

activities in the restrictive Phase II-type regimes in other countries, such as India.[55]

Similarly, the average ratio EER_x/EER_m also seems much closer to unity (at times even exceeding unity, but remaining closer to it) under the liberalized Phase IV- or V-type regimes than under the restrictive Phase II-type regimes.[56]

Thus, it would appear that, on both the degree and the pattern questions, distinguished earlier, the export-promoting countries with liberalized regimes seem to do better. For both types of allocative reasons, therefore, one could argue that the resulting reduction in allocative inefficiency must provide some of the explanation of the improved export performance that is observed for the liberalized-regime countries. But, in turn, one must ask the question as to why these incentives are less chaotic and more "neutral," by and large, under the liberalized trade regimes.

The reasons would seem to consist in the fact that the successful shift to export-promoting strategy (or Phase IV) generally takes place within the overall context of continuing exchange controls, and that the QR-caused bias against exports is offset by giving the import premia to exporters through schemes such as supply of imported materials at international prices, etc.,[57] and by using exchange rate adjustment more freely and thereby directly reducing import premia and hence the bias against exports. The result is generally (not always) to eliminate or reduce the bias against exports rather than to create excessive bias for exports. Because of budgetary considerations, cash subsidies that could conceivably create massive bias for exports are usually not substantial (though not unknown). On the other hand, the import-substituting strategy, especially via the mechanisms of import premia from QRs, can and has typically caused EER_m to get way out of line with EER_x (which was then determined almost exclusively by the exchange rate): and the costs of such a substantial rise in EER_m/EER_x above unity are generally not understood and, in any case, do not fall directly on the budget.

2. Next, the sheer improvement in export performance, following from the elimination of the bias against exports, must surely play the major role in the full explanation. The links here are possibly diverse.

i) The NBER studies suggest that there is little evidence that the export-promoting countries are technically more progressive or that they have higher savings rates because of a larger export sector.[58] The asymmetry in

[55] For a more detailed analysis, including statistical and analytical reasons for possible skepticism regarding this observation, consult Bhagwati (1978, chap. 8).

[56] In fact, Bhagwati (1978) therefore defines the export-promoting strategy as one where EER_x/EER_m is brought fairly close to unity.

[57] There is much documentation of these schemes of export promotion in the NBER studies. Cf., in particular, Bhagwati–Srinivasan (1975) on India and Frank, Westphal, and Kim (1975) on South Korea.

[58] These questions have been examined in detail, analytically and empirically, in Bhagwati (1978, chaps. 6 and 7).

the export-promoting and import-substituting countries' economic performance cannot thus be traced, at least on current evidence, to superiority of the one strategy over the other on these dynamic grounds, even though the proponents of each strategy often indulge in assertions to that effect.

ii) Part of the answer rather appears to be in the fact that a more comfortable balance-of-payments position, resulting from improved export incentives and earnings, generally eases up the excesses of the import-substituting strategy. This should be obvious from the well-known demonstration that, under a foreign exchange bottleneck (in the sense of Chenery), additional foreign exchange is more productive than under a savings bottleneck. But it is also apparent from the fact that it eases excess capacity (generated largely by the QR regime in the first place[59]), may reduce the need to hold excess inventories, and leads often to elimination of critical bottlenecks, etc. It is perhaps remarkable that these kinds of problems, attendant on economies in the restrictive Phase II, are rarely to be found in the liberalized Phase IV and V economies that have successfully transited to export-promoting strategy on a continuing basis.

iii) In regard to the general easing of the balance of payments (and hence of the losses that attend restrictive payments policies) under the export-promoting strategy, it is also worth noting that this effect is reinforced by the substantial inflow of foreign capital that can attend such a strategy. While political factors help to explain the substantial inflows of foreign private investment in South Korea, these are undoubtedly to be supplemented by economic factors. And here one probably ought to attribute to the export-promoting strategy itself the sizable magnitude of the inflow of nonaid foreign funds and its efficacy in promoting economic growth. By contrast, under import-substituting strategy, both the magnitude of the inflow and its social returns are likely to be lower. This contrast may be explained as follows.

Regarding magnitude, an export-promoting strategy, with its lack of discrimination against foreign markets, is likely to attract foreign firms essentially on the nineteenth-century pattern of factor-endowment advantages. Whereas in the nineteenth-century, this meant natural resources, today it means exploiting Heckscher–Ohlin style low wages. On the other hand, by creating artificial inducement to invest via tariffs and/or QRs, so that one gets "tariff-jumping" investments oriented to the domestic market alone, the import substituting strategy provides an artificially limited incentive to invest in the LDC. Furthermore, even the substantial official borrowings by South Korea and Brazil in the international capital markets surely must have been facilitated by the demonstration of a superior export performance (for, that would assuage fears of excessive borrowing and inability to repay).

Then again, in regard to efficiency, it is easy to show that "tariff-jumping"

---

[59] On this point, see the arguments in Bhagwati–Srinivasan (1975, chap. 13).

investments, induced under the import-substituting strategy, are more likely to imply social losses or (at minimum) reduced gains than investments attracted by Heckscher–Ohlinesque factors. That foreign capital inflow can be not merely less productive when inspired by QRs and/or tariffs, but actually immiserizing, has been shown elegantly by Brecher and Diaz–Alejandro in a recent paper.[60] For the traditional 2 × 2 model of trade theory, they show that social utility for the small country, having declined with the tariff, will decline further with the initial inflow of foreign capital when the importable good is capital-intensive. It will continue to decline with additional inflows of foreign capital until autarky is reached, then rise gradually to the level under free trade (a situation discussed by Mundell earlier),[61] remain at that level for further inflows and, finally, start rising after complete specialization in production is reached (a situation discussed by MacDougall earlier).[62]

While the factors noted in the preceding paragraphs would seem to be critical in defining the asymmetrical outcomes under the import-substituting and the export-promoting strategies, some additional factors may be cited that might contribute to the asymmetry, but for which no systematic evidence is yet available.

iv) Thus, one could argue that the export-promoting strategy may lead to a generally reduced reliance on direct or physical, as distinct from price, measures.[63] Direct controls have been argued with plausibility, in both the OECD and NBER studies, to be very costly in practice. It is possible that the general incidence of such direct controls may be significantly less under export promotion, because price, distribution, and other controls may make little sense to bureaucrats when firms' outputs are mainly addressed to overseas, rather than domestic, markets. A different, and perhaps more perceptive, formulation of this kind of contrast was well put by an economist familiar with both the Indian (Phase II) and the South Korean (Phase IV) trade regimes: the Indian regime consists mainly of "don'ts" whereas the Korean regime consists mainly of "do's." Whether these contrasts are, in a basic political sense, endemic to the two strategies being contrasted is not clear; but the NBER studies do suggest that they exist currently.

v) In the still more grey area, one may further argue that the export-promoting strategy must produce, through international competition, greater efficiency than the import-substituting strategy, with its sheltered markets. While this argument is plausible *a priori*, there is as yet no real

---

[60] Brecher and Diaz-Alejandro (1977). This possibility was noted, in the context of the same model, but less fully, in Uzawa (1969); Hamada (1974); Minabe (1974); and Bhagwati (1973).

[61] Mundell (1957).

[62] MacDougall (1958).

[63] The points in this paragraph and the next two were made, with slight differences in emphasis, in Bhagwati and Krueger (1973).

evidence at all on the subject. The issue is also complex, as the domestic competition may be sufficient to provide the incentive to efficiency under import-substitution, whereas exports may be to imperfectly competitive foreign markets or may simply be subsidized to the point necessary to offset any possible inefficiency-raised cost disadvantage.

vi) Finally, there is the factor of economies of scale, long recognized in international trade theory and policy discussions relating to customs unions, free trade areas, and similar areas where the size of the market is critical to the analysis of economic efficiency. In relation to export promoting strategy, it seems plausible to argue that the creation of incentives (or rather, the elimination of the disincentives) to enter the foreign markets augments the size of the market and hence should enable greater exploitation of economies of scale. Again, however, the issue is more complex insofar as the growth of firm size may be constrained by other policies and objectives (as in India), so that export promotion may take place from firms with constrained sizes by diversion from domestic production and/or by growth of new, licensed firms of small size. Again, therefore, the statistical evidence and analysis of this possible cause of asymmetrical advantage of the export-promoting strategy is not yet available in anything like a degree that would be reasonably compelling; but it does remain a plausible hypothesis.

It is finally important to note that once industrialization is on its way the basic difference between the two trade strategies is not in the degree of industrialization opted for; rather it is in the efficiency of the industrialization process. In fact, the export-promoting strategy merely implies a more rapid transition from import substitution to a substantial reduction of the bias against manufactured exports and, insofar as it is successful, may yield both more rapid and more substantial industrialization than the continued reliance on import-substituting strategy would. The familiar view in some developing countries and their policy-makers that the export-promoting strategy may result in reduced industrialization is therefore not based on an accurate understanding of the strategy and its precise contrast to the import-substituting strategy.

II. THE INTERNATIONAL TRADE SYSTEM: POLICY AND THEORETICAL PROBLEMS

While the preceding section underlines the developmental advantages that have accrued to the export-promoting countries, a necessary corollary to such a prescription for more than just a handful of LDCs is that the world trading system be reasonably open and accommodating to the trade needs of such a strategy. In fact, the problems that Japan has run into in regard to her international economic policy-making illustrate this point to advantage. It is thus not merely that Japan has often had an "undervalued"

Yen in the sense of generating a net surplus but also that, even if she was not building up exaggerated reserves and was instead spending all her export earnings, she would create waves because her growth rate, and the associated trade expansion, are just too great for the more sluggish rest-of-the-world to accommodate without serious disruptions of sectoral markets that lead to unceasing calls for VERs and other trade restrictions against Japanese exports.

Ragnar Nurkse, as we have seen, was quite aware of this problem for the export-promoting strategy; and the OECD project authors took the precaution also of stressing this when recommending against the import-substitution strategy. In fact, one cannot suppress the thought that the success stories of South Korea, Taiwan, Brazil, Singapore, and Hong Kong would not have been quite so impressive if they had not been built on the failures of the countries sticking overly long to import-substituting strategy and their consequent export (and associated economic) lag.

As it happens, the threats to a liberal international trade order come today from precisely the area of market disruption-related complaints in the DCs in regard to manufactures that must yield to growing imports and from the demands, in turn, from LDCs to extend restrictive arrangements to *primary commodities* as part of the New International Economic Order (NIEO). Both these threats are serious and both raise not merely policy but also theoretical issues of interest to international economists.

A. Market disruption-related threats

The political economy of tariff-making has received increasing attention recently, with empirical investigation by economists such as Cheh, Riedel, and Baldwin.[64] The result has been to focus on the nature of the adjustment costs that are likely to be imposed by shifts in trade policy or in trade environment, and therefore on the nature of the political opposition to the adoption or maintenance of open trade policies.

At the same time, trade theorists have tried to model the nature of adjustment costs. The model used by Mayer, in his recent work on the distinction between short-run and long-run equilibria, is based on the notion that, in the short run, the adjustment to commodity price change will be not along the usual transformation curve characterized by full mobility of factors but along one resulting from stickiness of capital in each activity and mobility of only labor.[65] On the other hand, we have argued recently that this notion of adjustment costs is too narrow; that the adjustment cost may exist because of, and in fact is more likely to reflect, the stickiness of real

---

[64] Cf. the pioneering paper of John H. Cheh (1974); James Riedel (1977); and the comprehensive and excellent paper by Robert E. Baldwin (1976).

[65] Cf. Mayer (1974). Of course, it is not the specificity of capital that causes adjustment problems, as suggested strongly by the work of Cheh (1974) and Riedel (1977), but rather the specificity of labor in the short run.

wages *à la* Brecher.[66] Equally, it may reflect stickiness of wages combined with initial unwillingness to move, with the former reducing as mobility also improves, so that the short run may well be realistically portrayed as the case where factors will not move and unemployment will ensue because of stickiness of wages.

From a theoretical standpoint, the interesting analytical issues that the threat of market disruption-related imposition of QRs and other trade restrictions poses are the following: (i) what should an exporting country that faces such a threat do by way of optimal policy intervention; and (ii) what should be the GATT rules govering the issue of market disruption-related invoking of trade restrictions? We have shown that the answer to the former question turns out to fall neatly into place in the traditional theory of distortions and welfare. Where the probability of the quota being invoked is endogenous to the level of (first-period) exports, clearly an optimal tariff argument follows: you need to take into account the increased probability of trade restraint, and hence loss of welfare, in the next period as a result of improved export performance in the first period. Moreover, if we also postulate a putty-clay model, such that first-period investments cannot be costlessly reassigned in the second period, clearly, a production tax-cum-subsidy will be required to take this additional complication into account: and this is, of course, nothing but the "adjustment costs" problem which, as just noted, may be modeled in different ways.[67] Building on this analysis, and the implied notion that the exporting country faces a loss in expected utility from the mere threat of trade restraints, Bhagwati has also suggested how the GATT Article XIX, which regulates (ineffectively, given VERs and bilateral deals) the exercise of market disruption-related invoking of trade restraints, may be revised and compensation rules be devised in regard thereto.[68]

On the other hand, the problem of revision of trade rules in regard to market disruption may be approached analytically by posing the question, not merely from the perspective of the exporting LDCs (just as the existing policies are largely reflecting only the importing DC interests *de facto*), but by considering the problem from the viewpoint of world optimality. If this is done, it is evident that the analytical problem is really one of determining the optimal assignment of adjustment costs between the country of

[66] Cf. Bhagwati and Srinivasan (1976), where the analysis of adjustment costs is general enough to embrace the different possibilities discussed in the text above. Among related papers of interest are Tolley and Wilman (1977); Mayer (1977); and Lapan (1976).

[67] Both these conclusions, of course, are consistent with the Bhagwati–Ramaswami–Srinivasan–Johnson type of conclusions that the optimal policy intervention should be in the markets where the problems arise. For details, see Bhagwati and Srinivasan (1976).

[68] For details, see Bhagwati (1977). The subject has also attracted proposals from other economists, notable among them being Hans Singer.

importation and the country of exportation, since one or the other must adjust. As such, the problem becomes analytically similar to the recent analysis of assignment of liability in the "law-and-economics" literature, with the adjustment costs, however, being spelled out by analytical specification of the nature of stickiness of wages, factor immobility, etc.[69]

B. Demands for commodity schemes

While the LDCs have been stressing the necessity to keep the DC markets open to increasing imports of manufactures from LDCs, they have simultaneously shifted recently to demanding restrictive and orderly arrangements in the markets for primary products. How is this paradox to be explained?

There are many explanations of the current LDC preference for commodity agreements, in their indexing form as distinct from their stabilization (of prices or perhaps earnings) form, but all would seem to miss the mark. Thus, it is often alleged that the commodity demands stem from the early Latin American preoccupation with the declining terms of trade of primary products, under the aegis of Prebisch and then UNCTAD (of which Prebisch was the first secretary-general). But if, indeed, this is so, one has to ask why it is only recently that such demands have come to the center of the stage: Sherlock Holmes did well to ask why the dog didn't bark! Alternatively, it has been suggested that the UNCTAD believes that economic progress is to be had by monopolistic cartelization and commodity schemes that rig prices at artificially high levels, rather than by the kinds of internal reform that attend on the economic advance in the presently developed countries. This too is a *non sequitur*. There is absolutely no contradiction between believing in the role of internal reforms (on whose dimensions, incidentally, most economists will disagree) and desiring a larger share of the gains from trade. The reasons why commodity schemes with the ultimate objective of indexing, and to be implemented by the LDCs and DCs in concerted action, have come to the forefront of the North–South negotiations have to be surely found elsewhere than in these theories.

There are, on the one hand, economic-philosophical reasons for these demands; on the other hand, there are also accidents-of-history type considerations here. Both must be understood if the demands are to be met by a reasonable response.

The economic-philosophical reasons are essentially the following. First, the LDC economists understand, what we have known with some clarity now since the developments in welfare economics since the 1940s, that the economics of the marketplace is about economic efficiency and not

---

[69] This has been noted in Bhagwati–Srinivasan (1976) and also happens to have been independently suggested by Gerald Meier in an undated paper.

about distributive justice. Thus, it is not intellectually foolish to argue that a price is unjust or unfair when the international income distribution that it reflects is unjust or unfair; rather, these economists know that it is naive to claim any more that opportunity cost is the touchstone of economic justice. Joan Robinson, despite her nascent radicalism, fell into the trap of calling "exploitation" the payment of a wage below the value of the factor's marginal product; she would probably burn *The Economics of Imperfect Competition* today! Second, many LDC economists find it increasingly baffling that DCs that have not been averse to resorting to indexing for their own constituencies on a massive scale—as with the U.S. agricultural price-support program—somehow find the idea to be an unacceptable violation of the principles of the marketplace when the idea is sought to be applied internationally: it seems reminiscent of the nineteenth-century English enthusiasm for free trade for the colonies and protection for domestic textiles. Finally, few LDC economists will accept the view that indexing by commodity agreements will disrupt competitive markets that currently assure economic efficiency. Here, there is room for further analysis, since it is not evident at all that the LDC economists' contention that these markets are already characterized by much intervention, willy nilly, and much monopolistic competition to the advantage of the DCs, is altogether bizarre. Thus, while the large number of oft-failing commodity agreements since World War II have been cited as evidence of the difficulty of getting such agreements designed and operated, they can equally well be cited as evidence of the considerable amount of intervention to which most commodity markets have been subjected during this period. Also, Gerry Helleiner has recently compiled the evidence on the degree to which market concentration operates in the world commodity trade and come up with what appeared to us at least to be substantially high figures of trade between related parties and of import concentration (in national markets) in the hands of a very small number of trading firms.[70] Of course, none of these latter facts automatically establish the existence of significant monopsonistic buying by DCs; we have all been sufficiently educated in the theory of entry, working competition, etc., to know that these facts are still consistent with the threat of entry by new firms and, therefore, competitive pricing may still be possible. However, in the face of this factual evidence on the existing structure of international trade in primary products, one needs to await systematic econometric analyses designed to enable us to choose among the two alternative hypotheses.

But if these factors account for why the LDCs are not persuaded that the market efficiency-based criticisms are well taken, the causes of their being wedded to the commodity schemes currently lie instead in political-economic factors that are probably the accidental results of the successes

[70] See, for example, his forthcoming paper, Helleiner (1977).

of the OPEC cartel. The OPEC cartel succeeded in unilaterally raising the price of a natural resource sevenfold in two years, against a backdrop of falling (real) aid flows from North to South and increasing sentiment that the path of moral suasion for raising the South's share in world income was unproductive. The OPEC seemed therefore to provide a new model: the LDCs, by acting jointly *qua* producers of commodities, would be able to raise their prices unilaterally. "Solidarity rather than charity" is the slogan that best captures this transition in the ethos in the South in the early post-OPEC years. Unfortunately, the LDCs were encouraged in this sentiment by DC economists who thought that this commodity power was nothing special to oil but really extended to other commodities: an argument that seems to have held only for bauxite in any significant degree. Thus, the initial shift in the South's strategy from that in the earlier UNCTAD Conferences and Group of 77 deliberations appears to have been toward the formation of producer groups to exercise unilaterally this alleged monopolistic power in individual commodities. Hence, the new-found focus on commodity schemes.

However, it was soon realized that the scope for such unilateral action was strictly limited and certainly self-destructing in the medium run because of induced-substitution possibilities. Since, however, the commodity schemes were "on" as the focal point of international negotiations, the emphasis soon shifted to making these commodity schemes joint LDC–DC, or producer-consumer, schemes, with the DC support being induced through political pressures brought from the South *en bloc* at UNCTAD, at CIEC, and so on. Thus, starting as the great new Southern weapon that would bring automatic and increased transfers of the incomes of the affluent countries to the poor ones, the commodity-scheme demands would appear to have become now the mere conduit through which transfers of resources would be made, these transfers to be induced by the exercise of political power, directly exerted by the LDCs *en bloc* at CIEC, and indirectly brought to bear on their behalf (with clearly much greater clout) by the OPEC members.

If this diagnosis is correct, the ultimate and true interest of the LDCs in commodity arrangements lies in their embodying some form of indexing (that would presumably procure higher, average terms of trade for the selected primary commodities than otherwise). This diagnosis would seem to derive additional support from two other observations: (i) the recent Group of 77 and UNCTAD documents, while carefully avoiding exclusive focus on indexing, never fail to include the notion in their proposed objectives for commodity schemes; and (ii) the commodities chosen for inclusion in the UNCTAD Integrated Plan for Commodities are not necessarily those characterized by severe (absolute or relative) instability in prices or earnings and, in fact, include items, such as tea, whose problem has always been that of low trend earnings.

It would thus appear that the alleged UNCTAD/CIEC willingness to negotiate stabilization, as against indexing, versions of commodity schemes is only tactical, designed to get some schemes going and then to make a move to indexing at an appropriate, future stage.

This judgment of LDC intentions is, of course, thoroughly compatible with the view that, by some strange quirk of coincidence, the price stabilization of commodities that are included in the UNCTAD Core Plan would yield a net transfer of resources from the stabilization *per se*: a view advanced recently by Jere Behrman on the basis of econometric analysis of the markets for these commodities.[71] Thus Behrman estimates that price stabilization for the commodities in the UNCTAD Integrated Plan would have created a modest resource transfer to the LDCs of the order of U.S. $5 billion in present value over the decade 1963–72. His simulations show that any buffer stock scheme intended to raise, rather than merely stabilize, prices is unlikely to succeed, since even a modest price increase of 2 percent annually in the secular price trends above their historical growth rates would result in accumulation of enormous stocks and would require unrealistically large financing.[72]

Turning then to the DCs, we may note that, if the DCs were faced with demands explicitly aimed at indexing, the prospects for commodity agreements would be negligible indeed. On the other hand, the DCs (and the United States specifically) have now indicated willingness to explore stabilization agreements. A cynical motivation behind this might well be to keep the North–South dialogue going for years to come, debating the rules and the specific commodities *ad nauseum*, while giving the appearance of responsiveness to LDC demands at relatively low cost. On the other hand, it appears that several DC policy-makers are of the view that price stabilization commodity schemes offer economic advantages to the DCs and that, therefore, here is an opportunity to grant an NIEO demand at a negative cost to the DCs, as long as indexing is firmly ruled out! There are really only two principal arguments underlying this view. First, that purchasers of primary products tend to be risk-averse and would favor price stability; and, second, that the inflationary effects of changes in primary product prices are asymmetrical and lead to a ratchet effect: primary product price

[71] Cf. Behrman (1977).

[72] The analysis in the text focuses on transfer of revenue to LDCs from the price-stabilization schemes. However, if we are interested in the welfare impact of price stabilization along conventional lines—it may be argued that welfare, as distinct from revenue transfer, impact is of interest only to economists rather than to LDC governments—then there is now an extensive literature on the distribution of welfare gains between producers and consumers from price stabilization, starting from the classic contributions of Waugh, Oi, and Massell. This literature has been surveyed recently by Turnovsky. The empirical issues, such as cost of stabilization, choice of commodities, as well as the econometrics underlying these are discussed among others by Behrman and Brook, et al. Cf. Waugh (1944); Oi (1961); Massell (1969); Turnovsky (1977); Brook, Grilli, and Waelbrook (1977); and Behrman (1977).

increases lead to overall price inflation, whereas their downturn does not reverse the overall price increase.

It is doubtful, however, that these arguments can support the case for an accommodation to the demands for commodity agreements, even if these are confined to stabilization arrangements. The risk-aversion that is admittedly rather strong at the moment surely reflects the phenomenally unusual commodity price boom of 1972–75: its remarkably unusual character having been noted and analyzed in the Cooper–Lawrence study for Brookings. Thus, they write:[73] "An extraordinary increase in commodity prices occurred in 1973–74. Even leaving aside crude oil as a special case, primary commodity prices on one index more than doubled between mid-1972 and mid-1974, while the prices of some individual commodities, such as sugar and urea (nitrogenous fertilizer), rose more than five times. While the timing differed from commodity to commodity, the sharp upward movement was widespread, affecting virtually all commodities. Most rose dramatically to twenty-year highs, and many went to historical highs." It is a fairly well-known generalization that when prices are on the upswing, consumers want price stability, whereas, producers want price stability on the downswing. Thus, one should probably treat as transient the present warmth toward price stability in the DCs. Nor is this judgment to be qualified by the argument that users, who fear quantitative shortfalls through withholding of supplies and embargos, would welcome price stability schemes: there is nothing in commodity agreements that would prevent such flow-disruptions and the appropriate method to approach the problem of export controls, so as to restrain their use to agreed rules of the game, may well lie in the general reform of GATT rules, whereby DCs agree to new market-disruption rules that restrain greatly their practice of clamping down on successful LDC exports and thus guarantee freer access by LDCs to DC markets, while LDCs reciprocally agree to a new set of rules that restrain their use of quantitative export controls on primary commodities and thereby maintain freer access by DCs to LDC supplies of primary products.

While, therefore, the risk-aversion argument in favor of price-stabilization commodity schemes is not particularly appealing to us, the macroeconomic argument on the ratchet effect is even less so. Admittedly, there is something to it: oil and wage goods obviously qualify for it. There even seems to be some empirical evidence in support of such a ratchet effect.[74] But, surely, it hardly applies to most of the commodities in which LDCs have invested their efforts for the commodity schemes. Again, just as LDCs made the mistake of generalizing from oil to other commodities in arrogating to themselves "commodity power" for unilateral price-raising, the DCs

---

[73] Cooper and Lawrence (1975).

[74] For detailed discussion, see the interesting papers of Nicholas Kaldor (1976), and Erik Lundberg (1977).

would appear to be making the mistake of generalizing the ratchet effect from oil, steel, and food to other commodities.

Our conclusions then are the following:

i) the LDCs have as their major objective an increase in the current transfer of resources from the rich to the poor countries;

ii) the LDCs stumbled mistakenly into commodity schemes as the new (OPEC-inspired) model for unilaterally achieving this objective;

iii) the LDCs, having realized that such unilateral power scarcely existed in a significant degree outside of oil, switched then to regarding commodity schemes as the conduit through which DCs could be politically pressured into transferring resources via indexing *à la* domestic price-support programs;

iv) the "true" objective of the LDCs is therefore to turn commodity agreements into indexing arrangements and the "noise" about stabilization etc. in UNCTAD/Group of 77/CIEC documents and demands is, at best, tactical;

v) the DCs, on the other hand, are opposed to indexing but are inclined, in some cases, to see in price-stabilization arrangements benefits to themselves;

vi) these benefits, however, are unlikely to be significant, have been mistakenly exaggerated, and will probably be seen to be so in the near future;

vii) the North–South willingness, if it crystallizes (as would seem imminent), to negotiate commodity schemes on the basis of price stabilization is then unlikely to lead to more than a transitory accommodation: the LDCs will soon wish to move to indexing, which the DCs will oppose and reject, whereas, the DCs will soon come to see even the stabilization schemes as nuisances, rather than as benefits, to themselves;

viii) therefore, far from promoting a smooth or amicable North–South relationship, the present focus on commodity schemes as part of the NIEO is a certain recipe for disorder: the LDCs will get next to nothing from the schemes while investing a massive political effort into getting them floated; and the DCs will have accomplished nothing worthwhile if they do mean to improve the flow of resources to the poor countries (though, those who aim at a no-give response should consider this to be a happy outcome, of course);

ix) therefore, it is of the utmost importance to bury the commodity schemes and to shift attention instead to the more traditional remedies for any of the problems that may be raised for LDCs by commodity revenue instability and to respond to NIEO demands by developing new and efficient resource-transfer proposals;

x) the traditional remedies for the problems associated with revenue instability include compensatory financing facilities for LDCs to tide over the periods of lean foreign exchange earnings, and domestic buffer stock schemes for those countries that wish to cushion their producers and/or consumers; this being the early, classic prescription of Ragnar Nurkse and also what has transpired satisfactorily with the successive augmentations of the special compensatory financing facilities at the IMF; and, finally, we may note that

xi) in regard to resource transfers, there are new resource transfer possibilities that amount either to taxing disexternalities (such as overfishing) or rents (such as from mining the seabeds or from skilled migration in the presence of severe immigration quotas) whose adoption could be explored.[75]

APPENDIX: DEFINITION OF PHASES IN THE NBER PROJECT

In order to demarcate in an analytically useful manner the evolution of a country's exchange-control regime, the NBER Project delineated a number of phases which were used in the country studies and are to be found in the two synthesis volumes as well. It should be noted that, while each study identifies the phases through which the country's payments regime passed, there is no presumption, and in fact the evidence shows there to be none as well, that the phases would be gone through necessarily in a predefined sequence.

Phase I: During this period, quantitative restrictions on international transactions are imposed and then intensified. They generally are initiated in response to an unsustainable payments deficit and then, for a period, are intensified. During the period when reliance upon quantitative restrictions as a means of controlling the balance of payments is increasing, the country is said to be in Phase I.

Phase II: During this phase, quantitative restrictions are still intense, but various price measures are taken to offset some of the undesired results of the system. Heightened tariffs, surcharges on imports, rebates for exports, special tourist exchange rates, and other price interventions are used in this phase. However, primary reliance continues to be placed on quantitative restrictions.

Phase III: This phase is characterized by an attempt to systematize the changes which take place during Phase II. It generally starts with a formal exchange-rate change and may be accompanied by removal of some of the surcharges, etc., imposed during Phase II and by reduced reliance upon quantitative restrictions. Phase III may be little more than a tidying-up operation (in which case the likelihood is that the country will re-enter Phase II), or it may signal the beginning of withdrawal from reliance upon quantitative restrictions.

Phase IV: If the changes in Phase III result in adjustments within the country, so that liberalization can continue, the country is said to enter Phase IV. The necessary adjustments generally include increased foreign-exchange earnings and gradual. relaxation of quantitative restrictions. The latter relaxation may

[75] For estimates and analysis, see the papers by Richard Cooper and Koichi Hamada in Bhagwati (1977). See also Bhagwati and Partington (1976).

take the form of changes in the nature of quantitative restrictions or of increased foreign-exchange allocations, and thus reduced premiums, under the same administrative system.

Phase V: This is a period during which an exchange regime is fully liberalized. There is full convertibility on current account, and quantitative restrictions are not employed as a means of regulating the ex ante balance of payments.

REFERENCES

Askari, H., and Corbo, V. 1976. "Export Promotion: Its Rationale and Feasibility." Mimeographed.

Balassa, B., and Associates. 1971. *The Structure of Protection in Developing Countries* (IBRD). Baltimore: The Johns Hopkins Press.

Baldwin, R. 1975. See NBER (3).

———. 1976. "U.S. Tariff Policy: Formation and Effects." *International Trade, Foreign Investment, Employment Discussion Papers*, U.S. Department of Labor, Bureau of International Labor Affairs.

Basevi, G. 1966. "The United States Tariff Structure: Estimates of Effective Rates of Protection of United States Industries and Industrial Labor." *Review of Economics & Statistics* 48: 147–60.

Behrman, J. 1976. See NBER (9).

———. 1977. "International Commodity Agreements." Overseas Development Council, *NIEO* Series.

Bergsman, J. 1970. See OECD (2).

Bhagwati, J. 1968. *The Theory and Practice of Commercial Policy: Departures from Unified Exchange Rates.* Frank Graham Lecture (1967); International Finance Section, Princeton University Special Papers No. 8.

———. 1972. "Trade Policies for Development." In *The Gap between Rich and Poor Nations*, Proceedings of an International Economic Association Conference in Bled, Yugoslavia. New York: Macmillan & Co.

———. 1973. "The Theory of Immiserizing Growth: Further Applications." In *International Trade and Money*, edited by M. B. Connolly and A. K. Swoboda. Toronto: University of Toronto Press.

———. 1976. *Protection, Industrialization, Export Performance and Economic Development.* UNCTAD, Geneva.

———. 1977. "Market Disruption, Export Market Disruption, Compensation and GATT Reform." In *The New International Economic Order: The North-South Debate*, edited by J. Bhagwati. Cambridge, Mass.: Massachusetts Institute of Technology Press.

———. 1978. *Foreign Trade Regimes and Economic Development: Anatomy and Consequences of Exchange Control Regimes.* See NBER (1978).

Bhagwati, J., and Desai, P. 1970. See OECD (3).

Bhagwati, J., and Krueger, A. 1973. "Exchange Control, Liberalization and Economic Development." *American Economic Review* (May): 419–27.

Bhagwati, J., and Partington, M. (eds.). 1976. *Taxing the Brain Drain: A Proposal.* New York: North-Holland Publishing Co.

Bhagwati, J., and Srinivasan, T. N. 1973. "Contribution to the Symposium on the Theory of Effective Protection in General Equilibrium." *Journal of International Economics* 3.

———. 1975. See NBER (6).

———. 1976. "Optimal Trade Policy and Compensation under Endogenous Uncertainty: The Phenomenon of Market Disruption." *Journal of International Economics* 6: 317–36.

Brecher, R., and Diaz-Alejandro, C. 1977. "Tariffs, Foreign Capital and Immiserizing Growth." *Journal of International Economics* 7: 317–22.

Brook, E. M., Grilli, E. R., and Waelbrook, J. 1977. "Commodity Price Stabilization and the Developing Countries: The Problem of Choice." World Bank Staff Paper No. 262.

Bruno, M. 1973. "Contribution to the Symposium on the Theory of Effective Protection in General Equilibrium." *Journal of International Economics* 3.

Cheh, J. 1974. "United States Concessions in the Kennedy Round and Short-Run Labor Adjustment Costs." *Journal of International Economics* 4: 323–40.

Cooper, R. 1971. *Currency Devaluations in Developing Countries.* International Finance Section, Princeton University Special Papers No. 86.

———. 1977. "Oceans as a Source of Revenue." In *The International Economic Order: The North-South Debate*, edited by J. Bhagwati. Cambridge, Mass.: Massachusetts Institute of Technology Press.

Cooper, R., and Lawrence, R. 1975. "The 1972–75 Commodity Boom." *Brookings Papers on Economic Activity* 3: 671.

Desai, P. 1970. *Tariff Protection and Industrialization: A Study of the Indian Tariff Commission at Work.* Delhi: Hindustan Publishing Corporation.

Diaz-Alejandro, C. 1975. "Trade Policies and Economic Development." In *International Trade and Finance: Frontiers for Research*, edited by P. Kenen. Cambridge: Cambridge University Press.

———. 1976. See NBER (8).

Dornbusch, R. 1974. "Tariffs and Nontraded Goods." *Journal of International Economics* 4: 177–85.

Dornbusch, P., Fischer, S., and Samuelson, P. 1977. "Comparative Advantage, Trade and Payments in a Ricardian Model with a Continuum of Goods." *American Economic Review* 67: 823–39.

Frank, C., Westphal, L., and Kim, K. S. 1975. See NBER (5).

Guisinger, S. 1971. "The Characteristics of Protected Industries in Pakistan." In *Effective Tariff Protection*, edited by H. G. Grubel and H. G. Johnson. Geneva: General Agreement on Tariffs and Trade.

Haberler, G. 1959. *International Trade and Economic Development.* Cairo: National Bank of Egypt.

Hamada, K. 1974. "An Economic Analysis of the Duty-Free Zone." *Journal of International Economics* 4: 225–41.

———. 1977. "Taxing the Brain Drain: A Global Point of View." In *The New International Economic Order: The North-South Debate*, edited by J. Bhagwati. Cambridge, Mass.: Massachusetts Institute of Technology Press.

Hansen, B., and Nashashibi, K. 1975. See NBER (7).

Helleiner, G. 1977. "Freedom and Management in Primary Commodity

Markets: U.S. Imports from Developing Countries." Forthcoming in *World Development*.

Hsing, M., Power, J., and Sicat, G. 1970. See OECD (5).

"Journal of International Economics Symposium on the Theory of Effective Protection in General Equilibrium." 1973. *Journal of International Economics* 3.

Kaldor, N. 1976. "Inflation and Recession in the World Economy." *Economic Journal* (December).

King, T. 1970. See OECD (6).

Kravis, I. 1970. "Trade as a Handmaiden of Growth: Similarities between the Nineteenth and Twentieth Centuries." *Economic Journal* (December).

Krueger, A. 1975. See NBER (1).

———. 1978. *Foreign Trade Regimes and Economic Development: Liberalization Attempts and Consequences*. See NBER (1978).

Lapan, H. 1976. "International Trade, Factor Market Distortions, and the Optimal Dynamic Subsidy." *American Economic Review* 66.

Leith, J. 1975. See NBER (11).

Lewis, S. 1970. See OECD (4).

Lewis, W. A. 1969. *Aspects of Tropical Trade: 1883–1965*, Wicksell Lectures. Stockholm: Almquist & Wicksell.

Little, I., Scitovsky T., and Scott, M. 1970. See OECD (1).

Lundberg, Erik. 1977. "World Inflation and National Policies." Stockholm: Institute for International Economic Studies Seminar Paper No. 80.

MacDougall, G. 1958. "The Benefits and Costs of Private Investment from Abroad: A Theoretical Approach." *Economic Record* 36: 13–35.

Massell, B. 1969. "Price Stabilization and Welfare." *Quarterly Journal of Economics* 83: 284–98.

Mayer, W. 1974. "Short-Run and Long-Run Equilibrium for a Small, Open Economy." *Journal of Political Economy* 82: 955–67.

———. 1977. "The National Defense Tariff Reconsidered." *Journal of International Economics* 7: 363–77.

Meier, G. "Externality Law and Market Safeguards." Undated, mimeographed.

Michaely, M. 1975. See NBER (2).

Minabe, N. 1974. "Capital and Technology Movements and Economic Welfare." *American Economic Review* 64: 1088–1100.

Mundell, R. 1957. "International Trade and Factor Mobility." *American Economic Review* 47: 321–35.

National Bureau of Economic Research (NBER). 1975, 1976. New York: Columbia University Press, 1975 (1)–(7); 1976 (8)–(9):

(1) A. Krueger, *Foreign Trade Regimes and Economic Development: Turkey*.

(2) M. Michaely, *Foreign Trade Regimes and Economic Development: Israel*.

(3) R. Baldwin, *Foreign Trade Regimes and Economic Development: Philippines*.

(4) J. Leith, *Foreign Trade Regimes and Economic Development: Ghana*.

(5) C. Frank, L. Westphal, and K. S. Kim, *Foreign Trade Regimes and Economic Development: South Korea.*

(6) J. Bhagwati and T. N. Srinivasan, *Foreign Trade Regimes and Economic Development: India.*

(7) B. Hansen and K. Nashashibi, *Foreign Trade Regimes and Economic Development: Egypt.*

(8) C. Diaz-Alejandro, *Foreign Trade Regimes and Economic Development: Colombia.*

(9) J. Behrman, *Foreign Trade Regimes and Economic Development: Chile.*

————. 1978. Cambridge: Ballinger Publishing Company.

   A. Krueger, *Foreign Trade Regimes and Economic Development: Liberalization Attempts and Consequences.*

   J. Bhagwati, *Foreign Trade Regimes and Economic Development: Anatomy and Consequences of Exchange Control Regimes.*

Nurkse, R. 1959. *Patterns of Trade and Development*, Wicksell Lectures. Stockholm: Almquist & Wicksell.

Oi, W. 1961. "The Desirability of Price Stability under Perfect Competition." *Econometrica* 29: 58–64.

Organization for Economic Cooperation and Development (OECD). 1970. Oxford: Oxford University Press:

(1) I. Little, T. Scitovsky, and M. Scott, *Industry and Trade in Some Developing Countries: A Comparative Study.*

(2) J. Bergsman, *Brazil: Industrialization and Trade Policies.*

(3) J. Bhagwati and P. Desai, *India: Planning for Industrialization.*

(4) S. Lewis, *Pakistan: Industrialization and Trade Policies.*

(5) M. Hsing, J. Power, and G. Sicat, *Taiwan and the Philippines: Industrialization and Trade Policies.*

(6) T. King, *Mexico: Industrialization and Trade Policies since 1940.*

Oyejide, T. A. 1971. "Tariff Protection and Industrialization via Import Substitution: An Empirical Analysis of the Nigerian Experience." *Bangladesh Economic Review* 1: 331–40.

Ramaswami, V. K., and Srinivasan, T. N. 1971. "Tariff Structure and Resource Allocation in the Presence of Substitution." In *Trade, Balance of Payments and Growth*, edited by J. Bhagwati et al. New York: North-Holland Publishing Co.

Riedel, J. 1977. "Tariff Concessions in the Kennedy Round and the Structure of Protection in West Germany: An Econometric Assessment." *Journal of International Economics* 7: 133–44.

Samuelson, P. A. 1964. "Theoretical Notes on Trade Problems." *Review of Economics & Statistics* (May): 145–54.

————. 1979. "Two-Country Ricardian Analysis for Discrete Goods and for a Continuum of Goods." Forthcoming in the *Journal of International Economics* (May).

Soligo, R., and Stern, J. J. 1965. "Tariff Protection, Import Substitution, and Investment Efficiency." *Pakistan Development Review* (Summer): 249–70.

Tolley, G. S., and Wilman, J. D. 1977. "The Foreign Dependence Question." *Journal of Political Economy* 85: 323–47.

Turnovsky, S. 1977. "The Distribution of Welfare Gains from Price Stabilization: A Survey of Some Theoretical Issues." Paper presented at Ford Foundation Conference on Stabilizing World Commodity Markets.

Uzawa, H. 1969. "Shihon Jiyuka to Kokumin Keizai [Liberalization of Foreign Investments and the National Economy]." *Economisuto*.

Viner, J. 1953. *International Trade and Economic Development*. Oxford: Clarendon Press.

Waugh, F. 1944. "Does the Consumer Benefit from Price Instability?" *Quarterly Journal of Economics*.

Comment

ROBERT E. BALDWIN

It is always a pleasure to have the opportunity to read a paper by Jagdish Bhagwati and T. N. Srinivasan. They combine great theoretical and econometric talents, a keen interest in policy issues, and a deep understanding of the complex economic and social forces that shape economic events in a manner that represents the best efforts of modern economists.

The paper begins by summarizing the rather large number of recent studies of individual developing countries that have evaluated the effectiveness of their economic development policies. Particular attention is devoted to the ten country studies and two synthesis volumes that make up the National Bureau of Economic Research project and in which Bhagwati and Srinivasan contributed a volume on India and Jagdish also wrote one of the synthesis studies.

It always has seemed remarkable to me how closely all of the authors in the NBER series agreed upon the notion that import substitution policies were carried too far in most of the countries studied and served to retard rather than accelerate growth. Moreover, it was generally agreed that, after a period, these policies worsened both the employment and income distribution problems. We also found that whenever trade and exchange rate liberalization measures were adopted in the economies, the pace of development tended to pick up. Those countries that followed export promotion policies most vigorously showed much better economic growth than those oriented toward import substitution. Perhaps the countries were somehow preselected, so that there was a bias toward these conclusions, but I do not think so. The conclusion is all the more impressive when one considers that the authors of the six countries constituting the OECD study arrived at the same general judgment.

One of the interesting questions Bhagwati and Srinivasan raise is why export promotion policies succeeded so well. It is not, as they point out, simply because they were administered so much better. Inconsistencies and mismanagement seem as prevalent in the success stories as the failures.

The authors give a series of interesting reasons why these outward policies may have succeeded so much better and they should provide the basis for further interesting work in the field. We also need theoretical work along these lines.

Another question that needs to be investigated further is why the developing countries tend to select the import-substitution route rather than export-promotion policies. It is by no means just a once and for all selection. Time and time again we found that after governments dismantled some of their import-substitution controls and moved in the direction of stimulating exports they slid back to import substitution within a few years. Why was this? Similarly, how did those few countries that succeeded in emphasizing exports maintain this policy? We must not make the mistake of believing that knowledge of the alternative results of the two development paths is all decision-makers need to know to make the right decision. For two hundred years, economists have been demonstrating the merits of liberal trade policies on theoretical, empirical, and historical grounds, yet the world is still dominated by trade barriers. If we are to affect policies, we must sometimes become political economists and try to understand the collection of forces that operate on decision-makers. Then, if possible, we must suggest policies that enable these decision-makers to adopt what we think are the proper long-run policies yet also handle some of the short-run economic and noneconomic pressures with which they must deal.

Without embarking on a long discussion of the subject, let me suggest that the import-substitution strategy was and is more politically acceptable and advantageous, especially in more democratically operated countries, than export promotion. Accepting industrialization as the major economic goal of the developing nations since the end of World War II, it seems that import substitution was the logical path to take toward this objective. First, it fit nicely in with the political goal of achieving a greater degree of independence from the developed countries that politically controlled so many of the developing countries. Increasing exports seemed to offer the prospects of substituting greater economic dependence for less political control, whereas replacing imports from developed countries with domestic production seemed to reduce both forms of dependence. Export orientation also promises—at least for many years—only a limited and highly selective form of industrialization. The early import-substitution programs, on the other hand, envisioned the creation of both textile and steel mills, and even machine tool factories. Financing development via the import-substitution route is also considerably more attractive politically. Tariffs, quotas, exchange controls, etc., provide an umbrella of protection that taxes the population in a hidden manner. For export promotion, on the other hand, governments must generally subsidize activities more openly in ways that involve politically difficult budget decisions. The burden of financing development can often be placed more easily on certain minority groups with import substitution. Foreigners, in particular, who move operations from their own countries to the protected domestic market, bear a larger part of the development costs. Providing outright subsidies to foreigners to establish export industries is also more difficult to do politically. Foreigners and other minority groups who often are very knowledgeable about exploiting export opportunities are sometimes discriminated against in developing countries and thus not regarded as desirable recipients of the kind of subsidies that export promotion schemes involve. And it is more difficult to exclude these groups from exporting than from producing for domestic use only.

There are a number of other reasons that could be cited for the bias toward import substitution, but I hope the above are sufficient to illustrate the nature and importance of understanding this bias. The lesson of the last twenty-five years seems clear, namely, we need more emphasis on export promotion in the developing countries. But now we must turn our attention toward understanding how we can get the developing countries to implement these policies and the developed countries to accept the greater exports of manufacturers from the poorer countries.

After one concludes that most of the developing countries seem to be on the wrong track with their import-substitution policies and then one looks at the policy changes these countries are seeking internationally with the New International Economic Order, one wonders if the developing nations don't have a built-in, self-destructive bias. For I would completely agree with Bhagwati and Srinivasan that the commodity agreements these countries seek will not bring the benefits they hope for, but will serve mainly to increase their degree of frustration and take away their energies from more important matters. Similarly, I think the emphasis on tariff preferences is unfortunate. They are playing into the hands of the protectionists in the industrial countries with their preoccupation with preferences. Instead they should be devoting their energies toward achieving significant MFN cuts in products of special interest to them and in trying to reduce the quantitative restrictions on labor-intensive products that many developed countries impose.

As far as commodity agreements are concerned, I think we can rightly turn around the usual phrase of so-called "practical men" about trade economists and say that commodity agreements are all right in theory but won't work in practice. By this I mean that if we accept the goal of these agreements, namely, to stabilize commodity prices over the trade cycle, we can say this stability is possible in theory but cannot be achieved in practice. The reason for their impracticality is simply because it is very difficult to disentangle cyclical and secular price movements and to estimate the length of any given price cycle. Moreover, producing and consuming nations are unwilling to commit the volume of resources that would prevent the schemes from breaking down when the cycles are very long, as they not infrequently are. For example, the floor and ceiling price that seemed reasonable to set for cocoa in 1973 was $.23 and $.32 per pound, respectively. Yet in recent months the price has been $1.50. What producer is now willing to accept $.23 as a price that is not too low as a floor for the long-run? Similarly, there are few consumers who don't think the long-run ceiling should be a lot closer to $.32 than $1.50. Moreover, why should consumers now agree to help maintain a floor, when the ceiling was exceeded to such an extent? That is, of course, why the Wheat Agreement broke down. Along the same general lines, a study of tin stabilization suggests that a buffer stock of something like 150,000 metric tons would have been necessary to hold the price of tin within a 15 percent annual price-change range. Yet the stock has never exceeded 20,000 metric tons.

In short, I think the developing countries will try to attach indexing schemes to commodity agreements and to raise the long-run average price of primary commodities. But the prospects for any significant success in these endeavors are not good, in my view. Moreover, they are diverting our attention from what I think is the only feasible way of narrowing the income gap between rich and poor and providing the employment opportunities so badly needed in the developing countries, namely, by concentrating on industrialization.

CHAPTER TWO

International Cartels and Monopolies in International Trade

RICHARD E. CAVES

The formal niceties of pure competition make it the stock-in-trade market structure in theoretical models of the international economy. Yet imperfect competition calls out for attention as a matter of international economic policy and, therefore, poses issues for theoretical and empirical research that cannot in good conscience be ignored. This chapter addresses two major ways in which imperfect competition impinges on the making of international economic policy. First, governments engage in or promote the formation of international cartels in order to maximize national monopoly gains, or they seek to evade exploitation by such cartels. Second, governments maintain competition in their national markets by means of policies that should recognize the presence or absence of international competition. The two main sections of this paper summarize the theory and empirical evidence relevant to governments' policy choices as exploiters of monopoly power and as enforcers of competition.

I. CREATION AND MAINTENANCE OF INTERNATIONAL CARTELS

By an international cartel, I shall mean an agreement among producers of a given good or service located in different countries and covering the bulk of the market decision variables that must be manipulated or constrained in order to achieve significant joint monopoly profits. Cartels have often been organized among private-sector producers. For this analysis, however, I shall assume that they are either the direct work of national governments or that governments enforce them in the pursuit of national economic objectives. This approach is responsive to the recent role of governments in forming or seeking to form primary-product cartels, and it focuses our attention on the behavioral conditions necessary for forming and maintaining cartels. That is, we can take the key structural conditions as given—a certain number of countries possessing bauxite deposits, for example—and concentrate on the game-theoretic depiction of their behavior that is the heart of traditional cartel theory. In the second part of this chapter, where we consider the problems of governments trying to maintain secure, effective, industrial performance, we shall be back in structuralist territory. The exposition of this section uses the microeconomic terminology that is standard for cartel theory. Some remarks about the process of translating the conclusions into the realm of national economies and general equilibrium come at the end.

Under what conditions do potential participants join a cartel? Once the cartel is under way, what are the incentives to defect, and what causes the parties to resist the temptation to cheat? It is useful to begin our answer by drawing upon the Cournot–Nash duopoly theory, in which Cournot's solution to the classic duopoly problem supplies a reference-point outcome for the case in which the parties achieve no cooperation. This solution of course is not in the core, but while we address the possibilities of a collusive bargain between sellers it is hardly unreasonable to put aside the possibility of a subsequent deal with the exploited buyers to supply them at marginal cost.[1]

The familiar "prisoner's dilemma" game explains why the Cournot solution emerges in single-period games. It would also emerge from a model involving trade in n successive periods, if trade in all periods is arranged by means of binding contracts reached on the initial day. More surprising, the Cournot solution also emerges in a market operating for a finite number of trading days, if sales are determined afresh each period and there is an enforcement mechanism that penalizes each period's noncolluders in the next time period. As Shubik (1959) and Telser (1972) have shown, this proposition is easily proved by backward induction. In the last (nth) time period, no punishment is possible for violators of a monopolistic consensus, and so the Cournot solution prevails in the nth period. But given that expected outcome, nothing can deter a party from cheating on that consensus in period $n - 1$, on the assumption that enforcement consists of reverting to the Cournot solution, which will obtain in period n in any case. The proof continues back to the initial period. The empirically interesting point that emerges from this analysis is that avoidance of the prisoner's-dilemma solution requires that the participants not know when the game is going to end. Telser develops this property by assuming that each duopolist supposes in each period that the game will continue for one (or more) additional periods with some exogenously

---

[1] Telser (1972, pp. 138–39) shows that the Cournot solution lies in the core of a reduced market—one in which the buyers extramarginal in the actual Cournot solution are assumed absent from the market.

given probability a. The temptation to cheat on a joint-monopoly consensus depends on the severity of punishment (modeled by Telser as retrogression for k periods to the Cournot outcome), but given that severity it is greater the smaller is a. Telser also points out that, if cheating is expected to be profitable, it will in this model be undertaken immediately; a joint monopoly once attained should be stable indefinitely if k and a values are stationary and high enough to deter cheating.[2]

The creation of cartels

The Shubik–Telser analysis, reported so far, is useful for introducing the central concerns of cartel theory—the essential terms of agreement and the conditions under which an agreement once reached will continue to be honored. Yet there is something peculiar about distinguishing the conditions under which sellers can reach an agreement from those under which they can sustain it. Why not suppose that potential cartel members correctly anticipate the enforcement loopholes of an agreement when it is first drafted? With that rationality assumed, we could predict a cartel would be undertaken if and only if the present value of its joint monopoly profit exceeds the present value of its expected costs of operation and enforcement. Outside interference apart, a potentially profitable cartel then is blocked only by its members' lack of inventiveness with devices that bind their commitment to follow the terms of the agreement. As Schelling (1960, especially chap. 5) points out, the strategies for achieving binding commitment may be rather rich. Nonetheless, the received body of cartel theory puts most of its emphasis on the problems of punishment and defection from incomplete cartel agreements without explaining why—aside from observed fact—this contractual incompleteness should pertain.

It is useful at this point to remind ourselves what is required for a contractually complete cartel. It is not enough to divide markets or agree on a common price. Joint profits from the cartel's activity cannot simply pass to each member as the net revenues resulting from his apportioned sales. Without pooling profits and dividing them according to some pre-agreed formula, the members will find that the allocation of production among themselves must meet an inconsistent set of objectives: it must minimize the aggregate cost of producing the joint-profit-maximizing output, and it must also generate whatever division of profits is consistent with the bargaining power of the parties. Without profit pooling, the feasible locus of efficient profit outcomes will contain many points that fall short of maximum joint profit. Only with profit-pooling or side-payments can the

---

[2] See Telser (1972, pp. 142–45). Recent developments in game theory seem to identify devices capable of sustaining collusive outcomes in noncooperative games that may have some empirical counterparts. They include the use of randomized strategies and the presence of differing subjective priors. Unfortunately, it is beyond the scope of this paper to survey these developments.

parties attain the maximum joint profit and divide the spoils in a way consistent with their bargaining power.[3] Securing a cost-minimizing distribution of outputs that sum to the group's profit-maximizing joint output level poses its own problems for the optimizing cartel. If the participants have different cost curves, the efficient distribution of output requires that all active producing units operate at a common marginal cost and that the output level of the least efficient unit in operation be such that its average cost is at a minimum.[4] Cartel members might obtain this efficient allocation by creating rights to produce given quantities of the profit-maximizing joint output, issuing these to the charter members as part of the basic agreement, and allowing them to be traded among sellers. Fully efficient trade would produce the optimal allocation of output just described.[5] Many decision variables besides the division of output and profits may affect the attainment of maximum joint profits, when output is heterogeneous and the transaction offered to the buyer can vary in a number of dimensions besides price.

When we consider these requirements for agreement, it is evident that contractual costs and uncertainties are an important potential limit on the ability of sellers to reach accord. The heterogeneity of sellers' preferences and of their perceived opportunity sets contributes to these costs. Oligopoly theory in the Fellner–Chamberlin tradition deals with these influences as limitations on how closely the market bargain can approach full joint profit maximization, and the field of industrial organization contains a large literature on the structural conditions and sellers' strategies capable of sustaining a noncompetitive market bargain. However, these valuable insights into the structural conditions for a cartel agreement do not generally take the form of deterministic cartel models, and so I reluctantly put them aside. Consider instead two formal propositions about the terms of cartel agreements.

First, a cartel agreement can potentially be made enforceable without an elaborate mechanism to defuse what would otherwise be a strong temptation to cheat. Osborne (1976) and Spence (forthcoming) show that the adoption by duopolists of reaction functions that commit them to maintaining constant shares of the value of total sales can lead them to a point on the contract curve with respect to their profits. That is, an agreement on market shares has a certain superiority over other forms of agreement on the key market variables.[6] The cartel's charter members can make other choices of terms that ease the enforcement burden. One frequently observed empirically is to divide markets (classes of customers, geographic areas,

---

[3] Telser (1972, chap. 5, esp. pp. 192–94).

[4] Patinkin (1947); Telser (1972, chap. 5).

[5] See Stigler (1952, chap. 14).

[6] Of course, the problem remains of finding a mutually agreeable set of market shares. See Cross (1969, pp. 207–14).

etc.) among the various members. Enforcement costs are then reduced to those of assuring that no one sells to a forbidden customer. There has been some analysis of optimally imperfect terms of agreement for cartels that cannot achieve complete joint maximization. For instance, Comanor and Schankerman (1976) point out that, for industries selling on the basis of bids on individual transactions, identical bids are less costly to enforce than a scheme of rotated bids that requires explicit agreement on market shares, so that we expect (and find) schemes involving the rotation of bids typically to encompass smaller numbers of sellers.

Second, a cartel may have a positive value to its members even if it achieves no long-run departure from a competitive market outcome. Consider the simple story often told in the institutional literature on cartels operated between World Wars I and II: A cartel is formed without the accession of all actual or potential producers of the good in question. The price is raised. The outsiders find price comfortably in excess of their marginal costs and expand output. Newcomers observe the elevated price to exceed their minimum attainable average costs and enter the industry. The cartel members start to lose market share, and the cartel-managed price gives way. The usual account then concludes that the cartel failed, and a soporific moral is drawn about the ultimate triumph of pure competition. The trouble is that the cartel members did expropriate consumers' surplus and cause deadweight losses of welfare while the cartel was in operation. And it could be rational to enter a cartel expected to be temporary (whether due to entry by outsiders or the defection of nominal signatories), even if the profits of the cartel members in the competitive period after the cartel's collapse are expected to be less than the competitive profits they earned before its formation.

The maintenance of cartels

Conventional cartel theory becomes more loquacious on the maintenance of a cartel agreement—the incentive to cheat, the chances that cheating will be detected, and the mechanisms of enforcement against the cheater. As the preceding discussion has suggested, this focus is unsatisfying because the enforcement problem results from the incompleteness of the cartel agreement—itself unexplained theoretically. Therefore, models of cartel enforcement float in an undefined structural context, and they are specific to an arbitrary set of initial conditions. I shall stress this problem of structural context in surveying these models.

The fundamental problem of maintaining cartel arrangements is that in order to obtain monopoly profits they must elevate price above producing members' marginal costs. In the absence of a common sales agency or binding profit-sharing arrangement, each member can potentially increase his own profits in the short run by any maneuver that lets him sell an extra unit for net revenue less than the official cartel price though greater than marginal cost. The factors affecting the net revenue gain expected by the potential cheater can be classified into three groups. First, consider the behavior of short-run marginal costs as the cartel members collectively restrict output and elevate the market price. The more steeply sloped their marginal cost curves in the neighborhood of the precartel output are, the greater becomes the gap between price and marginal cost. A familiar generalization is that a high level of fixed costs as a percentage of total costs should be associated with a steeply sloped marginal-cost curve.[7] Strictly speaking, the observation that fixed costs make up a large proportion of total costs tells us only about the magnitude of *total* variable costs— the integral under the marginal-cost curve up to the precartel output. Nonetheless, there is a probabilistic relation between high fixed costs and a steeply sloped marginal-cost curve, in that the average slope of the marginal-cost curve over its whole range must be steeper.

Another factor affecting the temptation to cheat is the elasticity of the cheater's demand curve, i.e., the responsiveness of the quantity he sells to whatever terms he offers to buyers. That responsiveness depends first on whether his product is a perfect substitute for those supplied by other members of the cartel. If it is differentiated in any way, or if transportation or other transaction costs differ for each buyer, depending on the seller chosen, the elasticity of the demand curve faced by the cheater will be reduced. The elasticity also depends on the method used by the price-cutter to lure extra business—an across-the-board announced price cut or clandestine price reductions to selected buyers. Between these extremes lie price cuts offered to all inquiring buyers but not publically announced and disguised price cuts in the form of quality or service improvements; these disguised improvements in the terms of the transaction can also be offered either selectively or to all buyers. The potential cheater presumably selects the method of defecting from the cartel agreement that has the highest expected present value. This is not necessarily the one corresponding to the most elastic demand curve for the cheater, because the behavior of costs and the likelihood of detection and enforcement also affect the calculation. The average sizes and size distribution of buyers are prominent among the factors determining the response of the quantity that the price-cutter sells to the terms he offers. A seller offering secret price cuts will certainly favor large buyers, if the likelihood that his cheating will become known depends on the number of buyers to whom cuts are offered and not their size. Conversely, the large buyer's threat to take his business elsewhere is more effective in forcing a selective price cut under any circumstances

---

[7] See Scherer (1970, pp. 192–98).

wherein the seller incurs some fixed contact cost per customer in securing new business.[8]

The third influence on the incentive to cheat is the probability of detection and the costliness of the enforcement that follows. One component is the expected lag between the offering of a reduced price and its detection by cartel members. The model developed by Orr and MacAvoy (1965) assumes that price information is transmitted only with a lag, so that the seller cutting price enjoys some increased profits before discovery, although reduced profits afterward. They show that if enforcement takes the form of matching the cheater's price cut, the potential cheater can calculate the optimal price cut (if any) to offer; and if the lag before detection is long enough, the present value of the profits expected from cheating will exceed those of remaining loyal to the cartel's terms. Besides the lag, the price-cutter's expected return will also depend on the chances of detection (within a given time) and the form of the punishment he expects. These features of cartel behavior demand treatment on their own.

The detection of cheating

The existence of a stochastic lag before cartel members detect cheating and a probability that they will discover it within a given period of time are alternative ways of formulating the same thing. The potential cheater who considers ways of offering price cuts in some sense seeks the one most effective in reaching buyers relative to its speed in reaching cartel-member competitors. Detection depends on the forms in which information passes through the market. If all prices are openly quoted, the same price must presumably be offered to all buyers (unless the structural conditions for price discrimination are present) and will become known to all buyers and sellers at the same time. If price quotations are made to individual buyers, the situation becomes more complicated. A favored buyer has an incentive to conceal his boon from other buyers, because their propensity to demand equally favorable treatment is probably hostile to the preservation of his own favored status. On the other hand, he may have an incentive to tattle about a below-market offer to other sellers in hope of getting a better price still. The seller who expects favored buyers to report the bonanza to other sellers will tend to refrain from cheating; the seller who expects them to switch to his custom and keep quiet will cheat more freely.

[8] Costs of switching to different trading partners, whether incurred by buyer, seller, or both, affect market equilibria in numerous ways that cannot be explored here. For example, the existence of switching costs for the seller are sufficient to guarantee large buyers a lower price, even if there are no scale economies in the transaction itself. If the buyer has no incentive to enter into a long-term supply contract with a particular seller, he can never be deprived of a credible threat to switch suppliers, and thus the seller in each market period rationally offers a discount that depends on the size of these contact costs and the difference between the sizes of the large and the average buyers.

In the face of these diverse possibilities, one model that has attracted much attention is Stigler's (1964) "A Theory of Oligopoly," which is really a theory of the detection of cheating under rather specific conditions. Stigler assumes that each seller recognizes his regular customers and can perceive whether or not he is losing an abnormally large percentage of them in a given time period. Stigler's sellers do not, however, know the prices that other sellers are charging, although these price offers are disseminated by any given seller both to the established customers of other sellers and to buyers new to the market. The Stiglerian seller may hear indirectly about price cutting, with a probability that increases with the number of buyers contacted—hence cheating grows more likely, the fewer buyers per seller. Cartel members' main defense against cheating, however, is to stand guard with probability tables in hand, inferring cheating from any movements of customers in the market that are sufficiently improbable if all sellers are maintaining the agreed price. These movements include the following: the loyal seller can lose too many old customers; the price-cutter can be observed to retain too large a fraction of his own old customers; or the price-cutter can be found attracting too many of the customers new to the market. The latter two tests of violation generally require that the loyal sellers pool their information, and there is always some gain to the loyalists from pooling. It emerges from this model that cheating is more likely to occur the more numerous the sellers, the fewer customers are present per seller, and the more random shifting of buyers among suppliers normally taken place (i.e., shifts not motivated by price cuts). The likelihood of cheating is reduced where large loyal firms are present, because the gains to equal-size firms from pooling information about customer movements are equivalent to the advantages in statistical confidence enjoyed by the large-firm observer of the market.

The process of enforcement

The process of detecting cheating in cartels holds no importance unless there is some mechanism to punish cheaters. And, as Yamey (1973) pointed out, even with a mechanism identified, we still require an explanation why it is in the interest of some cartel members to apply the indicated punishment.

In formal duopoly models it is usually assumed that the punishment for cheating on the cartel consensus is a reversion to the Cournot solution, either permanently or for some predetermined number of time periods. If there are lags in detecting a member's price cut, even a threat of permanent reversion to the Cournot solution will not deter cheating in all cases. To end the cartel, however, is an analytically uninteresting form of punishment, and there are other possibilities to consider:

1. The optimal price response of loyal cartel members is not necessarily to revert to the Cournot solution. In the model of Orr and MacAvoy (1965), where information lags permit price differentials between sellers to persist, matching the cutter's price is neither a sufficient deterrent nor optimal for the cartel. Rather, a reaction-function equilibrium can emerge between the price-cutter and the cartel members, and Orr and MacAvoy show that it is stable under certain conditions. This adaptive behavior between price-cutter and cartel members is reminiscent of a pattern observed empirically in industries with an oligopolistic core or dominant firm but also a fringe of price-taking small firms. The fringe cannot be kept from undercutting the core group's price by some amount. However, some constraints restrict the rate at which fringe firms can expand their joint market share; usually unspecified, these constraints might result either from information lags or adjustment costs in adding capacity for the fringe. The core holds to its collusive price (or perhaps chooses an optimal differential over the fringe) and loses market shares over time.[9] Finally, Salant (1976) develops the properties of an optimal reaction by a natural-resource cartel to the existence of noncooperative fringe producers. The essence of monopolistic exploitation of a natural resource is to charge a higher price initially than would competitive exploiters, but to raise it less rapidly over time and to make the resource last longer. Where a competitive fringe takes the cartel's behavior as parametric, Salant shows that the cartel maximizes its present value by producing nothing, or very little, until the competitive extractor's resources are exhausted, then producing on a schedule that maximizes the present value of the cartel's resource stock. An analysis somewhat similar to Salant's is provided by Hnyilicza and Pindyck (1976), who assume different discount rates for the fringe and core of the resource-extracting producers and thereby provide the basis for a Pareto-optimal extraction schedule that maximizes a weighted average of the welfare functions for the two groups.

2. A punishment more onerous than a return to a noncooperative equilibrium is a threat to ruin a price-cutter, and a formal analysis of games of survival can be employed to identify possible patterns.[10] Telser (1966) develops this analysis in the context of the capital structures of business firms. The firm in an uncertain environment, facing a rising marginal supply price of funds, must keep a portion of its capital in liquid assets for unforeseen contingencies. These liquid funds defend the value of the firm's fixed capital (to be exact, its value in use over its salvage value) by permitting it to operate for a period with its variable but not its fixed costs covered. If this firm is caught cutting prices, the cartel's enforcer may be able to put

9 See Worcester (1957); Stigler (1968, chap. 9).
10 See Shubik (1959, chap. 10).

prices lower still and force fatal losses on the price-cutter. The cost of predation to the potential monopolistic survivor is at least the liquid assets of the potential victim plus the present value of the profits lost by the enforcer during the period of price warfare. The feasibility of such enforcement is greater, the shorter the victim's liquid reserves and credit lines, and the higher the victim's minimum average variable costs relative to the long-run average costs of the enforcer. If the enforcer's fully allocated costs are actually less than the victim's variable costs, the victim's enterprise in any case has no economic value. Certain structural conditions in the market increase the feasibility of price warfare for eliminating a price-cutter. For instance, the price-cutter may operate in a more limited market segment that the enforcer; or the enforcer may be able to identify the price-cutter's "regular" customers and direct his retaliatory price cuts only at them. These conditions make predation a more feasible enforcement strategy, but they do not necessarily make it optimal; the factors determining the minimum cost of the attack to the enforcer are still the victim's liquid reserves plus foregone profits on some quantity of sales.

3. An enforcement strategy potentially preferable to predatory attacks on a price cutter is to buy him out, or to offer a bribe to induce him to leave the market. There is room for such a deal, as an alternative to a predatory attack, because the price-cutter is better off taking a price (or bribe) slightly greater than his liquid reserves, whereas the potential monopolist is better off paying anything up to these same liquid reserves plus the present value of the monopoly profits he expects to lose during a predatory attack. Telser (1966) shows, however, that the lower limit to the merger price or bribe just stated may be too small. This is because the cost to the potential monopolist of extending an actual price war for another time period always exceeds the cost to the price-cutter (because the former equals the latter plus the present value of the monopolist's foregone profits). Therefore, the price-cutter, as a blockade to monopoly profits, is a valuable market asset, and the price-cutter should be able to secure outside funds to enable him to hold out for at least the value of his total capital, not just the value of his liquid funds. The proposition remains that it is generally more profitable for a cartel to dispose of a single price-cutter through a bribe than through predatory action. However, a vital qualification is that the effects of the two strategies on the profits expected by potential entrants are quite opposite. The supply of potential entrants must be limited for the bribe strategy to be superior.

Although cartel theory identifies these possible enforcement strategies, it is reticent about what structural conditions might mark one seller a price-cutter, another an enforcer of a joint-maximization agreement. Among the few clear factors is relative size. The larger the firm's share of sales under the joint-maximization agreement, the smaller are its potential gains from diverting additional sales by price cutting (because there is less to divert), and the larger are its losses from foregoing monopoly profits.[11] Another discriminant sometimes listed is the relative efficiency of firms; the reasoning holds that for two otherwise identical cartel members, the one with the lower marginal cost curve will experience the greater gap between market price and marginal cost and thus the greater temptation to snatch at extra sales. The trouble with this inference is that the assumed difference in marginal costs at the outputs stipulated in the cartel arrangement indicates that the cartel members are not minimizing their total costs of production, and it also implies that they would not have identical preferences for the common cartel price. The cartel agreement thus is incomplete, to begin with. A few other factors might discriminate between price-cutters and loyalists. Short time horizons or high discount rates dispose participants toward price-cutting; the price-cutter trades short-run profits against long-run sacrifices, whereas the trade for the enforcer is of foregone short-run profits against the preservation of long-run monopoly returns.

In conclusion, these mechanisms for detecting and punishing cheaters are specific to the terms of the cartel agreement within which the behavior takes place. The mechanisms may be interesting if cartel agreements in fact do contain incomplete provisions for policing their terms. However, the reasons why the terms should be incomplete are left unexplained. If punishment *A* is an insufficient deterrent to cheating, why does the cartel not employ heavier punishment *B*? The loyalists can afford the punishment costs, because the seller who cheats on an optimal cartel destroys more surplus for the loyalists than he annexes for himself.

Strategic responses to cartels

What of the buyers in a cartelized market? Traditional cartel theory offers them little but the option to bribe the cartel to sell at marginal cost. The possibility of a mutually beneficial arrangement rests on the familiar conclusion that the gain to the cartel (its monopoly profits) is less than the loss to the buyers (monopoly profits plus deadweight loss), except in the case of perfect price discrimination. Recently Nichols and Zeckhauser (1977) have revived Abba Lerner's (1944) proposal of government counterspeculation as an antidote to monopoly. Lerner pointed out that public authority could hold a stock of a monopoly's output, offering to sell unlimited quantities at long-run marginal cost, and thereby force the monopolist to accept marginal-cost pricing. Nichols and Zeckhauser deal with the problem that the government must first acquire a stock of the cartel's output before this strategy can be employed. Working with simulations based on two-period and multiperiod models, they analyze a strategy that basically reduces to the following. With the full knowledge of the cartel, the consuming-country government (or governments) purchases on

[11] This analysis assumes that the cartel members do not pool profits, so that individual members' profits are related to their sales.

the market in the first period and sells its holdings in the second period. This strategy can be mutually beneficial, despite the existence of storage and holding costs for the consumer-nation government, because the cartel gets its profits moved forward in time (from the second period to the first) and the consuming nation averts enough deadweight loss in the second period to offset the holding and storage costs and any increase in the cartel's profit-maximizing price that occurs during the first period. (It is not even necessarily optimal for the cartel to raise the first-period price when it knows stockpiling is taking place.) If several importing countries independently undertake counterspeculation, it will be underprovided, because part of the gain from *A*'s stockpile sales is in surplus for *B*'s consumers.

Because the cartel nations must benefit from the occurrence of stockpiling,[12] the cartel is actually worse off when stockpiling is underprovided and will lower its initial period price somewhat as a partial offset to this underprovision. To that extent, the "weakness" of divided (noncollusive) consuming nations becomes a virtue.

Cartels in the international economy

The preceding analysis has mainly dealt with firms as actors and proceeded in a microeconomic context. However, translating the conclusions to the circumstances of countries cartelizing their exports is generally a straightforward process. The process of monopolizing barter trade for a single country is familiar from the theory of optimal tariffs, and joint monopolization by several countries is merely a matter of calculating the optimal export tax from the joint foreign reciprocal demand curve. The analysis of countries combining to exploit joint monopoly power is closely related to customs-union theory, in which the welfare-maximizing country seeking a customs-union partner is simply a general-equilibrium discriminating monopolist looking for the submarket with the elastic demand curve, and the rest of the world becomes the loser from price discrimination.[13]

A good deal of current writing on international primary-product cartels implicitly employs the analysis of cartel agreements developed above. Without attempting a full survey, some points of contact can be noted.

1. The structural requisites for reaching initial agreement have been discussed in terms reminiscent of Fellner's (1949) analysis of oligopolistic bargains. Because the objectives of national governments are multiple and vaguely defined, a shared set of values (e.g., a common religion) may be more helpful than purely economic facilitating factors, such as a small number of participants. Sharing profits—or even defining them exactly—is

---

[12] They cannot be excluded from benefits because the cartel can always frustrate the stockpiling strategy by charging the no-stockpiling monopoly price each period.

[13] The relation between customs-union theory and price discriminating monopoly is developed by Caves (1974*a*).

not an easy matter when governments are traders, so the quest for cartels is constrained to agreements in which profits can be acceptably shared as the outcome of the division of output. Potential participants seem conscious that cartel efforts are unproductive where the demand curve and/or the supply of potential entrant producers is elastic.[14]

2. Because of the incompleteness of observed and practicable cartels, policing and enforcement become major problems. When the agreement is simply to raise price, total demand declines, while individual participants are motivated to expand their outputs; the cartel is visible only if dominant members possess extra-economic threat capabilities or are willing themselves to make the necessary output cutbacks. The latter course has apparently been followed by the largest oil-exporting countries. The international aluminum industry employs a consortium arrangement to buy up the otherwise unsold supplies of fringe producers.[15]

3. Another important implication of incomplete agreements is that the distribution of output cannot be rationalized and marginal costs equalized among the producers. This incompleteness either prevents agreement on a joint-maximizing price at the start, or brings about divisive disputes when the price is subsequently adjusted. Producers whose output has been expanded to its long-run equilibrium level, or the extraction of whose stock resource is far advanced, experience a high perceived marginal cost and therefore prefer high prices, even if all sellers are in agreement about the elasticity of demand. One systematic (and rational) divergence does occur, however, in estimates of the demand elasticity facing individual producers. For selling countries in which buyers have already invested in fixed plant to extract the resource, the relevant demand elasticity for price increases is reduced by the sunk character of this plant. For producer countries whose deposits are not yet developed, the operative elasticity of derived demand reflects the buyer's ability to vary the combination (and location) of complementary inputs.[16]

4. International governmental cartels were often formed between World Wars I and II at times when market price had dropped to a very low level, due to declining demand or the intrusion of substitutes. Although this source of cartelization efforts is often attributed to a psychological propensity to "do something" when and only when the existing situation has become unsatisfactory, a more economic rationale can be found in cartel theory. At such times the proportional gap (and probably the absolute

[14] See Rowe (1965, part IV), Bergsten (1974), Krasner (1974), and Mikdashi (1974).

[15] See Litvak and Maule (1975), on aluminum, and Blair (1967), on quinine.

[16] See Greene (1977), on the International Bauxite Association. Greene also shows that the presence of concentrated buyers complicates the formation of a sellers' cartel, because a series of arm's-length prices and price differentials between buyers' locations does not exist. The cartel must grope with limited information not only for a price level but also for a price structure.

gap) between Cournot profits and joint-maximum profits increases. It becomes rational for the potential cartel member to incur higher policing costs, higher risks of retaliation, or whatever costs might probabilistically be incurred in pursuit of elevated profits.

5. The debate over importing-country policies toward the Organization of Petroleum Exporting Countries touches upon the policing of cartel arrangements and the detection of cheating. Adelman (1972) has argued that the OPEC countries' use of a "tax" as a nonnegotiable base for pricing oil and the intermediary roles of the international oil companies have reduced the opportunity for the importing countries to exert their bargaining power as large buyers. There is ground for dispute, however, whether that bargaining power is better exercised by conversion of the crude-oil market into one of bilateral monopoly or by a number of large but independent buyers who can exploit the intrinsic difficulties of policing the cartel.[17]

6. Hexner (1945, chap. 4) demonstrates how the risks of failure in a cartel create distrust that further reduces the completeness of the cartel agreement that can be achieved. For instance, optimal allocation of output to a changing group of customers generally requires a collective mechanism to assign customers to suppliers. However, individual suppliers are apt to prefer keeping their old customers in order to build loyalty against the day of the cartel's collapse.

II. POLICY TOWARD COMMERCIAL MONOPOLY

In the balance of this chapter I consider the policy-making country not as a participant in an international cartel or an adversary of other nations forming cartels, but rather as a welfare maximizer dealing with commercial monopoly in national product markets. Market monopoly may pose three issues for the national policy-maker: (1) it may affect the nation's gains from trade and its efficient participation in international trade; (2) trade policy provides an instrument of competition policy by limiting or extinguishing monopoly in national markets; (3) patterns of collusion in noncompetitive markets may affect the short-run dynamics of the economy's response to changes in the international economy.

Monopoly and the gains from trade

A small country participating in international trade by definition faces an externally determined world price ratio. If one of its domestic industries is monopolized, it therefore follows that exposure to trade will eliminate the monopolist's perceived distinction between price and marginal revenue and force him to act as a pure competitor on the world market. This effect, which amplifies the conventional gains from trade, will be

---

[17] Compare Adelman (1972) and Roberts (1974).

considered in the next section. What must be recognized first, however, is that the standard propositions about gains from trade acquire some important qualifications if monopoly extends beyond a single industry in a small country. Melvin and Warne (1973) analyze the conventional two-by-two general-equilibrium model in which one or both of the two sectors is monopolized in each country. (It turns out not to matter whether monopolistic control affects both industries in each of the two countries, or only one industry—the same one—in each.) Their model employs explicit utility functions which assure that at any relative price ratio demand elasticities for a given good are the same in both countries.[18]

In this model, one trading country must wind up worse off than with purely competitive free trade, and both can wind up worse off. More alarmingly, one country can experience a lower level of welfare with trade carried on by monopolies than it would with monopolized production and no trade at all. The potential loser can be identified—the country having a comparative advantage in the good with the higher elasticity of demand at equilibrium world prices. If only one sector (the same one) is monopolized in each country, the nation with a comparative advantage in the competitively produced good may suffer from the introduction of trade. These conclusions from a two-by-two model do not translate easily into policy conclusions for an *n*-sector trading nation, but they provide a suitable cautionary note about the effect of monopolies that persist in the presence of international trade.

Some significant findings about monopoly and the gains from trade have been developed in a partial-equilibrium context. Corden (1967) considered the problem of a decreasing-cost industry—a natural monopoly—facing import competition. When should such an industry be established, given that the country can instead acquire its product through international trade? Corden shows that there is a critical import price that makes its establishment just socially desirable; that price lies below the one that would allow the monopoly to cover its average costs and above the one that would prevail in an equilibrium with price equal to its marginal costs. When the world price lies below the monopoly's average-cost price, however, the gain from establishing the natural monopoly is contingent on a lump-sum transfer arrangement that permits (forces) it to price at marginal cost. Corden demonstrates that a tariff can play no useful role in this situation. Raising the landed price of imports by less than the amount needed to establish the industry merely costs consumers' surplus. Raising it to or above the price that permits the monopoly to cover its costs permits it to price at or above average cost and impose a welfare loss.

---

[18] In this model the introduction of trade does not change the degree of monopoly; the two national producers of any given good behave as if they were jointly monopolizing the world market, with their market shares determined by the general-equilibrium adjustment of trade to tastes and factor endowments.

Corden assumed that his decreasing-cost firm was somehow probihited from expanding to minimum-cost scale and charging forth into export markets. Basevi (1970) and Pursell and Snape (1973) point out that an export market affects the decision to establish a decreasing-cost industry, even if the net world price received by the exporter is below his minimum attainable long-run average cost with all scale economies exhausted. Their case is essentially that of the decreasing-cost producer who can cover his costs only through price discrimination. Domestic demand by itself is not substantial enough to permit the industry to cover its costs at any level of output. And the world-market price, as mentioned, lies below the minimum attainable average cost. Nonetheless, if the activity is carried on by a discriminating monopolist, output may be sufficiently expansible through foreign sales that a higher price in the domestic market will yield enough profits to cover total costs. Thus, there can be cases in which welfare is increased by permitting a decreasing-cost monopolist to discriminate between home and foreign markets, as the price of bringing him into existence. As in Corden's case, a tariff is no help for reaching the optimum, and indeed an import subsidy may be desirable to curb excess monopoly price in the domestic market. Frenkel (1971) points out that discrimination against the domestic market is not always necessary; the cost reduction attainable through selling on price-elastic export markets may make a natural monopoly viable, charging a single price at home and abroad. White (1974) indicates some consequences of monopolized production of exportables for the volume of goods exported. The discriminating monopolist who sells at a competitive world price will supply more exports than would a competitive industry experiencing the same costs, because he elevates the domestic price, reducing demand at home and freeing more goods for the world market. If the monopolist of exportable goods cannot price-discriminate, however, the quantity he exports will be at most equal to what a competitive industry would supply, and he may opt for exporting nothing at all.[19]

In this section we have taken as a given either a monopolized market or decreasing costs as a structural basis for natural monopoly. Empirical research in industrial organization treats markets not as dichotomously monopolistic or competitive, but as capable of showing degrees of "market power," i.e., departing by varying amounts from conditions of pure competition. There is, in fact, a feedback loop running from the structural conditions that create market power to the pattern of a country's foreign trade, because certain fundamental characteristics of technology and demand underlie both comparative advantage and market power. The specific

---

[19] White also points out that a risk-neutral import-competing monopolist will produce less than a risk-neutral competitive industry facing the same distribution of expected import supply prices.

relation between trade patterns and market structure must, of course, vary from country to country because not all countries can export the same thing, and so the evidence will not be summarized here.[20] Instead we turn to international trade as a limit on market power.

International trade and competition policy

Eliminating a market distortion due to monopoly is an extra dividend that may be associated with the gains from trade. Put the other way around is the old American saying, "the tariff is mother of the Trusts." The two-sector general equilibrium model provides some simple comparative-statics findings about the effect of opening an economy to competitive trade when one industry is initially monopolized. If the monopolized sector is the export industry at externally given world prices, that sector's output will definitely expand, but the pretrade domestic price could either rise or fall. If the monopolized sector turns out to be import-competing, the domestic price will definitely fall, but the pretrade output could either expand or contract. In any of these cases, the world's gains from trade are greater than if the economy had been initially competitive.[21] In each instance, unrestricted international trade is a sufficient remedy for monopolistic distortions of domestic markets, in the sense that the marginal conditions for a competitive welfare optimum will hold after the introduction of trade. Feenstra (1977) points out, however, that international trade is not a complete remedy to monopolistic distortions in this general-equilibrium case, if the monopolist also exercises his monopsony power in national factor markets.[22]

The last few years have brought a burst of statistical research on the effect of international trade on monopoly or—more generally—the extent of market power exercised by oligopolistic industries. These studies examine rates of profit on equity capital or price-cost margins as indicators of the fruits of exercised monopoly power. These dependent variables are related by means of multivariate regression analysis to assorted measures of trade exposure for a sample of manufacturing industries. There is a problem of how to evaluate the extent of import competition facing an industry—

[20] Relevant studies are Pagoulatos and Sorenson (1976*b*), Caves and Khalilzadeh-Shirazi (1977), and Caves et al. (1977).

[21] See Caves (1974*c*); also Melvin and Warne (1973).

[22] Feenstra (1977) demonstrates that monopsony in the two-by-two general equilibrium case could be exercised in two ways. The conventional monopsonist recognizes his influence on individual factor markets, depressing the relative price of the factor used intensively in the monopolized industry and forcing the economy onto an inferior transformation curve. The "multiplant monopolist" buys factors of production competitively (say, because branch plant managers fail to recognize their collective influence on the price of each individual factor); however, the monopolist recognizes (as numerous pure competitors in the same industry would not) that expansion of his output along a convex transformation surface drives up his marginal cost. The multiplant monopolist's decisions leave the economy on its competitive transformation curve, though not at the optimal output, either with or without free trade.

specifically, how to proxy the position and elasticity of the excess-supply curve of competing goods importable into the national market. Reliable econometric estimates of import-supply elasticities are not found in droves. Most researchers have settled for using the share that imports comprise of domestic production or domestic disappearance as a proxy for the missing parameters. The proxy could obviously be faulty; e.g., the import-supply curve might be perfectly elastic, and yet domestic supply might fall just slightly short of domestic demand at the world price, making the import share very small. Still, given that the "industries" identified in published statistics and used in these statistical analyses only roughly approximate homogeneous markets, the import-share proxy is probably not a bad indicator of what proportion of the finely defined goods marketed by a group of sellers actually face close competition from foreign suppliers.

In any case, this variable has been found to have a statistically significant negative influence on measures of monopolistic distortion in several studies. Effects of import competition for U.S. manufacturing industries were reported by Esposito and Esposito (1971) and Pagoulatos and Sorenson (1976a). Both studies cover relatively large samples of manufacturing industries and secure statistical results that seem robust to minor changes in statistical specifications.[23]

With such strong results found for the large and relatively closed U.S. economy, one would expect even clearer findings for the smaller industrial nations. The pattern has been a bit murky, however. Khalilzadeh-Shirazi (1974) undertook a similar analysis of U.K. manufacturing industries and secured a regression coefficient for the import-share variable that was correctly signed, but only marginally significant. Hart and Morgan (1977) found no significant relation in their analysis of U.K. data for 1968. A very likely explanation for their negative result is the 1967 devaluation of the pound sterling, which raised the landed price of competing imports and should have given import-competing industries a temporary windfall. Pagoulatos and Sorenson (1976c) studied the determinants of price-cost margins for France, Italy, Germany, the Netherlands, and Belgium–Luxembourg in 1965, reporting a significant negative influence of import competition for all but Italy. Adams's (1976) coefficient for a transnational sample of large companies is negative, but not always significant. For Canada, Schwartzman (1959) employed a different research design that involved comparing the performance of more concentrated Canadian manufacturing industries to their less concentrated U.S. counterparts. He recognized that higher concentration in Canada should lead to higher price-cost margins only when the Canadian industry's trade exposure is

---

[23] The Espositos report separate regressions for consumer and producer-good industries. When a correction has been made for heteroscedasticity, the import variable appears significant for the consumer goods but not the producer goods.

attenuated. However, the concentration-profit relation that he found for the trade-sheltered industries became even more significant when the import-competing industries were added to the sample. Jones, Laudadio, and Percy (1973) chose to represent import competition by dummy variables designating high (imports over 30 percent of domestic shipments) and medium (imports between 15 and 30 percent) import competition with Canadian manufacturing industries. Their medium-imports dummy proved insignificant, their high-imports dummy *positive* and significant.[24]

Two modifications of these analyses may help to explain their incomplete support for the hypothesis that import competition limits the exploitation of monopoly positions. Most important of these is Bloch's (1974) development of the proposition that import competition should affect industries' profitability only if their seller concentration is indeed high enough that excess profits would be taken in the absence of foreign rivals. Bloch's own statistical work, discussed below, deals with the effect of tariffs rather than import competition. In research in progress on Canadian industrial organization,[25] we find that monopoly profits are significantly related to a variable that is a measure of seller concentration divided by imports as a percentage of domestic-industry shipments. There is not a significant relation to either concentration or the import share when they are included separately in a regression equation. Because the import share is a small fraction with a skewed distribution, the interaction variable tends to "turn on" concentration as an influence on profits only when import competition is low.[26] Another modification recognizes the weakness of the import-share variable as a proxy for the parameters of the excess-supply curve of imports. Turner (1976, chap. 4) utilized the 1967 devaluation of sterling, which provided a substantial disturbance to the import competition faced by U.K. manufacturing industries, as an opportunity to improve this specification. Given that the devaluation should have elevated world prices relative to U.K. domestic prices and costs by about the same proportion in all industries, variations among industries in the change in imports' share of the market in the years immediately following devaluation years should be correlated with the elasticity of the unobserved excess-supply function.

---

[24] For this they offer an unsatisfactory explanation that might apply to a short-run time-series analysis, but not to a cross-sectional analysis in which (one normally assumes) the entities are observed only randomly displaced from their long-run equilibria.

[25] This study, undertaken jointly with M. E. Porter, M. Spence, and J. T. Scott, draws upon a data base constructed with the support of the Royal Commission on Corporate Concentration. Caves et al. (1977) provides a preliminary report on this project that does not include the result mentioned in the text.

[26] Pagoulatos and Sorenson (1976c) also employ an interaction between concentration and import share, but they inappropriately formulate it as a product rather than as a quotient. Naturally, it is not significant.

Turner seeks to explain variations in price-cost margins in 1973 both by imports as a percentage of domestic disappearance in 1973 and by the recent change in a somewhat similar variable, the proportional change in import share. He finds that the change in imports has much more explanatory power.[27] Pagoulatos and Sorenson (1976a) employ a somewhat similar variable, the proportional change in the level of imports 1963–67 as an alternative to the 1973 share of imports for explaining price-cost margins in 1967; the rate of import growth is marginally significant, but appears to have considerably less explanatory power than the level of the import share.

Some evidence from surveys and case studies supports and extends these statistical findings about imports and monopoly in the United States. Sichel (1975) queried large manufacturing firms in the United States as to the identity of their three principal competitors—foreign or domestic. At least one foreign company was listed among the principal rivals of 23 percent of his respondents, although only 5 percent listed a foreign firm as the leading rival. When the respondents were classified to their principal industries, at least one response in 42 of 69 industries designated a foreign company among the chief competitors. Frederiksen (1975) studied several highly concentrated U.S. industries that had experienced increased foreign competition since World War II, finding that foreign rivals had increased price competition in two industries selling undifferentiated products, but that foreign rivalry had been less effective in two differentiated-product industries for which a significant proportion of imports are "captive" purchases by the leading companies in the U.S. industry.

The evidence on import competition, taken together, suggests that imports are a substantial limit on monopolistic distortions. A principal implication of this finding is that tariffs facilitate the collusive behavior of domestic sellers in concentrated industries and can thereby cause welfare losses in such markets that are greater than the familiar deadweight losses expected when a purely competitive industry receives protection. The proposition that tariffs increase the incidence of monopolistic distortion has been tested directly in some statistical studies. Pagoulatos and Sorenson (1976a) report a significant and correctly signed regression coefficient for a variable indicating the proportion of competing imports that are subject to nontariff barriers, but nominal tariff rates are not significant. For Canada, McFetridge (1973) found no influence of effective rates of protection on price-cost margins. Bloch (1974) likewise found that the gross profits of heavily protected Canadian industries, relative to the gross profits of their U.S. counterparts, were no higher than for industries with low tariffs. He did find, however, that selling prices of the heavily protected industries

---

[27] It makes no important difference whether the change is calculated for 1968–73, 1970–73, or 1971–73.

were higher, suggesting that the effect of tariff protection may be on efficiency rather than profitability.[28] We return to this question below.

This analysis provides a strong case against tariffs because they can amplify the scope for monopolistic distortion. But the policy implications go beyond a preference for free trade over tariffs. Vicas and Deutsch (1964) point out that the government could force even a monopoly not facing import competition to price at marginal cost by offering a subsidy to imports equal to the difference between the higher world price and the monopolist's marginal cost at the output that equates his marginal cost to price. If his average costs are covered, the monopolist would produce the "competitive" output, and no imports would actually enter.

The theory of the effect of trade exposure on monopoly indicates that the consequences for a small country's domestic monopoly should be the same whether the industry emerges as competing with imports or making net exports. Either way, it faces a parametric price on the world market. In a sample of actual industries, however, two factors could upset the implied prediction of a negative relation between the proportion of an industry's output exported and its rate of profit. For a concentrated and collusive industry, dumping may be possible, so that the presence of international trade is associated with discriminating monopoly. This would imply (if anything) a positive relation between exporting and profitability. Second, under some microeconomic assumptions efficiency rents could accrue to exporting firms, even if they lack shared monopoly power. For instance, if the industry's product is differentiated, the presence of foreign markets should shift the demand curve facing the average seller outward and lift the profit rate above the normal rate of return implied by the Chamberlinean tangency solution. Hence we have no determinate empirical prediction about the effect of export-market participation on profitability.

Actual statistical results have turned out correspondingly diverse. For the United States, Pagoulatos and Sorenson (1976a) report no consistent relation (even as to sign) between profit rates and exports as a percentage of the industry's value of shipments. In their study of five European countries, Pagoulatos and Sorenson (1976c) get negative signs for all five countries, but the coefficients are significant only for France and Italy. Consistent with this, Jenny and Weber (1976) secure a significant negative relation for France, and the result is robust when several alternative measures of profit are empolyed as the dependent variable. Adams's (1976)

---

[28] There are reasons, having to do with sample properties, why the theoretically certain effect of tariffs on an industry's potential market power fails to show up in cross-section studies. As Bloch's (1974) analysis suggests, protecting an industry results in excess profits only if free entry of domestic sellers does not compete away the resulting rents. Nonetheless, governments may choose to ignore this fact and award high tariffs to many sectors that are purely competitive or employ large quantities of low-wage labor. Some of the highest tariffs therefore may generate no monopoly profits.

transnational sample gives an insignificant negative result. The outlier is the United Kingdom, for which Khalilzadeh-Shirazi (1974) found a significant positive relation between exports and price-cost margins. Additional exploration of this result by Caves and Khalilzadeh-Shirazi (1977) suggests the following interpretation: (1) for the United Kingdom, like other countries,[29] there is a strong relation between export participation and the sizes of companies and manufacturing establishments; (2) because U.K. exports run heavily to differentiated goods, efficiency rents associated with larger scale might be captured by the companies rather than dissipated through competitive entry; (3) the positive statistical relation between exports and profits, rationalized in this way, is weaker in the more concentrated industries, consistent with export-market participation having some dampening effect on the exercise of monopoly power. Taken together, the evidence on the exports and profitability of manufacturing industries suggests that extensive participation in foreign markets is (*ceteris paribus*) hostile to effective achievement of monopoly power in the domestic economy, and that it may also bring dividends in the achievement of more efficient scales of production.

A brief account is needed of the relation of the multinational company to monopoly and international trade.[30] Foreign direct investment tends to occur in industries where the average firm is large and sellers are concentrated. Although there are ways in which high concentration can promote foreign investment, and the presence of multinationl companies can increase the degree of monopoly, probably the most important fact is that concentration and foreign investment share a number of common fundamental causes. We can develop, however, some more positive propositions about the behavior of the multinational company that are relevant to international economic policy. It is seldom recognized that the multinational company is a favored entrant to industries with high barriers to entry. Monopoly is a long-run problem only where entry barriers deter the elimination of monopoly profits through entry, and analysis of the differing incidence of multinational companies from industry to industry establishes that the firm-specific assets that induce them to invest abroad tend to be what is needed for scaling the principal sources of barriers to entry (ample supplies of funds, established ability to differentiate their products, and perhaps other forms of technical and marketing skill). Thus the multinational company is a likely potential entrant into national industries that might otherwise be cloistered by even higher entry barriers.[31] When a foreign auto company begins assembly in the U.S. market, or a steel company develops

---

[29] Sue, for example, Scherer et al. (1975, p. 396).

[30] Brief because I have dealt with the subject at length elsewhere; see Caves (1974*b*) and Caves (1974*c*, pp. 17–28).

[31] Gorecki (1976*a*) demonstrates that multinational companies are not halted by the same entry barriers that affect other companies.

an iron ore deposit in a difficult piece of terrain, it may be providing an additional market participant that could come from few other sources. Besides its ability to enter a market, there is also some possibility that the multinational may be an entrant particularly disruptive of an oligopolistic consensus, especially in the early period of its presence. Its alien status may make it initially less sensitive to signals about an oligopolistic consensus emanating from established native firms. And its superior access to information about alternative returns to resources placed elsewhere in the world may make it less risk-averse than firms dependent on a single market.

The analysis so far supports a general policy of openness to market entry by multinational companies. The case is not completely clear-cut, however, for some considerations run the opposite direction. If the multinational company is good at scaling existing industrial barriers to the entry of new firms, it is also good at building up such barriers. The resources required to contrive such barriers (maintaining excess capacity, integrating forward to control distributive outlets, advertising heavily, accelerating the frequency of "model changes," etc.) are often found in the portfolios of multinational companies. It is also true that the multinational possesses the "long purse" that might drive out single-market rivals (see preceding section).[32] Of course, the most direct approach of public policy to such offensive forms of market behavior is to regulate or prohibit the behavior directly rather than blocking the very presence of international ownership links. Conduct designed to reduce the competitiveness of an industry is socially undesirable whatever sort of firm undertakes it.

One policy instrument that appears to have strong leverage on the activity of multinational companies is the tariff, in the case of companies whose foreign subsidiaries normally produce the same line of goods as the parent. A tariff elevates a company's cost of landing its goods within a national market relative to the cost of producing them there through a subsidiary, and hence tends to increase the flow of foreign investment. Many historical accounts affirm this effect of increased tariff rates. The statistical evidence, except for Horst (1972), is less consistent, but a cross-section statistical analysis is ill-suited for testing the hypothesis.[33] If we nonetheless accept the hypothesis, it has interesting implications about monopoly in national markets. Multinational-company entrants are likely to be a significant competitive force in industries that are protected from import competition by tariffs. The same holds for industries subject to

[32] Statistical research on the profitability of U.S. manufacturing industries suggests that profit rates are higher, the larger is the extent of foreign investment by member firms in the industry, after we control for the extent of monopoly or market power. This profit increment could represent the return to intangible assets garnered by working them in foreign markets, or it could measure the effect of additional monopolistic distortion due to international entry-barrier building or similar practices.

[33] Because some industries lack the structural requisites for direct investment to occur, and so no tariff is high enough to induce significant foreign investment.

product differentiation of the Chamberlinean stripe, in which multinational companies flourish on the basis of their success in establishing intangible good-will assets. Conversely, international trade is a more effective curb on monopoly where tariffs are low and where products are homogeneous, so that elaborate marketing organizations are not necessary to sell substantial quantities in a foreign market.

In considering international trade as a restraint on monopoly, economic analysis habitually concentrates on costs of allocative inefficiency—the deadweight loss due to monopoly. However, where competition is imperfect, trade—and trade restrictions—can have important effects on the degree to which costs are minimized. It is a commonplace that the welfare gains from policy changes that reduce unit costs can easily exceed those due to the recapture of deadweight-loss triangles. I shall concentrate on the relation between trade and cost minimization through attaining efficient scales of production.[34]

Trade changes the effective size of the market in which the firm sells. The connections can be illustrated by the firm in the position of the Chamberlinean monopolistic competitor, facing its individual, downward-sloping demand curve though not necessarily taking part in oligopoly. The total size of the market affects the typical firm's scale of production by changing the slope or position of the demand curve that it faces. Access to export markets shifts the curve outward and may also render it more elastic, if the firm's output faces closer substitutes in the international market than in the domestic market. Both changes tend to move the monopolistic competitor's profit-maximizing scale toward that which minimizes long-run average cost. The presence of competing imports has an ambiguous effect, shifting the import-competing seller's demand curve to the left, but also making it flatter, with an indeterminate effect on its profit-maximizing scale of production.[35]

This analysis can also be applied to the organization of Chamberlinean industries marked by either of the following conditions: (1) each "variety" of the product is subject to the same production function, but buyers' preferences are distributed unevenly among the varieties (some are popular, some are not); (2) each of n varieties is preferred by $1/n$ buyers when all varieties sell at the same price, but production functions differ so that some varieties are subject to greater scale economies than others (i.e., must

[34] This is only one channel through which competition and technical efficiency may be interrelated. Others are the outright inefficiency of the enterprise that employs more inputs than necessary to produce a given output and—a special case of this—chronic excess capacity.

[35] In referring to a Chamberlinean industry, I am assuming that entry by new firms propels existing ones *toward* the tangency solution but not invariably *to* it. Oligopoly (mutual dependence recognized) is assumed absent, but the average firm can still command a rent. Enlargement of market size can enlarge the rents of those firms not pressed to the tangency solution.

attain larger volumes to achieve minimum average cost). With free trade, the international distribution of production will be influenced from the cost side by the classic forces of comparative advantage. Given those forces, however, production in the small national market will tend to be confined to popular varieties and those subject to minimal scale economies (in the sense just defined). Large countries will tend to specialize in the unpopular varieties and those subject to extensive scale economies.[36] The effect of tariff protection for any national market—though especially a small one— is to make viable the production of less popular varieties demanded domestically in smaller quantities. Also, domestic production may become viable for varieties subject to more extensive economies of scale. Taking these effects together, it is possible that surrounding a small national market with tariff protection actually reduces the average size of enterprises. And it necessarily follows that tariffs imposed by any country tend to reduce the average scale of production for the world industry as a whole.[37]

A good deal of statistical evidence has accumulated that provides at least indirect support for these propositions about trade, scale, and efficiency. Scherer et al. (1975, pp. 117–20), analyzing the branches of twelve manufacturing industries located in six industrial countries, found that the extent to which plants attain minimum efficient scale in manufacturing industries depends sensitively on the proportion of total shipments that is exported. Eastman and Stykolt (1976, chap. 3) and Gorecki (1976*b*, chap. 5) report similar results for Canadian manufacturing industries. Owen (1976) found an association for pairs of European countries between the relative sizes of manufacturing plants and the balance of trade. Relatively larger plants (though not larger firms) are associated with larger net exports, although Owen's analysis does not clearly identify the direction of causation between the variables. Other studies have noted a simple correlation between the proportion of output exported and the average sizes of plants and firms,[38] and Pryor (1973, chaps. 5, 6) finds for a large sample of countries that the average sizes of both plants and companies (measured in various ways) are associated with the share of output exported after controlling for the size of the national market. On the import side, we saw that the effect of trade (and its impediment by tariffs) on efficient scale is ambiguous. Scherer's six-country study correspondingly finds that the extent to which an industry's plants achieve efficient scale is negatively but in-

[36] The analysis assumes that transportation and transactions costs are greater between than within national economies.

[37] This relation between trade policy and efficient scale depends on the individual firm facing a downward-sloping demand curve, and economists enchanted with the siren song of pure competition may suppose that this is an uncommon market condition. Therefore, I must stress the abundance of evidence supporting the principal corollary of the preceding analysis, namely, that the sizes of plants and firms will be related to the size of the national market in which they are embedded; for example, Pryor (1973, chaps. 5, 6).

[38] Caves and Khalilzadeh-Shirazi (1977); Caves et al. (1977, chap. 7).

significantly related to the extent of import competition. For Canada, however, several studies lean toward the conclusion that tariffs reduce the average plant scale of production or the degree to which efficient scale is attained.[39] Broadly speaking, the evidence confirms that trade restrictions reduce the average scale of production in an industry worldwide, but they may increase it within the markets of some tariff-imposing countries.

Monopoly and short-run adjustments

A final consequence of monopoly in open economies is that it may change the path of short-run adjustment to disturbances from what would prevail in the presence of pure competition. The difference arises not from the behavior of the theoretical pure monopolist but rather mainly from the pricing practices employed in oligopolies with incomplete collusive arrangements. Such industries' prices may be relatively sticky in the short run, because each change in list prices incurs the risk of a breakdown in the oligopolistic consensus. Such pricing behavior can affect both the imports and exports of the country in question.

If an industry's comparative advantage is deteriorating, or if the nation's money price and cost structure is getting too high relative to its fixed exchange rate, the short-run inflexibility of a domestic price can have the effect of inflating the volume of imports. This consequence has been documented for U.S. steel imports by Krause (1962), who found the prices of domestically produced steel products insensitive to changes in import prices and market shares. Rowley (1971, pp. 220–21) describes a period in which the U.K. steel industry showed similar behavior.

Other possibilities pertain to the concentrated exporting industry. Suppose that prices in the domestic market are maintained at a sticky collusive level, while the producers also sell as pure competitors on the world market. First of all, this behavior inflates the average volume of exports above what a competitive industry would sell abroad, as White (1974) pointed out. It can also influence the variability of exports. If the domestic price is inflexible in the face of shifts in the demand curve for the product, the induced fluctuations in the volume of exports will have a greater amplitude than if the domestic price adjusted competitively. Such competitive adjustments in the domestic price would reduce the variability of the quantity sold in the domestic market by a sticky-price oligopoly. Given the position of the sellers' marginal-cost curves, larger fluctuations in the volume of exports are implied by greater fluctuations in the oligopoly's domestic sales.

The presence of product differentiation also affects the adjustment of trade flows. Differentiated goods by definition lack perfect substitutes in

---

[39] Gorecki (1976*b*, chap. 5) reports an insignificant negative influence of tariffs. Eastman and Stykolt (1967) and English (1964) stressed the tendency of the tariff to hold an umbrella over firms that were inefficient for whatever reason, and the proclivity of multinational companies to locate inefficiently small-scale production facilities behind a tariff wall.

foreign markets. What adjustments are made to their export prices following a devaluation therefore can depend on pricing practices and market conditions in the domestic market. Turner (1976, chap. 3) found that after the 1967 devaluation U.K. producers of differentiated goods raised their domestic-currency prices of exports significantly less than producers of homogeneous goods.[40] The lower increase by itself does not prove a noncompetitive response, of course, but it does establish a potential influence for collusive practices in the domestic market.

The normative significance of monopoly for short-run adjustments in international trade is not clear and probably varies from one situation to the next. The point is simply that paths of adjustment can be different where elements of monopoly are present.

National and international policy toward monopoly

An "optimum tariff" serves the interest of the single country imposing it, but it imposes a net cost on the rest of the trading world. A similar problem of national versus international welfare arises in the making of national policy toward competition in an open economy. Consider first an industry that is monopolized and sells all of its output abroad. Suppose that some application of antitrust policy by the nation's government can potentially force the industry to sell competitively at a price equal to marginal cost. If, for simplicity, we assume that marginal cost is constant, application of the policy will have two effects. It relieves foreign consumers of a deadweight loss, and it transfers the monopoly profits formerly earned by the monopoly to the consumers' surplus of foreign buyers. The nation enforcing competition is necessarily a net loser, although the world as a whole is better off. If the monopoly has been selling some of its output at home (without import competition) and some abroad, the same antitrust policy now eliminates some deadweight loss at home. Given elasticities of demand in the home and foreign markets, one could evidently identify a share of output exported just small enough that the country would become a net gainer by enforcing competition for its exportable-goods monopolist.[41] The optimal national policy would, of course, be to establish competition in the industry, while applying an optimal export tax.[42] Without that

[40] Also see Hague, Oakeshott, and Strain (1974).

[41] This critical export share could be larger if the country attaches some utility to the redistribution of income from domestic profit recipients to domestic final buyers.

[42] That governments are not indifferent to the joys of monopoly profits taken from foreigners hardly needs to be argued in the days of OPEC. Less familiar, however, is the common practice of permitting domestic companies to collude on export sales, even when such behavior is illegal in the domestic market. In the United States the Webb–Pomerene Act is the vehicle for the exercise of joint monopoly in international trade. Part of the Act's rationale was to assist small companies to meet the heavy transaction costs of exporting through joint associations—a sensible policy by itself. However, Larson (1970) has shown that the Act has primarily benefitted already concentrated industries, and that the Webb–Pomerene associations have assisted in monopolizing the domestic as well as foreign markets.

option, however, the government must choose between the potential national gains from cartel participation outlined in the first part of this chapter and the advantages of domestic-market competition attainable partly through appropriate international economic policies.

This problem can be analyzed formally in terms of optimal competition policy for the exporting industry, on the assumption that policy instruments can secure any outcome from pure competition to pure monopoly, but must accept the same degree of monopoly in both domestic and export markets (Auquier and Caves, 1978). The larger the export market relative to the domestic market, the less competition should be enforced to maximize national welfare. The optimal degree of competition is greater, the more elastic is domestic demand and the less elastic is demand in the export market.[43] These partial-equilibrium conclusions can be transplanted to a general-equilibrium setting, using the model of Melvin and Warne (1973). For instance, if the same degree of competition characterizes a given industry in each country (the degrees may differ between industries, though), a nation can lose by entering into international trade either because its exportable good faces an elastic demand (Melvin–Warne's conclusion) or because a high level of competition in its export industry allows that industry to claim little of its potential monopoly profit. If the home country's industries are monopolized, while those abroad are competitive, the home country can lose from entering into international trade.

The general clash between national and international interests considered in this formal analysis has many simple implications for competition policy. A familiar form of international cartel agreement is for sellers in countries *A* and *B* to divide up world markets, with *C*'s market assigned to *A*, and *D*'s market assigned to *B*. Countries *A* and *B* may well be net beneficiaries of the cartel. *C* and *D* could potentially bribe them to terminate it, but handing over voluntary tribute to a foreign exploiter is not a policy proposal that commonly wins elections. The divergence of national interests bears not just on policy toward outright monopolies and collusive arrangements but also toward potentially monopolistic practices engaged in by multinational companies. It was pointed out above that the practices generating good-will assets that permit companies profitably to invest abroad also can create or augment contrived barriers to entry into their industry—whether in the multinational's home market or in the market where its subsidiary operates. Once again, prohibiting the practices might not be in the interest of the home-country government.[44]

A different problem of divergent national interests can arise when a multinational company in country *A* acquires or merges with a national firm in a country *B* engaged in producing the same line of goods. Suppose

---

[43] A related analysis demonstrates the use of an optimal export tax or subsidy on the assumption that competition policy is inoperable and the degree of monopoly must be taken as given.

[44] Other examples are discussed in Caves (1975).

that A's producer has not previously been exporting to country B, and that each country's competition authorities regulate mergers only on the basis of the effect on seller concentration in the national market. Concentration conventionally measured is unaffected by the merger in either of the national economies, yet there has been an increase for the two markets taken together. If concentration should be high enough in the international market, this merger could impose real costs on the trading world as a whole. Even if the producer in A has previously been exporting to B, the same misperception could occur if B's competition authorities follow the common practice of watching concentration ratios calculated only over domestic production and not over all sellers present in the domestic market.

Actual antitrust policy in the United States has been fairly sensitive to such spillovers from anticompetitive actions—even in cases where the United States is the beneficiary from monopoly rents. United States companies have been stopped from acquiring foreign companies that are their actual or potential competitors in the U.S. market (and elsewhere). United States and British companies in one instance were prosecuted for agreeing jointly to monopolize the Canadian market.[45] The internationalized competition policy of the European Economic Community has dealt with a number of cases that probably had divergent effects on the national economic welfare of Common Market members (see de Jong, 1975). Despite these favorable patterns, divergent national and international interests in competition create a general problem similar to the problem of tariff reduction addressed by the General Agreement on Tariffs and Trade. A possible (though not necessary) interpretation of that agreement is that countries agree to multinational tariff reduction on the conjecture that the losses they incur from reducing their own tariffs below "optimal" levels will be more than offset by their gains in consumers' surplus (including reduced deadweight losses) from foreign countries' reductions of monopolistic tariffs. One can imagine a similar declaration of faith in the averaging out of gross losses that could occur if all countries agreed that each would apply its competition-policy instruments to whatever monopolistic structures or practices lay within its reach, wherever the resulting social benefits might be felt.

The provisions of competition policy dealing specifically with international trade pose a somewhat different set of issues. All industrial countries allow their domestic sellers greater freedom to collude in the export market than at home, and most of them restrict monopolization of their export trades little or not at all.[46] This policy represents a consistent pursuit of national welfare maximization, in the sense that the prices charged abroad

[45] For details see Brewster (1958).

[46] See Organization for Economic Cooperation and Development (1974) and Gribbin (1976). Jacquemin (1974) suggests that the EEC takes a symmetrically tough line against foreign firms with market power in member-country markets.

by monopolistic exporters could in principle be identical to the "optimum tax" on exports. The only qualm about this policy for a government maximizing its own national welfare lies in the possibility that collusion among exporters may unavoidably spill over and increase distortions in the domestic market. In that case, the country faces the same tradeoff identified above between capturing consumers' surplus abroad and suffering deadweight losses at home. There has been little or no public recognition of the divergence between national and global welfare resulting from these policies, and the policies open to the individual country to combat foreign monopolization of its imports are limited (see the first section of this chapter).

The familiar applications of competition policy to imports are generally concerned not with getting them more cheaply but with restricting the sale of imported goods whose prices are affected by dumping or export subsidies. There is generally little or no foundation for such policies in the maximization of national welfare. The restriction of dumping from a nationalistic point of view makes sense only in the special case of short-run predatory dumping.[47] From an international viewpoint the case is more complicated, because dumping as a form of monopolistic price discrimination is efficient only if total costs can be covered in that way and no other. The case of an export subsidy is somewhat different, assuming that the exporting industry itself is competitive and the subsidy creates rather than removes a market distortion. The importing country maximizes its national welfare by doing nothing and accepting the improvement in its terms of trade. From an international viewpoint, however, all importing countries should impose a counter-vailing duty to offset the distortion induced by the subsidy, and this duty should not be contingent on the occurrence of injury to import-competing domestic producers.

III. CONCLUSIONS

This chapter has surveyed policy toward monopoly in the open economy. The national government may find itself dealing with two classes of issues. First, the nation may possess monopoly power over its export goods, if it colludes successfully with other producing nations. The literature of cartel theory, which concentrates on the conditions for sustainable collusion, supplies a number of useful predictions about the circumstances that render such alliances stable and supply countries with a self-interest in joining them. Some helpful hints are also available for nations whose terms of trade have been worsened by cartels; a version of counterspeculation may retrieve a portion of their losses.

Countries may also find themselves using international economic policy

[47] See Barcelo (1972).

to deal with imperfections in their national markets for goods and services. Where natural monopoly exists due to extensive scale economies, tariffs are no help; however, dumping may sometimes be desirable, and the analysis indicates conditions under which it is desirable to offer lump-sum subsidy to an import-competing monopolist. The power of unrestricted international trade to eliminate market distortions due to monopoly has recently been subject to extensive empirical testing. The general conclusion is that import competition (definitely) and export opportunities (probably) reduce the ability of concentrated industries to exercise their joint monopoly power. Conversely, tariffs augment or preserve this power and may also induce organizational patterns in industries that are inconsistent with cost minimization. The multinational company offers the advantage of being a well-equipped entrant into national product markets surrounded by high entry barriers, but it may also contribute in some ways to long-run anticompetitive conditions.

These two strands of national policy-making can be brought together around the situation of a national authority contemplating its policy toward a monopolized export industry. If the industry sells only in foreign markets, the national (though not global) welfare is served by allowing it to extract the rents available to it. On the other hand, if it sells partly in the domestic market, there is an offsetting deadweight loss to domestic consumers that might be greater than the profits corresponding to surplus captured from foreign buyers. The best nationalistic policy is to make the industry competitive, but levy an optimal tax on exports. If this cannot be done (e.g., because the monopoly power is holistic, due to patents or trademarks, and cannot be preserved one place but not another), a choice must be made by weighing the foreign loss against the domestic gain from enforcing competition. National competition policies implicitly recognize this dilemma by permitting collusion more freely in foreign than domestic markets. United States antitrust policy shows some tendency to recognize international competition and treat it in order to maximize global rather than national welfare.

REFERENCES

Adams, W. J. 1976. "International Differences in Corporate Profitability." *Economica* 43: 367–79.
Adelman, M. A. 1972. *The World Petroleum Market*. Baltimore: The Johns Hopkins University Press for Resources for the Future.
Auquier, A., and Caves, R. E. 1978. "Monopolistic Export Industries and Optimal Competition Policy." Harvard Institute of Economic Research, Discussion Paper No. 607.
Barcelo, J. J. 1970. "Antidumping Laws as Barriers to Trade—the United States and the International Antidumping Code." *Cornell Law Review* 57: 491–560.

Basevi, G. 1970. "Domestic Demand and Ability to Export." *Journal of Political Economy* 78: 330–37.

Bergsten, C. F. 1974. "The Threat Is Real." *Foreign Policy*, no. 14, pp. 84–90.

Blair, J. M. 1967. "Statement," in U.S. Senate, Committee on the Judiciary, Subcommittee on Antitrust and Monopoly, *Prices of Quinine and Quinidine*, Part 2, Hearings pursuant to S. Res. 26, 90th Cong., 1st sess., pp. 180–223. Washington, D.C.: Government Printing Office.

Bloch, H. 1974. "Prices, Costs, and Profits in Canadian Manufacturing: The Influence of Tariffs and Concentration." *Canadian Journal of Economics* 7: 594–610.

Brewster, K. 1958. *Antitrust and American Business Abroad*. New York: McGraw–Hill.

Caves, R. E. 1974a. "The Economics of Reciprocity: Theory and Evidence on Bilateral Trading Arrangements." In *International Trade and Finance: Essays in Honour of Jan Tinbergen*, edited by W. Sellekaerts, pp. 17–54. London: Macmillan & Co.

————. 1974b. "Industrial Organization." In *The Multinational Enterprise and Economic Analysis*, edited by J. H. Dunning, pp. 115–46. London: George Allen & Unwin.

————. 1974c. *International Trade, International Investment, and Imperfect Markets*, Special Papers in International Economics, no. 10. Princeton, N.J.: International Finance Section, Princeton University.

————. 1975. "International Enterprise and National Competition Policy: An Economic Analysis." In *International Conference on International Economy and Competition Policy*, edited by M. Ariga, pp. 183–90. Tokyo.

Caves, R. E., and Khalilzadeh-Shirazi, J. 1977. "International Trade and Industrial Organization: Some Statistical Evidence." In *Welfare Aspects of Industrial Markets: Scale Economies, Competition and Policies of Control*, edited by A. P. Jacquemin and H. W. de Jong, pp. 111–27. Leiden: Martinus Nijhoff.

Caves, R. E., et al. 1977. *Studies in Canadian Industrial Organization*. Ottawa: Information Canada.

Comanor, W. S., and Schankerman, M. A. 1976. "Identical Bids and Cartel Behavior." *Bell Journal of Economics* 7: 281–86.

Corden, W. M. 1967. "Monopoly, Tariffs and Subsidies." *Economica* 34: 50–58.

Cross, J. G. 1969. *The Economics of Bargaining*. New York: Basic Books.

de Jong, H. W. 1975. "EEC Competition Policy towards Restrictive Practices." In *Competition Policy in the UK and EEC*, edited by K. D. George and C. Joll, chap. 2. Cambridge: Cambridge University Press.

Eastman, H. C., and Stykolt, S. 1967. *The Tariff and Competition in Canada*. Toronto: Macmillan & Co.

English, H. E. 1964. *Industrial Structure in Canada's International Competitive Position*. Montreal: Canadian Trade Committee.

Esposito, L., and Esposito, F. F. 1971. "Foreign Competition and Domestic Industry Profitability." *Review of Economics and Statistics* 53: 343–53.

Feenstra, R. C. 1977. "Trade, Competition, and Efficiency: A General Equilibrium Analysis." Senior honors thesis, University of British Columbia.

Fellner, W. 1949. *Competition Among the Few*. New York: Knopf.

Frederiksen, P. G. 1975. "Prospects of Competition from Abroad in Major Manufacturing Oligopolies." *Antitrust Bulletin* 20: 339–76.

Frenkel, J. A. 1971. "On Domestic Demand and Ability to Export." *Journal of Political Economy* 79: 668–72.

Gorecki, P. K. 1976a. "The Determinants of Entry by Domestic and Foreign Enterprises in Canadian Manufacturing Industries: Some Comments and Empirical Results." *Review of Economics and Statistics* 58: 485–88.

————. 1976b. *Economies of Scale and Efficient Plant Size in Canadian Manufacturing Industries*, Research Monograph No. 1, Bureau of Competition Policy. Ottawa: Department of Consumer and Corporate Affairs.

Greene, R. S. 1977. "Cartel Action and Forward Integration by the Bauxite Producing Nations." Senior honors thesis, Harvard College.

Gribbin, J. D. 1976. "Review of OECD, *Export Cartels*." *Antitrust Bulletin* 21: 341–50.

Hague, D. C., Oakeshott, A., and Strain, A. 1974. *Devaluation and Pricing Decisions*. London: Allen & Unwin.

Hart, P., and Morgan, E. 1977. "Market Structure and Economic Performance in the United Kingdom." *Journal of Industrial Economics* 25: 177–93.

Hexner, E. 1945. *International Cartels*. Chapel Hill, N.C.: University of North Carolina Press.

Hnyilicza, E., and Pindyck, R. S. 1976. "Pricing Policies for a Two-Part Exhaustible Resource Cartel: The Case of OPEC." *European Economic Review* 8: 139–54.

Horst, T. 1972. "The Industrial Composition of U.S. Exports and Subsidiary Sales in the Canadian Market." *American Economic Review* 62: 37–45.

Hu, S. C. 1975. "Uncertainty, Domestic Demand, and Exports." *Canadian Journal of Economics* 8, 258–68.

Jacquemin, A. P. 1974. "Application to Foreign Firms of European Rules on Competition." *Antitrust Bulletin* 19: 157–79.

Jenny, F., and Weber, A. P. 1976. "Profit Rates and Structural Variables in French Manufacturing Industries." *European Economic Review* 7: 187–206.

Jones, J. C. H., Laudadio, L., and Percy, M. 1973. "Market Structure and Profitability in Canadian Manufacturing Industry: Some Cross-Section Results." *Canadian Journal of Economics* 6: 356–68.

Khalilzadeh-Shirazi, J. 1974. "Market Structure and Price-Cost Margins in United Kingdom Manufacturing Industries." *Review of Economics and Statistics* 56: 67–76.

Knickerbocker, F. T. 1973. *Oligopolistic Reaction and Multinational Enterprise.* Boston: Division of Research, Harvard Business School.

Krasner, S. D. 1974. "Oil Is the Exception." *Foreign Policy*, no. 14, pp. 68–83.

Krause, L. B. 1962. "Import Discipline: the Case of the United States Steel Industry," *Journal of Industrial Economics* 11: 33–47.

Larson, D. A. 1970. "An Economic Analysis of the Webb–Pomerene Act." *Journal of Law and Economics* 13: 461–500.

Lerner, A. P. 1944. *The Economics of Control.* New York: Macmillan & Co.

Litvak, L. A., and Maule, C. J. 1975. "Cartel Strategies in the International Aluminum Industry." *Antitrust Bulletin* 20: 641–63.

McFetridge, D. G. 1973. "Market Structure and Price-Cost Margins: An

Analysis of the Canadian Manufacturing Sector." *Canadian Journal of Economics* 6: 344–55.

Melvin, J. R., and Warne, R. D. 1973. "Monopoly and the Theory of International Trade." *Journal of International Economics* 3: 117–34.

Mikdashi, Z. 1974. "Collusion Could Work." *Foreign Policy*, no. 14, pp. 57–67.

Nichols, A. L., and Zeckhauser, R. J. 1977. "Stockpiling Strategies and Cartel Prices." *Bell Journal of Economics* 8: 66–96.

Organization for Economic Cooperation and Development. 1974. *Export Cartels—Report of the Committee of Experts on Restrictive Business Practices*. Paris: OECD.

Orr, D., and MacAvoy, P. W. 1965. "Price Strategies to Promote Cartel Stability." *Economica* 32: 186–97.

Osborne, D. K. 1976. "Cartel Problems." *American Economic Review* 66: 835–44.

Owen, N. 1976. "Scale Economies in the EEC: An Approach Based on Intra-EEC Trade." *European Economic Review* 7: 143–63.

Pagoulatos, E., and Sorenson, R. 1976a. "International Trade, International Investment and Industrial Profitability of U.S. Manufacturing." *Southern Economic Journal* 42: 425–34.

———. 1976b. "Domestic Market Structure and International Trade: An Empirical Analysis." *Quarterly Review of Economics and Business* 16: 45–60.

———. 1976c. "Foreign Trade, Concentration and Profitability in Open Economies." *European Economic Review* 8: 255–67.

Patinkin, D. 1947. "Multi-Plant Firms, Cartels, and Imperfect Competition." *Quarterly Journal of Economics* 61: 173–205.

Pryor, F. L. 1973. *Property and Industrial Organization in Communist and Capitalist Nations*. Bloomington, Ind.: Indiana University Press.

Pursell, G., and Snape, R. H. 1973. "Economies of Scale, Price Discrimination and Exporting." *Journal of International Economics* 3: 85–91.

Roberts, M. J. 1974. "Review of Adelman, *The World Petroleum Market*." *Journal of Economic Literature* 12: 1363–68.

Rowe, J. W. F. 1965. *Primary Commodities in International Trade*. Cambridge and London: Cambridge University Press.

Rowley, C. K. 1971. *Steel and Public Policy*. London: McGraw–Hill.

Salant, S. W. 1976. "Exhaustible Resources and Industrial Structure: A Nash–Cournot Approach to the World Oil Market." *Journal of Political Economy* 84: 1079–93.

Schelling, T. C. 1960. *The Strategy of Conflict*. Cambridge, Mass.: Harvard University Press.

Scherer, F. M. 1970. *Industrial Market Structure and Economic Performance*. Chicago: Rand McNally.

Scherer, F. M., et al. 1975. *The Economics of Multi-Plant Operation: An International Comparisons Study*. Cambridge: Harvard University Press.

Schwartzman, D. 1959. "The Effect of Monopoly on Price." *Journal of Political Economy* 67: 352–67.

Shubik, M. 1959. *Strategy and Market Structure: Competition, Oligopoly, and the Theory of Games*. New York: John Wiley.

Sichel, W. 1975. "The Foreign Competition Omission in Census Concentration Ratios: An Empirical Evaluation." *Antitrust Bulletin* 20: 89–105.

Spence, M. (forthcoming). "Tacit Coordination and Imperfect Information." *Canadian Journal of Economics.*

Stigler, G. J. 1952. *The Theory of Price*, rev. ed. New York: Macmillan & Co.

———. 1964. "A Theory of Oligopoly." *Journal of Political Economy* 72: 44–61.

———. 1968. *The Organization of Industry.* Homewood, Ill.: Richard D. Irwin.

Telser, L. G. 1966. "Cutthroat Competition and the Long Purse." *Journal of Law and Economics* 9: 259–77.

———. 1972. *Competition, Collusion, and Game Theory.* Chicago: Aldine-Atherton.

Turner, P. P. 1976. "Some Effects of Devaluation: A Study Based on the U.K.'s Trade in Manufactured Goods." Ph.D. dissertation, Harvard University.

Vicas, A. G., and Deutsch, A. 1964. "The Paradox of Employment Creation through Import Subsidies." *Economic Journal* 74: 228–30.

White, L. J. 1974. "Industrial Organization and International Trade: Some Theoretical Considerations." *American Economic Review* 64: 1013–20.

Worcester, D. A., Jr. 1957. "Why 'Dominant Firms' Decline." *Journal of Political Economy* 65: 338–46.

Yamey, B. S. 1973. "Notes on Secret Price-Cutting in Oligopoly." In *Studies in Economics and Economic History: Essays in Honour of Professor H. M. Robertson*, edited by M. Kooy, pp. 280–300. London: Macmillan & Co.

Comment

ALAN V. DEARDORFF

Professor Caves has provided us with a useful survey of the literature on the role of imperfect competition in the international economy. From his remarks there appears to be a difference between the two topics that he treats, in terms of the extent to which distinctly international considerations are important for understanding and dealing with the market imperfections discussed. In the second part of his paper, he cites considerable evidence of how international trade can influence domestic market power and of how such market power, in turn, can affect the gains from trade. But in the first part of the paper he analyzes international cartels with the tools that are used for the study of purely domestic cartel arrangements, and leaves the impression that there is little that is distinctly international in the character of international cartels. While I do not dispute his claim that the same analytical framework is appropriate for both domestic and international cartels, I would like to amplify and extend his short section on "Cartels in the international economy." Specifically I shall suggest three issues that have occurred to me as posing difficulties for the maintenance of international cartels, difficulties that would not arise in a purely domestic context.

1. Caves mentions briefly the difficulty of defining the objectives of an international cartel when, as is likely to be the case, the participants either are themselves, or are abetted by, national governments. A "shared set of values" may, as he says, be helpful, but these values may well contradict the basic nature of a cartel, which is to restrict output so as to raise price. A concern for employment is the obvious example. Governments are often notoriously willing to stimulate inefficient production in order to sustain employment and may therefore be reluctant to enter or abide by a cartel agreement which requires that output be reduced. This suggests that international cartels are most likely to succeed among governments that feel no such responsibility to their people, and in industries where labor requirements are minimal.

2. Members of an international cartel face another difficulty that is reminiscent of one long faced by economists in determining the efficient pattern of trade: they must decide among various measures of cost in determining the output to be provided by each member. This problem does not arise in a domestic cartel where all members share a common currency. But the distinction between money cost and opportunity cost can be troublesome for cartel members that operate out of different countries. Suppose, for example, that money wages rise in the country of one of the members. A member firm, looking at money costs, will react to the change by reducing output, but from the national point of view opportunity cost is unchanged and output should not be curtailed. This suggests the need for coordination of macroeconomic policies among cartel member governments if the cartel is to function smoothly.

3. Finally, Caves points out that "joint monopolization by several countries is merely a matter of calculating the optimal export tax from the joint foreign reciprocal demand curve." This particularly simple means of setting up a cartel is, of course, not available to domestic cartels, and therefore suggests that cartels are more easily formed in the international context. It is not even necessary that the number of producing firms be small—only that the number of governments that are party to an agreement be limited. But if an export tax can be used to form a cartel, this also suggests a devious means of cheating on the cartel that would also not be available in the domestic context. For we know from Lerner's symmetry theorem that anything that can be done by an export tax can be undone by a reduction in tariffs.[1] For symmetry to be perfect, of course, the export tax must apply to all exports, but cartel member countries are often highly specialized in their exports, and even if they were not a tariff reduction

[1] See A. P. Lerner (August 1936) "The Symmetry between Import and Export Taxes," *Economica* 3: 306–13.

could be expected to partially offset the effect of an industry-specific export tax. Thus the enforcers of an international cartel must not only see that export taxes are effectively maintained in the member countries but also that tariff reductions (and perhaps other policy changes as well) are not used to undermine the agreement. One could object that member governments are unlikely to have read Lerner and to be aware that this means of cheating is at their disposal. But if the cartel succeeds in increasing export revenue, tariff reductions may be undertaken without the knowledge that they interfere with the cartel.

These remarks are only intended to be suggestive of the special problems that may face an international cartel. I would hope that these and other issues that are unique to the international cartel will be given further scrutiny by those economists, such as Caves, whose expertise covers both industrial organization and international trade.

CHAPTER THREE

Trade and Direct Investment: Recent Policy Trends

RACHEL McCULLOCH

I. INTRODUCTION

Overview

International economists have readily accepted some credit for the dramatic growth in world trade and investment that has occurred since World War II. Yet the policies actually chosen by most industrialized countries during that period comprised both liberal and protectionist elements, and, in any case, it is unlikely that whatever liberalizing changes were made reflected the persuasiveness of academic arguments.[1] Furthermore, clear evidence is now accumulating of renewed interest in protectionism—a political trend that certainly does not find its roots in recent scholarly output. Indeed, despite the strong policy orientation of international economists in the days of Ricardo, Mill, and Hume, little research in recent years has been motivated by or responsive to current problems as they are perceived by policy-makers. For example, even Corden's (1974) excellent and very comprehensive treatise on the theory and practice of trade policy contains but a few paragraphs on quantitative restrictions. However, encouraging trends are visible in new work. In particular, studies integrating the political and economic sides of policy formation, as well as those dealing with such hitherto neglected topics as short-run consequences, adjustment, and income distribution, now come at least within striking distance of the considerations policy-makers believe to be paramount.

This chapter does not attempt a thorough survey of the literature on

[1] Baldwin (1976), page 5.

Financial support for this chapter was provided by the National Science Foundation under Grant No. SOC–19459. I would also like to acknowledge a great intellectual debt to my friend and teacher Harry Johnson, who first stimulated my interest in the subjects discussed in this chapter.

trade and investment policy.[2] My purpose has been to identify areas in which the policy problems posed by trade and investment, or the solutions offered by international economists, have changed significantly in recent years. What follows is, therefore, highly selective, an assessment of the policy areas in which something new is happening, either in terms of problems or of solutions. Because of the very large range of possible issues to be considered, I have further narrowed the field by restricting my attention to major policy concerns of the United States and other industrialized nations. Thus, I have considered trade and investment problems of the developing nations only to the extent that these have had an important influence on the policies of industrialized nations.

Retreat from interdependence

Today every component of the international economic system is in a state of transition. After an extended period of progress toward international economic integration, the momentum of liberalization appears to be spent. In the decade since Richard Cooper wrote *The Economics of Interdependence*, economic and political events have amply underscored the central message of that book, and the world's nations have become painfully conscious of the costs of interdependence. Current and proposed changes in the institutions that set rules governing international transactions, as well as the policy changes of individual nations, are aimed largely at coping with the consequences of increased interdependence, while retaining at least some of the celebrated benefits of an integrated world economy. The abandonment of the Bretton Woods system in favor of a flexible exchange rate regime was promoted as a way of increasing national economic hegemony. The developing nations, even as they strive for a rapid increase in their share of world trade, are seeking new economic arrangements to free them from dependence upon the good will of the industrialized nations. Thus, the Organization of Petroleum Exporting Countries (OPEC), with its record of unilateral success in achieving a vast improvement in the economic and political fortunes of its members, has become the symbol of Third World aspirations. The Tokyo Round of Multilateral Trade Negotiations, stalled in efforts to further the cause of trade liberalization, seems destined at best to limit damage resulting from new national safeguard measures. In the area of direct foreign investment, the need for international guidelines governing the behavior of multinational corporations and of home and host governments has been acknowledged

---

[2] International economics has not suffered from a lack of surveys. Of particular interest to students of trade and direct investment policy are Stern (1973) on trade control, Corden (1974) on trade and investment, and Johnson (1975) on investment. Whitman's (1977) survey of current policy developments covers trade and investment as well as macroeconomic issues.

by all interested parties—although an early consensus on the substance of such guidelines appears improbable.

To call the current phase of international economic policy a "retreat from interdependence" is perhaps misleading, as it suggests that national and international policies were the driving force behind the prolonged period of increasing international economic integration. In fact, the postwar period has not been characterized by steady progress in the elimination of nationally imposed barriers to international transactions. Rather, the record has been mixed, with some important advances—particularly the restoration of currency convertibility and elimination of exchange controls during the earlier part of the period and the extensive tariff reductions negotiated during the 1960s—and many steps backward—most notably the proliferation of nontariff barriers to trade, especially the "voluntary" and "negotiated" bilateral arrangements of recent years.

More important in stimulating the growth of international transactions than the adoption of liberal policies have been rapid improvements in technology. Technological advances have facilitated and stimulated international linkages in at least three ways. First and most obvious are those advances resulting in reduced costs of transport and communication. A second important technological force has been the development of advanced techniques of large-scale management, which has facilitated the growth of multinational corporations. Finally, development of new product and process technology of all kinds typically entails relatively high initial outlays and marginal production costs that decline as cumulative output rises. This cost configuration offers a profit inducement to innovating firms to increase the size of their effective markets through trade, foreign direct investment, or licensing.[3]

While technological developments, rather than the gradual elimination of nationally imposed barriers, provided the driving force behind the increase in interdependence that followed World War II, national policies still played a key—if largely passive—role. Although technological advances facilitated and stimulated trade and investment, it was, nevertheless, a matter of national policy to allow these developments to take their course, rather than to stop them at the national borders with increasingly restrictive measures.[4] During most of the postwar period, the main trend of national policies was to provide mild reinforcement of, rather than resistance to, the growth in trade and investment; the evident gains from increased flows of goods, capital, and technology appeared to outweigh whatever costs were entailed. The technological gap between the United States and other industrialized countries, and between the industrialized

---

[3] Conversely, the opportunity to exploit new technology through these channels also increases the profitability of investments in research and development.

[4] Keohane and Nye (1975).

and less developed countries, was narrowed with surprising speed. Wages and per capita incomes rose rapidly throughout the industrialized world and in many developing nations.

In recent years, however, the political and economic gains from world integration through foreign trade and investment ties have come to be taken largely for granted, while the costs incurred through this interpenetration of national economies have become increasingly apparent. International linkages are now perceived as severely delimiting national hegemony, undermining the ability of national governments to achieve their own domestic macroeconomic and sectoral policy objectives. A number of recent polemic works have provided elaborate if sometimes selective documentation of the erosion of the power of individual nations to control their economic and political destinies.[5]

Trade and investment linkages also provide a channel for the international transmission of disturbances originating abroad. The transfer of advanced technology through foreign direct investment and licensing, together with explicit and disguised export promotion policies, have resulted in rapid changes in trading patterns. These, in turn, have caused massive sectoral dislocations for some industries and regions in the industrialized nations. Persistent high overall unemployment rates in these nations have exacerbated the adjustment problems associated with rapid growth of manufacturing capacity abroad, particularly in the developing countries; as a result, the new exporters of manufactured products have been faced with an increasing likelihood of abrupt export market closures.

While disturbances of foreign origin are part of a far larger class of disruptions that cause domestic adjustment problems in the industrialized nations, characteristically the immediate victims of shock from abroad are more visible and better represented than those who stand to gain from perpetuation and extension of liberal trade and investment policies.[6] In the United States, the labor unions have become an important pressure group favoring restrictive measures. The AFL–CIO helped to formulate and gave its enthusiastic support to the frankly protectionist Burke–Hartke Bill, legislation that would have instituted a broad system of import quotas as well as severe restraints on direct foreign investment and technology transfer by U.S.-based firms.

Recent gyrations in the markets for primary commodities have underscored yet another way in which international linkages may force costly adjustments upon national economies. The Arab oil boycott of late 1973 amply demonstrated the potential for political exploitation of economic interdependence, and the subsequent success of OPEC in maintaining a

---

[5] Servan-Schreiber (1968), Barnet and Müller (1974), Gilpin (1975).

[6] However, exporting nations threatened with the loss of lucrative markets often mount a substantial lobbying effort.

greatly increased price of oil indicates the possibility of joint exporter action for mutual economic gain. While few economists now expect that OPEC will be but the first in a sequence of long-lived raw material cartels, the increased likelihood of severe temporary dislocations, whether politically or economically motivated, is apparent. The industrialized nations have made their own contribution to increased uncertainty in the markets for primary commodities with occasional resort to export controls as an emergency measure to suppress conspicuous price increases, and extreme weather conditions such as drought (wheat) and frost (coffee) have been responsible for some large price movements in recent years. In general, the risk of supply interruptions and sizable price fluctuations, whether man-made or resulting from natural causes, is now viewed as a major source of uncertainty, increasing the effective cost of primary commodity imports.

The combined effect of these and related developments has been to turn, policy-makers in the direction of measures to limit or even reverse, rather than to facilitate, the growth of international linkages. The costs of inter-dependence have made themselves evident more slowly than the benefits, but they have made themselves evident, and a process of reaction is now underway.

II. TRADE POLICY DEVELOPMENTS

Politics and international economic policy

The political and economic forces confronting those who shape international economic policy have been transformed dramatically by the events of recent years. Perhaps most important among the changes is the altered role of the United States in the international system. At the close of World War II, the United States emerged as unquestioned world leader in terms both of military power and of economic strength. Heroic wartime feats had also won for the Americans a role of moral leadership in the world community. Vigorous recovery and growth in the other industrialized nations have now narrowed the military and economic gap, while the events of the Viet Nam era served to dissipate any remaining claim to moral leadership by the United States. Today the nation remains the world's foremost power, but it is now better described as first among equals. The decline in U.S. power and prestige means that the nation is less able than in the past to impose its own values on the policies of other nations of the Organization for Economic Cooperation and Development (OECD) and on the institutions that set rules governing the conduct of international transactions.[7]

A second crucial structural change in the international community is

[7] Whitman (1977).

the increasing integration into the mainstream of world trade and investment flows of new members: Japan, the Soviet Bloc nations and China, and the less developed countries (LDCs). A concomitant of this development has been the growth of the political and economic power of the international institutions, particularly those dominated by the developing nations. The new entrants all bring to the world community strong antimarket traditions, thus reinforcing the position of those who favor greater restrictions on international transactions.

A third important development is the emergence within the nations of the OECD group of strong new internal pressures for closure. The perceived role of trade and investment as undermining the ability of national governments to achieve domestic goals, particularly high employment, satisfactory wage growth, and control of inflation, has become a key political issue in the United States and other industrialized nations. While the pressures for restraints on trade and investment emerge from many quarters, the most vocal advocates in recent years have been the labor unions. The unions have, however, won some strong allies in the academic community; the academics generally support restriction of trade and investment to combat their undesirable effects on the (internal) distribution of income.

An important related development of the postwar period is the increasing politicization of international economic issues.[8] While political considerations have always been crucial determinants of economic policy choices, political pressures have become increasingly potent. In large part, this reflects the expansion over time of the role of the state in the regulation of economic activity, beginning with measures enacted in response to the special circumstances of the Great Depression and World War II, but which have tended to remain in place thereafter. This trend has shifted into the political arena many decisions previously left to private market forces. And, internationally, industrialized and developing nations alike have increasingly sought to link political and economic issues.

Perhaps in response to the increasing politicization of trade and investment policy, more economists are now studying the political determinants of economic policy decisions. In comparison with previous contributions to this area of research,[9] current work is typically narrower in its focus, applying standard techniques of economic analysis to questions that have been ignored by most contemporary economists. Brock and Magee (1973) have developed a model that incorporates bribes and public lobbying along with distributional effects in predicting political outcomes. Several empirical studies have used political variables to explain tariff structure—the relative height of tariffs across industries—or changes in that structure. Fieleke

---

[8] One objective measure of politicization used by political scientists is the number of inches of newspaper coverage accorded to these issues.

[9] Gerschenkron (1943), Hirschman (1945), and Kindleberger (1951).

(1976) examined interindustry differences in nominal tariff heights for U.S. manufacturing in 1965 and 1972 (before and after the Kennedy Round tariff cuts took effect). He found low-wage industries were more likely to have high tariff rates; however, all the traditionally accepted political measures together accounted for only a small percentage of total variation. In contrast, Cheh (1974) was able to explain up to one-half the interindustry variation in exemptions from across-the-board 50 percent tariff cuts imposed in the Kennedy Round with variables proxying short-run labor adjustment costs. Cheh's findings were supported in a subsequent study by Bale (1977), in which the proxies used by Cheh were replaced by actual estimates of labor adjustment costs. In yet another study of Kennedy Round tariff concessions, this time for West Germany, Riedel (1977) found no evidence that labor adjustment costs determined tariff cuts. Riedel concluded that West Germany has been more successful than the United States in replacing trade barriers by domestic subsidies and tax allowances as means of alleviating adjustment problems. However, coordination of tariff cuts among members of the European Economic Community was probably of major importance in determining the German outcome. Thus, a model that looks only at domestic labor adjustment costs is less appropriate for Germany than for the United States.

Caves (1976) examined the pattern of tariffs protecting Canadian secondary manufacturing industries in 1963. Three models of political behavior, which alternatively pose reelection, interest group pressure, and collective national preferences (represented by groups of relevant explanatory variables and hypothesized signs of effects) were tested; the results, while highly qualified, give greatest support to the interest group model. Results were stronger for effective than for nominal rates. Pincus (1975) investigated the role of pressure groups in obtaining favorable tariffs under the U.S. Tariff Act of 1824. He obtained strong confirmation of the effectiveness of pressure group activity, with geographical and industrial concentration and low proprietorial income (a proxy for a small number of proprietors) all leading to significantly higher tariff rates. Pincus hypothesized that the Tariff Act of 1824 was a more accurate reflection of group pressure than contemporary tariffs, since such benefits as "subsidies, tax credits, military procurements, freeways, etc." may be more easily secured or more attractive than import restriction. In a study with a somewhat different focus, Baldwin (1976) has examined the political forces determining the overall course of U.S. trade policy during the postwar period. Baldwin's statistical analysis of Congressional voting on the Trade Act of 1974 showed that import-competing industries were able to marshal congressional support for their interests, while export-oriented industries were less successful.

Recognition of the ability of pressure groups and individuals to influence government action for private benefit has given rise to new work on the social costs of rent-seeking behavior. Economists have never been fully satisfied with measured costs of protection as calculated by the standard Marshallian approach—the "tiny triangles" of lost consumers' and producers' surplus.[10] A new approach to the cost of protection, one which focuses on rent creation rather than static efficiency effects, has been advanced by Tullock (1967) and Krueger (1974). This argument concedes that many markets do satisfy one or more of the well-known conditions under which intervention may increase economic efficiency.[11] But tariff or quota protection, subsidies, and special tax treatment can be beneficial to *any* industry or special interest group, irrespective of whether these measures contribute to the efficiency of the economy as a whole. Thus, a government receptive to arguments for intervention in the name of increased efficiency will receive petitions from all sectors of the economy, based on claims by each firm and industry group that it also falls into one or another of these categories. The net effect is to turn economic activity away from the production of goods and services available to the final consumer and toward attempts to influence the legislative and administrative process. While these attempts may include bribery and other illegal transactions, the process can be totally legal and economically wasteful nonetheless. The loss thus incurred is probably far greater than any of the present estimates of the cost of protection; for every successful applicant, many others who have made similar investments have been turned away. Although it never became law, the Burke–Hartke Bill had a substantial social cost.

Krueger provides empirical estimates of the costs of "rent-seeking" behavior for Turkey and India. However, her calculations capture only the estimated costs of competition for *existing* rents, not the cost of resources— possibly far larger in total—which are devoted to promotion of new rent-creating restrictions by the would-be beneficiaries of such policies.

Trade and the distribution of income
The view that trade and investment policy should be designed to maximize national income without regard to its distribution has never won many adherents outside the economics profession. Today, most international economists themselves recognize that the separation of international economic policy from its internal (or even external) income-distribution consequences is unrealistic and sometimes counterproductive.[12] The traditional approach assumes that the problems of efficient adjustment and

[10] Increased competition and scale economies have been cited as further benefits from unrestricted trade. Leibenstein's (1966) *x*-efficiency concept gave a name to such benefits.
[11] For a summary, see Bhagwati and Ramaswami (1963) and Johnson (1965).
[12] Baldwin (1976, pp. 23–24).

redistribution have already been solved; in fact, they remain high on the agenda of critical unfinished business.

Even when liberal trade and investment policies yield clear aggregate benefits, these benefits are never evenly distributed. Measures that increase overall economic efficiency are likely to yield rather small benefits to large numbers of consumers and potential exporters, while inflicting costs— smaller in total than the national gains—upon a more concentrated group of factor owners. Broad programs of trade liberalization like the Kennedy Round do bring some compensating benefits to those hurt in their role as producers through lower prices for many goods they consume. Nevertheless, the distributional consequences of trade and investment policies cannot be ignored. From the standpoint of equity, a policy is not unambiguously beneficial for the country as a whole when its benefits are widely distributed but its costs borne by a small group;[13] from the practical point of view, proponents of restrictive policies are often politically powerful and well organized, so that liberal trade and investment policies can be made politically feasible only by coupling them with means of achieving a more even distribution of benefits and costs.

The internal dislocations resulting from rapid changes in trading patterns are frequently offered as a justification for temporary protective measures, and this principle is well established in U.S. and international trade law. However, international trade theorists see this practice as entailing excessive social costs; also, "temporary" measures have a predictable way of becoming permanent fixtures. The approach endorsed is a free trade policy, augmented by adjustment assistance when adjustment would otherwise be slower than optimal, and lump-sum compensation of "losers" from general tax revenues. However, success in redistributing income through taxes and transfers has been very limited, and public resistance to explicit redistribution policies is far greater than that (if indeed there is any)[14] to curbs on foreign competition designed to maintain employment in import-competing industries. Furthermore, optimism concerning the role of trade adjustment assistance programs as a means of smoothing adjustments to changes in international trading patterns appears to have been premature. In fact, an important reason for the resurgence of protectionist sentiment in the United States is that little success has been achieved in promoting prompt adjustment to sectoral demand changes resulting from import competition —or from any other type of disturbance, for that matter.[15] Policies intended

---

[13] Such a change could constitute a welfare improvement according to the potential compensation criterion.

[14] Political pressure for trade liberalization comes primarily from wholesale importers and from actual and potential exporters rather than from consumers.

[15] Dislocations stemming from import competition have a highly visible cause, however, and discrimination against foreign competitors is considered more acceptable than discrimination against lower-cost domestic competitors.

to compensate displaced workers have actually tended to retard, rather than to speed, adjustment.[16]

The Trade Expansion Act of 1962 broke new ground by providing trade adjustment assistance (TAA) for groups of workers injured by competition from new imports.[17] Under this legislation, injured workers could be eligible for extended unemployment compensation; counseling, retraining, and placement services; and assistance in relocation to obtain new employment. Labor's enthusiasm for adjustment assistance was short-lived. The eligibility criteria proved so stringent that not a single petition for assistance was approved until 1969, when the criteria were reinterpreted. Even after 1969, long delays between application and approval, along with administrative obstacles to the usefulness of some provisions, left most displaced workers, even those eventually judged eligible, to adjust without assistance. The Trade Reform Act of 1974 liberalized and simplified eligibility criteria somewhat, reducing the delay between application and approval for those eligible. The Act also introduced adjustment assistance for communities adversely affected by import competition. However, TAA still does little to smooth the adjustment process itself. The present program emphasizes extended unemployment benefits, leaving largely to the workers themselves the problem of finding new jobs.

TAA could be strengthened by inclusion of special benefits for older workers, who typically encounter the greatest difficulty in finding new employment; more efficient administration and an "early warning" system to help firms and workers anticipate dislocations; and expanded attention to retraining and employment counseling. These measures constitute active steps to assist displaced workers in finding suitable employment. It is worth emphasizing that these proposals would be beneficial in assisting workers displaced through any type of change in economic conditions, not merely those injured as a result of import competition.

Three empirical studies of adjustment under TAA have lent support to organized labor's claim that the program "neither adjusts nor assists." McCarthy (1975) made a careful study of the experience of workers displaced in the Massachusetts shoe industry—the largest concentration of adjustment assistance cases, both geographically and in a single industry. TAA was found to be ineffective in promoting adjustment for several reasons: strict eligibility criteria eliminated many injured workers and firms; the long time lag between application for and receipt of benefits left workers to adjust on their own; many workers did not know what benefits were available, while some were simply not interested. About one-quarter of

[16] This is not surprising, since the programs provide mainly larger unemployment compensation payments for a longer duration. Recent studies by labor economists have confirmed a positive supply response of unemployment to such payments.

[17] Injured firms were also eligible for assistance in the form of preferential tax treatment, loans and loan guarantees, and technical advice.

those displaced, usually older and female workers, never found another job. To calculate costs of labor displacement, Bale (1976) used data on workers who applied for TAA benefits. As in McCarthy's study, long delays between the date of layoff and receipt of assistance were apparent, so that few workers were able to take advantage of the nonpecuniary benefits available. A study by Neumann (1978) for the U.S. Department of Labor surveyed trade-impacted workers and compared the experience of those receiving assistance with a control group.[18] Again, many displaced workers failed to find new jobs; furthermore, the length of time between jobs was unusually high for TAA recipients. However, Neumann found some evidence that the longer period of unemployment was used productively for job search, since TAA males became reemployed at a significantly higher wage rate than the control group. This effect was much weaker for women.

Theorists examining the relationship between trade and the distribution of income have concentrated their efforts on the long run.[19] Because short-run effects are likely to have a larger impact on policy, theorists have had some difficulty in reconciling the main results of the long-run theory with observations of actual behavior on the part of interest groups. For example, in an empirical analysis of U.S. pressure group behavior, Magee (1976) found that labor and management work together on the question of protection—in contradiction to the patterns predicted by the Stolper–Samuelson theorem. Two recent papers by Mayer (1974) and Mussa (1974) have developed short-run analyses of income changes in a model based on the long-run Heckscher–Ohlin–Samuelson approach.[20] The short run is characterized by immobility of one factor. Results obtained are consistent with observed interest group behavior; for example, Mayer and Mussa show that a tariff on competing imports is likely to yield short-run benefits to both capital and labor in the affected industry.[21]

Trade theorists have recognized that immobile factors and rigid wages may cause unemployment when the terms of trade change. The prescribed second-best solution is, however, a production subsidy rather than a tariff on import-competing production.[22] In a recent paper, Lapan (1976) has argued that too large a subsidy removes any incentive for intertemporal reallocation of resources. He has used an optimal control approach to

[18] The choice of an appropriate control group poses obvious problems, however.

[19] The classic paper is Stolper and Samuelson (1941). Jones (1965) has presented these income distribution effects in a model now used extensively in international trade theory.

[20] Jones (1965).

[21] Mayer and Mussa both assumed freely mobile labor and flexible wages. Under these conditions, labor is always fully employed and earns the same wage in both industries. McCulloch (1977) has extended the analysis to the case in which a rigid wage prevents attainment of full employment.

[22] Haberler (1950) first proposed this analysis, later refined by a number of writers on distortion theory.

develop an alternative "dynamic subsidy," which results in eventual adjustment; when the social discount rate is not too high, losses from unemployment will be offset by gains from movement toward the long-run optimum.

A number of recent quantitative studies, most supported by the U.S. Department of Labor, have estimated the impact of trade flows on labor earnings and employment.[23] Baldwin and Lewis (1978) estimated trade and employment changes for the United States and eighteen other industrialized countries from a uniform 50 percent tariff reduction on most goods by these countries. The study reported detailed employment changes for the United States by occupation group, state, and industry. The authors' main conclusion was that a substantial multilateral tariff cut could be undertaken by the United States without causing significant adverse effects on aggregate trade or employment.

Bale (1976) made estimates of the private and social costs to U.S. workers displaced as a consequence of trade liberalization. The costs calculated include the effects of temporary unemployment as well as temporarily or permanently lower wages after new employment is obtained. Under alternative assumptions, private cost to an average displaced worker could be negative or close to $10,000, while social cost estimates ranged from about $1,000 to $8,000. A study by Jacobson (1978) emphasized long-term effects of job displacement on earnings. He found that the loss (private cost) for an average prime-age male displaced from one of the high-wage industries, such as automobiles or steel, could be as high as $17,000.

Horst and McCulloch (1977) analyzed the relationship between earnings of workers in manufacturing industries and the import shares of those industries. Results based on industry average earnings and individual earnings both showed a significant negative correlation between earnings and industry imports, in addition to the expected effects of such worker characteristics as race, education, and experience. (High-import industries are concentrated in the South and employ a disproportionate share of female, minority, and unskilled workers.) The industry results do not include costs of displacement for workers who lose their jobs, since the data were for workers currently employed in the industry. The individual data, for older males, showed that few in this group became unemployed or changed jobs; no significant link between imports and unemployment was found for this group.

Nontariff barriers to trade

Since the acclaimed success of the Kennedy Round of Multilateral Trade Negotiations in lowering the tariff walls of the industrialized nations,

[23] The pioneer among such studies was Salant and Vaccara (1961).

international economists have focused their attention increasingly on the role of nontariff barriers to trade. There are at least four related but distinct reasons for this renewed interest in quantitative restrictions and other, more elusive, forms of nontariff protection of domestic industries. Most obviously, the Kennedy Round tariff reductions increased the relative importance of existing nontariff barriers as deterrents to the free movement of goods. Second, nontariff barriers are characteristically ambiguous in their effects, including their consequences for the terms of trade and for the overall distribution of gains and losses. Thus, it was immediately evident that the negotiating formula used in arriving at multilateral tariff reductions had no easy counterpart in the negotiated elimination of nontariff barriers. Third, while important tariff reductions have been achieved, the underlying domestic policy objectives of the industrialized countries, such as maintenance of incomes and employment in particular import-competing industries, remain largely unchanged. Some tendency has therefore arisen to substitute nontariff measures for tariffs as means of achieving these objectives. Finally, as decisions concerning trade policy have become increasingly politicized, the very ambiguity of the effects of nontariff barriers makes them more likely than tariffs to provide a compromise acceptable to all parties. This is especially true of the recent trend toward voluntary export restraints and orderly marketing agreements; these measures allow rents created by trade restriction to be captured by exporters, thus providing partial compensation for losses inflicted on them by market closure.

A theoretical literature comparing tariffs and quotas has grown up in recent years, the major message of which is that no direct equivalence can be drawn except in certain restrictive cases. Bhagwati (1965) was the first to trace systematically the differences between the effects of tariffs and quotas under a variety of noncompetitive market situations, demonstrating nonequivalence when any one of the affected markets is monopolized.[24] Equivalence was defined by Bhagwati in terms of the relationship between the internal and world price of the protected product—the implicit tariff rate. Subsequent papers by Shibata (1968), Yadav (1968), Bhagwati (1968), Finger (1971), and McCulloch (1973) refined the original analysis, taking into account alternative definitions of equivalence in terms of effects on domestic production, imports, or profits; Holzman (1969) questioned the usefulness of the implicit tariff rate as a measure of import restriction, particularly in the case of Soviet Bloc nations. McCulloch and Johnson (1973) demonstrated that the distribution of import licenses was crucial to the outcome. Rodriguez (1974) and Tower (1975) analyzed equivalence when retaliation occurs. Shibata made the important point

[24] Although Bhagwati was the first to provide a systematic analysis, Heuser (1939) indicated that the use of import quotas might transform a potential monopoly into an actual one, and Meade (1950) showed that market structure would be one determinant of the impact of a quota.

that voluntary export restraints allow the exporting government to capture the rent created by trade barriers; the effects of such export quotas—which have proliferated in recent years—were considered in much greater detail by Bergsten (1975).

Another strand of literature has brought changes in demand and supply conditions into the analysis. Kreinin (1970) and Walter (1971) have pursued the question of (non)equivalence when demand or supply schedules for the imported good shift. Fishelson and Flatters (1975) and Pelcovits (1976) introduced uncertainty explicitly into the analysis. Anderson (1978) has pointed out that a specific tariff is fully equivalent to a state-dependent quota. In contrast to a fixed quota, the specific tariff in effect permits arbitrage of import licenses across alternative supply-and-demand conditions.

Bhagwati (1978) has explored the precise relationships among many of these nonequivalence results. As he has noted, all the cases rest upon the breakdown of the implicit assumption of given supply and demand schedules. When schedules shift exogenously, equivalence can be reestablished with a flexible quota. However, if shifts are endogenous—induced by trade restriction itself—equivalence breaks down regardless of flexibility. Actual administrative practices in a number of countries result in other types of nonequivalence. An example cited by Bhagwati is the allocation of raw material quotas in proportion to installed production capacity of domestic users.

The standard reference on nontariff barriers is Baldwin (1970), an analytical study that also contains a wealth of institutional material. Magee (1972) and Bergsten (1972) have calculated measures of the welfare cost of U.S. import restrictions. Magee's estimate was based on the standard Marshallian analysis, while the Bergsten study focused on cost to consumers in the form of higher prices, a somewhat misleading cost measure. Krueger (1974) has made rough estimates of the costs of Indian and Turkish import quotas on the basis of her rent-seeking approach.

Recent studies of specific U.S. quota arrangements include Dam (1971) and the Cabinet Task Force on Oil Import Control (1970) on oil, Johnson (1974) on sugar, and Jondrow (1976) on steel. The voluntary quotas on steel exports by Japan and the European Economic Community to the United States, which were in effect from 1969 until 1973, offer an opportunity to analyze empirically some of the questions of nonequivalence that have dominated the theoretical literature, but Jondrow simply calculated without comment an implicit tariff rate and did not consider the distribution of rents created by the quotas.

Discriminatory trading

Although nondiscriminatory trade is said to be one of the cornerstones of the General Agreement on Tariffs and Trade (GATT), preferential—

i.e., discriminatory—trading arrangements have become increasingly important in recent years. The GATT rules accorded a specific exemption from most-favored-nation (MFN) requirements to full customs unions and free trade areas; the rules were recently amended to permit extension of preferential treatment of developing country manufactured exports by the industrialized nations.

Most important among existing preferential arrangements is the European Economic Community (EC). The United States heartily endorsed the establishment of the EC for largely strategic reasons. Today, strategic considerations seem less important, and now that the EC's staged internal tariff reductions have been completed, exclusion from this large and affluent market is increasingly vexing to U.S. exporters. (As of 1977, the last remaining tariffs were also eliminated on trade between the EC and the seven members of EFTA,[25] creating a free trade area encompassing more than one-fifth of total world trade.) Although the EC's common external tariff on manufactured imports from the United States and other non-preferred nations is modest for most goods, even a low tariff wall around such a large market is a significant barrier. However, the primary focus of U.S. discontent is the EC's Common Agricultural Policy (CAP); on agricultural trade issues, the EC remains far more protectionist than the United States.[26]

The Europeans have also been active in establishing significant preferential ties with developing countries, beginning with former colonies. Virtual free access to the EC market is now available to fifty-two developing nations under the Lomé Convention, a wide-ranging trade and aid package, which also includes an export-earnings stabilization plan (Stabex) for raw material exporters. Reverse preferences were a part of prior arrangements —and another source of disgruntlement for U.S. exporters—but have been eliminated under the Lomé pact.

A number of trade preference schemes among the less developed nations themselves are now in effect. Of these, the oldest is the Latin American Free Trade Area (LAFTA), established in 1960. A more comprehensive Latin American regional trading bloc (SELA) was formed in 1975. Other preferential arrangements, mainly regional in membership, have been created in Central America, the Caribbean; Africa, Asia, and among the Arab states. As yet, these regional trading blocs are of relatively small importance in the trade of the industrialized nations, since intradeveloping nation trade constitutes just a small fraction of total world trade—around 6 percent in 1974 (excluding trade of nonmarket economies), and trade

[25] Members of the European Free Trade Area (EFTA) are Austria, Switzerland, Portugal, Iceland, Norway, Sweden, and Finland. The EC also has preferential ties with a number of Mediterranean countries.

[26] The prospects for negotiations between the EC and the United States on agricultural issues have been appraised by Whitman (1977).

between non-OPEC developing nations was only 2.5 percent of world trade. Nevertheless, as developing nations gain a larger voice in the international decision-making process, their wish to maintain and expand discriminatory trading arrangements is likely to further undermine the MFN principle.

The developing nations have also challenged the principle of nondiscrimination as unfair to the later starters (themselves) in the world trading community. Accordingly, they have demanded and received—after a decade of foot-dragging by the developed countries—a Generalized System of Preferences (GSP). GSP schemes now in effect allow many manufactured products of developing nations preferential access to the protected markets of the industrialized nations. Although the plans vary in coverage and in some cases appear to yield only token benefits, the effect of the establishment of these arrangements is to further erode the MFN principle. Also, since the benefits to eligible nations depend on the height of the MFN tariff of the importer, there has been some lack of enthusiasm on the part of LDCs for further MFN tariff reductions. The LDCs have requested compensation—in the form of increased GSP product coverage, for instance—for reduction of benefits resulting from negotiation of new MFN tariff cuts.

There is a well-established theoretical literature on discriminatory trading arrangements, mainly in the context of customs union, but the implications of reciprocity are rarely taken into account. Although most writers have acknowledged potentially important gains from increased competitiveness and economies of scale within a customs union, the traditional framework highlights static efficiency gains and losses. These correspond to the now familiar concepts of "trade creation" and "trade diversion" introduced by Viner (1950). That analysis has been refined in many ways, including the application of general-equilibrium techniques.[27] A basic problem with the traditional analysis was first pointed out by Cooper and Massell (1965). Whatever gains are made are in effect gains from a movement toward free trade. Nothing in the model explains why a country is initially away from free trade or why it chooses customs union rather than unilateral elimination of all tariffs. To avoid overstating the gains, a consistent model of the consequences of discriminatory trading must incorporate the motive for the initial level of protection.

IMF (1977) has summarized briefly the status of current preferential trading arrangements. On the EC, Swann (1975) has provided a comprehensive institutional study; many further references are included. Krause (1968) addressed the effects of the EC on U.S. economic welfare. Balassa (1967) estimated trade-creation and trade-diversion effects of the EC. Basic features of the major national GSP arrangements have been outlined

---

[27] The literature has been surveyed by Krauss (1972). More recent contributions have been made by Michaely (1976), Kemp and Wan (1976), and Corden (1976).

in IMF (1975, 1977). Cooper (1972), Murray (1973), and McCulloch (1973) have appraised the significance of restrictions limiting preferential access. Cline, Kawanabe, Kronsjo, and Williams (1977) have compared LDC benefits from preferential trading to gains from MFN trade liberalization, concluding that LDCs would benefit from the most complete liberalization possible.

Trade as a source of uncertainty

Recent events have underscored the role of international transactions as a major source of uncertainty for trading nations. However, trade and investment linkages also provide some insurance or risk-sharing opportunities for trading nations. The role of uncertainty in the analysis of trade policy has been raised in a number of contexts. Because each is discussed at some length in other chapters in this volume, I will simply list them here.

First, a large body of recent theoretical literature has examined the validity of the basic theorems of international trade under various types of uncertainty. These papers, focusing on such themes as the gains from trade and the direction of trade, are not oriented toward issues of trade policy, but nevertheless have implications for the effectiveness of alternative policies in achieving desired objectives. Some recent work, surveyed in a previous section, has introduced uncertainty into a comparison of the effects of tariffs and quotas. Second, there has been increasing recognition that the safeguard measures of the industrialized nations are a major source of uncertainty for LDC exporters of manufactured goods. Bhagwati and Srinivasan (1976) have analyzed the policy implications. Finally, the area that has attracted the greatest attention among policy-makers concerns the use of buffer stock arrangements and export-earnings stabilization schemes to minimize commodity price fluctuations and to mitigate their effects. Although this topic is a venerable one in the literature of international economic policy, recent large fluctuations in the prices of internationally traded raw materials have stimulated renewed interest.

III. DIRECT INVESTMENT ISSUES

The foreign direct investment controversy

The rapid growth of foreign direct investment (FDI) is perhaps the most controversial international economic development of recent years. The role of multinational corporations (MNCs) based in the United States and, to a lesser extent, in other industrialized nations, has been questioned on many grounds, sometimes mutually contradictory.[28] Efforts are now underway to

---

[28] This is particularly true for complaints concerning the distribution of benefits between home and host countries.

develop international rules guiding the conduct of the MNCs, as well as of home and host country governments.

Criticisms reflect four distinguishing characteristics of MNCs. Some attacks focus on the international mobility of MNC operations. Mobility is said to permit these firms to evade the national authority of both home and host governments, thus complicating the conduct of fiscal and monetary policy. International mobility of MNC production facilities likewise undermines the bargaining power of national labor unions, leading to income gains for capital at the expense of labor. A second class of criticisms is aimed at the size of the typical MNC, seen as a threat to competitive forces; the MNC practice of expanding by buying up locally owned firms is one form of anticompetitive behavior often cited.[29] A third category of issues suggests that MNC operations enable the home country to achieve economic and political benefits at the cost of the host nation, or the reverse. Most issues of taxation, transfer pricing, employment, and technology transfer lie within this group. Finally, and most removed from economic analysis, is the role of the MNC as an international transmitter of sometimes unwelcome cultural values.

Identification of the subject is itself a somewhat thorny problem for students of FDI. The hallmark of direct investment is, of course, control over operation of the enterprise. However, this definition is difficult to translate into a set of objective and easily observable characteristics, particularly ones that can be applied to a body of empirical data rather than on a case-by-case basis. Theorists attempting to assess the validity of claims regarding the effects of FDI have also encountered some difficulty in modeling the investment process. Typically, a direct foreign investment will include the international transfer of technology (here defined broadly to include trademarks and other means of product differentiation), managers and other skilled workers, and often, but not necessarily, physical capital equipment or financial capital (purchasing power). That the transfer of physical and financial capital need not be entailed is apparent from complaints by Europeans prior to the devaluation of the dollar that American MNCs were buying up European firms with funds borrowed on local capital markets.

Because FDI has become the center of a heated controversy, an overwhelming body of literature has accumulated on its causes, consequences, and control. Of the many surveys now available, Hufbauer (1975) on empirical evidence, Johnson (1975) on theoretical and policy issues, and Vernon (1976) on past and present MNC practices, deserve special mention. The following sections single out for consideration the issues that have received most attention from U.S. policy-makers in recent years.

---

[29] Caves (1974) has provided a useful overview of theoretical and empirical evidence.

Taxes and international capital flows

Tax treatment of foreign investment income by home and host countries has important implications for the efficiency of international capital flows and for the internal and international distribution of the returns to invested capital. In the United States, much recent attention has focused on the role of the foreign tax credit, which allows U.S. corporations a tax credit for taxes paid to foreign governments on earnings of investments abroad.[30] The tax deferral provision, which permits U.S. firms to postpone payment of U.S. taxes until profits are repatriated, has also become the object of increased scrutiny. The deferral in effect makes tax rates somewhat lower on foreign-source income than on similar income generated domestically whenever applicable foreign tax rates are lower than U.S. rates.

The effect of the foreign tax credit, leaving aside deferral, is to equalize the *after-tax* rate of return to the firm on capital invested at home and abroad. But in the case of domestic investment, the full gross return on capital accrues to the United States, since taxes paid are part of the national return, while with capital invested abroad, the United States receives only the after-tax return. Thus, national benefits from foreign investment are less than from investment at home.[31] On the basis of this analysis, Musgrave (1969) concluded that the foreign tax credit results in a misallocation of American investment. She has recommended that the United States abolish the foreign tax credit in favor of a deduction similar to that now in effect for state taxes. The argument assumes that firms do in fact choose between investing a dollar at home and in a foreign operation, and that the volume of investment is independent of the after-tax rate of return to the firm. Furthermore, as Hartman (1977) has noted, there is nothing in the Musgrave analysis that takes into account the characteristics of foreign direct investment apart from its role in facilitating the transfer of capital.

The issue of the distribution of capital income between home and host countries has also been raised in theoretical literature extending the logic of the optimum tariff analysis to the case in which capital as well as goods can move internationally. A larger flow of capital abroad means a lower rate of return on inframarginal units, so that the lending nation can gain through some degree of restriction of capital exports. MacDougall (1960) introduced this idea in a partial-equilibrium model. Kemp (1966), Jones (1967), and Gehrels (1971) have used general-equilibrium models with two countries and two sectors to derive optimal restrictions on capital exports. However, none of these contributions has taken explicit account of the characteristics that differentiate direct from portfolio investment.

---

[30] A detailed descriptive account of the taxation of foreign-source income has been presented by Musgrave (1969).

[31] An issue rarely raised in this connection is the marginal cost of services provided to the investor by the government of the country in which production or other facilities are located.

In addition to the international distribution of returns from capital, critics of U.S. tax policy are also concerned about the consequences of foreign investment flows for the distribution of income between capital and labor within the United States. Foreign investment is claimed to benefit capital at the expense of labor for three reasons. The first is a simple factor-proportions argument. To the extent that foreign investment lowers the capital-labor ratio in the United States, a one-sector model of competitive wage determination predicts a resulting reduction in the return to labor.[32] This argument is due to MacDougall (1960). Two other arguments focusing on the distributional consequences of foreign investment turn on the erosion of the bargaining power of national labor unions and on domestic employment effects. These arguments, frequently used by U.S. organized labor in promoting curbs on foreign direct investment by U.S. corporations, are appraised in a subsequent section.

Musgrave (1975) has made empirical estimates of the distributional consequences of a transfer back into the United States of U.S.-owned capital now invested abroad. While the estimated effect on aggregate national income is not large, the distributional consequences are noteworthy. Under Musgrave's assumptions, the share of national income received by U.S. labor would rise by 7 to 12 percent, while capital's share would decline by 7 to 9 percent. As Hartman (1977) has observed, Musgrave's (1975) estimates understate the potential gains in national income from restriction of capital outflows, since she has analyzed the case in which all U.S.-owned capital is returned, rather than the gains from optimal restriction of capital outflows. This method also produces a larger distributional shift than under an optimal policy. Thurow (1976) has used a simulation model to analyze the gains from a policy of optimal capital outflow restriction of the Kemp–Jones type; the distributional shifts estimated are similar to those obtained by Musgrave.

Hartman (1977) has developed a general-equilibrium simulation model incorporating the role of the direct foreign investor as a foreign producer. Production is assumed to be shifted abroad because of a cost advantage, with the effects of taxes as well as local factor costs taken into account. According to the analysis, significant national income gains can be achieved through appropriate tax policies, but the optimal tax rate may be substantially higher *or lower* than the current U.S. domestic rate. The optimal tax rate depends on the fraction of funds U.S. firms are able to borrow abroad, the size of the cost advantage of U.S. firms, the capital intensity of foreign production, and restrictions on trade. In contrast to the results obtained by Musgrave and Thurow, Hartman found that re-

---

[32] With two or more sectors, of course, a fall in the overall capital-labor ratio has no necessary implications for industry factor-use ratios or competitively determined wages.

striction of foreign investment may lower labor's share at home if foreign investors produce the capital-intensive good. He concluded that much additional statistical information would be required to tailor U.S. tax policy to achieve desired consequences for national income or its distribution.

International technology transfer

Multinational firms have been the main channel for the international transfer of new product and process technology; indeed, foreign direct investment has been characterized by Stobaugh (1974) as "primarily a movement of knowledge rather than a movement of funds." Most of the international flow of new technology has been from the United States to the rest of the world, first to other industrialized countries and more recently to the developing nations. Despite cutbacks in government support, the United States is still spending more for research and development than all other OECD countries combined. However, other nations, particularly Germany and Japan, are now the source of substantial U.S. technology imports.

In recent years, the transfer abroad of American technology, whether through foreign direct investment or licensing, has become a focus of increasing concern. Critics of U.S. policy argue that technology transfers erode U.S. comparative advantage based on technological superiority and are particularly detrimental to the interests of domestic labor. Organized labor's position on technology transfers was made explicit in its support of the Burke–Hartke Bill, which would have allowed the President to prohibit any holder of a U.S. patent from manufacturing the patented product abroad or licensing its use outside the United States, if in his judgment this prohibition would contribute to increased employment in the United States.

Advanced technology has long been recognized as an important determinant of U.S. trading patterns.[33] The United States has been a "high-wage" economy for many years. However, it is not wages but labor costs that are relevant in determining the ability of an industry to compete internationally. In many industries, high wages are more than offset by higher productivity, in large part due to superior technology. But in some industries, particularly those employing less-skilled workers, the cost disadvantage is too great to be offset by higher productivity. Wage rates in textiles, footwear, and apparel are relatively low in all the industrialized countries, but they are far lower still in less developed areas, such as Taiwan, Hong Kong, and Brazil, which have gained a rapidly increasing share of the world market for these products despite formidable barriers to trade.

[33] The empirical evidence has been summarized by Johnson (1975).

A systematic link between technology transfer and changing patterns of trade was suggested by Vernon (1966). The trade product cycle hypothesis posits a sequence of events that begins with investment in research and development aimed at home production. Exporting to foreign markets is the next step if the innovation proves successful at home. New products from the high-technology industries are likely to have no close competitors in foreign markets. The United States, with its giant (in absolute terms) research establishment and abundant supply (both in absolute and relative terms) of skilled labor, scientists, and engineers, has enjoyed a temporary world monopoly position for many unique products. As standardization progresses and the entry of imitators increases the importance of cost minimization relative to other considerations, production facilities are established abroad. While wage rates are clearly one component of the relevant international cost comparison, tax rates and import barriers may also play an important role in the location decision. Finally, if the cost advantage of foreign production is sufficiently important, the cycle may end with imports back into the home market of goods produced by foreign subsidiaries. This sequence has been confirmed empirically for many new products, including pharmaceuticals, synthetic fibers, and consumer electronics. The product cycle is, however, not so much a theory as a suggestive empirical generalization, since it offers no way of predicting how long each step in the sequence will take. Some observers believe that the product cycle has been speeding up in recent years, so that the period in which the innovating country has a comparative advantage in the new product is becoming shorter.

The product cycle sequence implies a corresponding employment sequence for the innovating industry. Initiation of the cycle is normally accompanied by growth of employment, which may accelerate after the new product is widely accepted in home and foreign markets. Even if world demand grows rapidly, however, the later parts of the cycle are likely to entail job displacement in the innovating industry at home. This job cycle has suggested the possibility of slowing down the international transmission of technology, so as to prolong the phases that create employment in the domestic innovating industry. Among measures proposed are legal restraints (such as those contained in the Burke–Hartke Bill) on the rights of innovating firms to exploit their unique technology through foreign direct investment or licensing of foreign production. Such suggestions tend to overlook the dynamic nature of the product cycle. Investments in research and development depend on the expected profits from future exploitation, including foreign production. Although it would perhaps be possible to delay the shift abroad of production of particular goods, restraints on the use of new technology diminish the profitability of innovative activity and are likely to reduce the flow of new products with which the cycle commences.

Labor's case against technology transfer centers on job losses and wage reductions in the industries directly affected, a partial-equilibrium analysis of the resulting gains and losses. However, such an approach is of limited value in assessing overall benefits for the economy or even for the domestic labor force. The transfer abroad of a particular industry's technology will in most cases reduce the returns to immobile factors in that industry in the short run. But while such losses constitute a legitimate policy concern in themselves, they shed little light on the longer-run distributional effects of technology transfer. Although dissemination of technology leads to a contraction of output in the affected industries, it also stimulates production in other sectors of the economy as a consequence of changed production patterns and increased incomes abroad. Full adjustment to altered sectoral demands may bring about higher real wages or expanded aggregate employment. Using a general-equilibrium approach, McCulloch and Yellen (1976) have shown that labor will derive long-run benefits from technology transfer if the new product is relatively capital-intensive and factors are immobile internationally. For a fully employed economy, the gains take the form of increased real wages; in the presence of unemployment, benefits accrue through job creation. With internationally mobile capital, however, labor is likely to experience no long-run gains or losses as a consequence of technology transfer.

A number of recent theoretical papers have analyzed a second policy issue relating to the international transfer of technology, the price at which technology is sold to foreign producers. Rodriguez (1974) derived an optimal royalty-tariff policy for the case in which factors of production are fully employed and immobile internationally and technology is disembodied. Optimal royalty policies in the case of labor unemployment and international capital mobility were analyzed by McCulloch and Yellen (1976); however, their model assumed free trade and thus did not address the joint royalty-tariff policy choice. Magee (1977) used a dynamic limit pricing model to derive the optimal price strategy for a firm that develops an embodied innovation. Berglas and Jones (1977) derived optimal national and private pricing policies for transfer of an embodied technology under free trade. They found that the optimal national policy in some cases entailed a subsidy rather than a tax on transfer of technology.

Employment and wage effects of direct investment

Foreign direct investment may affect domestic labor through a number of direct and indirect channels. As previous sections have suggested, the effect may come through resulting changes in capital-labor ratios at home or through effects on imports and exports. Unions have argued that establishment of foreign subsidiaries diverts the attention of managers, so that less effort is put into improving economic performance in home production facilities. The ability of MNCs to move production facilities abroad is also said to undermine the bargaining power of labor unions in the United States.

A number of empirical studies have attempted to measure the impact of foreign investment on domestic employment. Estimates depend critically on the assumptions made by researchers concerning relevant alternatives, so that studies sponsored by U.S. labor unions have been able to show massive job losses, while Harvard Business School researchers have found important increases in employment resulting from foreign investment activities of U.S. multinationals.[34] Even Barnet and Müller (1974), while hardly disposed to think well of the effects of MNCs, hesitated to conclude that the evidence supported the existence of important detrimental employment effects.

A good summary of the reasons why estimates can diverge so dramatically is presented by Horst (1978). His own estimates for the period 1965 to 1971 indicate no consistent statistical relationship, positive or negative, between U.S. investments abroad and domestic employment. In a related study, Horst and McCulloch (1977) found that industry foreign investment activity was usually positively correlated with wages, when labor and industry characteristics (including trade variables) were also included. This effect, while not strong, suggested that whatever harmful censequences FDI might have for domestic wages must come through induced changes in imports or exports.

A recent study by Frank and Freeman (1978) of the short-run employment effects of FDI focused on sectoral export displacement estimates. They concluded that a ban on foreign investment would be likely to produce an increase in domestic employment demand. This was true even though the authors estimated that sales in foreign markets would shrink by more than one-half as a result of such a ban. (In contrast, cross-sectional studies of wages and employment have generally shown a significant negative effect of imports but no significant impact, positive or negative, of exports.) Frank and Freeman also derived short-run sectoral estimates of demand reductions from FDI by manufacturing industry and have broken down employment-demand effects by occupational categories. The latter analysis showed that FDI is associated with much larger reductions in blue-collar than white-collar employment—a result that is consistent with the product cycle scenario.

REFERENCES

Anderson, James E. 1978. "Specific Taxes Are Usually Preferred to Mean Equivalent Quantitative Restrictions under Uncertainty." Unpublished manuscript, Boston College.

[34] See Barnet and Müller (1974) for references.

Balassa, Bela. 1967. "Trade Creation and Trade Diversion in the European Common Market." *Economic Journal* 77: 1–21.

Baldwin, Robert E. 1970. *Nontariff Distortions of International Trade.* Washington: The Brookings Institution.

———. 1976. "The Political Economy of Postwar U.S. Trade Policy." *Bulletin*, 1976–4. New York: New York University Graduate School of Business Administration.

Baldwin, Robert E., and Lewis, Wayne E. 1978. "U.S. Tariff Effects on Trade and Investment in Detailed SIC Industries." In *The Impact of International Trade and Investment on Employment: A Conference on the Department of Labor Research Results*, edited by William G. Dewald. Washington: Government Printing Office.

Bale, Malcolm D. 1976. "Estimates of Trade-Displacement Costs for U.S. Workers." *Journal of International Economics* 6: 245–50.

———. 1977. "United States Concessions in the Kennedy Round and Short-Run Labour Adjustment Costs: Further Evidence." *Journal of International Economics* 7: 145–48.

Barnet, Richard J., and Müller, Ronald E. 1974. *Global Reach.* New York: Simon and Schuster.

Berglas, Eitan, and Jones, Ronald W. 1977. "The Export of Technology." In *Carnegie-Rochester Conference Series on Public Policy*, Vol. 7, edited by Karl Brunner and Allan H. Meltzer. Amsterdam: North-Holland.

Bergsten, C. Fred. 1972. *The Cost of Import Restrictions to American Consumers.* New York: American Importers Association.

———. 1975. "On the Non-Equivalence of Import Quotas and 'Voluntary' Export Restraints." *Toward a New World Trade Policy: The Maidenhead Papers*, edited by C. Fred Bergsten. Lexington, Mass.: D. C. Heath.

Bhagwati, Jagdish N. 1965. "On the Equivalence of Tariffs and Quotas." In *Trade, Growth and the Balance of Payments—Essays in Honor of Gottfried Haberler*, by Robert E. Baldwin et al. Chicago: Rand McNally.

———. 1968. "More on the Equivalence of Tariffs and Quotas." *American Economic Review* 58: 142–46.

———. 1978. *Anatomy and Consequences of Exchange Control Regimes.* New York: National Bureau of Economic Research.

Bhagwati, Jagdish N., and Ramaswami, V. K. 1963. "Domestic Distortions, Tariffs, and the Theory of the Optimum Subsidy." *Journal of Political Economy* 71: 44–50.

Bhagwati, Jagdish N., and Srinivasan, T. N. 1976. "Optimal Trade Policy and Compensation under Endogenous Uncertainty: The Phenomenon of Market Disruption." *Journal of International Economics* 6: 317–36.

Brock, William A., and Magee, Stephen P. 1973. "An Economic Theory of Institutional Change: The Case of Tariffs—Some Empirical Formulations." Unpublished manuscript, University of Rochester and The Brookings Institution.

Cabinet Task Force on Oil Import Control. 1970. *The Oil Import Question.* Washington: Government Printing Office.

Caves, Richard E. 1971. "International Corporations: The Industrial Economics of Foreign Investment." *Economica* 38: 1–27.

———. 1974. "International Trade, International Investment, and Imperfect Markets." *Special Papers in International Economics*, 10. Princeton: International Finance Section, Department of Economics, Princeton University.

———. 1976. "Economic Models of Political Choice: Canada's Tariff Structure." *Canadian Journal of Economics* 9: 278–300.

Cheh, John H. 1974. "United States Concessions in the Kennedy Round and Short-Run Labor Adjustment Costs." *Journal of International Economics* 4: 323–40.

Cline, William R., Kawanabe, Noboru, Kronsjo, T. O. M., and Williams, Thomas. 1977. *Trade, Welfare, and Employment Effects of Multilateral Negotiations in the Tokyo Round.* Washington: The Brookings Institution.

Cooper, C. A., and Massell, Benton F. 1965. "A New Look at Customs Union Theory." *Economic Journal* 75: 742–47.

Cooper, Richard N. 1968. *The Economics of Interdependence: Economic Policy in the Atlantic Community.* New York: McGraw–Hill.

———. 1972. "The European Community's System of Generalized Tariff Preferences: A Critique." *Journal of Development Studies* 8: 379–94.

Corden, W. M. 1974. *Trade Policy and Economic Welfare.* Oxford: Oxford University Press.

———. 1976. "Customs Union Theory and the Nonuniformity of Tariffs." *Journal of International Economics* 6: 99–106.

Dam, Kenneth W. 1971. "Implementation of Import Quotas: The Case of Oil." *Journal of Law and Economics* 14: 1–60.

Fieleke, Norman S. 1976. "The Tariff Structure for Manufacturing Industries in the United States: A Test of Some Traditional Explanations." *Columbia Journal of World Business* 11: 98–104.

Finger, J. M. 1971. "Protection and Domestic Output." *Journal of International Economics* 1: 345–51.

Fishelson, Gideon, and Flatters, Frank. 1975. "The (Non)Equivalence of Optimal Tariffs and Quotas under Uncertainty." *Journal of International Economics* 5: 385–93.

Frank, Robert H., and Freeman, Richard T. 1978. "The Distributional Consequences of Direct Foreign Investment." In *The Impact of International Trade and Investment on Employment: A Conference on the Department of Labor Research Results,* edited by William G. Dewald. Washington: Government Printing Office.

Gehrels, Franz. 1971. "Optimal Restrictions on Foreign Trade and Investment." *American Economic Review* 61: 147–59.

Gerschenkron, Alexander. 1943. *Bread and Democracy in Germany.* Berkeley: University of California Press.

Gilpin, Robert. 1975. *U.S. Power and the Multinational Corporation.* New York: Basic Books.

Haberler, Gottfried. 1950. "Some Problems in the Pure Theory of International Trade." *Economic Journal* 60: 223–60.

Hartman, David. 1977. "The Effects on National Income and Its Distribution of Taxation of Foreign-Source Investment Income." Harvard Institute of

Economic Research. Discussion Paper Number 539. Harvard University.

Heuser, Heinrich. 1939. *Control of International Trade.* London: George Routledge and Sons.

Hirschman, Albert O. 1945. *National Power and the Structure of Foreign Trade.* Berkeley: University of California Press.

Holzman, Franklyn D. 1969. "Comparison of Different Forms of Trade Barriers." *Review of Economics and Statistics* 51: 159–65.

Horst, Thomas. 1978. "The Impact of American Investments Abroad on U.S. Exports, Imports and Employment." In *The Impact of International Trade and Investment on Employment: A Conference on the Department of Labor Research Results,* edited by William G. Dewald. Washington: Government Printing Office.

Horst, Thomas, and McCulloch, Rachel. 1977. "International Trade and Investment and the Earnings of U.S. Workers." Unpublished manuscript, Harvard University.

Hufbauer, G. C. 1975. "The Multinational Corporation and Direct Investment." In *International Trade and Finance: Frontiers for Research,* edited by Peter B. Kenen. Cambridge University Press.

International Monetary Fund. 1975 & 1977. *IMF Survey* 4: 188–89; and 6: 205–14.

Jacobson, Louis S. 1978. "Earnings Losses of Workers Displaced from Manufacturing Industries." In *The Impact of International Trade and Investment on Employment: A Conference on the Department of Labor Research Results,* edited by William G. Dewald. Washington: Government Printing Office.

Johnson, D. Gale. 1974. *The Sugar Program: Large Costs and Small Benefits.* Washington: American Enterprise Institute.

Johnson, Harry G. 1965. "Optimal Trade Intervention in the Presence of Domestic Distortions." In *Trade, Growth and the Balance of Payments— Essays in Honor of Gottfried Haberler,* by Robert E. Baldwin et al. New York: Rand–McNally.

———. 1968. *Comparative Cost and Commercial Policy for a Developing World Economy: Wicksell Lectures.* Stockholm: Almquist & Wiksell.

———. 1970. "The Efficiency and Welfare Implications of the International Corporation." In *The International Corporation,* edited by Charles P. Kindleberger. Cambridge: Massachusetts Institute of Technology Press.

———. 1975. *Technology and Economic Interdependence.* London: Macmillan & Co.

Jondrow, Jim. 1976. "The Impact of the Steel Tariff and Quota 1969–1973." Unpublished manuscript. Public Research Institute, Center for Naval Analyses.

Jones, Ronald W. 1965. "The Structure of Simple General Equilibrium Models." *Journal of Political Economy* 73: 557–72.

———. 1967. "International Capital Movements and the Theory of Tariffs and Trade." *Quarterly Journal of Economics* 81: 1–38.

———. 1970. "The Role of Technology in the Theory of International Trade." In *The Technology Factor in International Trade,* edited by Raymond

Vernon. New York: Columbia University Press.

Kemp, Murray C. 1966. "The Gain from International Trade and Investment: A Neo-Heckscher-Ohlin Approach." *American Economic Review* 56: 788–809.

Kemp, Murray C., and Wan, Henry Y., Jr. 1976. "An Elementary Proposition Concerning the Formation of Customs Unions." *Journal of International Economics* 6: 95–97.

Keohane, Robert O., and Nye, Joseph S. 1975. "Eagle Entangled: America in an Era of Complex Interdependence." Unpublished manuscript, Harvard University.

Kindleberger, C. P. 1951. "Group Behavior and International Trade." *Journal of Political Economy* 59: 30–46.

Krause, Lawrence B. 1968. *European Economic Integration and the United States.* Washington: The Brookings Institution.

Krauss, Melvyn B. 1972. "Recent Developments in Customs Union Theory: An Interpretive Survey." *Journal of Economic Literature* 10: 413–36.

Kreinin, Mordechai E. 1970. "More on the Equivalence of Tariffs and Quotas." *Kyklos* 23: 75–79.

Krueger, Anne O. 1974. "The Political Economy of the Rent-Seeking Society." *American Economic Review* 64: 291–303.

Lapan, Harvey E. 1976. "International Trade, Factor Market Distortions, and the Optimal Dynamic Subsidy." *American Economic Review* 66: 335–46.

Leibenstein, Harvey. 1966. "Allocative Efficiency vs. 'X-Efficiency'." *American Economic Review* 56: 392–415.

MacDougall, G. D. A. 1960. "The Benefits and Costs of Private Investment from Abroad: A Theoretical Approach." *Economic Record* 36: 13–35.

Magee, Stephen P. 1972. "The Welfare Effects of Restrictions on Economic Activity." *Brookings Papers on Economic Activity* 3: 645–701.

———. 1976. "An Empirical Test of the Stolper-Samuelson Theorem." Unpublished manuscript, University of Chicago.

———. 1977. "Application of the Dynamic Limit Pricing Model to the Price of Technology and International Transfer of Technology." In *Carnegie-Rochester Conference Series on Public Policy*, Vol. 7, edited by Karl Brunner and Allan H. Meltzer. Amsterdam: North-Holland.

Mayer, Wolfgang. 1974. "Short-Run and Long-Run Equilibrium for a Small Open Economy." *Journal of Political Economy* 82: 955–68.

McCarthy, James E. 1975. *Trade Adjustment Assistance: A Case Study of the Shoe Industry in Massachusetts.* Boston: Federal Reserve Bank of Boston.

McCulloch, Rachel. 1973. "When Are a Tariff and a Quota Equivalent?" *Canadian Journal of Economics* 6: 503–11.

———. 1977. "Technology, Trade, and the Interests of Labor: A Short Run Analysis of the Development and International Dissemination of New Technology." Harvard Institute of Economic Research Discussion Paper Number 489. Harvard University.

McCulloch, Rachel, and Johnson, Harry G. 1973. "A Note on Proportionally Distributed Quotas." *American Economic Review* 63: 726–32.

McCulloch, Rachel, and Yellen, Janet L. 1976. "Technology Transfer and the

National Interest." Harvard Institute of Economic Research Discussion Paper Number 526. Harvard University.

Meade, James. 1951. *The Theory of International Economic Policy*, Vol. 1. Oxford: Oxford University Press.

Michaely, Michael. 1976. "The Assumptions of Jacob Viner's Theory of Customs Unions." *Journal of International Economics* 6: 75–93.

Murray, Tracy. 1973. "How Helpful is the Generalized System of Preferences to Developing Countries?" *Economic Journal* 83: 449–55.

Musgrave, Peggy B. 1975. *Direct Investment Abroad and the Multinationals: Effects on the United States Economy*. Prepared for the Committee on Foreign Relations, U.S. Senate. Washington: Government Printing Office.

————. 1969. *United States Taxation of Foreign Investment Income: Issues and Arguments*. Cambridge: Harvard Law School International Tax Program.

Mussa, Michael. 1974. "Tariffs and the Distribution of Income: The Importance of Factor Specificity, Substitutability, and Intensity in the Short and Long Run." *Journal of Political Economy* 82: 1191–1203.

Neumann, George R. 1978. "The Direct Labor Market Effects of the Trade Adjustment Assistance Program: Evidence from the TAA Study." In *The Impact of International Trade and Investment on Employment: A Conference on the Department of Labor Research Results*, edited by William Dewald. Washington: Government Printing Office.

Pelcovits, Michael D. 1976. "Quotas Versus Tariffs." *Journal of International Economics* 6: 363–70.

Pincus, J. J. 1975. "Pressure Groups and the Patterns of Tariffs." *Journal of Political Economy* 84: 757–78.

Riedel, James. 1977. "Tariff Concessions in the Kennedy Round and the Structure of Protection in West Germany: An Econometric Assessment." *Journal of International Economics* 7: 133–43.

Rodriguez, Carlos. 1974. "The Non-Equivalence of Tariffs and Quotas Under Retaliation." *Journal of International Economics* 4: 295–98.

————. 1975. "Trade in Technological Knowledge and the National Advantage." *Journal of Political Economy* 83: 121–37.

Salant, Walter S., and Vaccara, Beatrice. 1961. *Import Liberalization and Employment*. Washington: The Brookings Institution.

Servan-Schreiber, Jean-Jacques. 1968. *The American Challenge*. New York: Atheneum.

Shibata, Hirofumi. 1968. "A Note on the Equivalence of Tariffs and Quotas." *American Economic Review* 58: 137–42.

Stern, Robert M. 1973. "Tariffs and Other Measures of Trade Control: A Survey of Recent Developments." *Journal of Economic Literature* 11: 857–88.

Stobaugh, Robert B. 1974. "A Summary and Assessment of Research Findings on U.S. Transactions Involving Technology Transfers." In *The Effects of International Technology Transfers on U.S. Economy*. Papers and Proceedings of a Colloquium Held in Washington, D.C., November 17, 1973. Washington, D.C.: National Science Foundation.

Stolper, Wolfgang F., and Samuelson, Paul A. 1941. "Protection and Real

Wages." *Review of Economic Studies* 9: 58–73.

Swann, Dennis. 1975. *The Economics of the Common Market*. Harmondsworth, England: Penguin.

Thurow, Lester C. 1976. "International Factor Movements and the American Distribution of Income." *Intermountain Economic Review* 2: 13–24.

Tower, Edward. 1975. "The Optimum Quota and Retaliation." *Review of Economic Studies* 42: 623–30.

Tullock, Gordon. 1967. "The Welfare Cost of Tariffs, Monopolies, and Theft." *Western Economic Journal* 5: 224–32.

Vernon, Raymond. 1966. "International Investment and International Trade in the Product Cycle." *Quarterly Journal of Economics* 80: 190–207.

———. 1977. *Storm Over the Multinationals*. Cambridge: Harvard University Press.

Viner, Jacob. 1950. *The Customs Union Issue*. New York: Carnegie Endowment for National Peace.

Walter, Ingo. 1971. "On the Equivalence of Tariffs and Quotas: A Comment." *Kyklos* 24: 111–12.

Whitman, Marina v. N. 1977. "Sustaining the International Economic System: Issues for U.S. Policy." *Essays in International Finance*, No. 121. Princeton: International Finance Section, Department of Economics, Princeton University.

Yadav, Gopal J. 1968. "A Note on the Equivalence of Tariffs and Quotas." *Canadian Journal of Economics* 1: 105–10.

Comment

RONALD W. JONES

In surveying the issues relevant to policy choices in the field of commercial policy generally and in the problems surrounding foreign direct investment in particular, Rachel McCulloch has noted that underlying trade models are sometimes of the long-run Heckscher–Ohlin variety and, at other times, of the short-run type characterized by the sectoral immobility of some factors of production. As she appropriately stresses, renewed interest in the impact of commercial policy upon the internal distribution of income highlights the fact that the short-run interest for a factor of production may run counter to the long-run model's forecast.

It is the long-run Heckscher–Ohlin model of trade that has been used to bring general equilibrium analysis to bear upon the optimal policy choices for a country involved in direct foreign investment.[1] Alternatively, a general equilibrium approach stressing specificity of, say, capital as between occupations could be taken in investigating the effects of direct foreign investment on national incomes.[2] How would such an analysis

---

[1] McCulloch cites, in particular, the articles by Kemp [10], Jones [7], and Gehrels [5].

[2] The short-run sector specific model is described in Jones [8], Mayer [11], Mussa [12] or Caves and Jones [3, chapter 6].

compare with the Heckscher–Ohlin approach? In this note I shall argue that the conclusions of the earlier "long-run" literature on foreign investment are robust with respect to the specification of intersectoral mobility of factors.[3] Furthermore, I shall point out how the potential for conflict between protection of commodity trade and capital exports, present in both short- and long-run versions of the model, is intimately linked to the final stages of Ray Vernon's product cycle [13].

Suppose the home country exports the first commodity in a two-sector model and also exports capital, in the sense that some of its owned capital stock is located in production facilities in the foreign country. Any change either in the commodity terms of trade p_1^* (the foreign price of commodity 1 with the second commodity serving as *numéraire*) or the foreign return to capital located abroad r_i^* (where i indicates the sector in which the capital is placed abroad) must affect home real incomes. To these "terms-of-trade" effects must be added the "volume-of-trade" effects if an export tax or subsidy causes p_1^* to differ from home price p_1, or the foreign return to capital in sector i, r_i^*, to differ from home r_i. Let E_1^* represent foreign imports of the first commodity, K_i the volume of home capital located abroad, and dy the change in home real income. Then a formal expression for the combination of terms-of-trade and volume-of-trade effects on home welfare is shown by:

$$(1) \quad dy = \{E_1^* dp_1^* + K_i dr_i^*\} + \{(p_1^* - p_1)dE_1^* + (r_i^* - r_i) \cdot dK_i\}.$$

This expression was formally derived for the Heckscher–Ohlin model in Jones [7]. In such a case, the i subscript for the capital flow and rate of return to capital can be ignored. Capital is not specific to either sector and earns the same return in both. By contrast, I assume that if capital is sector-specific, it is nonetheless internationally mobile, but only in one sector, i.[4] In what follows, I shall show that it makes a difference whether sector i refers to the home country's export sector (1) or import sector (2). The general form provided by equation (1) is independent of the assumptions made in the underlying model as to the intersectoral mobility of capital.

Certain properties of the model (s) can be exploited to develop expression (1) so that it shows the dependence of home welfare only upon the commodity terms of trade and the volume of capital exports. The first of these links the volume of foreign imports both to the terms of trade (as illustrated by the foreign offer curve for a given amount of foreign investment) and to the quantity of home capital located abroad. The impact that a change in K (or K_i) has on foreign imports at unchanged terms of

[3] For earlier work on foreign investment using models with sector-specific capital, see Corden [4], Caves [2], and Berglas and Jones [1].

[4] Caves [2] briefly discusses this model with sector-specific capital internationally mobile in both industries.

trade does depend upon the particular specification of the model. For example, in a Heckscher–Ohlin setting, with capital nonspecific as to sector, suppose the foreign country is incompletely specialized. Then, an increase in K will, at constant terms of trade, cause production of the capital-intensive industry abroad to expand. Should this be the foreign import sector (1), a capital outflow serves to cut foreign demand for imports through this production effect. No direct impact on demands for commodities abroad is registered, however, since with incomplete specialization the foreign rate of return r^* is uniquely linked to the given commodity terms of trade p_1^*. Although the increase in K serves to increase the value of foreign production, this increase (per unit of K) is precisely captured by r^*, which must be repatriated to home capitalists. Therefore, there is no change in foreign real incomes triggered by the capital flow.

Alterations in this account are required if the foreign country is completely specialized (in its export commodity, 2), since the increase in K now serves to drive down the return to capital r^*, even at given commodity terms of trade. Thus, foreign real income rises (and with it the demand for imports of commodity 1). But foreign production of commodity 1 remains constant, since none of this good is (by assumption) produced.

The model in which capital is sector-specific reveals an impact of an increase in capital exports that parallels the effects in the Heckscher–Ohlin model *both* with incomplete specialization and with complete specialization. Suppose the foreign country receives (at unchanged p_1^*) an increase in capital used specifically in its import sector. Then, as in the incomplete specialization version of the Heckscher–Ohlin model, production in the foreign import-competing sector rises. But, as in the completely specialized case, foreign real incomes (and therefore foreign demand for importables) are favorably affected, since even with commodity prices frozen a change in factor supplies changes factor prices.

This is the second property of the model alluded to above. The foreign rate of return to capital in the Heckscher–Ohlin model depends either upon the commodity terms of trade p_1^* (if the foreign country is incompletely specialized), or upon the volume of capital flow K (if specialization is complete), but not both. By contrast, both p_1^* and K have an impact on the foreign rate of return in the specific-capital model. More formally put,

$$(2) \quad \hat{r}_i^* = \gamma_i^* \hat{p}_1^* + \delta_i^* \hat{K}_i.$$

In the Heckscher–Ohlin model the subscript i should be ignored as capital is not sector-specific. If the first sector abroad produces a positive quantity of output (thus assuring incomplete specialization), and if this sector is capital-intensive, γ_i^* exceeds unity.[5] Furthermore, by the factor-price

---

[5] This is the magnification effect discussed in Jones [6]. A circumflex over a variable indicates the relative change in that variable: $\hat{x}$ is dx/x.

equalization reasoning, δ_i^* is zero. If the foreign country ceases to produce commodity 1, γ^* vanishes, while δ^* becomes negative, since the factor-price equalization result no longer applies when productive factors (labor and homogeneous capital) exceed in number the distinct kinds of output produced. In the specific capital model, the number of factors exceeds the number of commodities, so that δ_i^* is negative, but commodity prices also exert an influence on factor prices, so that γ_i^* does not vanish.

These two properties state that in equation (1) dr_i^* and dE_1^* can be expressed in terms of dp_1^* and dK_i. Letting η_1^* represent the (negative value of the) foreign country's elasticity of demand for imports along its offer curve (as of given value for K_i) and m_i^* the foreign marginal propensity to comsume commodity i, substitution for dr_i^* and dE_1^* into (1) yields (3):

$$(3) \quad dy = \frac{\partial y}{\partial p_1^*} dp_1^* + \frac{\partial y}{\partial K_i} dK_i,$$

where

$$\frac{\partial y}{\partial p_1^*} = E_1^* \left\{ 1 + \mu^* \gamma_i^* + \frac{(p_1^* - p_1)}{p_1^*} \eta_1^* \right\}$$

$$\frac{\partial y}{\partial K_i} = \left[1 + \left(\frac{p_1}{p_1^*} m_1^* + m_2^* \right) \delta_i^* - \frac{(p_1^* - p_1)}{p_1^*} \gamma_i^* \right] r_i^* - r_i.$$

In these expressions, the term μ^* is the ratio of home earnings on capital located abroad, $r_i^* K_i$, to home earnings from exports, $p_1^* E_1^*$. Expression (3) is precisely the same as equation (9) in [7] for the long-run Heckscher–Ohlin model.[6] But, as stressed above, the value either of γ^* or δ^* is zero in the Heckscher–Ohlin model, depending upon the degree of specialization. In the short-run specific factors model, neither parameter vanishes.

More insight into the similarity and differences between these two models can be obtained by considering the important case in which no taxes on capital or commodity flows are initially imposed, so that at the outset $p_1^* = p_1$ and $r_i^* = r_i$. In particular,

$$(4) \quad \frac{\partial y}{\partial p_1^*} = E_1^* \left\{ 1 + \mu^* \gamma_i^* \right\}.$$

This expression is useful in revealing whether the home country can benefit by levying an export tax (which would raise p_1^*) or an export subsidy (which would lower p_1^*).[7] It was at this stage of the argument for the Heckscher–Ohlin model in [7] that the question of factor-intensity was crucial. If γ^* is positive, the first commodity is produced by capital-intensive techniques abroad. If so, an increase in p_1^* (engineered by the imposition

---

[6] However, in [7] commodity 1 was the *numéraire* and the home country exported commodity 2.

[7] An import duty would be equivalent to an export tax.

of an export tax) not only is directly beneficial, but, because r^* is raised as well, there is a further gain from the higher return earned on all capital located abroad. This secondary effect is obviously more important the larger the capital outflow (or value of $E_1{}^*\mu^*$). A conflict between these two terms of trade effects would ensue if γ^* were negative, which is the case in which the commodity imported abroad is produced by labor-intensive techniques. Indeed, if capital flows are important enough, it might in such a case prove optimal for the home country to subsidize its capital exports.

It is perhaps tempting to suppose that the foreign country, assumed to be an importer of capital, must also import the capital-intensive commodity. That is, an initial shortage of capital both stimulates a direct capital flow and an inflow of commodities in which capital is the important input. But the capital inflow causes a magnified expansion in production of the capital-intensive commodity. That is, home exports of capital serve to expand foreign production capabilities in the commodity that the home country might initially export. A sufficient flow of capital could serve to establish the foreign country as the important producer of (and exporter of) the capital-intensive commodity. This result corresponds to the final stages of what Ray Vernon has termed the "product cycle" [13]. With direct investment having established a strong foreign production base, optimal commercial policy in the home country could be aimed at worsening the home country's commodity terms of trade in order to raise the foreign price of the capital-intensive commodity (now exported from the foreign country) and, with it, the return to foreign direct investment.

The concept of factor intensity, which played a crucial role in this Heckscher–Ohlin argument, ceases to be important in the model in which capital is sector-specific.[8] But the kind of conflict apparent in equation (4), when $\gamma_i{}^*$ is negative, can arise for different reasons. In the early stages of the product cycle, the home country has accumulated capital specific to a sector and established its own productive base. It starts by exporting the commodity and also exporting some of this capital to establish a production facility abroad. Any increase in the price of this export commodity would be doubly welcome: the commodity terms of trade improve and the return to foreign investment is also driven up—by a magnified amount. As more capital is shipped abroad, the home country's export position is threatened, and toward the end of the product cycle the trade pattern can be reversed. Let the "new" home export commodity be commodity 1, with capital exports of the type used in the second commodity. In (4), $\gamma_2{}^*$ must be negative; an increase in $p_1{}^*$ drives down the return to capital used in the second sector. If foreign investment is sufficiently im-

---

[8] As I have argued in [8] and [9], distributive labor shares can be compared in the specific-factor model in order to make a factor intensity ranking. But for present purposes such a ranking is not crucial.

portant (so that μ^*, equal to $r_2^*K_2/p_1^*E_1^*$, exceeds $-1/\gamma_2^*$), it would pay the home country to subsidize trade flows (a negative optimal tariff) in order to raise the return earned by its capital placed abroad.

To conclude, note that the crucial similarity in these two models is the relationship between a nation's trade pattern and its stance as a foreign investor. Investment abroad develops a nation's production potential. At early stages of the product cycle, a country may be in sole possession of a type of capital specifically used in producing a certain commodity. In such a case, capital and commodity exports would initially go hand-in-hand and an improvement in export prices (through restrictive policies) would serve to raise the return to capital exports. The Heckscher–Ohlin model is less capable of capturing the technological specificity of capital. However, it does link trading patterns to overall location of homogeneous capital and, at early stages, associates abundance of home-owned capital with exports of the capital-intensive commodity. In both models, a switch in the trading pattern occurs when sufficient export of capital has taken place to support production and export abroad of the commodity intially exported from the home country. With this new trading pattern it is no longer the case that commercial policy designed to raise the world price of home exportables will also raise the return to home-owned capital located abroad. There is a conflict between these two terms of trade changes, and optimal policy depends on the relative importance of trade flows and capital exports.

REFERENCES

1. Berglas, Eitan, and Jones, R. W. 1977. "The Export of Capital." In Brunner and Meltzer (eds.), *Optimal Policies, Control Theory and Technology Exports*. Amsterdam: North-Holland Publishing Co.
2. Caves, Richard E. 1971. "International Corporations: The Industrial Economics of Foreign Investment." *Economica* (February).
3. Caves, Richard E., and Jones, Ronald W. 1977. *World Trade and Payments*, second edition. Little, Brown.
4. Corden, W. Max. 1967. "Protection and Foreign Investment." *Economic Record*, June.
5. Gehrels, Franz. 1971. "Optimal Restrictions on Foreign Trade and Investment." *American Economic Review*, March.
6. Jones, Ronald W. 1965. "The Structure of Simple General Equilibrium Models," *Journal of Political Economy*, December. Reproduced as chap. 4, in R. W. Jones, *International Trade: Essays in Theory*. Amsterdam: North-Holland Publishing Co., 1978.
7. ———. 1967. "International Capital Movements and the Theory of Tariffs and Trade." *Quarterly Journal of Economics*, February; reproduced as chap. 12, in R. W. Jones, *International Trade: Essays in Theory*. Amsterdam: North-Holland Publishing Co., 1978.
8. ———. 1971. "A Three-Factor Model in Theory, Trade and History."

Chapter 1 in Bhagwati, Jones, Mundell, and Vanek, *Trade, Balance of Payments and Growth*; and reproduced as chap. 6, in R. W. Jones, *International Trade: Essays in Theory*. Amsterdam: North-Holland Publishing Co., 1978.

9. ———. 1975. "Income Distribution and Effective Protection in a Multi-Commodity Trade Model." *Journal of Economic Theory*, August.
10. Kemp, Murray C. 1966. "The Gain from International Trade and Investment: A Neo-Heckscher-Ohlin Approach." *American Economic Review*, September.
11. Mayer, W. 1974. "Short-run and Long-run Equilibrium for a Small, Open Economy." *Journal of Political Economy*, October.
12. Mussa, Michael. 1974. "Tariffs and the Distribution of Income: The Importance of Factor Specificity, Substitutability, and Intensity in the Short and Long Run." *Journal of Political Economy*, December.
13. Vernon, Ray. 1966. "International Investment and International Trade in the Product Cycle." *Quarterly Journal of Economics*, May.

CHAPTER FOUR

Uncertainty and International Trade

JOHN POMERY

I. INTRODUCTION

This chapter will assess some recent developments in the literature on uncertainty and international trade. Coverage will be selective both by choice and as a consequence of difficulties in placing natural boundaries on the topic. It is almost exclusively an exercise in pure theory, reflecting in part the fact that much of the selected literature is neither strongly policy-oriented nor empirical in content.

Restricting attention to single-period models, observe that the introduction of randomness creates a presumption that economic agents will desire to transform via trade and/or production across states of the world and not merely across physical commodities (as is exclusively the case in nonrandom models). This observation is clearly nonoperational in that, except in special cases, the "randomness rationale for transformation" is inextricably interwoven with the "commodity rationale for transformation." Nonetheless, it does suggest a fundamental new feature introduced by the presence of randomness and will provide an implicit theme for this survey.

Almost all the models covered will be simple (i.e., relatively highly aggregated) single-period models based on microeconomic optimization behavior, since these models are particularly suited to handle the interaction of the randomness and commodity rationales for transformation. Monetary and macroeconomic models will be largely ignored, although at the current level of aggregation the distinctions between these types of models becomes blurred. For example, a two-asset two-commodity financial model by Heckerman (1973) discussing exchange-rate randomness could equally well be viewed as a real model involving randomness in relative commodity price. A more important omission arises from the exclusion of many models with nontrivial intertemporal aspects—including the literature on

I am grateful to T. N. Srinivasan and Bill Ethier for their thoughtful comments, and to others for advice and for information about some significant papers widely circulated in unpublished form. Also thanks to Wolfgang Mayer for comments on the original version. All errors, omissions and misconceptions are nontradable liabilities of the author.

buffer stocks and on international forward markets in foreign exchange or commodities. Some of these topics might be covered more profitably when the nontrade literature on so-called speculative markets has developed further.

Models falling within the scope of the survey will be classified according to the timing of production and trade decisions relative to the realization of values of ex-ante random variables and according to the explicit market structure in commodity and/or asset trade. It will also be important to isolate assumptions about the groups of decision-makers involved in producing or trading randomness. In some models, these assumptions can be viewed as implying restrictions on implicit domestic markets for trading randomness—an idea that has been broadly hinted at in the literature (e.g., Kemp 1976c, note 1), but not fully explored. One reason that relative timing and the identity of decision-makers are both important is that they determine constraints and preferences concerning transformation of randomness vis-à-vis transformation of physical commodities.

There are a variety of two-stage decision models, and Section II will focus on models with ex-ante production decisions and ex-post trade in physical commodities. The purpose of these models is to capture the effect of lags in production in the presence of randomness. The literature encompasses the Heckscher–Ohlin–Samuelson (HOS) model and the Ricardian model, as well as papers that work with a general well-behaved, neoclassical, production-possibility frontier. Randomness has been introduced at almost every conceivable point in the basic structure of these models, although the most popular choices have been either randomness in an exogenous world-price ratio or a single source of multiplicative (technological) randomness in production. The production decision has been allocated to a representative individual consumer, a representative entrepreneur, the owners of one of the physical factors of production, and in effect to entrepreneurs available in perfectly elastic supply.

The predominant concern in these ex-ante production and ex-post trade models has been the robustness in the presence of randomness of propositions originating from nonrandom trade theory. In the HOS model, discussion has covered the Rybczynski, Stolper–Samuelson, factor-price equalization and (to lesser extent) Heckscher–Ohlin theorems. The major concern in the Ricardian model has been necessary and/or sufficient conditions for determining the pattern of production (and in particular situations of specialization in production). New comparative static exercises have been introduced, including the impact on production of introducing randomness or of imposing a mean-preserving spread on an existing source of randomness. With the aid of recent work by Helpman and Razin (1976, 1977b, and, especially, 1977a), which is also discussed in Section II, the literature is moving toward an examination of the role of implicit domestic or explicit international markets for trading randomness. Neglect of this aspect by earlier authors can be ascribed to their commodity-oriented approach; Section II attempts to throw some light on this issue.

Part (i) of Section III briefly covers explicit portfolio models. Here one thinks not only of relatively isolated papers, such as Grubel (1968), but also about the rapidly expanding literature on international applications of the Sharpe–Lintner capital-asset-pricing model (CAPM). Although the international version of the CAPM has been particularly useful in providing empirical estimates of the scope for international diversification of risk (as in Solnik [1975] and other papers in Elton and Gruber [1975]), discussion will be very limited. For the purposes of the current paper, the Arrow–Pratt expected-utility framework provides a more natural method of extending nonrandom trade theory. In the Arrow–Pratt context brief mention will be made of the randomness-oriented approach to uncertainty and international trade adopted in Pomery (1976).

Section III, part (ii), discusses "commitment models," where trading decisions are made ex-ante, but the realized terms of trade depend on a price ratio for ex-post trade. A nonrandom quantity of one commodity is committed to be exported (or imported) in return for an ex-ante random quantity of imports (exports) of the second commodity. The random component of the exchange is assumed to depend on the exogenous world-price ratio that is also random, and in some models commitments are permitted in both commodities simultaneously. It is not clear how authors discussing the commitment model intend this form of trade, and the assumption of an exogenous random price, to be extended from a single price-taking country to a general-equilibrium model of the world economy. The commitment is difficult to interpret as a bilateral contract and seems to be predicated on the need to commit exports to market (because of, say, transportation lags) prior to knowledge of market price in a world without forward markets.

Since the implicit market structure for the market as a whole is left ambiguous, the status of welfare propositions, even for a single price-taking economy, also remains ambiguous. The central result in this area is the theorem on the nonoptimality of autarky under unconstrained joint commitments, as derived in Ruffin (1974a), which is in essence a proposition about gains from trade. It is not surprising that there are numerous welfare propositions in the entire literature on uncertainty and international trade, since the topic combines potential gains from ex-ante and/or ex-post trade (and possibly from ex-post substitution in production), with potential adverse effects for risk-averters from owning and consuming randomness.

Models where all decisions are made ex-post are covered in Section IV. "Fluctuation models" belong to the same family as those discussed by Waugh, Oi, and Samuelson (for which Samuelson [1972] provides an introduction). Particular interest is focused on the relation of work of

Massell (1969, 1970) and others to this nontrade literature. Section IV also encompasses the tariff-vs.-quota literature under uncertainty, work by Kemp and Khang (1975) on the implications for income distribution in an HOS model with fluctuations in exogenous world price, and some preliminary work by Johnson (1974, 1976) on a general-equilibrium approach to speculation.

Section V includes some papers that, while suggesting useful alternative directions for research, do not fit easily into our simple classification scheme. Also there are some brief final remarks on the state of the literature.

As mentioned earlier, the literature surveyed here is not strongly policy-oriented. A stimulating early paper by Brainard and Cooper (1968) discusses the costs of uncertainty, the possibility of divergencies between private and social attitudes to risk, and the extent to which a government (particularly in a less-developed economy) might have reason to intervene in the market to create a socially-desirable pattern of diversification in production. Subsequent authors have concentrated on extending the theoretical background rather than adopting an actively policy-oriented approach. A significant exception is the paper of Bhagwati and Srinivasan (1976), covered in Section V, where the level of exports of one country endogenously determines the probability of retaliation in subsequent periods by its trading partner and, hence, may create an additional rationale for government intervention. Other topics, such as the differential impact of tariff and quota under uncertainty, should have direct relevance for policy-makers, but in general the literature seems to be moving through a phase of theoretical integration that (hopefully) precedes wider policy applications.

The empirical aspects of the literature are even more sparse. Again, Brainard and Cooper gave a lead by considering, in a mean-variance portfolio framework, the possibilities for diversification in production for less-developed countries, based on correlations among world prices for suitable products. The international version of the capital-asset pricing model provides a useful tool for estimating the scope for diversification of portfolios across national boundaries. In the empirical category, one might include the estimate by McCulloch (1975) of the quantitative (in)significance of "the Jensen's inequality phenomenon" in the context of forward-exchange markets, and work on the implications of the Brock–Magee (1976, 1977) theory of campaign contributions and tariff determination for factor specificity as reported in Magee (1976). However, this appears to exhaust the current bounds of empiricism.

The main purpose of the majority of the literature has been the development of new theoretical results. In this respect there has been considerable success—almost too much success, as the availability of results has run ahead of a deeper analysis of implicit assumptions that might affect the interpretation of these results. While it might be argued that uncertainty has only a minor role to play in trade theory, especially in the context of the basic HOS and Ricardian models, an emphasis on the new role of the randomness rationale for transformation gives an alternative perspective. Models of uncertainty and international trade appear too strongly rooted in nonrandom trade theory and insufficiently linked to related nontrade models involving uncertainty. Thus some results that are new to trade theory are in essence applications of elementary propositions of Arrow–Pratt portfolio theory and, in at least one case, several authors have examined a model for which the formal structure had been exhaustively analyzed in a nontrade context a few years earlier. The commodity-oriented approach has partially impeded the assimilation of intuition from nontrade uncertainty literature (particularly portfolio theory, but also in some cases game theory and the theory of information) that would appear essential to the development of a more general theory of uncertainty and international trade. As a byproduct, this intuition shows that significant parts of the formal structure of nonrandom trade models can be adapted and/or reinterpreted for the case of uncertainty.

II. MODELS WITH EX-ANTE PRODUCTION AND EX-POST TRADE DECISIONS

i) Overview

A number of authors have considered the impact of uncertainty for economies where production decisions are made ex-ante, while trade decisions are made ex-post. Such models may differ according to the production structure employed. Batra (1975b, chaps. 1–5), Mayer (1976), Lapan (1977), and Kemp (1976c) all employ the HOS model; Helpman and Razin (1977a) concentrate on the HOS model, while explaining the implications of their analysis for the Ricardian model.[1] Kemp (1976b) uses a "fixed coefficients" version of the HOS model, with a concluding reference to the Ricardian model. Ruffin (1974b) and Turnovsky (1974) employ Ricardian models—as in effect does Stiglitz (1970) in a different context. Anderson and Riley (1976) and Brainard and Cooper (1968) are less specific, appealing to a convex production technology and a well-behaved, neoclassical, production-possibility frontier respectively. Kemp and Liviatan (1973) consider modified Ricardian economies with intermediate goods, i.e., Leontief–Ricardian hybrids.

A second difference between models arises from alternative sources of

---

[1] Batra (1974, 1975a) will not be discussed independently of Batra (1975b); cf. Das (1977) in this context, also Ruffin (1976). The work of Helpman and Razin is currently in unpublished and on-going form, and for this reason discussion will be ꞏnfined to an available version of Helpman and Razin (1977a), which is central to ꞏr discussion and believed to be in a final version in terms of publication (if not ꞏecessarily for their on-going research).

randomness. With the exception of the robust model of Helpman and Razin (1977*a*), there has been virtually no attempt to incorporate more than a single source of randomness. Batra (1975*b*, chaps. 1–5), Kemp (1976*c*), and Lapan (1977) consider multiplicative randomness in production for a single industry in a price-taking economy, although under additional assumptions Kemp considers the situation for an economy levying an optimal tariff. Ruffin (1974*b*), Mayer (1976), Anderson and Riley (1976)—and, in effect, Stiglitz (1970)—work with randomness in exogenous world price. Turnovsky (1974) considers both forms of randomness, although not simultaneously. Kemp (1976*b*) covers randomness in factor endowments and in technology, again not simultaneously, while Kemp and Liviatan (1973) introduce what is in effect preference-induced randomness in a world price that is exogenous for one of the two countries in their model.

A third major difference is generated by alternative assumptions about the identity of the group of risk-averse decision-makers who choose production levels in the face of randomness. Batra (1975*b*, chaps. 1–5) can be viewed as working with a representative entrepreneur for the random industry. Mayer (1976) argues for what appears to be a perfectly elastic supply of entrepreneurs at a (positive) risk premium that equates the expected utility of profits with the utility associated with zero profits. Lapan (1977) assigns the decision to owners of capital and, depending on the labor endowments of individual capitalists, this can vary from a representative-consumer model to that of a representative labor-free capitalist. Kemp (1976*b,c*), Kemp and Liviatan (1973), Ruffin (1974*b*), Turnovsky (1974), and Anderson and Riley (1976) all operate with a representative individual consumer, while Stiglitz (1970) models a single price-taking individual. The contribution of Helpman and Razin (1977*a*) can be viewed in two stages. First, an explicit domestic stock market is introduced, based on the work of Diamond (1967), which allows trade in "real equity" claims generated in production and which provides a foundation for the representative individual assumption. Second, these real equities are internationally traded under the assumptions that the home country. is a price-taker in both asset and ex-post trade and that randomness is identically distributed across countries for the same industry. The implications of these two components of Helpman and Razin's model are discussed separately in this section. Another potential assumption, not used in this context but employed elsewhere by Batra and Russell (1974) and Rothenberg and Smith (1971), is that of risk neutrality on the part of entrepreneurs.

Given the variety of assumptions employed in this segment of the literature, it is not surprising that there is an abundance of propositions—not always pointing in the same direction. Helpman and Razin have clarified the implicit domestic stock market foundations for the representative individual model, and here it is suggested how other models can also be interpreted as implicitly assuming a (restricted) domestic market for trading randomness. These ideas are not totally unanticipated in the literature, and a formal exposition is not possible within the constraints of the survey; it should be noted that the suggested approach is least helpful when randomness bearing cannot be isolated from domestic income redistribution.

In the subsequent discussion attention is focused primarily on the HOS model. The technique involves taking a characterization of the nonrandom HOS model developed in Jones (1965) and reinterpreting this structure in the case of randomness. Jones employs input-output coefficients of the two physical factors of production relative to unit isoquants in the two industries in order to capture the market-clearing conditions for those two factors and also the competitive-profit conditions for the two industries (under the assumption that the economy is not specialized). These input-output coefficients vary with the wage-rental (i.e., factor price) ratio, and for the purposes of local comparative static exercises these changes can be handled, using the definitions of the elasticities of substitution around the unit isoquants and an envelope property implied by cost minimization.

The factor market-clearing conditions can be adapted trivially to include multiplicative randomness in production. Following Helpman and Razin, assume this multiplicative random variable takes on a positive value in each of a finite number of states of the world. In addition, choose the physical units so that this random variable has expected value of unity. Then the factor market-clearing relations go through if expected outputs replace previously nonrandom output levels.

The competitive-profit conditions, which imply that in each producing industry unit costs exactly equal unit revenue (or output price) and, hence, the industry is zero profit, are of greater interest. The concept of competitive equilibrium in the nonrandom HOS model involves a sufficiently long time frame to allow domestic-factor mobility to clear factor markets and also to allow freedom of entry and exit to guarantee zero entrepreneurial profits. This time frame may be inappropriate for many economic issues, with or without the presence of randomness, but it would seem natural to generalize the HOS model to include randomness in a manner that is consistent with this concept of competitive equilibrium.

In the nonrandom HOS model the entrepreneurial role is, in a sense, degenerate, since entrepreneurs wash out in a competitive equilibrium with zero profits. The model behaves as though entrepreneurs enter (exit) any industry that offers positive (negative) profit; this expands (contracts) industry output precisely to the point where the change in factor prices resulting from increased (decreased) demand has driven profits to a zero level. Now define a *pure entrepreneurial role* in a random version of the HOS model in an analogous fashion. Pure entrepreneurs enter (or exit) an industry as a consequence of a positive (or negative) return in all states of the world, and a competitive equilibrium requires that when an industry produces the pure entrepreneurs receive a zero return in all states.[2]

This approach preserves the concept of competitive equilibrium embodied in the nonrandom HOS model and implies that pure entrepreneurs play the same degenerate role with zero return in a competitive equilibrium. Moreover, it implies that whoever bears the randomness in this economy, it is certainly not the pure entrepreneurs, since their guaranteed zero return in a competitive equilibrium is unambiguously nonrandom. In effect, the standard production-possibility frontier of the nonrandom HOS model has become a production-possibility frontier in expected output space. All that remains is to define the wage and rental, the returns to the two physical factors, in such a way that in a competitive economy the ratio of unit costs attributable to the physical factors between the two industries is exactly equal to the marginal rate of transformation in expected output space. If this can be done, then unit costs in each industry attributable to physical factors of production play a role in the random HOS model analogous to that of output prices in the competitive-profit conditions of the nonrandom HOS model.

Although in the version of Helpman and Razin (1977*a*) currently available the authors do not emphasize the competitive-profit conditions per se, their stock market model pursues this analogy perfectly. Helpman and Razin show that, even with differing expectations, preferences and initial endowments within an economy, a competitive equilibrium for a random HOS model of the representative individual type can be viewed as the outcome of the workings of a domestic stock market; hence, by implication, local comparative static exercises for such a representative individual economy effectively abstract from the impact of domestic income redistribution created by those differences. For Helpman and Razin, factor payments are made in the form of proportional claims on the (possibly random) output of the corresponding industry. These claims have been termed "real equities" and are tradable on a domestic stock market, thus allowing factor prices to be equalized across industries when measured in units of a *numéraire* real equity. Note that both factor prices and, hence, unit costs attributable to those factors can be measured in terms of some *numéraire* real equity; also under our earlier normalization, real equities can be measured in units of expected output for the corresponding industry.

In a competitive equilibrium in the Helpman and Razin model, all randomness is borne by owners of the physical factors of production and none by entrepreneurs (or shareholders). This is exactly as it should be,

---

[2] This criterion would be ill-defined if it were impossible to guarantee that a pure entrepreneur received a positive (respectively zero, negative) return in one state of the world, if and only if he received a positive (respectively zero, negative) return in all states. At least for the models considered here, this is no problem.

since (a) the two physical factors of production are effectively producing real equities under conditions of constant returns to scale and value of marginal product pricing, and (b) in a competitive equilibrium the representative individual obtains all his income, and absorbs randomness generated via production, from the remuneration of the physical factors.

Thus if output levels are replaced by expected output levels and physical commodity prices by real equity prices, then the entire formal structure of the production side of the nonrandom HOS model is preserved with randomness. The (possibly random) commodity prices and attitudes to risk both enter on the preferences side of the model, and this represents the major theoretical alteration from introducing randomness into the HOS model.

ii) A single source of multiplicative randomness in production

While the Helpman–Razin stock market model is equally robust for price randomness or multiplicative technological randomness (or both simultaneously)—although the preference side will differ in each case—other models that do not adopt the representative individual assumption are best seen in the simplest possible context. In each of these alternative models, it is as though pure entrepreneurs pay a nonrandom return (in units of some *numéraire* physical commodity) to both physical factors of production and, simultaneously, sell the randomness generated from production. The claim to random gross revenue per unit of expected output is exchanged for a nonrandom claim that in a competitive economy will just be sufficient to cover unit costs attributable to the physical factors of production; this exchange occurs in a competitive market between the pure entrepreneurs and a designated group of "randomness-bearers."

The case of a country facing exogenous nonrandom world prices, but producing with multiplicative randomness in one of two industries, is particularly expedient. With constant output price ratio, the model can be aggregated into a one-good form; factor payments can be denominated in units of a *numéraire* physical commodity that can be considered as measuring income. The effect of introducing randomness is to create an implicit third factor of production, which provides the service of bearing randomness, and in a competitive equilibrium the market-clearing return to this factor (per unit of expected output) creates a wedge between unit costs attributable to the physical factors and revenue (i.e., output price) per unit of expected output. In the context of nonrandom world prices and a single source of production randomness, it is natural to think of this market-clearing return to the third factor as a form of unit-risk premium.

Derived demand for the services of this third factor will be a strictly decreasing function of the unit-risk premium. At constant output price ratio a rise in the unit-risk premium forces down physical-factor unit costs in the random industry, while unit costs in the nonrandom industry remain constant. Thus, exactly as in the standard supply response of the non-random HOS model, there is a change in the marginal rate of transformation in expected output space, such that production in the random industry is reduced. The offer of randomness-bearing services will also be a function of the unit-risk premium, but the precise nature of the offer curve will depend on the designated group of randomness-bearers.

Batra (1975*b*, chaps. 1–5), in effect, has a representative entrepreneur in the random industry maximizing the expected utility of profits. Conceptually, it is as though the pure entrepreneurs in the random industry sell the randomness to a fixed group, who happen to be identified as a fixed initial set of entrepreneurs in that industry. In their joint role of pure entrepreneur and also randomness-bearer, these entrepreneurs face a standard portfolio problem. They choose the level (of expected output) at which to go short in a safe asset (with nonrandom return reflecting unit costs attributable to the physical factors) in return for a risky asset (with random return equal to gross unit revenue from production). Batra's assumption of nonincreasing absolute risk aversion guarantees the risky asset is not inferior[3] (and *a fortiori* is non-Giffen), although it does not exclude a backward-bending supply curve for the safe asset. The two central aspects are the implicit assumptions (a) of a fixed stock of ran-domness-bearers, and (b) that these individuals have no other source of income except that generated as bearers of randomness.

Lapan (1977) suggests an alternative formulation, because of two potentially unattractive features of the Batra model. Recognizing the exist-ence of an additional implicit and scarce factor in the random industry, Lapan points out that proportionate growth in the endowments of the physical factors at constant output prices will not lead to equiproportionate growth in the levels of expected output in the two industries. Leaving aside the question of whether such a balanced-growth property is either plausible or desirable in a world involving randomness, the reason for the result is clear. At constant unit-risk premium and constant output prices, balanced growth in physical endowments would lead to balanced growth in expected output for the two industries. However, the fixed stock of randomness-bearers will not be willing to absorb this additional randomness at constant unit-risk premium. In a stable market, the excess demand for services of randomness-bearers will force up the market-clearing unit-risk premium, and this will alter the marginal rate of transformation in expected output space, so as to reduce expansion in the random industry relative to balanced growth.

Lapan's other objection is that the bet taken by the designated group of randomness-bearers will necessarily achieve a negative return in some state(s) of the world, and hence this group must either possess unspecified alternative assets or must default in payments to the physical factors of production. In either case, the model appears incomplete if this is not explicitly taken into account.

Both objections can be evaded by attributing production decisions to the fixed stock of owners of one physical factor—capitalists for Lapan—and by assuming that the total return to each capitalist (possibly including wage income) is sufficient in all states of the world to cover contractual obligations to labor (excluding any self-imputed wage). Consider, for simplicity, the special case where capitalists have no labor endowment, although this is not crucial. It is possible to impute a pure nonrandom return to capital in the random industry that must be equal to the return to capital in the nonrandom industry; the residual return to capitalists in the random industry is nothing but a risk premium that (when measured per unit of expected output) creates the wedge between output price and nonrandom unit costs in the random industry. It is as though the pure entrepreneurs, with zero return in a competitive equilibrium, hire labor and capital at nonrandom rates and then sell the randomness competitively at exactly the unit-risk premium required to induce the designated group of (capitalist) randomness-bearers to hold the amount produced.

Unfortunately for our purposes, the separation of randomness-bearing and supply of factors of production is not as complete, and hence not as useful, as for a representative individual or a representative entrepreneur. The production-possibility frontier can be presented in expected output space as before, with a marginal rate of transformation equal to the ratio of (imputed) nonrandom unit costs attributable to the physical factors of production in the two industries. However, there appears to be no way of representing preferences of a representative capitalist (who is not also a representative individual) in this space by an indifference map that is independent of the prevailing wage and rental.

In Lapan's model, while the stock of randomness-bearers is fixed, they do possess a source of nonrandom income generated by the nonrandom return to capital (and possibly labor) owned. Thus, if there is proportionate growth in the endowments of labor and capital, but the stock of capitalists remains fixed, then equiproportionate growth in expected output at constant output prices and constant unit-risk premium would imply that the representative capitalist would be bearing a proportionately larger amount of randomness, but would have a proportionately larger amount of nonrandom income. (Here again assume capitalists do not possess labor endowments.) From the work of Arrow (1971), we know that the unit-risk premium must rise (respectively remain constant, fall) as the representative capitalist exhibits increasing (respectively constant, decreasing) relative risk aversion.

The possibility of balanced growth under constant relative risk aversion is not attainable in the Batra model.

Note that the above example of balanced growth should not be confused with the situation where labor, capital, and the number of (identical) randomness-bearing capitalists all grow in the same proportion. In this latter situation, the economy is being replicated with respect to all three factors of production, and in this case we require that expected output levels also grow equiproportionately in the face of constant output prices.[4]

Mayer (1976) suggests an alternative method of modifying Batra's model; this is done in the context of price randomness, but the analysis does not appear to lose anything in the translation to production randomness, and we will consider the latter case. Mayer points out that the implicit assumption of a fixed number of entrepreneurs in the random industry contravenes the assumption of freedom of entry and exit in that industry and, hence, violates an integral part of the concept of competitive equilibrium. Instead of a fixed stock of entrepreneurs, Mayer, in a sense, introduces a perfectly elastic supply of entrepreneurs at a positive risk premium, such that the expected utility of profits equals the utility of zero profits with certainty. Apart from the explicit mention of a risk premium, Mayer's paper is valuable since the case of perfectly elastic supply contrasts strongly with the fixed stock of randomness-bearers implicit in assuming either a representative individual, a representative entrepreneur, or a representative capitalist.

Under our distinction between pure entrepreneurs and entrepreneurs as designated bearers of randomness, it is clear that the restrictive nature of Batra's assumption does not lie in the denial of freedom of entry or exit for pure entrepreneurs. Rather it is as though pure entrepreneurs have freedom of entry or exit, but are required to sell their randomness to a fixed group (identified as the initial set of entrepreneurs in the industry).

Mayer uses the first-order condition for expected utility maximization by individual firms, and also the familiar envelope property implied by cost minimization, to show that for comparative statics exercises the basic structure of the (differentiated) "competitive-profit conditions" is unchanged. The analogs of the nonrandom HOS competitive-profit conditions are here the conditions that expected utility of profits equals the utility of inaction for each firm. In terms of the portfolio situation for a given entrepreneur, as discussed earlier in the case of the representative entrepreneur of Batra, each firm adjusts in the face of a comparative static change, so that it remains in asset space on the same indifference curve, namely, the in-

---

[4] I am grateful to Wolfgang Mayer for pointing out that in an earlier version of this chapter I had not made explicit the distinction between expanding the amount of labor per individual and expanding the amount of labor and individuals equally; this in the context of a representative individual model.

difference curve passing through the origin; this is guaranteed via the simultaneous entry or exit of (identical) entrepreneurs. This approach neatly eliminates the unit-risk premium from comparative statics exercises, preserving the formal structure of the production side of the nonrandom HOS model in the form essential for the Rybczynski and Stolper–Samuelson theorems. However, the determination of the unit-risk premium is left somewhat up in the air, and this raises a question.

The source of the problem arises from the assumptions of constant returns to scale for each individual firm, risk-aversion, and freedom of entry and exit for the random industry. From the fundamental propositions of Arrow (1971) that, relative to nonrandom autarky, risk-averters take some part of an actuarially favorable bet, but no part of a fair or unfavorable bet, it follows that all entrepreneurs will want to enter the random industry at a positive risk premium, but all will want to exit at a zero or negative risk premium. It is as though the aggregate offer curve for services of randomness-bearers has a discontinuity at zero premium, excluding the possibility of finding a market-clearing situation. Put another way, with constant returns to scale and entrepreneurial risk-aversion, the industry is analogous to a nonrandom industry of price-taking firms with decreasing returns to scale throughout; under competitive pressures the size of each individual firm must approach zero, but the limit of zero production by all firms is not an equilibrium situation.[5] It is difficult to see how this problem could be avoided by allowing potential entrepreneurs to have an alternative of working as contractual labor, particularly if the supply is to be perfectly elastic. Relaxing the assumption of constant returns to scale at the level of the individual firm would appear more hopeful, although even with U-shaped average cost curves (both in terms of physical-factor costs and augmented by an average risk premium at each level of expected output) it is not clear that in a general equilibrium setting one would anticipate a perfectly elastic supply of randomness-bearers.

In order to see exactly how theorems such as those of Rybczynski and Stolper–Samuelson could be preserved, return to the portfolio problem of a typical entrepreneur maximizing the expected utility of profits. In terms of the *numéraire* commodity (which we will choose to be the output of nonrandom industry two with $p_2 = 1$), the entrepreneur commits $uc_1 \cdot \bar{x}_1$ by going short in the safe asset representing physical-factor unit costs and has an expected return from the risky asset of $p_1 \cdot \bar{x}_1$; here $\bar{x}_1$ is expected output for this firm. By choosing to measure the bet in terms of units of expected output, the unit-risk premium becomes $(p_1 - uc_1)$. However, it

---

[5] This problem of introducing risk-aversion into a competitive industry of firms operating under conditions of constant returns to scale has been recognized in the nontrade literature; cf., Rosett in Borch and Mossin (1968), pp. 274–77. Note that the problem arises not from optimization behavior of an individual firm within the industry, but from the impact of entry and exit for that industry in the presence of constant returns.

would also be possible to measure the scale of the bet in units of the *numé'-aire* commodity, in which case the unit-risk premium becomes $(p_1/uc_1) - 1$.

In the Rybczynski proposition, with output prices constant, the distinction between constancy of the two measures of unit-risk premium does not arise. A Mayer-style argument would presumably suggest that if the labor endowment expanded at constant output prices, then all firms in the random industry could operate at the same scale as before (and hence hold the same portfolio as before), and identical firms would enter or exit the industry until the new level of aggregate expected output equaled that predicted by the Rybczynski proposition. This adjustment is consistent with individual entrepreneurial optimization and perfectly elastic supply at an unchanged level of expected utility of profits, such that not just output prices but also the unit-risk premium (in either sense) and hence physical-factor unit costs remain constant, while expected output alters at the industry level.

For the Stolper–Samuelson proposition, it is advisable to insist on a constant unit-risk premium in terms of the *numéraire* commodity, not per unit of expected output. Then an increase in output price in the random industry could bring about a new equilibrium with constant unit-risk premium (in the *numéraire* sense) and unchanged portfolio holding (and hence unchanged expected utility) in each firm if (a) unit costs rise in the same proportion as output price in the random industry, (b) expected output falls for each individual firm in the same proportion, and (c) firms enter or exit the industry to achieve the requisite aggregate-supply response.

It should be clear from the discussion in this section to date that there is no simple answer to the question of whether propositions from non-random trade theory are robust in the presence of randomness. The structure of the random versions of the HOS (and the Ricardian) model depends crucially upon what assumptions one is prepared to make in terms of the supply of services of bearing randomness, and hence about the additional market implicit in the model—whether it be a Helpman–Razin domestic stock market or a more restricted situation with only a designated subgroup of the economy allowed to bear randomness.

For single-country HOS propositions, such as the Rybczynski or Stolper–Samuelson theorems, the key is to obtain a constant unit-risk premium (in terms of *numéraire* commodity for the latter). This rigidly links proportionate changes in output prices to equiproportionate changes in the ratio of physical-factor unit costs in the two industries. It is this ratio of unit costs that determines the marginal rate of transformation in expected output space for a competitive economy, and it is the marginal rate of transformation, *not* the ratio of output prices, which is important for these HOS propositions. Despite reservations about the precise formalization of his model, Mayer's paper is valuable in highlighting the sensitivity of conclusions to supply conditions for designated bearers of randomness. Helpman and Razin (1977*a*) achieve the same end by assuming that real equities are traded internationally and that the economy is a price-taker in the equity market. Both Mayer's approach and that of Helpman and Razin can be viewed as alternative methods of preserving the underlying logical structure of the Rybczynski and Stolper–Samuelson propositions (and of the associated magnification effects). Alternative approaches disrupt the formal structure and lose some but not all of the qualitative conclusions (as in Batra 1975*b*, chaps. 1–5; Das 1977).

Two-country propositions such as the factor-price equalization theorem require more structure. A sufficient condition for factor-price equalization is that the marginal rate of transformation in expected output space be equalized across the two countries, given identical technologies and no factor-intensity reversals. In turn, this can be guaranteed if, in addition, both countries are incompletely specialized, face identical output prices (from free ex-post trade), and identical unit-risk premia. However, in general, the equalization of risk premia across countries would be coincidental, since even with identical distributions for random variables across countries the equilibrium risk premium would also depend on expectations and preferences of randomness-bearers and the relative size of this designated group to the amount of randomness generated by the random industry for each country. Here the missing link is supplied by the brilliantly simple assumption of Helpman and Razin that real equities are freely traded across countries. With identically distributed randomness across countries, so that real equities from a given industry are perfect substitutes, this guarantees equalization of real-equity prices and hence of the marginal rates of transformation in expected output space. Factor-price equalization requires free trade to equalize prices for "preference-contaminated" goods as a prerequisite to appealing to the basic univalence property of the two-by-two system in the absence of intensity reversals.

Other results in the literature can be seen clearly in models with a fixed stock of identical risk-averse domestic bearers of randomness, with no ex-ante international trade in randomness, and with no income redistribution effects. For example, consider the proposition that the introduction of a single source of multiplicative production randomness into a previously nonrandom HOS economy will reduce production in the random industry relative to the certainty-equivalent case. The wedge created by the positive risk premium between output price and physical-factor unit costs would imply, via a form of Stolper–Samuelson logic, a reduction in the return to the physical factor intensive in the random industry and an improvement for the other physical factor. The result that a risk-averter relative to non-random autarky takes some part of a favorable bet, but no part of a fair or unfavorable bet, implies that the random industry will produce at a positive level with randomness if and only if it would produce in the certainty-equivalent situation. Results of this nature can be found in Kemp (1976c) for the representative individual model.

A risk-averse individual choosing between a risky and a safe asset in a one-good world will, under nonincreasing absolute risk aversion, exhibit a change in his marginal rate of substitution in asset space if there is a mean-preserving spread on the random return of the risky asset (and holding of the risky asset is nonzero). A greater quantity of the risky asset is required to compensate for the loss of a given amount of the safe asset. From consideration of the preference map and the production-possibility frontier in asset space (i.e., expected-output space), production in the random industry will fall with consequent adverse effect for the intensive factor in that industry—although production will not cease. This conclusion, based on properties of the preference map in asset space, appears to be valid so long as there are no income-redistribution effects entering preferences of the designated group of randomness-bearers, as occurs in Lapan's model. Presumably, income distribution is the basis for Kemp's apparent scepticism in the somewhat cryptic footnote 1 of Kemp (1976c). An increase in risk-aversion, defined following Pratt (1964) as a monotonic increasing strictly concave transformation of the utility function of the representative randomness-bearer, has a similar effect on the marginal rate of substitution in asset space—irrespective of the behavior of the coefficient of absolute risk-aversion—and hence generates similar conclusions.

In the Ricardian model, the proposition that a risk-averter from non-random autarky takes some part of a favorable bet implies that if an economy is unambiguously specialized in one industry in the certainty equivalent case, then it may diversify but will not specialize entirely in the other industry when randomness occurs in the first one. This is because from the point of specialization in the nonrandom industry a move toward diversification represents a favorable bet. Similarly, because a risk-averter from nonrandom autarky takes no part of an actuarially fair or unfavorable bet, it follows that specialization (including the borderline case) in one industry in the certainty-equivalent case will imply unambiguous specialization in the same industry, if randomness is introduced in the other industry. (These propositions can be found in Turnovsky [1974]; note that Turnovsky's proposition 9 is clearly false as stated.) Proposition 3 of Kemp (1976b) appears to contradict the first of the two propositions stated in this paragraph. The problem arises because in the statement of the theorem on page 288 of Kemp (1976a) and in the preamble on page 286, it is assumed that the exogenous world-price ratio differs, albeit "only very slightly," from the slope of the production-possibility frontier, while in the diagram and sketched proof on page 287, the two ratios are treated as identical. Since the proposition concerning a risk-averter taking some part of a favorable bet is a statement about the ultimate dominance of a nonzero, first-order term (representing the favorable bet) over the second-order term (reflecting risk-aversion) as the scale of the bet becomes arbitrarily small, it is not legitimate to treat only very slightly favorable bets as exactly fair bets in this context.

iii) Randomness in exogenous world price

We now turn to the case of an economy possessing nonrandom technology and endowments, but facing randomness in the exogenous world-price ratio. The randomness in the price ratio destroys the single-good aspect of models with technological randomness but nonrandom exogenous world price, and this makes the theory noticeably different. For example, an approach that has entrepreneurs maximizing the expected utility of profits and paying physical factors a nonrandom return is less easy to defend. Profits, wage, and rental would all be measured in units of a *numéraire* commodity, implying an implicit price of unity for that commodity in all states of the world; however, nonrandom wage or rental in terms of the *numéraire* commodity does not imply nonrandom real income (unless only the *numéraire* commodity is consumed), and it is unclear why entrepreneurial decision-making does not involve an indirect utility-function approach in the general case. Kemp (1976c, footnote 7), and Riley (1976) are among those pointing out the need for an indirect utility function in the general case.

If entrepreneurs in the non-*numéraire* industry, with random price, were to maximize the utility of *numéraire* profits, then the problem would be formally identical to the case with multiplicative technological randomness. For the entrepreneur, *qua* bearer of randomness, it is a matter of indifference whether randomness in gross revenue arises from the price or the quantity side. This implies that, in such a world, production in the presence of randomness in non-*numéraire* price can only lead to a reduction of production in that industry relative to the certainty-equivalent case; with a representative individual's indirect-utility function, it will be seen that production can move in either direction relative to the certainty-equivalent case. Thus the indirect utility-function approach unambiguously generates a richer, and more plausible, spectrum of outcomes; attention will be restricted to such a representative individual model.

A second source of complexity arises from the application of Jensen's inequality. If relative price is random, and if we define $p \equiv p_1/p_2$ and $q \equiv p_2/p_1 = 1/p$, then from the convexity of the reciprocal function it follows that $Ep \cdot Eq > 1$ (where E is the expectation operator). This can be looked at in several related ways. If relative price is random, and we seek a certainty-equivalent benchmark, then it is possible to use p identical to Ep in all states or q identical to Eq in all states, but not both simultaneously. Conversely, if we start from a nonrandom price $\bar{p} = 1/\bar{q}$, it is possible to introduce a positive multiplicative random variable $\epsilon_1(s)$ (where s runs over the finite number of states of the world) with expected value unity so that $p(s) = \bar{p} \cdot \epsilon_1(s)$ or alternatively a positive multiplicative random variable $\epsilon_2(s)$ with expected value unity, so that $q(s) = \bar{q} \cdot \epsilon_2(s)$; however, Jensen's inequality implies that these are two distinct conceptual experiments.

In effect, the introduction of multiplicative randomness in a rate of transformation such as a price ratio must improve the actuarial tradeoff in at least one direction with ex-post substitutability. Consider an economy with a locally constant marginal rate of transformation along the production-possibility frontier given by α, and assume in a nonrandom setting α equals $\bar{p}$. (or equivalently $1/\bar{q}$). Compare the cases of introducing (a) $\epsilon_1(s)$ with mean unity, and (b) $\epsilon_2(s)$ with mean unity as discussed in the previous paragraph. Take a circular bet denominated in units of commodity one: production is reduced by a single unit of commodity one, the resources released produce α units of commodity two, which are exchanged for either (a) $\alpha/\bar{p} \cdot \epsilon_1(s)$ or (b) $\alpha \cdot \bar{q} \cdot \epsilon_2(s)$ units of commodity one in the world market. Noting $\alpha = \bar{p} = 1/\bar{q}$ and the initial nonrandom stake for this circular bet is one unit of commodity one, the bet is actuarially favorable in case (a), since $E[1/\epsilon_1] > 1/E\epsilon_1 = 1$, but actuarially fair in case (b), since $E\epsilon_2 = 1$. For the reverse circular bet, where one unit of commodity two is removed from production to obtain either (a) $\bar{p} \cdot \epsilon_1(s)/\alpha$ or (b) $1/\alpha \cdot \bar{q} \cdot \epsilon_2(s)$ units of commodity two, the bet is actuarially fair in case (a), but actuarially favorable in case (b).

In either case, the introduction of randomness must create a favorable bet in one direction. This implies that if the nonrandom economy is at autarky initially, and the random variable has sufficiently small higher moments so that income effects from nonzero net-trade positions can be ignored, then the economy will reduce production in industry one relative to autarky in case (a), but will reduce production in industry two relative to autarky in case (b).

Having drawn attention to this distinction, let us ignore the second possibility and concentrate on case (a). Let $\bar{p}$ be the expected value of the relative price of commodity one, so that we can write $p(s) = \bar{p} \cdot \epsilon_1(s)$. Define $\bar{q}$ as the expected value of the relative price of commodity two, so that $q(s) = \bar{q} \cdot \epsilon_2(s)$, where both $\epsilon_1(s)$ and $\epsilon_2(s)$ have mean unity. Note that from Jensen's inequality $\bar{p} \cdot \bar{q}$ exceeds unity, and, hence, although $p(s) = 1/q(s)$ for all states of the world, we have $\bar{p} \neq 1/\bar{q}$.

As is well-known in the literature, if α represents the marginal rate of transformation via production at the optimum, then maximizing the induced expected-utility function defined over the levels of output of the two commodities (i.e., effectively maximizing an objective function defined over quantities of two assets) subject to the production-possibility frontier constraint requires for an interior optimum:

(1) $[(\bar{p}/\alpha) - 1] + (\bar{p}/\alpha \cdot EU_2) \cdot \text{cov}(U_2, \epsilon_1) = 0$

or equivalently:

(1′) $[\bar{q} \cdot \alpha - 1] + (\bar{q} \cdot \alpha / EU_1) \cdot \text{cov}(U_1, \epsilon_2) = 0.$

Here $U_j, j = 1, 2$, is the marginal utility of the jth commodity (which is state-dependent), and E is the expectation operator. These are merely alternative statements of the standard condition that marginal rate of substitution equals marginal rate of transformation in output (i.e., asset) space; it is easy to show that boundary solutions are characterized by the usual inequalities in (1) and (1′).

The first term on the left-hand side of each of these equations can be thought of as a marginal betting term, while the second term can be considered more loosely as a marginal insurance term. Thus, in (1) the covariance term is positive if ϵ_1 tends to be above average in states where marginal utility for *numéraire* commodity two is high. Such a positive term would imply opportunities for additional marginal insurance (in terms of the *numéraire*), which remain unexploited at an optimum because of the offsetting actuarially unfavorable nature of the bet. Marginal utility of the *numéraire* commodity is a function of the random variable and monotonicity of this relation is sufficient to sign the covariance term. The effect of the random variable on marginal utility can be decomposed into a substitution effect and an income effect; with a symmetry property it yields:

(2) $(\epsilon_1/U_2) \cdot (dU_2/d\epsilon_1) = - \theta_{c1} \cdot e_{1M} + (\theta_{c1} - \theta_{x1}) \cdot \gamma$

(2′) $(\epsilon_2/U_1) \cdot (dU_1/d\epsilon_2) = - \theta_{c2} \cdot e_{2M} + (\theta_{c2} - \theta_{x2}) \cdot \gamma .$

Here $\theta_{c1} = 1 - \theta_{c2}$ and $\theta_{x1} = 1 - \theta_{x2}$ are the financial shares of commodity one in consumption expenditure and national income respectively, e_{jM} is the income elasticity of demand for commodity $j, j = 1, 2$, and γ is the coefficient of relative risk aversion. Variants of these equations can be found in Ruffin (1974b) and Anderson and Riley (1976), for example.

Virtually every result in the literature is based on equations (1), (1′), (2) and (2′). Suppose that initially the economy faces nonrandom prices and is at an optimum with marginal rate of transformation α equal to $\bar{p}$. Now, introduce $\epsilon_1(s)$ with mean unity and hold production fixed temporarily, so that the betting term on the left-hand side of (1) vanishes at the (now suboptimal) original production point. If the economy is a net exporter of commodity one in all states of the world, and commodity one is noninferior, then the marginal insurance term in equation (1) is negative and the economy will reduce production of commodity one. If the economy is a net importer of (noninferior) commodity one in all states, then the sign of the covariance term is ambiguous, although if risk-aversion is strong, then the income effect will dominate in (2), the covariance term will be positive, and production of commodity one will increase. As an unambiguous net exporter of commodity one, a reduction in production of commodity one implies an increased reliance on nonrandom domestic production and a decreased reliance on random foreign trade for acquiring commodity two for consumption. As an unambiguous net importer of commodity one, such a reduction in production would increase reliance on random sources for consumption of commodity one. An economy may be a net exporter of commodity one in one state and a net importer in another state, but the presumptive bias of strong risk-aversion via the income effect is a move toward autarky.

One can see the result of Anderson and Riley (1976) that an economy may have a production bias toward one commodity relative to autarky in a nonrandom situation, but a production bias in the opposite direction when randomness occurs. For example, assume homotheticity, so that $e_{1M} = 1$, and start from the situation where autarky is exactly optimal in the non-random situation and introduce $\epsilon_1(s)$ (with small variance and mean unity); the substitution term in (2) will dominate, the covariance term will be negative, and the economy will reduce production of commodity one relative to autarky. However, via continuity of the marginal betting and insurance terms, a move in this direction would still be optimal, even if the betting term had been slightly positive at autarky, and that positivity would imply a move toward increased production of commodity one in the nonrandom case. A similar argument will establish the proposition, to be found in Turnovsky (1974) and Anderson and Riley (1976), that in the Ricardian model an economy may completely reverse its specialization in production under price randomness—unlike the situation with a single source of multiplicative production randomness.

In the context of the Ricardian model, Ruffin (1974b) has considered conditions for determining the pattern of production in the face of price randomness. Recalling that the marginal rate of transformation α is constant in the Ricardian model, it is easy to see from the betting terms in equations (1) and (1$'$) that if α exceeds $\bar{p}$, and *a fortiori* α exceeds $1/\bar{q}$, then the bet of shifting production into commodity one is actuarially unfavorable in terms of commodity two, while the bet of shifting production into commodity two is actuarially favorable in terms of commodity one. Similarly, if α is less than $1/\bar{q}$, and *a fortiori* α is less than $\bar{p}$, then the first bet is actuarially favorable, while the second bet is unfavorable. If α lies between $\bar{p}$ and $1/\bar{q}$, then both bets are actuarially unfavorable.

A sufficient condition for specialization in say commodity one in production is that at the point of specialization the bet of shifting into commodity two, using commodity one as *numéraire*, is actuarially fair or unfavorable, while the corresponding insurance term is also nonpositive. From the previous discussion and equations (1$'$) and (2$'$), this requires

$\alpha \leqq 1/\bar{q}$ and $\gamma \leqq e_{2M}$, noting that $\theta_{x2} = 0$, when production is specialized in commodity one. Similarly, a sufficient condition for specialization in commodity two is that $\alpha \geqq \bar{p}$ and $\gamma \leqq e_{1M}$.

As Ruffin notes, in the case of constant coefficient of relative risk-aversion equal to unity, the marginal insurance term vanishes at the specialization points, since $\gamma = e_{1M} = e_{2M} = 1$.[6] In this case, the impact of Jensen's inequality in generating a range of diversification can be seen, since diversification occurs if $\bar{p} > \alpha > 1/\bar{q}$ and only if $\bar{p} \geqq \alpha \geqq 1/\bar{q}$. High levels of risk-aversion tend to expand the range of diversification, while low levels tend to contract it. If the coefficient of relative risk-aversion lies between the two income elasticities, then the range of diversification is shifted, so that there is an increased specialization range for the commodity with low-income elasticity of demand.

Ruffin derives results of this type and employs them to suggest the potential impact on trade patterns between developed and less-developed countries on the basis of attitudes to risk (possibly dependent on levels of wealth) and of income propensities for commodities likely to be exported by the two groups of countries. Even in this two-country model there is no explanation of the ultimate source of price randomness in trade between two (groups of) countries with nonrandom technologies and endowments.

Kemp and Liviatan (1973) examine comparative-advantage theory in a two-country context. Their economies are mixed Leontief–Ricardian, with fixed coefficients, a single primary factor, and two final (and intermediate) commodities. The introduction of intermediate goods largely obscures the issue, although it does provide an ingenious method of inducing price randomness from randomness in preferences. Each country has an ex-ante decision allocating labor along the long-run production-possibility frontier, and ex-post this can only be adjusted along short-run production-possibility frontiers by discarding some of the labor already allocated. The slopes of these short-run frontiers depend on the intermediate good input-output coefficients.

The sole purpose of the short-run frontiers in one (dominant) country is to provide a two-state distribution for world price as preferences fluctuate in that country. For the counterexample to the theory of long-run comparative advantage (i.e., specialization according to the long-run transformation frontiers), the second small country is assumed to be nonrandom and with no intermediate goods in production. Thus we are back with the situation of a Ricardian economy with nonrandom autarky in the face of exogenous random price. The specific counterexample chosen involves a homothetic logarithmic utility function, which implies that $\gamma = e_{1M} = e_{2M} = 1$ and, hence, from Ruffin's work, that specialization can be determined solely

---

[6] Recall that a globally constant coefficient of relative risk-aversion implies homotheticity for preferences in commodity space; cf. Stiglitz (1969).

from the betting term. Thus all that is required is a two-state price generated by the large country so that the specialization pattern under uncertainty for the small country reverses that implied by the (now irrelevant) long-run frontier of the large country.

Kemp and Liviatan also consider the same model where trade occurs through futures markets rather than spot markets. Once again examples of reversal of specialization in the small country can be created. Kemp and Liviatan assume in this case that the small country is nonrandom, but that it has intermediate inputs in production; further, they claim that "the direction of specialization in [the small country] depends partly on the ease of short-run adjustment in that country" (Kemp and Liviatan 1973, page 226; or page 276 of Kemp 1976*a*).

However, the role of short-run substitution in production is essentially redundant. Income acquired from contingent sales in one state is a perfect substitute for income acquired in the second state and the optimum occurs where total income is maximized. Except in a borderline case, total income is maximized at one or other specialization point on the long-run transformation frontier; the only role of the parameters of the locus of short-run production possibilities lies in the fact that it is impossible to determine the geometric location of the two specialization points (and, hence, total income attained at each) without these parameters. Thus it appears that the role of short-run production possibilities does not play an essential role anywhere in the behavior of the small country.

The most exhaustive treatment of the formal structure of the Ricardian model in the face of price randomness occurs outside the trade literature. The paper by Stiglitz (1970) escaped the notice of the subsequent trade literature, because its nominal topic is the term structure of interest. However, the model of Stiglitz is mathematically equivalent to that of Ruffin and others, and contains Ruffin's central result on criteria for specialization within a broader discussion.[7]

Stiglitz considers a single individual with a utility function defined over consumption in two periods, nonrandom wealth, and the option to buy one-period or two-period bonds at given market prices. One-period bonds yield a certain return for consumption in period one and two-period bonds yield a certain return for consumption in period two. The initial allocation of wealth between one-period and two-period bonds in period zero corresponds to the Ricardian allocation of labor. However, when period one arrives the individual has the option of selling some of his two-period bonds to use for consumption in period one or of using some of the proceeds of his income from initial one-period bonds to buy new one-period bonds that will provide income for consumption in period two. The terms of trade for these period-one transactions are unknown when the initial wealth alloca-

---

[7] Cf. Stiglitz (1970), especially equation (30), p. 333.

tion is made in period zero, and the period-one transactions correspond to the ex-post trade and consumption decision in the Ricardian model. The analogy is complete.

Stiglitz is careful to state the limitations of a model with no explicit supply side. We cannot give the entire content of such an extensive paper here, but Stiglitz starts from the optimal position under autarky, i.e., the preferred position on the nonrandom transformation frontier, as a benchmark. At least for small variability in price, if $\alpha < 1/\bar{q}$ then all individuals will speculate on commodity one by moving production in that direction relative to autarky, although the more risk-averse will speculate less; if $\alpha > \bar{p}$, then all individuals bias production toward commodity two, an unambiguously actuarially favorable move. If α lies in the intermediate diversification range, then nothing can be said in general.

If the production-possibility frontier is viewed as a transformation frontier in asset space, then Stiglitz starts from the case of certainty, where the indifference map in asset space is trivially identical to that in commodity space, and implicitly asks how the slope of the indifference curve in asset space through the prerandomness autarkic production point alters with the introduction of price randomness. Ruffin's analysis concentrates exclusively on the behavior of the indifference map at the points of specialization.

iv) *Concluding remarks*

Price and technological randomness dominate but do not exhaust the literature. For example, Kemp (1976*b*) considers a two-stage production decision in a fixed coefficients version of the HOS model for an economy facing a nonrandom exogenous world-price ratio. Randomness occurs in the supply of one factor and the proportions of that factor allocated to the two industries must be decided ex-ante, although the second factor is allocated ex-post. The issue is whether randomness can create or destroy a situation of specialization relative to the nonrandom case. If the world-price ratio lies outside the range of marginal rates of transformation for the two factors, or if one constraint is always binding despite the randomness, then the problem is trivial, but in the nontrivial situations Kemp concludes that it is possible to create or destroy a specialization optimum by introducing randomness.

The destructive impact of the presence of randomness on the robustness of propositions in nonrandom trade theory is emphasized throughout Kemp's work, and in the situation with no ex-ante trade, this conclusion has strong support. The significance of the papers by Helpman and Razin lies in the more positive conclusions created by the introduction of ex-ante trade in real equities. The Helpman–Razin approach also draws attention to the domestic microeconomic foundations of the representative individual approach, and in doing so will almost certainly establish the stock market model as the centerpiece of the theory of trade and uncertainty. We would argue that, especially prior to the work of Helpman and Razin, the literature was hampered by failure to emphasize the introduction of the randomness rationale for transformation and by a consequent strongly commodity-oriented approach. Greater attention to the uncertainty roots of the theory and to the associated nontrade uncertainty literature might have produced a faster awareness of portfolio aspects of the models, both domestically and internationally, and developed a more uncertainty-oriented intuition to accompany the results.

III. MODELS WITH EX-ANTE TRADE

i) Explicit portfolio models

There is a significant literature on portfolio models based on the Sharpe–Lintner capital-asset-pricing model as applied to an international environment. This literature has relevance for trade theorists, although it is usually presented and interpreted in a manner that can best be described as finance-oriented rather than trade-oriented. As an example, Black (1974) has a clean presentation of the impact of international barriers to investment on the basic portfolio separation theorem of the CAPM. Black considers three groups, taxed individuals in each of the two countries and internationally tax-exempt individuals. It is shown that within each group there is a common composition for the portfolio of risky assets, and this composition differs between groups and (in a systematic and plausible way) from what would be the globally common (market) portfolio of risky assets with unrestricted asset trade.

Numerous references could be given for this growing literature; the interested reader can refer to the volume edited by Elton and Gruber (1975) and the citations therein. The main advantage of the CAPM is its suitability for empirical work, and perhaps the most valuable work using this model in an international context arises from estimates of scope for diversification in assets across national boundaries. Of course, this raises issues of the type discussed by Black, with potential barriers to international mobility in the form of explicit regulatory policies and also from limited information about foreign assets or from increased danger of expropriation. Another advantage of the CAPM is that it effectively aggregates all risky assets into a composite representing the market portfolio. The work of Hart (1975) and Cass and Stiglitz (1972) implies that the Arrow–Pratt expected-utility portfolio models, which in principle are more general than a mean-variance approach, are not very robust in obtaining comparative static results outside of certain special cases. The aggregation problems associated with more than one source of randomness are in general at least as complex as other aggregation problems that have been traditionally minimized in much of trade theory—as evidenced by the search for gross substitutability conditions (Blanchard and Plantes 1977). In any event the CAPM appears destined to play a useful role in the theory of uncertainty and international trade, to the mutual benefit of finance theory and trade theory.

Bearing in mind the (perhaps excessively) central role of simple general equilibrium models in nonrandom trade theory and also the presence of the randomness rationale for transformation once uncertainty is introduced, the current author has examined a sequence of simple two-country models of ex-ante trade based on the Arrow–Pratt expected-utility theory. The purpose of these models is to complement the existing commodity-oriented literature on uncertainty and international trade by first isolating the randomness rationale for transformation in highly aggregated one-commodity models of exchange and then production, and then by introducing two physical commodities. The seminal work by Arrow (1971) on risk-aversion can be viewed as analyzing a single market participant endowed with an asset with nonrandom return and participating in a market where both the nonrandom asset and an asset with random return are available. This leaves open the question of behavior of other market participants, some of whom presumably own the randomness embodied in the second asset. The models of Pomery (1976) were designed to view such markets from a simple trade theoretic and general equilibrium perspective. The high level of aggregation is intended to abstract from internal-risk diversification and to isolate differences in expectations, attitudes to risk or endowments of risk across rather than within countries. The work of Helpman and Razin, based on the relatively sophisticated stock market model of Diamond, rather than the minimal portfolio structure of Arrow's risk-aversion paper, suggests that this type of model can be integrated into the literature without too much difficulty. While Helpman and Razin are interested in production issues and in propositions such as factor-price equalization that emphasize similarities between countries, the less sophisticated models of Pomery (1976) emphasize exchange aspects originating from differences between countries.

ii) *Commitment models*[8]

Commitment models involve an ex-ante trade decision, either in an exchange context or in combination with an ex-ante production decision. Although the ex-ante trade decision can be partially interpreted as a form of asset trade, the explicit market structure involves trade in commodities. Brainard and Cooper (1968) introduced this type of model where a country determines the quantity of exports (of its natural export commodity) prior to knowing the realized value of world price. Thus a nonrandom claim to consumption of the exportable is exchanged for a

---

[8] Some parts of this subsection express views similar to those found in the survey paper of Helpman and Razin (1977*b*).

random claim to consumption of the importable, with world price determining the terms of trade and providing the randomness.

The purpose of this framework is to model economies where as a result, for example, of transportation lags and long distances between the point of production and the international market, export decisions must be made before world price is known. Brainard and Cooper place their analysis in an applied context with discussion of the possible detrimental effects of randomness in export earnings for a less developed country, of the possibility of divergence between social and private attitudes to risk, and of the possibilities for diversification in production based on observed correlations between world prices in various commodities.

The subsequent literature has neglected the applied aspects, as well as abandoning the quadratic utility function and, in some cases, the production decision of Brainard and Cooper. Batra (1975*b*, chap. 7), and Batra and Russell (1974) consider commitment models involving ex-ante production decisions and an export commitment in one commodity. In Batra and Russell's paper the producers are risk-neutral while consumers are risk-averse, a combination that raises some question about the interpretation of policy conclusions. Also one should treat with caution the remark (Batra and Russell 1974, page 1048) that risk-averse consumers will tend to overconsume the commodity in which the export commitment is made. In the special case of a boundary solution in production where only commodity one is produced, this version of the commitment model becomes formally equivalent to a two-commodity skewed endowment share-trading model in Pomery (1976). It can be shown that under certain situations the asset embodying the commodity that is random in consumption may be treated by risk-averse consumers as the "safe asset;" i.e., a higher proportion of output (the nonrandom asset) is exported when there is randomness in the imported asset than in the certainty equivalent case, and also an increase in risk-aversion generates a shift toward the random imported asset at constant price. Sufficient conditions for these outcomes include an additive constant elasticity of substitution utility function with σ less than unity. Thus risk-aversion need not imply overconsumption of commodity one in either of these senses.

The most interesting result in the commitment model literature has arisen in the exchange context, with a theorem on the nonoptimality of autarky in Ruffin (1974*a*). The derivation and interpretation of this result for a single price-taking country are fairly straightforward, but it raises other questions as to how the model is intended to be viewed as part of a global, general equilibrium model and to what extent it is based on implicit omission of certain international markets.

In a two-commodity exchange model, it is easy to see that an export commitment places the country on a second-best form of offer curve, which we may call a "commitment curve." The second best nature arises from inability to adjust the realized marginal rate of substitution to the realized marginal rate of transformation in trade.

Formally, if (x_1, x_2) represents the fixed endowment bundle and non-negative e_1 the export commitment for exportable commodity one, then consumption is given by $c_1 = x_1 - e_1$ and $c_2 = x_2 + p \cdot e_1$. Here $p \equiv p_1/p_2$ is the relative price of the exportable in the world market and is the source of randomness.

As can be seen from Figure 1, the commitment curve will not coincide with the standard offer curve except in special cases. One such special case is with skewed endowment (i.e., $x_2 = 0$) and a utility function that (ordinally) is Cobb–Douglas in form; for all positive prices a fixed quantity of commodity one would be exported ex-post, and hence there is a unique optimal ex-ante choice irrespective of the distribution of world price and irrespective of attitude to risk.

Since the commitment curve is a second-best offer curve, and since offer curves rarely exhibit the special form exhibited in Figure 1, it is natural to consider simultaneous export commitments (non-negative e_1, e_2) in both commodities. Thus consumption is given by:

$$(3) \quad c_1 = x_1 - e_1 + (e_2/p)$$

$$c_2 = x_2 - e_2 + p \cdot e_1 .$$

By eliminating price from these two equations, the commitment curve can be seen to be a rectangular hyperbola relative to the translated origin $(x_1 - e_1, x_2 - e_2)$ that passes through the endowment point when $p = e_2/e_1$, as with curve CC in Figure 2. Clearly, a joint export commitment is at least as good as a single export commitment, and usually strictly better.

Ruffin (1974a) took this argument to a natural conclusion by dropping

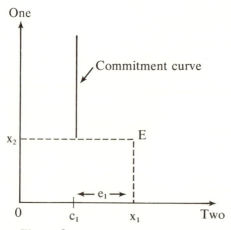

Figure 1

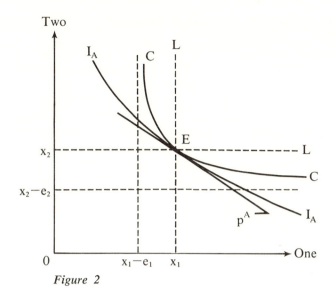

Figure 2

the non-negativity constraints on e_1 and e_2 (where negative values represent autonomous imports). In this situation, autarky, i.e., the solution with $e_1 = e_2 = 0$, is never optimal.

This result can be justified somewhat loosely, by a graphical illustration of Ruffin's Theorem 2. Assume that the utility function has sufficient continuity for the autarkic indifference curve ($I_A I_A$ in Figure 2) to be well behaved in the neighborhood of endowment point E, and that the range of prices is bounded. Now freeze the ratio of positive e_1 and e_2, so that e_2/e_1 is always equal to the autarkic marginal rate of substitution p^A. This implies that the commitment curve and the autarkic indifference curve have the same tangent hyperplane at the endowment point.

Reducing e_1 and e_2 toward zero, while preserving the ratio, pulls each point on the commitment curve toward the endowment point E. The commitment curve approaches the right-angled curve LL (although, of course, it vanishes in the limit when $e_1 = e_2 = 0$); for sufficiently small positive values of e_1 and e_2, the commitment curve lies entirely inside the autarkic indifference curve (except for the common position at E, when world price equals the autarkic marginal rate of substitution).

This shows that a sufficiently small, positive, joint-export commitment can always be found to dominate the choice of autarky, but it does not imply that the optimal values of e_1 and e_2 are both positive. Ruffin derives sufficient conditions in his Theorem 3 for optimal e_1 and e_2 to be positive simultaneously. Note that since Ruffin has already assumed strict concavity of the utility function (and not just strict quasiconcavity) earlier in the paper, the additional condition of weak Pareto complementarity ($U_{12} \geqq 0$)

is not required, and a sufficient condition is that $E(p) > p^A > [E(1/p)]^{-1}$.[9] In this situation, bets involving positive export commitments are simultaneously favorable in both directions.

Ruffin considers the case where a forward market exists allowing trade at certain price in this market as well as unrestricted joint commitments. The economy always possesses the option of using the forward market for standard trade purposes, attaining a new pseudoautarkic endowment point, where marginal rate of substitution equals p^f (the relative price in the forward market), and then playing the same joint-commitment game relative to the new endowment point. Thus Ruffin shows that the zero-commitment option is never optimal, and that if $E(p) > p^f > [E(1/p)]^{-1}$, then both optimal commitments are positive.

Models of the commitment type have appeared elsewhere, particularly in the literature on savings and uncertainty (e.g., Levhari and Srinivasan 1969; Sandmo 1970, 1974; Dreze and Modigliani 1972; Leland 1968; and, in passing, Rothschild and Stiglitz 1971; Kihlstrom and Mirman 1974).

The typical intertemporal model involves two periods, a single commodity, and a single price-taking individual. The individual has a non-random endowment in the first period, a (possibly zero) endowment in period two, and the option to forego some consumption in the first period and to use the proceeds (accumulated at an exogenous interest rate) to augment second-period consumption.

Recalling the opposing income and substitution effects of an interest-rate change in a deterministic setting, the issue is whether the introduction of randomness in the interest rate or in the second-period endowment—but not both simultaneously—encourages or discourages saving relative to the certainty-equivalent benchmark. The case of interest-rate randomness is precisely the exchange-commitment model with random terms of trade, although the intertemporal context has encouraged concentration on models where a single commitment is allowed. Since the first period good must be exported (i.e., e_1 non-negative and e_2 zero) the savings and uncertainty literature has not incorporated Ruffin's result. Rather it has tended to become immersed in the question of the appropriate concept of decreasing absolute risk-aversion for a utility function defined over two commodities, a line of enquiry encouraged by the common assumption of additive utility in intertemporal models.

Although the commitment model implies trade decisions are made ex-ante, it is difficult if not impossible to interpret the commitment as a bilateral contract. If it were a bilateral contract, there would be no reason to make the realized terms of exchange dependent on the spot price prevailing at the time of delivery, since the two markets are conceptually distinct. Even making allowance for this, the model involving a single

---

[9] Note that this p is the reciprocal of that in Ruffin (1974a), p. 253, equation (13).

price-taking country with nonrandom autarky appears incomplete. If the nonoptimality of autarky theorem is to have impact, it must surely represent more than a suboptimal way of realizing gains from trade that exist independently of the commitment-trading structure. When all countries are nonrandom, but price is random with $E(p) > p^A > [E(1/p)]^{-1}$, then all countries will want to make positive joint commitments simultaneously, and in a system of bilateral contracts there is no country willing to hold the reverse commitments; the market fails to clear because in effect there are no explicit asset prices to adjust.

If one country owned randomness in its supply structure, and this induced randomness in world price, then it is necessary to discuss the possible existence of explicit markets for trading randomness, and whether the gains from trade in the nonrandom country are related to an implicit risk premium paid by the random economy for acquiring randomness through trade. This last argument applies equally well whether commitment trade involves bilateral contracts or not. An alternative interpretation is that there need not be any owned randomness in the system, and that no bilateral contracts are involved.[10] Rather all exports are determined ex-ante and sent to a central market where the market-clearing terms of trade are determined from these fixed supplies. This interpretation appears to imply the absence of any forward markets, since, if all countries are nonrandom, the optimal solution is to trade entirely through such a market. In a nonrandom world, any intention to trade not just via the forward market but also via a random spot price is either based on illusion (if the spot price is in fact nonrandom) or, in effect, implies artificially generated price randomness that must be globally detrimental, using arguments of Samuelson (1972) discussed in Section IV.

As with much of the trade and uncertainty literature, the assumption of randomness in exogenous world price leaves questions about the implicit market structure for trading randomness. From a general-equilibrium viewpoint, price is traditionally treated as an endogenous variable, and it would be useful to know whether authors consider price randomness to be generated endogenously from random preferences or supply structure, or arising purely from the inability of the market to provide sufficient information at the time of decision-making, or even from strategic introduction of randomness in a game-theoretic sense. By and large the source of randomness in world price is not important to a price-taking country, but, in terms of extending the model from a single country to the global economy, and of asking which markets are implicitly assumed not to exist, the distinctions are important. And if the general-equilibrium model depends on implicit assumptions about the existence or nonexistence of world forward

---

[10] I am grateful for Bill Ethier's patient insistence that commitment models need not be interpreted in terms of ex-ante bilateral contracts; he is not liable for the comments here.

markets or world markets for trading owned-randomness, or about the existence or nonexistence of randomness in other countries, then welfare statements will be contingent upon these assumptions. Thus, even for a single price-taking country, there is a presumption that general-equilibrium aspects of the model should be made explicit.

IV. FLUCTUATIONS MODELS

Fluctuations models permit ex-post decisions and focus on the normative comparison of situations of randomness versus situations where the random variable is stabilized at its mean. This type of instantaneous-adjustment model "is, of course, absurdly unrealistic, but it does enable us to separate and highlight some of the irreducible effects of variability, with all the complications of uncertainty skimmed off" (Kemp 1976a, page 76; c.f. also Kemp and Khang 1975).

Mathematically, the issue is whether the objective function, usually utility, is strictly convex (strictly concave) as a function of the random variable after allowing for ex-post adjustment. If the function is strictly convex (strictly concave), then expected utility with randomness is greater (less) than utility evaluated at the expected value of the random variable; hence fluctuations are superior (inferior) to stabilization at the mean value.

Economically, there may occur some ambiguity over the interpretation of these results, particularly in the case of fluctuations in exogenous world price. As is shown in Figure 3, a country facing with certainty price p^A (which happens to be the autarkic price ratio in order to eliminate income effects) would unambiguously be better off if instead it faced prices p^1 and p^2

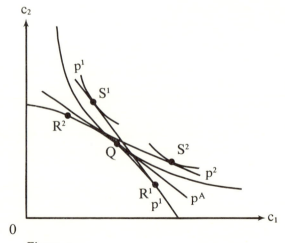

Figure 3

with expected value p^A. The opportunity to substitute in production and in consumption allows it to achieve consumption points S^1 and S^2 respectively, so that in each case (and hence on average) it is better off than at autarkic Q. However, this cannot be the complete story if price fluctuations are endogenously induced by owned randomness in the supply structure of one of the countries.

The nontrade fluctuations literature originates from work by Waugh (1944, 1966) and Oi (1961). The gains from substitution in consumption (around autarky) in Figure 3 reflect the fact that minimum expenditure required to achieve a given level of utility is a strictly concave function of relative price; this property provides the basis of Waugh's analysis. The gains from substitution in production arise from the fact that maximum national income subject to the transformation-frontier constraint is a strictly convex function of relative price. Oi's paper rests on the related property that maximum profit subject to a production function constraint is a strictly convex function of relative price, implying that a single price-taking firm receives higher expected profits from fluctuating output price than when price is stabilized at its mean.

Samuelson (1972) strongly emphasizes the partial equilibrium nature of these results, pointing out that a closed nonrandom economy neither could (nor should) attempt to create such a mean-preserving randomness of price. Put another way, in an exchange model with risk-averse individuals, if any economy owns randomness in its endowment structure then the world is worse off in the sense that the world (expected) utility-possibility frontier is contracted toward the origin relative to the situation where the endowment takes on its expected value with certainty. Thus, if randomness is owned, then any analysis that considers only a nonrandom economy facing induced price randomness, and not the dominant ownership loss of the random economy, is normatively incomplete.

A simple example illustrates the source of gains and losses from randomness. Gains from the opportunity to substitute ex-post conflict with losses for risk-averters from ownership of randomness. Consider a single decision-maker producing a single output by two production processes that draw on a fixed supply of a single input. Each production process exhibits diminishing returns (as well as monotonicity and sufficient differentiability), one or other process—but not both simultaneously—involves multiplicative randomness, and the input allocation decision can be made ex-post. Trivially, interior optimization implies equating the marginal rate of transformation to unity. If $\epsilon_j(s)$ is the (positive) value in state s of a multiplicative random variable in process j with expected value unity, then it is easy to show that randomness in process j is beneficial (adverse) if

(4) $\quad -\theta_{xj} \cdot \gamma + \theta_{xi} \cdot \sigma_S$

is positive (negative) in all states. Here $i, j \, \epsilon \{1, 2\}, i \neq j, \theta_{xj} = 1 - \theta_{xi}$ is the "share of industry j in national income," γ the coefficient of relative risk-aversion, and σ_S the elasticity of substitution around the (expected) transformation frontier.

The first term in (4) reflects the fact that the randomness in production causes randomness in consumption of the single final output. A closed economy owns this randomness, and the randomness is more adverse to the extent that process j is a large part of national income and/or the economy is highly risk-averse. With no ex-post substitution, the economy is unambiguously worse off. However, to the extent that it has strong substitution possibilities, and the nonrandom process is a large part of national income, there will be a significant beneficial effect from what Samuelson terms "betting after the event." Indeed, a risk-neutral economy is unambiguously better off if it can substitute ex-post.

If process one is random, the sufficient condition for this to be beneficial is that everywhere σ_S/γ exceeds θ_{x1}/θ_{x2}, while, in contrast, if process two is random then the sufficient condition requires σ_S/γ to exceed θ_{x2}/θ_{x1}. From earlier discussion we know that if $E\epsilon_1 = 1$, then from Jensen's inequality $E(1/\epsilon_1) > 1$, and if $E\epsilon_2 = 1$, then $E(1/\epsilon_2) > 1$. Once again multiplicative randomness is being introduced into a ratio representing the slope of a transformation frontier, and if the rate of transformation is kept actuarially unchanged in one direction, then it must be actuarially improved in the other direction; this property appears in relation to the opportunity to substitute ex-post.

Clearly, a similar type of argument will apply to multiplicative randomness in world price, since this permits substitution along the transformation frontier represented by the perfectly elastic foreign-offer curve. However, the analysis is complicated by the existence of both substitution and income terms in a world of two (or more) commodities. Note, however, that income effects will arise not from the ultimate ownership of randomness, say in endowments, but from any nonzero net-trade position, which implies an "induced" ownership of randomness.

If p is the random relative price of commodity one, equations of the following form have been derived by many authors, e.g., Anderson and Riley (1976) equation (10), Turnovsky (1974) equation (40), Pazner and Razin (1974) equation (8).

$$(5) \quad (p^2/U_2 \cdot Y) \cdot (d^2U/dp^2)$$
$$= \theta_{c1} \cdot \theta_{c2} \cdot \sigma_D - 2 \cdot (\theta_{x1} - \theta_{c1}) \cdot e_{1M} - (\theta_{x1} - \theta_{c1})^2 \cdot \gamma ,$$

where $Y = p \cdot x_1 + x_2$ is national income in units of commodity two; θ_{xj}, θ_{cj}, $j = 1, 2$, are the production and consumption financial shares respectively of commodity j in national income; σ_D is the elasticity of substitution around an indifference curve; e_{1M} is the income elasticity of demand for commodity one.

Equation (5) is for an endowment model; adding substitution in production merely adds an extra positive substitution term. For fluctuations in the neighborhood of autarky, the economy is unambiguously better off, as the last two terms vanish. The last term on the right-hand side of (5) represents the unambiguously adverse effect of owning randomness, if the net trade position is nonzero and the economy is risk-averse. The middle term represents the combined income effect on consumption of commodity one and substitution effect on the marginal utility of (*numéraire*) income, and depends on both the direction of trade and whether commodity one is normal. Reversing the *numéraire* and considering randomness when the expected value of $1/p$ is kept at unity implies an analog of equation (5), which has the beneficial substitution term and the adverse risk-aversion term unchanged (noting that $\theta_{x1} - \theta_{c1} = \theta_{c2} - \theta_{x2}$). However, the middle term will be altered and have reverse sign if both commodities are normal.

Thus the basic intuition of beneficial-substitution opportunities versus adverse-ownership effects in the presence of randomness is in a sense only partially changed by moving from production randomness to price randomness—and that as a consequence of the tedious cross-effects. However, in the case of production randomness, we observed the ultimate source of randomness. With price randomness, any ultimate owned source of randomness is omitted, and we know that this ultimate ownership effect dominates to the extent that at least one country—and the world as a whole—must be worse off.

The work on fluctuations in a trade context is not subject to this partial equilibrium misinterpretation, although much of the work has been partial equilibrium analysis in the sense that it works with producer and consumer surplus in a single industry. (Anderson and Riley [1976] object to the use of such analysis on the grounds that it eliminates a proper role for risk-aversion in the analysis.) The trade-fluctuations literature has focused on the benefits of stabilizing price at its expected value in a world of linear demand and supply functions and additive randomness in the intercepts of these functions.[11] Explicit reconciliation of this assumption with randomness in underlying preferences or production structure might be beneficial. The earliest papers are those of Massell (1969, 1970), followed by Hueth and Schmitz (1972) and Bieri and Schmitz (1973). Massell (1969) shows in a closed economy that buyers benefit from supply-side randomness and sellers benefit from demand-side randomness, but that the "owners" of the randomness would prefer stabilization to neutralize the price fluctuations— and could compensate the other half of the market.

Note that the normative comparison is not one between randomness and the random intercept stabilized at its mean, but between laissez faire randomness and a policy that stabilizes price at its mean. This stabilization is actuarially feasible with linear functions, if we assume zero storage costs

---

[11] Note the cautionary paper by Turnovsky (1976) on the differences between the linear additive case and multiplicative randomness for (nonlinear) demand or supply.

and no rate of discount over time. However, in a sense, actuarial feasibility is insufficient, since commodities cannot be transformed backwards in time. If the seven years of famine precede the seven years of plenty (rather than vice versa), it is not clear how a buffer stock is to be accumulated, and with any finite level of buffer stock there is always nonzero probability that it will prove inadequate in subsequent periods.

The nature of Massell's result can be suggested in a general equilibrium framework for a closed economy with additive randomness in the production of commodity one. To mimic the consumer surplus approach, assume constant marginal utility of *numéraire* commodity two (in the sense that the marginal propensity to consume commodity one is zero).

In Figure 4 consider a distribution with two equi-probable states, with A representing the autarkic optimal solution when the additive randomness in production takes on its expected value with certainty. When the additive random variable takes on its high value, at stabilized price producers will wish to move to C^1 and, given this income, consumers will wish to be at B^1 on the vertical income-consumption path through A. When the random variable takes on its low value, production at stabilized price is at C^2 and consumption at B^2. With congruence of the triangles AB^1C^1 and AB^2C^2, stabilization is actuarially feasible. Without stabilization, production would equal consumption at points D^1 and D^2. Since D^j is inferior to B^j for $j = 1, 2$, stabilization dominates the laissez faire solution. Ignoring income effects, consumers benefit from the ability to make (compensated) ex-post adjustments to price; however, the supply side adjustment implied by

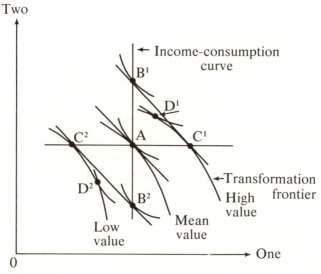

Figure 4

adjustment to D^1 and D^2 in production creates a dominating adverse fall in real income.

The stabilization literature was extended to a two-country framework by Hueth and Schmitz (1972), who found that under free trade the owners of the randomness (i.e., the buyers or the sellers in one of the countries) are the only beneficiaries from price stabilization—but could compensate all remaining market participants. Intuitively, all nonowners appear to benefit from a laissez faire policy, because of the ability to make (compensated) adjustments as price changes, but this is dominated by the ownership loss analogous to that in Figure 4. As Hueth and Schmitz note, compensation across national boundaries may be even less plausible than compensation within an economy. (Hueth and Schmitz also consider simultaneous free trade in intermediate and final commodities under simplifying assumptions.)

Bieri and Schmitz (1973) modify the previous analysis by introducing an optimal tariff for the importing country. Normative comparisons are undertaken by considering consumer surplus, producer surplus, and tariff revenue. With randomness in the tariff-imposing country, the conclusion is unaltered from the free trade case; the exporting country prefers the undamped fluctuations, although with compensation the stabilization policy is globally preferable. However, if randomness occurs in the exporting country, not merely the owners of the randomness but also (after considering the impact on tariff revenue) the tariff-imposing country prefers stabilization (even prior to compensation). Apparently, by imposing an optimal tariff and treating the nonlinear foreign offer curve as an explicit constraint, the importing country has internalized some of the ownership loss by creating a fall in real income when the unstabilized price creates movement around this constraint frontier.

Bieri and Schmitz also consider the case of a marketing board in the exporting country. The purpose of the board is to maximize returns to producers. In this model the importing country benefits from nonstabilized fluctuations from abroad, but the situation in the exporting country is more complex.

The fluctuations approach has been employed by other authors. For example, Berry and Hymer (1969) analyze the relative effects on utility (and other variables) of price fluctuations for economies with and without ex-post flexibility in production. Both Fishelson and Flatters (1975) and Pelcovits (1976) consider the relevance of fluctuations for the growing literature on the (non)equivalence of tariff and quota.

The tariff-quota models do not represent pure fluctuatations in the sense that, although market participants have complete ex-post flexibility, the tariff or quota is fixed ex-ante. The agnostic nature of the conclusions are captured in the closing sentence of the introduction of Fishelson and Flatters (1975, page 387): ". . . there is no general presumption in favor of one instrument over the other under conditions of uncertainty."

The ambiguity in contrasting the two policy instruments lies in the fact that a given shift in the foreign-offer curve can make the previously equivalent (and optimal) tariff and quota bracket the new optimal point on the altered offer curve. In the familiar case of linear demand and supply in the import market, Fishelson and Flatters conclude that if randomness arises in the demand intercept, then a tariff is preferable to a quota, but with randomness in the supply intercept, a tariff is superior to a quota if and only if the supply of imports is elastic.

Pelcovits uses the Fishelson–Flatters framework, where the foreign supply curve is perfectly elastic and where (for noneconomic reasons) expected imports are constrained to a given level. With randomness in foreign supply, the tariff allows beneficial (compensated) adjustment on the demand side—unlike the quota—but the associated "tariff revenue" for the two instruments must also be taken into account; the latter effect may be sufficient to make a quota superior. With demand side randomness, the tariff always dominates.

This literature on tariffs versus quotas might be clarified by an analysis which, perhaps in a general equilibrium framework, focuses on the conflict between opportunities to make (compensated) ex-post substitution and the (direct and internalized) ownership effects, similar to those seen in Figure 4, which would have required adverse adjustments in the absence of stabilization.

In an entirely different fluctuations context, Kemp and Khang (1975) take the case of an HOS economy facing randomness in exogenous price and consider the impact on the returns to each factor of production. (A slightly modified and extended version of this paper appears as Chapter 6 of Kemp [1976*a*].) Recall that national income is a strictly convex function of relative price, and note that Kemp and Khang are concentrating on the decomposition of this beneficial substitution effect in production among the factors of production.

In general, with n outputs (with quantities x_j, prices p_j, $j = 1 \cdots n$) and m inputs (with exogenous quantities v_k, endogenous prices r_k, $k = 1 \cdots m$), it can be shown from the national income identity relating value of output to value of factor payments that—with, say, the nth output as *numéraire:*

$$(6) \quad \sum_{i=1}^{n-1} \sum_{j=1}^{n-1} (\partial x_i / \partial p_j) \cdot dp_i \cdot dp_j$$

$$= \sum_{k=1}^{m} v_k \cdot \left[\sum_{i=1}^{n-1} \sum_{j=1}^{n-1} (\partial^2 r_k / \partial p_i \cdot \partial p_j) \cdot dp_i \cdot dp_j \right].$$

The strict convexity of national income implies the left-hand side of (6) is positive (almost everywhere) for all nonzero changes in relative price.

Kemp and Khang work in the context of two outputs and two inputs; if p is the relative price of commodity one, x_1 output of commodity one,

L, T labor and land endowments respectively, and w, r the wage and rental, then equation (6) becomes:

(7) $\quad \partial x_1/\partial p = L \cdot (\partial^2 w/\partial p^2) + T \cdot (\partial^2 r/\partial p^2)$.

Thus at any point on the production-possibility frontier at least one factor, and possibly both, has its return behaving locally as a strictly convex function of relative price.

Kemp and Khang find that, if we assume for concreteness that industry one is labor-intensive, both factor returns will be strictly convex in (either) relative price if everywhere we have $\theta_{L1}/\theta_{L2} > \sigma_2/\sigma_1 > \theta_{T1}/\theta_{T2}$. Here θ_{ij}, $i = L, T, j = 1, 2$, is the financial share of factor i in industry j, and σ_j is the elasticity of substitution in that industry. However, if, say, σ_2/σ_1 exceeds θ_{L1}/θ_{L2} everywhere, then wage is strictly concave in relative price.

These results seem to say that in order to jump on the bandwagon of beneficial substitution effects from exogenous price it pays to be the intensive factor in the industry that has the relatively high ability to substitute. Once again, ex-post substitution pays. It might be interesting to see analogous results not in a general $n \times m$ context but rather in a two-output model with one mobile and two specific factors of production; unfortunately, this model is less straightforward for such exercises.

The final application of fluctuations-type analysis is that of Johnson (1974, 1976), who has considered what might be termed globally-artificial fluctuations as an approach to "reversed international transfers" and to preliminary models of speculative behavior. In these exchange models, transfers of commodities are made in one period with an identical reverse transaction made in the second period. However, the two partners to this transaction can trade after each transfer, implying that, in general, a new market equilibrium will be created in both periods.

The problem is similar to the standard transfer problem in many respects. Assume risk-neutral Cobb–Douglas utility functions, following Johnson, and let the home country have a taste bias for commodity two. In Figure 5, let C be the initial equilibrium, p' the equilibrium relative price, EE the common budget line through C at price p', and OD, O^*D^* the respective income-consumption paths through C. If the transfers of the given commodity bundle keep income constant at price p', i.e., the two moves are in either direction from C along EE, then there is no effect, since ex-post trade returns both economies to the original equilibrium at C.

Suppose that the first period transfer does raise income for the home country at the initial prices. For any move into region A, there is excess demand for commodity two at the initial price and the terms of trade will move in favor of the home country. For infinitesimal moves the region A can be extended toward the line FF, which is tangential to the contract curve at C; compare the standard transfer problem analysis. The reverse transfer in the second period will also turn the terms of trade in favor of the

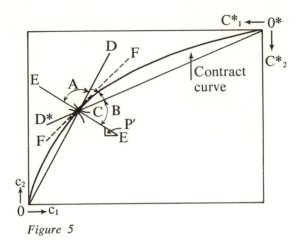

Figure 5

home country, although it is worse off than at C. Similarly, if the transfer shifts the home country into region B (extended to meet FF for infinitesimal changes), the terms of trade move against the home country in both periods.

With constant and equal marginal utility of income in both countries, a reversed transfer at constant price p' leaves expected utility unchanged in both countries. However, constant price implies markets fail to clear, if initial movements along EE are excluded, and the change in equilibrium price unambiguously benefits one country for (finite) changes in regions A or B, harms the other, and leaves the world as a whole with a deadweight loss.

Figure 6 illustrates the world utility-possibility frontier, which is smoothly bowed out, given the cardinal assumptions on utility functions.[12] If point X corresponds to initial equilibrium C in Figure 5, then a transfer, where at constant price p' the home country benefits in period one, will result in equal shifts to Y^1 (in period one) and Y^2 (in period two). Expected utility is unchanged for both countries, and hence for the world as a whole, but neither Y^1 nor Y^2 is feasible. In the absence of intertemporal transfer of utiles along the lines of the stabilization in Figure 4 earlier, output price must change to attain a market-clearing equilibrium and hence a feasible point on the utility-possibility frontier. Aggregate utility unambiguously falls in both periods, although if we are in region A in period one, say, then the move will be to feasible Z^1 and Z^2, where the home country benefits.

In Johnson's models stabilization, analogous to that discussed earlier in relation to the work of Massell, would prevent the losses in aggregate

---

[12] Cf. Johnson (1974), Fig. 3; also Jones (1972) for an explicit statement of this activity analysis approach to welfare economics. Constant marginal utilities of income equal across countries implies unit slope for the objective function in Fig. 6.

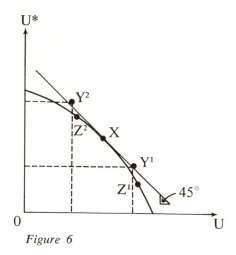

Figure 6

welfare. However, Johnson's point is that this deliberate destabilization may be inherent in some activities. Thus on the view that "speculative transactions" do not remove resources from the global economy, and that each speculative transaction requires a nonspeculator willing to consumate the transaction, Johnson suggests that this type of model can capture an essential aspect of speculative behavior.

This view that the two-sided nature of a speculative transaction makes it difficult to distinguish speculators and nonspeculators in a general-equilibrium context has support in the literature; consider for example the distinction between "price risk" and "quantity risk" in Hirshleifer (1975). Also the intuition that speculative behavior cannot be explained outside of a general equilibrium framework appears sound. It is unfortunate that we will not know how these preliminary models would have been extended to permit additional insights into the nature of speculation.

V. CONCLUSION

i) *Miscellany*

There are a number of papers that have investigated aspects of the theory of uncertainty and international trade that do not fit easily into the categories employed in Sections II–IV, usually because of intertemporal or game-theoretic aspects. Nsouli (1975) considers uncertainty in the context of trade and growth, employing a dynamic stochastic programming approach in a Ricardian-cum-accumulation model for a single price-taking country. This country can export a (consumption) good at random terms of trade for imports of the other (capital) good, which acts as the sole input in production. Kemp (1976a, chaps. 24, 25) addresses the topical issue of utilization of a wasting resource, where the size of the stock is uncertain; issues discussed include the scope for initial gains from trade and of using international borrowing as in effect a means of exporting randomness.

Bhagwati and Srinivasan (1976) tackle the problem of how uncertainty about imposition of a retaliatory quota by a trading partner in subsequent periods can affect current export policy. Since fear of retaliation is based on the exporter's perception of its trading partner, this model would involve strategic uncertainty in an explicit general-equilibrium context. The inter-temporal nature gives the model a two-stage decision structure; current production and trade decisions are decided ex-ante, and decisions in the subsequent period will be made ex-post. Also the probability of retaliation is endogenous, in the sense that the perceived probability increases with the level of current exports.

Bhagwati and Srinivasan consider the case where production can be freely adjusted in both periods through situations where limited (or zero) flexibility is available in the second period. With zero adjustment costs the exporting country has an incentive to impose a tariff to discourage exports below the competitive level. This reflects the increasing probability of retaliation ignored by private traders, and is in addition to any optimal tariff introduced for the standard reason of monopoly power in trade. With zero flexibility in production, the tariff solution is inadequate, since the first-period production decision should take into account the potential impact of a quota on second-period consumption, as opposed to reflecting the marginal rate of substitution in period one alone. Bhagwati and Srinivasan show that the presumption that a tariff alone will be insufficient extends to the case of partial production flexibility, and also that the model can be extended to an infinite horizon under reasonable assumptions.

The paper of Brito and Richardson (1976) represents preliminary work on a scheme to tackle intertemporal and game-theoretic aspects of un-certainty in an international context. Relatively sophisticated mathematical techniques are to be used to study a range of issues involving intertemporal strategic behavior; hopefully, this will provide new perspectives on topics such as the extent of governmental incentive to manipulate stocks of commodities or of foreign exchange reserves in order to create credible threats and hence induce favorable adjustments in key international prices.

Perhaps the most innovative and radical departure from the mainstream of the literature on uncertainty and international trade is to be found in Brock and Magee (1976, 1977). A game-theoretic approach to two-candidate political elections is adopted where the choice variable for each candidate is the level at which he declares support for a tariff. Each candidate knows that a high level of support relative to his opponent will improve campaign contributions from the relevant lobbyists (and hence, *ceteris paribus*, increase his probability of election) but will reduce voter support (for a given level of campaign contributions) from the rest of the electorate.

In effect, the tariff levels can be viewed as endogenous prices that clear political markets. Magee (1976) has used this theory as a basis for empirical testing of the 2 × 2 model. The main question is whether the two factors, labor and capital, behave as though both are industry-specific, as if both are mobile (as in the HOS model), or as if one is mobile and one specific (as in the models of Mussa [1974] and Mayer [1974]). Based on lobbying behavior, Magee finds that his tests lean in the direction of factor specificity for both labor and capital, with capital tending to be more specific than labor.

ii) *Final remarks*

The papers discussed in the previous subsection are an indication that the literature on uncertainty and international trade is beginning to expand in a number of different and potentially useful new directions. We do not intend to speculate on the end product of these and other as yet unplanned avenues of inquiry, but it is clear that the role of uncertainty in international trade need not be confined to providing another minor variation for the standard trade models.

The bulk of this chapter has discussed a selective group of models closer to the mainstream of international trade theory. A theme of this survey has been that the literature, while producing a variety of results, has tended to ignore or underemphasize randomness-oriented aspects of these models. Further exploitation of parallel models in the nontrade literature, and of the accompanying intuition, would be beneficial. As is natural in a new literature, implicit assumptions about domestic or international markets for trading randomness and global general-equilibrium aspects of models of price-taking economies have been slow to obtain proper discussion; this is a consequence of a commodity-oriented approach, which should benefit from the recent work of Helpman and Razin in particular.

So long as the literature embodies hidden assumptions, answers to questions about robustness of theorems or policy implications arising from the theory must remain of dubious status. At this moment it appears that the literature is in the midst of an integrative phase and will soon move into a more mature and productive stage of development. I have attempted to contribute to the process of integration not only by emphasizing randomness-oriented aspects of the literature but also by suggesting, as in Section II, that in some situations the formal structure of familiar trade models can be adapted and reinterpreted to handle the introduction of randomness.

REFERENCES

Anderson, J., and Riley, J. G. 1976. "International Trade with Fluctuating Prices." *International Economic Review* 17 (1): 76–97.
Arrow, K. J. 1971. "The Theory of Risk Aversion." In *Essays in the Theory of*

Risk Bearing, by K. J. Arrow. New York: Markham.

Batra, R. N. 1974. "Resource Allocation in a General Equilibrium Model of Production under Uncertainty." *Journal of Economic Theory* 8 (1): 50–63.

————. 1975a. "Production Uncertainty and the Heckscher-Ohlin Theorem." *Review of Economic Studies* 42: 259–68.

————. 1975b. *The Pure Theory of International Trade under Uncertainty.* New York: Halsted Press.

Batra, R. N., and Russell, W. R. 1974. "Gains from Trade under Uncertainty." *American Economic Review* 64 (6): 1040–48.

Berry, R. A., and Hymer, S. H. 1969. "A Note on the Capacity to Transform and the Welfare Costs of Foreign Trade Fluctuations." *Economic Journal* 79 (136): 833–46.

Bhagwati, J. N., and Srinivasan, T. N. 1976. "Optimal Trade Policy and Compensation under Endogenous Uncertainty: The Phenomenon of Market Disruption." *Journal of International Economics* 6 (4): 317–36.

Bieri, J., and Schmitz, A. 1973. "Export Instability, Monopoly Power, and Welfare." *Journal of International Economics* 3 (4): 389–96.

Black, F. 1974. "International Capital Market Equilibrium with Investment Barriers." *Journal of Financial Economics* 1 (4): 337–52.

Blanchard, O. J., and Plantes, M. K. 1977. "A Note on Gross Substitutability of Financial Assets." *Econometrica* 45 (3): 769–71.

Borch, K., and Mossin, J. (editors). 1968. *Risk and Uncertainty.* N.Y.: St. Martin's Press.

Brainard, W. C., and Cooper, R. N. 1968. "Uncertainty and Diversification in International Trade." *Food Research Institute Studies* 8 (3): 257–85.

Brito, D. L., and Richardson, J. D. 1976. "Money, Power, and Bilateral Trade." Social Sciences Research Institute Discussion Paper 7603, University of Wisconsin at Madison.

Brock, W. A., and Magee, S. P. 1976. "The Campaign Contribution Specialization Theorem." Unpublished manuscript.

————. 1977. "Equilibrium in Political Markets on Pork-Barrel Issues: The Case of the Tariff." Working Paper 77–50, The University of Texas at Austin, Graduate School of Business.

Cass, D., and Stiglitz, J. E. 1972. "Risk Aversion and Wealth Effects on Portfolios with Many Assets." *Review of Economic Studies* 39: 331–54.

Das, S. K. 1977. "Uncertainty and the Heckscher-Ohlin Theorem: A Comment." *Review of Economic Studies* 44: 189–90.

Diamond, P. A. 1967. "The Role of a Stock Market in a General Equilibrium Model with Technological Uncertainty." *American Economic Review* 57 (4): 759–76.

Dreze, J. H., and Modigliani, F. 1972. "Consumption Decisions under Uncertainty." *Journal of Economic Theory* 5 (3): 308–35.

Elton, E. J., and Gruber, M. J. (editors). 1975. *International Capital Markets.* Amsterdam: North-Holland Pub. Co.

Fishelson, G., and Flatters, F. 1975. "The (Non)equivalence of Optimal Tariffs and Quotas under Uncertainty." *Journal of International Economics* 5 (4): 385–93.

Grubel, H. G. 1968. "Internationally Diversified Portfolios: Welfare Gains and Capital Flows." *American Economic Review* 58 (5 part 1): 1299–1314.

Hart, O. D. 1975. "Some Negative Results on the Existence of Comparative Statics Results in Portfolio Theory." *Review of Economic Studies* 42: 615–21.

Heckerman, D. 1973. "On the Effects of Exchange Risk." *Journal of International Economics* 3 (4): 379–87.

Helpman, E., and Razin, A. 1976. "Welfare Aspects of International Trade in Goods and Securities." Working Paper no. 13–76, The Foerder Institute for Economic Research, Tel-Aviv University.

―――. 1977a. "Uncertainty and International Trade in the Presence of Stock Markets." Manuscript, revised February 1977. (Forthcoming in *Review of Economic Studies*.)

―――. 1977b. "International Trade under Uncertainty: A Select Survey of Recent Developments." Manuscript, revised June 1977.

Hirshleifer, J. 1975. "Speculation and Equilibrium: Information, Risk and Markets." *Quarterly Journal of Economics* 89 (4): 519–42.

Hueth, D., and Schmitz, A. 1972. "International Trade in Intermediate and Final Goods: Some Welfare Implications of Destabilized Prices." *Quarterly Journal of Economics* 86 (3): 351–65.

Johnson, H. G. 1974. "The Welfare Effects of Reversed International Transfers." In *Trade, Growth and Macroeconomics: Essays in Honor of Lloyd A. Metzler*, edited by G. Horwich and P. A. Samuelson. New York: Academic Press.

―――. 1976. "Destabilizing Speculation: A General Equilibrium Approach." *Journal of Political Economy* 84 (1): 101–08.

Jones, R. W. 1965. "The Structure of Simple General Equilibrium Models." *Journal of Political Economy* 73 (6): 557–72.

―――. 1972. "Activity Analysis and Real Incomes: Analogies with Production Models." *Journal of International Economics* 2 (3): 277–302.

Kemp, M. C. 1976a. *Three Topics in the Theory of International Trade*. Amsterdam: North-Holland Pub. Co.

―――. 1976b. "Patterns of Production and Trade under Conditions of Resource Uncertainty." Chapter 21 of Kemp (1976a).

―――. 1976c. "Some General-Equilibrium Implications of Technological Uncertainty." Chapter 22 of Kemp (1976a).

Kemp, M. C., and Khang, C. 1975. "A Convexity Property of the Two-by-Two Model of Production." *Journal of International Economics* 5 (3): 255–61.

Kemp, M. C., and Liviatan, N. 1973. "Production and Trade Patterns under Uncertainty." *Economic Record* 49 (126): 215–27.

Kihlstrom, R. E., and Mirman, L. J. 1974. "Risk Aversion with Many Commodities." *Journal of Economic Theory* 8 (3): 361–88.

Lapan, H. E. 1977. "More on General Equilibrium Models of Uncertainty and Trade." Seminar Paper no. 81, Institute for International Economic Studies, University of Stockholm.

Leland, H. E. 1968. "Savings and Uncertainty: The Precautionary Demand for Saving." *Quarterly Journal of Economics* 82 (3): 465–73.

Levhari, D., and Srinivasan, T. N. 1969. "Optimal Savings under Uncertainty." *Review of Economic Studies* 36: 153–64.

Magee, S. P. 1976. "Three Simple Tests of the Stolper-Samuelson Theorem." Unpublished manuscript.

Massell, B. F. 1969. "Price Stabilization and Welfare." *Quarterly Journal of Economics* 83 (2): 284–98.

————. 1970. "Some Welfare Implications of International Price Stabilization." *Journal of Political Economy* 78 (2): 404–17.

Mayer, W. 1974. "Short-Run and Long-Run Equilibrium for a Small Open Economy." *Journal of Political Economy* 82 (5): 955–67.

————. 1976. "The Rybczynski, Stolper–Samuelson, and Factor–Price Equalization Theorems under Price Uncertainty." *American Economic Review* 66 (5): 797–808.

McCulloch, J. H. 1975. "Operational Aspects of the Siegel Paradox." *Quarterly Journal of Economics* 89 (1): 170–72.

Mussa, M. 1974. "Tariffs and the Distribution of Income: The Importance of Factor Specificity, Substitutability, and Intensity in the Short and Long Run." *Journal of Political Economy* 82 (6): 1191–1203.

Nsouli, S. M. 1975. "Theoretical Aspects of Trade, Risk and Growth." *Journal of International Economics* 5 (3): 239–53.

Oi, W. Y. 1961. "The Desirability of Price Instability under Perfect Competition." *Econometrica* 29 (1): 58–64.

Pazner, E. A., and Razin, A. 1974. "Welfare Aspects of Exchange Rate Uncertainty." *Economica* n.s. 41 (163): 256–68.

Pelcovits, M. D. 1976. "Quotas versus Tariffs." *Journal of International Economics* 6 (4): 363–70.

Pomery, J. G. 1976. "International Trade and Uncertainty: Simple General Equilibrium Models Involving Randomness." Ph.D. dissertation, Univ. of Rochester.

Pratt, J. W. 1964. "Risk Aversion in the Small and in the Large." *Econometrica* 32 (1–2): 122–36.

Riley, J. G. 1976. "On the Risk-Spreading Role of Domestic Markets with International Price Uncertainty." Unpublished manuscript.

Rothenberg, T. J., and Smith, K. R. 1971. "The Effect of Uncertainty on Resource Allocation in a General Equilibrium Model." *Quarterly Journal of Economics* 85 (3): 440–59.

Rothschild, M., and Stiglitz, J. E. 1971. "Increasing Risk: II. Its Economic Consequences." *Journal of Economic Theory* 3 (1): 66–84.

Ruffin, R. J. 1974a. "International Trade under Uncertainty." *Journal of International Economics* 4 (3): 243–59.

————. 1974b. "Comparative Advantage under Uncertainty." *Journal of International Economics* 4: 261–73.

————. 1976. "Review of *The Pure Theory of International Trade under Uncertainty*," by R. N. Batra. *Journal of International Economics* 6 (2): 226–27.

Samuelson, P. A. 1972. "The Consumer Does Benefit from Feasible Price Stability" and "Rejoinder." *Quarterly Journal of Economics* 86 (3): 476–93, 500–03.

Sandmo, A. 1970. "The Effect of Uncertainty on Savings Decisions." *Review of Economic Studies* 37: 353–60.

————. 1974. "Two-Period Models of Consumption Decisions under Uncertainty: A Survey." In *Allocation under Uncertainty: Equilibrium and Optimality,* edited by J. H. Dreze. New York: Halsted Press.

Solnik, B. H. 1975. "The Advantages of Domestic and International Diversification." In *International Capital Markets,* edited by E. J. Elton and M. J. Gruber. Amsterdam: North-Holland Pub. Co.

Stiglitz, J. E. 1969. "Behavior Towards Risk with Many Commodities." *Econometrica* 37 (4): 660–67.

———. 1970. "A Consumption Oriented Theory of the Demand for Financial Assets and the Term Structure of Interest Rates." *Review of Economic Studies* 37: 321–51.

Turnovsky, S. J. 1974. "Technological and Price Uncertainty in a Ricardian Model of International Trade." *Review of Economic Studies* 41: 201–17.

———. 1976. "The Distribution of Welfare Gains from Price Stabilization: The Case of Multiplicative Disturbances." *International Economic Review* 17 (1): 133–48.

Waugh, F. V. 1944. "Does the Consumer Benefit from Price Instability?" *Quarterly Journal of Economics* 58 (4): 602–14.

———. 1966. "Consumer Aspects of Price Instability." *Econometrica* 34 (2): 504–08.

Comment

WILFRED ETHIER

Recent years have witnessed the appearance of many studies of international trade and uncertainty, and so the area has been badly in need of a survey. John Pomery has given us a masterly paper that is at once a comprehensive and insightful survey and also a significant contribution itself.

The typical line of attack in this area has been the designation of one or more ingredients of standard models as random, followed by straightforward manipulation. The uncertainty introduces a motive for diversification that cancels against the standard trade theory's message of specialization; complicated analysis and ambiguous conclusions thus naturally result.

Pomery's contribution is to point out that these problems should be examined in the context of markets for risk sharing. Consider, for example, the stock market analyzed by Diamond. Pomery has classified the papers he surveys according to the source of uncertainty; also instructive is an alternative organization according to the implicit role of stock markets. These are of three classes. (1) Those papers allowing free international trade in both stocks and goods (Helpman and Razin and Pomery's own work). (2) Those in which neither domestic nor international stock markets exist (Batra, Lapan, Mayer). (3) Those in which a domestic stock market implicitly exists, but in which stocks cannot be traded internationally (most of the rest of the literature).

This classification brings out the point that the subject is concerned in an essential way with the degree of substitutability between trade in goods and trade in securities. Looked at in this way, there is a clear analogy with much of the deterministic theory of international trade.

Pomery emphasizes (and properly so) the recent work of Helpman and Razin which, alone of all the contributions surveyed, shares Pomery's concern with trade in randomness. Also they show, again uniquely, that the basic trade theorems are preserved. Pomery identifies the reason for this as their assumption "that randomness is identically distributed across countries for the same industry." It is important to be clear as to just what this means. The assumption is essentially equivalent to requiring internationally identical production functions in all states of the world, i.e., 66.9 inches of rain will in fact fall on wheat planted in India if, and only if, 66.9 inches falls on wheat planted in America. The Heckscher–Ohlin assumption of identical technology is carried to its extreme limit. In such a world there is obviously nothing to be gained by diversifying production across countries, and so the pure theory's message of specialization once again reigns supreme. More generally, if uncertainty is industry-specific and not country-specific, then (regardless of whether technology is in other respects identical) such uncertainty will not tend to vitiate the standard results. Helpman and Razin have provided a valuable and enlightening insight, but it should be kept in mind that they obtain their results by assuming away the problems that other papers in the area have been concerned to grapple with.

Let me now say a few words about the commitment models, which display in sharp relief several difficulties common to the entire literature.

Pomery identifies (appropriately) Ruffin's nonautarky theorem as the basic result in this area. He then criticizes Ruffin's model, and the commitment models generally, on the grounds that a general equilibrium of such countries would necessarily have undesirable properties. Such criticism is natural, and I have the impression that many share it. I do not. As Pomery suggests, one can imagine a collection of Ruffin-type countries making commitments to a central market, which then finds a price at which the commitments in the aggregate balance out, either with each other or with the nonrandom offer curve of a residual country. Examples can be constructed for which no such price exists, so restrictions must be placed on tastes or on output or commitment possibilities. But note that a balancing price exists if all countries choose non-negative export commitments of both goods; hence, the restrictions should not rule out the nonautarky theorem.

Relevant examples do exist (e.g., the export of bananas to be auctioned for what they will fetch in large marketing centers). While I am not tempted to try to force all of world trade into such a mold, the model's relevance does not differ significantly from that of others dealing with uncertainty and trade.

Ruffin has argued that forward markets would not preclude commitments, but simply assuming away forward markets is a valid exercise. After all, every paper dealing with trade and uncertainty is based in an essential way on the arbitrary exclusion of one or more potential markets.

Individual countries would form subjective probability distributions for the ultimate price. These would reflect neither illusion nor artificial randomness, but simply the lack of complete information (the ultimate source, I suppose, of all randomness). The price system should convey information; if individual commitments must precede price formation, all relevant economic information is not conveyed. The randomness reflects this. Such a framework is not only acceptable but also relates the uncertainty to economic fundamentals.

One can imagine the Ruffin-style equilibrium as one stage in a dynamic process where the realized price in one period is used in forming subjective probability distributions for the next. Long-run equilibrium would feature all countries trading desired amounts at nonrandom prices. Alternatively, the model can be interpreted as representative of a continuously changing world where full information is never obtained.

While I am not uncomfortable with the relation of commitment models to general equilibrium, I am bothered by another characteristic: their sensitivity to the specification of allowable commitments. Pomery's survey brings out this sensitivity quite well. The algebraic treatment might give the impression that Ruffin's model is a limiting case or "logical conclusion." This is not so. Geometrically, countries trade by specifying a "commitment curve" of possible trades, one of which will be randomly chosen. The models differ in the prior constraints placed on these curves. In the limiting case of no constraints, each country would specify its offer curve and thus end up trading exactly what it would have chosen had it known the price. Thus the constraint on acceptable commitment curves is what actually gives significance to imperfect information. Ruffin's model is just one arbitrary specification. The results generated by these models, including the nonautarky theorem, are crucially dependent on the commitment allowed.

One might be tempted to class the arbitrariness with the universal arbitrary exclusion of markets and let it go at that. But I think rather that work on the commitment models cannot be interesting unless it pursues at least one of three possibilities. (i) It could aim to model some real-life situation that would dictate the commitments allowed. Pomery points out that some of the earlier work was in this spirit, but that more recent papers are decidedly not. (ii) It could systematically relate constraints on the commitment curve to the nonexistence of specific markets. (iii) It could develop an endogenous theory of such constraints. To my knowledge, no paper has pursued either of the latter two alternatives.

CHAPTER FIVE

Macroeconomic Interdependence and the Exchange Rate Regime

MICHAEL MUSSA

I. INTRODUCTION

The purpose of this chapter is to review the theory of the transmission of macroeconomic disturbances under fixed and flexible exchange rates. Attention is focused on the transmission of disturbances that affect levels of employment and output as well as prices. Included within the class of such disturbances are the policy actions of national governments taken in pursuit of the objectives of internal and external balance. Indeed, an issue of central importance in this essay is the extent to which monetary and fiscal policies adopted by one government generate disturbances in the rest of the world. Another focus of concern is the extent to which a flexible exchange rate insulates an economy from disturbances in the rest of the world.

The procedure adopted in this chapter is to organize the discussion of major developments in the theory of the international transmission of disturbances by using a single, integrated analytical framework. This is possible because there is widespread agreement concerning the analytical framework that it is appropriate to use in dealing with issues in open-economy macroeconomics. This area of agreement is embodied in what might be termed "the standard two-country macroeconomic model." The basic structure of this model is summarized in Section II.

In Section III, this model is used to analyze the transmission of disturbances when there are no private flows of capital between countries. This analysis yields the strong conclusion that a flexible exchange rate insulates an economy from disturbances in the rest of the world, including the policy actions of the foreign government. This conclusion is illustrated by considering two disturbances originating in the foreign country, disturbances that could either be the result of decisions by the private sector or of policy actions by the government: a reduction in desired expenditure by foreign residents (contractionary fiscal policy) and a reduction in the foreign money supply or an increase in foreign money demand (contractionary monetary policy). Under a fixed exchange rate, these disturbances are transmitted through the trade balance and affect output in the home country. Under a flexible exchange rate, the trade-balance linkage is cut off, and home country output is completely insulated from these disturbances. This result of complete insulation, however, is shown to be sensitive to the precise specification of the model. In particular, some transmission of these disturbances to the home country can be shown to occur if desired expenditure in the home country is affected by the terms of trade, or if import prices affect the demand for money, or if import prices directly affect the cost of domestic output.

Section IV reviews the results concerning the implications of capital mobility for the transmission of disturbances and the conduct of policy. It is shown that a flexible exchange rate affects the way in which foreign disturbances are transmitted to the home economy, but does not insulate the home country from such disturbances. Further, the extent of insulation provided by a flexible exchange rate is shown to depend critically on the nature of the disturbance. An expenditure disturbance in the foreign country (perhaps resulting from a fiscal policy action of the foreign government) is likely to be transmitted with greater force to the home economy under a flexible exchange rate than under a fixed exchange rate. In contrast, a monetary disturbance in the foreign country (perhaps resulting from a monetary policy action of the foreign government) will have opposite effects on foreign and home output under a flexible exchange rate and will move both outputs in the same direction under a fixed rate. Moreover, international mobility of capital has important implications for the appropriate conduct of economic policy

Section V considers the implications of three recent developments in macroeconomics and in balance-of-payments and exchange rate theory. First, the monetary approach to the balance of payments focuses attention on the consequences of changes in asset stocks that result from balance-of-payments deficits and surpluses, particularly with respect to the longer-run consequences of policy actions and other disturbances. Second, recent experience with inflation and developments in the theory of inflation suggest serious reservations concerning conclusions that are based on the assumption that the position of the aggregate supply curve remains fixed for long periods. Third, the asset market view of the exchange rate introduces changes in the expected future exchange rate as a potentially important source of disturbance to the world economy and as a potentially important channel for the transmission of disturbances between national economies.

Finally, Section VI considers three key issues that seem likely to play important roles in the development of open-economy macroeconomics during the next decade. First, there is the "mobility and substitutability issue," which concerns the ease with which goods and assets in one country move to other countries and the extent to which goods and assets of one country are substitutable with those of another. Second, there is the "speeds of adjustment issue," which concerns the relative speeds with which prices and quantities in different markets adapt to changing economic circumstances and the implications of significantly different speeds of adjustment in different markets. Third, there is the "information issue," which concerns the way in which economic agents receive and process new information and the manner in which new information impinges on the behavior of the economic system.

II. A TWO-COUNTRY MACROECONOMIC MODEL

In order to analyze the transmission of disturbances between national economies, it is useful to employ the standard, two-country macroeconomic model. This model has a long tradition in international economics, dating back to the contributions of Harberger (1950), Laursen and Metzler (1950), Machlup (1955), and Meade (1951). It plays a prominent role in the writings of Fleming (1962), Johnson (1958), Mundell (1968), Pearce (1961), and Tsiang (1961). More recently, its influence is apparent in the work of Brunner and Meltzer (1975), Cooper (1969), Floyd (1969), McKinnon and Oates (1966), and Swoboda and Dornbusch (1973), to name but a few.

The world consists of two countries:[1] the home country, H, and the foreign country, F. Variables referring to H appear without an asterisk (*) and the corresponding variables referring to F appear with an asterisk (*). In each country there are four fundamental functional relationships among the critical macroeconomic variables: the aggregate supply function, the asset market equilibrium condition, the desired expenditure function, and the import demand function. For simplicity, these relationships will be described only for the home country, with the understanding that similar relationships apply for the foreign country.

The national output of H is denoted by Q, and is assumed to be physically distinct from the national output of F. The price of a unit of H's output in terms of H's money is denoted by P. The aggregate supply function,

(1) $Q = S(P/W), \partial S/\partial(P/W) > 0,$

[1] Much of the literature on open-economy macroeconomics treats the case of a small country that faces given prices for all internationally traded goods. In some models, there is a single traded good that is shared by two countries and, in addition, each country produces and consumes its own nontraded good. For the expository purposes of this chapter, however, the most convenient and useful assumption is that there are two countries, each of which produces its own distinct national output.

specifies how output increases in response to increases in P relative to the parameter W. In the long run, there is a normal value of the ratio P/W, say, $\bar{p}$. Corresponding to $P/W = \bar{p}$, there is a long-run normal level of output $\bar{Q} = S(\bar{p})$. One interpretation of the aggregate supply function is that W represents the (temporarily) fixed nominal wage rate (or structure of nominal wage rates) that defines the position of the short-run labor supply function, and $\bar{w} = 1/\bar{p}$ represents the long-run equilibrium value of the real wage.[2] Given W, an increase in P shifts up the labor demand curve, resulting in an increase in output and employment. An alternative interpretation is that W represents the "expected price level," and $\bar{p} = 1$.[3] When P exceeds W, individual producers are fooled into believing that the relative price of their particular output has risen and respond by increasing output above its normal level. For convenience in subsequent discussion, it is useful to invert the aggregate supply function and write it in the form of the price response function,

(2) $\quad P = h(Q; W), \partial h/\partial Q > 0, (W/P)(\partial h/\partial W) = 1.$

Asset market equilibrium requires that people be satisfied with the division of their marketable wealth between money and bonds. Because of the balance-sheet constraint, the asset market equilibrium condition can be expressed in terms of the requirement that the demand for money must equal the supply available; that is,

(3) $\quad k(i, a) \cdot (P \cdot Q) - M = 0, \partial k/\partial i < 0, 0 < \partial k/\partial a < 1.$

For simplicity, it is assumed that the demand for money is proportional to the nominal value of domestic output, $P \cdot Q$, with a factor of proportionality, k, which declines with increases in the nominal interest rate, i, and increases with increases in the real marketable wealth of domestic residents, a. Real marketable wealth is the sum of real money balances, M/P, and real bond holdings, b:

(4) $\quad a = (M/P) + b.$

Substitution of (2) and (4) into (3) yields an equation that implicitly determines the nominal interest rate as a function of Q, given M, b, and W, say,

(5) $\quad i = \bar{i}(Q; M, b, W).$

---

[2] This assumption is employed in Harberger (1950) and Meade (1951) and is characteristic of many "Keynesian" models. An alternative and somewhat simpler assumption is that the price of each country's output is fixed in terms of its own money. This assumption yields essentially the same implications as the assumption that the wage rate is fixed.

[3] This version of the aggregate supply function was developed by Lucas and Rapping (1969). A more refined basis for this specification has been provided by Lucas (1972). See also Raasche (1973) and Friedman (1976).

Desired expenditure of domestic residents, measured in units of national output, E, depends on real national income, Y, the real interest rate, r, the real marketable wealth of domestic residents, a, and a shift parameter, g, which represents both exogeneous changes in desired expenditure by the private sector and changes in fiscal policy:

(6) $E = E(Y, r, a; g), 0 < \partial E/\partial Y < 1, \partial E/\partial r < 0$

$$\partial E/\partial a > 0, \partial E/\partial g = 1.$$

Real national income is equal to domestic output plus real interest earnings on the excess of domestic holdings of bonds, b, over the domestic issue of bonds, $\bar{b}$; that is,

(7) $Y = Q + r \cdot (b - \bar{b}).$

The real interest rate is equal to the nominal interest rate, i, less the expected rate of inflation, π:

(8) $r = i - \pi.$

Substituting (7) and (8) into (6) and making use of (5), we obtain the reduced form desired expenditure function,

$$\tilde{E}(Q; g, M, b, \bar{b}, W, \pi)$$

(9)

$$= E[(Q + (i - \pi)(b - \bar{b})), i - \pi, ((M/h(Q; W)) + b); g].$$

The amount that domestic residents will spend on imports, I, measured in units of domestic output, is assumed to depend on total desired expenditure, E, and on the relative price of foreign output in terms of domestic output, t:[4]

(10) $I = I(E, t), \partial I/\partial E > 0, \partial I/\partial t < 0.$

The relative price of foreign output in terms of domestic output is determined by the prices of the two outputs in terms of their respective national monies and by the exchange rate, e, defined as the price of a unit of F's money in terms of H's money:

(11) $t = e \cdot P^*/P = e \cdot h^*(Q^*; W^*)/h(Q; W)$

$$\equiv \tilde{t}(e, Q, Q^*; W, W^*).$$

Substituting (9) and (11) into (10), we obtain the reduced form import expenditure function,

(12) $\tilde{I}(Q; e, g, M, b, \bar{b}, W, \pi) = I(\tilde{E}, \tilde{t}).$

---

[4] This is a very strong assumption. It implies that the price elasticity of import demand is greater than unity in absolute value. This is more than sufficient to insure that an increase in the relative price of foreign goods will improve the home country's trade balance (the Marshall–Lerner condition).

The excess of F's desired purchases of H's output over H's desired expenditure on F's output is the (desired) trade balance of H, measured in units of H's output:

(13) $\quad T = t \cdot I^* - I.$

Making use of the reduced form import expenditure functions for H and F and of (11), we obtain the reduced form trade balance function,

(14) $\quad \tilde{T} = \tilde{t} \cdot \tilde{I}^* - \tilde{I}.$

For an economy to be in equilibrium, the demand for its output must equal the available supply. The demand for H's output, D, is the sum of what home residents wish to spend on their own output plus the import demands of foreigners:

(15) $\quad D = E + T.$

Similarly, the demand for F's output can be expressed as

(16) $\quad D^* = E^* - (1/t) \cdot T.$

Using the reduced form relationships $\tilde{E}$, $\tilde{E}^*$, and $\tilde{T}$ to substitute for E, E^*, and T, we obtain the reduced form demand functions

(17) $\quad \tilde{D} = \tilde{E} + \tilde{T};$

(18) $\quad \tilde{D}^* = \tilde{E}^* - (h(Q; W)/e \cdot h^*(Q^*; W^*)) \cdot \tilde{T}.$

The variables and parameters affecting both $\tilde{D}$ and $\tilde{D}^*$ are Q, Q^*, e, g, g^*, M, M^*, b, b^*, $\bar{b}$, $\bar{b}^*$, W, W^*, π, and π^*. To reduce complexity in subsequent discussion, only those variables and parameters that are of immediate interest will be included in the expression of the reduced form relationships derived in this section. Further, in order to produce concrete results in a number of circumstances in which results would otherwise be ambiguous, it will be assumed that residents of each country have a marginal preference for their own goods. This means that when desired expenditure in a country declines, this has a stronger effect on the demand for domestic goods than on the demand for foreign goods.[5]

III. THE MEADE PARADIGM

At least up until the early 1960s economists' thinking concerning the transmission of disturbances between national economies was dominated by the type of analysis that reached its most refined form in the outstanding contribution of James Meade (1951). In this line of analysis, it is assumed that for the span of time that is relevant for the formulation and conduct of macroeconomic policy, wage rates at home and abroad may be treated

[5] This assumption is related to the "transfer problem criterion," which has extensive application to many questions in international economics; see Johnson (1958).

as fixed (W and W^* are fixed), and fluctuations in demand influence output and employment as well as prices. No inflation is anticipated (π and π^* are both zero). Interest-bearing assets are not mobile internationally (b and b^* are both fixed and equal, respectively, to $\bar{b}$ and $\bar{b}^*$). When exchange rates are fixed, official settlements surpluses and deficits are assumed to have no effect on national money stocks (M and M^* are treated as policy parameters under both fixed and flexible exchange rates).[6]

A. Macroeconomic independence under flexible rates

To understand the implications of the Meade Paradigm for the transmission of disturbances between national economies, it is convenient to start with the case of flexible exchange rates and then consider the case of fixed exchange rates. Under flexible exchange rates, there are no official reserve flows to balance trade surpluses or deficits. Since domestic residents do not hold foreign money, and vice versa, and since interest-bearing assets are not mobile internationally, the trade balance must always be zero:

$$(19) \quad T = \tilde{T}(Q, Q^*; e) = 0.$$

Since the trade balance is zero, the equilibrium requirement that each country's output equal the demand for that output implies the conditions:

$$(20) \quad \tilde{E}(Q; g, M) = Q$$

$$(21) \quad \tilde{E}^*(Q^*; g^*, M^*) = Q^*.$$

It is noteworthy that the equilibrium level of Q determined by (20) depends only on the values of parameters referring to the home country and is independent of Q^* and of all of the parameters referring to the foreign country. Indeed, the equilibrium level of Q is precisely the same as the equilibrium level of output that would prevail if the home country were a completely closed economy; and a similar statement applies to the equilibrium level of Q^*. This implies that the level of output and all other variables in the home country (except t and e) are unaffected by any type of disturbance taking place in the foreign country, and vice versa. Given a disturbance in F, the exchange rate adjusts so that (19) remains satisfied at the values of Q and Q^* determined independently by (20) and (21). Thus, under flexible exchange rates, there is complete macroeconomic independence between H and F.

This phenomenon of macroeconomic independence may be illustrated by considering the consequences of two disturbances originating in the

---

[6] The implicit assumption is that the monetary authorities are sterilizing foreign exchange inflows and outflows. In some models, this policy of sterilization is dictated by the assumption that governments pursue a monetary policy that insures "internal balance." For discussion of this point, see Corden (1960) and Tsiang (1961).

foreign economy. First, consider a reduction in desired expenditure in F (a reduction in g^*). This disturbance reduces foreign demand for both goods. The reduction in foreign demand for H's goods produces an incipient trade-balance surplus for the foreign country and an incipient trade-balance deficit for the home country. Under flexible exchange rates, without capital mobility, however, trade imbalances are not possible. Instead, the incipient trade-balance deficit of H causes the value of its money to depreciate relative to foreign money (that is, e rises). This causes the price of F's goods to rise relative to the price of H's goods and shifts demand in both countries away from F's goods and toward H's goods. Ultimately, when equilibrium is established, the incipient trade imbalance will be eliminated. This means that e will rise by enough so that the implied increase in t restores the demand for H's goods to the level that prevailed before the disturbance. H's output, therefore, is completely insulated from the reduction in desired expenditure in F, and the full effect of this disturbance falls on F's output.

Second, consider a reduction in the money supply in F. At given output and prices, this disturbance requires an increase in the foreign interest rate in order to restore equilibrium between money demand and money supply in F. This increase in i^* reduces desired expenditure in F. From here on, the analysis is the same as for the reduction in g^*. The reduction in desired expenditure in F induces an incipient trade-balance surplus for F and trade-balance deficit for H. This incipient trade imbalance is prevented from becoming an actual trade imbalance by the adjustment of the exchange rate. The increase in e increases the relative price of F's goods and shifts demand away from these goods and toward H's goods. In the new equilibrium, the trade balance is zero, the demand for H's goods is restored to its previous level, and the full effect of the disturbance falls on F's output.

In both cases, the domestic economy is insulated from the disturbance occurring in F, because equilibrium requires that the trade balance always be zero. With a zero trade balance, equilibrium in H requires that desired expenditure in H equal output in H. Since there is no direct effect of either of the disturbances in F on the level of desired expenditure in H, output is unaffected by these disturbances. The two disturbances have the same effect on foreign output (they reduce it) and the same effect on the exchange rate (they increase e) and on the relative price of F's goods in terms of H's goods (they increase t). The disturbances differ only in their effect on the foreign interest rate. In terms of the standard *IS–LM* model, the reduction in g^* results in an inward shift of the *IS* curve in F and hence in a decline in i^*. In contrast, the reduction in M^* results in an inward shift of the *LM* curve in F and hence in an increase in i^*. This difference between the two disturbances in their effect on i^* has no further consequences, because capital is not free to flow in response to interest rate differentials between

H and *F*. As shall become apparent, however, this difference is of substantial importance under conditions of international capital mobility.

The strong conclusion of complete macroeconomic independence under flexible rates is, of course, sensitive to the assumptions that are embodied in the model set forth in Section II. Five assumptions are of special interest. First, it has been assumed that changes in the terms of trade, *t*, have no direct effect on desired expenditure. The contrary assumption leads to types of conclusions derived by Laursen and Metzler (1950). In particular, suppose that a deterioration of a country's terms of trade (an increase in *t* for *H* and a reduction in *t* for *F*) increases desired expenditure, measured in terms of domestic output. Under this assumption, disturbances in *F* will be transmitted to *H*. A reduction in either *g** or *M** reduces *t* and hence increases *E*, thus increasing the equilibrium level of *Q*. Second, it has been assumed that the demand for money depends only on the price of domestic goods. An alternative assumption is that the demand for money depends on a price index that includes the price of imports as well as domestic goods. Under this alternative assumption, we would get exactly the reverse of the results just described for the case where desired expenditure responds positively to a deterioration of the terms of trade. Third, it has been assumed that import prices have no direct effect on the aggregate supply function. It could be assumed, however, that increases in import prices increase the price of domestic output at a given level of that output. This would be likely if wages responded rapidly to increases in the price of imported consumption goods, or if producers passed through increases in the prices of imported intermediate goods. Under the assumption that increases in import prices increase the price of domestic goods, a reduction in either *g** or *M** would induce an upward shift of *H*'s price-response function and, hence, result in a reduction in the equilibrium level of *Q*. Fourth, it has been assumed that each country produces its own distinct national output. An alternative assumption is that both countries produce the same two traded goods.[7] Under this assumption, disturbances may be transmitted through their effects on relative commodity prices. Fifth, it has been implicitly assumed that factors of production are not internationally mobile. An alternative assumption is that labor moves between countries in response to variations in employment opportunities, perhaps due to explicit government policies directed at employment of foreign workers. Such movements affect both aggregate demand and aggregate supply in both countries and thereby provide an important channel for the international transmission of disturbances.

---

[7] An alternative assumption is that both countries produce the same traded good and, in addition, each country produces its own nontraded good; see, for instance, Dornbusch (1973*a*, 1973*b*), Komiya (1967), Salter (1959), and Swan (1960). In this type of model, changes in the exchange rate obviously cannot affect the terms of trade. Nevertheless, a flexible exchange rate does insulate an economy from foreign disturbances.

B. Macroeconomic interdependence under fixed rates

Under fixed exchange rates, when interest-bearing assets are not internationally mobile, trade-balance surpluses and deficits are financed by flows of official foreign exchange reserves. Since the trade balance need not be zero, the equilibrium conditions for the case of flexible exchange rates, (19), (20), and (21), no longer apply. Instead, the equilibrium conditions that jointly determine the equilibrium levels of Q and Q^* are

$$(22) \quad \tilde{D}(Q, Q^*; e) \equiv \tilde{E}(Q) + \tilde{T}(Q, Q^*; e) = Q;$$

$$(23) \quad \tilde{D}^*(Q^*, Q; e) \equiv \tilde{E}^*(Q^*) - (h/e \cdot h^*) \cdot \tilde{T}(Q, Q^*; e) = Q^*.$$

In these equations, e is a parameter that is determined by the fixed value of the exchange rate and maintained by the willingness of central banks to convert domestic money into foreign money at the officially fixed price.

The relationship between the equilibrium conditions (22) and (23) and the equilibrium conditions (20) and (21) may be illustrated with the aid of Figure 1.[8] Under flexible exchange rates, the equilibrium value of Q is determined by the equilibrium condition (20), $\tilde{E}(Q) = Q$. Since the value

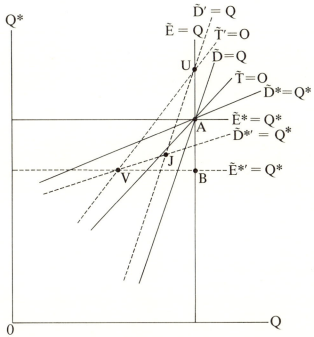

Fig. 1.   The Effects of a Reduction in g* or M* with capital immobility.

[8] This diagram is borrowed from Swoboda and Dornbusch (1973), who credit its initial development to Robinson (1952).

of Q that satisfies this condition does not depend on Q^*, the combinations of Q and Q^* that are consistent with this condition are shown by the vertical line labeled $\tilde{E} = Q$. Similarly, the combinations of Q and Q^* that are consistent with the equilibrium condition (21) are shown by the horizontal line labeled $\tilde{E}^* = Q^*$. Under fixed exchange rates, the equilibrium value of Q is determined by the condition (22), $\tilde{D}(Q, Q^*; e) = Q$. Since increases in Q^* increase D through their effect on F's demand for H's output, the combinations of Q and Q^* that are consistent with this equilibrium condition are shown as the solid, positively sloped line labeled $\tilde{D} = Q$. Similarly, the combinations of Q and Q^* that are consistent with the equilibrium condition (23) are shown by the solid, positively sloped line labeled $\tilde{D}^* = Q^*$.[9]

The intersection of the $\tilde{E} = Q$ line and the $\tilde{E}^* = Q^*$ line determines the equilibrium values of Q and Q^* under flexible exchange rates. The intersection of the $\tilde{D} = Q$ line and the $\tilde{D}^* = Q^*$ line determines the equilibrium values of Q and Q^* under fixed exchange rates. For simplicity, these initial intersection points are assumed to be the same point A. Under flexible exchange rates, the value of e that prevails at A must be such that the trade balance is zero. Under fixed exchange rates, the trade balance need not be zero in equilibrium. But, for convenience, it is assumed that the value of the exchange rate that is fixed by the monetary authorities is the rate that is consistent with trade-balance equilibrium. This assumption is signified by the fact that the line labeled $\tilde{T} = 0$, which shows the combinations of Q and Q^* that are consistent with the condition $\tilde{T}(Q, Q^*; e) = 0$, for the fixed value of e, passes through A. The $\tilde{T} = 0$ line is positively sloped because an increase in Q^* tends to improve H's trade balance by increasing F's demand for H's output, while an increase in Q tends to worsen it by increasing H's demand for F's output. Above and to the left of the $\tilde{T} = 0$ line, the home country has a trade surplus; below and to the right of the $\tilde{T} = 0$ line, the home country has a trade deficit.

Figure 1 may also be used to illustrate the transmission of disturbances under flexible and under fixed exchange rates. Specifically, consider a reduction in desired expenditure in F (a reduction in g^*). Under flexible exchange rates, this disturbance is reflected in a downward shift of the $\tilde{E}^* = Q^*$ line to the dashed line labeled $\tilde{E}^{*\prime} = Q^*$. The new equilibrium occurs at the point B, where the new $\tilde{E}^{*\prime} = Q^*$ line intersects the original $\tilde{E} = Q$ line. As previously described, H's output is unaffected by the disturbance, and the full effect of the disturbance is absorbed by a reduction in F's output. This result is achieved because the exchange rate rises in order to maintain trade-balance equilibrium. This increase in e rotates the $\tilde{T} = 0$

---

[9] The slope of the $D = Q$ line, with respect to the Q-axis, is given by $(1 - (\partial E/\partial Q) + (\partial I/\partial Q))/t \cdot (\partial I^*/\partial Q^*)$. The slope of the $D^* = Q^*$ line, with respect to the Q^*-axis, is given by $(1 - (\partial E^*/\partial Q^*) + (\partial I^*/\partial Q^*)) \cdot t/(\partial I/\partial Q)$. Since $1 - (\partial E/\partial Q)$ is positive and $1 - (\partial E^*/\partial Q^*)$ is positive, it follows that the $D = Q$ line is steeper than the $D^* = Q^*$ line.

line in a clockwise direction until it passes through the point B. This clockwise rotation occurs because at given values of Q and Q^*, an increase in e decreases H's demand for F's goods and increases F's demand for H's goods. To maintain trade-balance equilibrium, therefore, either Q must rise (increasing H's demand for F's goods) or Q^* must fall (decreasing F's demand for H's goods).

Under fixed exchange rates, the reduction in g^* is not permitted to increase e. The $\tilde{T} = 0$ line does not rotate in a clockwise direction, but rather in a counterclockwise direction to the dashed line labeled $T' = 0$. This is because, at a given value of e, a reduction in g^* reduces F's demand for H's output and induces a trade-balance deficit for H. To restore trade-balance equilibrium, at a fixed e, either Q must fall or Q^* must rise. Because H's trade balance is in deficit at the point A after the reduction in g^*, this point no longer satisfies the equilibrium conditions $\tilde{D} = Q$ and $\tilde{D}^* = Q^*$. The reduction in g^* shifts the $\tilde{D} = Q$ line upward and to the left, to the dashed line labeled $\tilde{D}' = Q$.[10] This shift occurs because the deterioration in H's trade balance at the point A must be corrected either by a reduction in Q or by an increase in Q^* in order to restore equilibrium between the level of H's output and the demand for that output. The reduction in g^* shifts the $\tilde{D}^* = Q^*$ line downward and to the right, to the dashed line labeled $\tilde{D}^{*\prime} = \tilde{Q}^*$.[11] This shift occurs because the reduction in g^* directly reduces F's demand for its own output, requiring either a reduction in Q^* or an increase in Q to restore equilibrium between the level of F's output and the demand for it.

The new equilibrium following the reduction in g^*, under fixed exchange rates, is at the intersection J of the $\tilde{D}' = Q$ line and the $\tilde{D}^{*\prime} = Q^*$ line. At J, both Q and Q^* are lower than they were at A. Q^*, however, is higher than it would be under flexible exchange rates. Thus, under fixed exchange rates, the effect of a reduction in desired expenditure in F is not restricted to a reduction in F's output: part of the effect of this disturbance is transmitted to H's output and the effect on F's output is thereby moderated. The channel of transmission of the disturbance from F to H is through the trade balance. At the initial equilibrium point, A, there is an incipient trade-balance deficit for H and a trade-balance surplus for F. This incipient trade imbalance is not eliminated through adjustment of the exchange rate. Indeed, at the new equilibrium point J, the home country still has a trade-balance deficit and the foreign country still has a trade-balance

---

[10] The $\tilde{D}' = Q$ line must always pass through the point U at which the new $\tilde{T} = 0$ line intersects the vertical line $\tilde{E} = Q$. This is so because when $\tilde{T} = 0$, the equilibrium level of Q is determined by the condition $\tilde{E} = Q$. The reduction in g^* does not affect the position of the $\tilde{E} = Q$ line.

[11] The $\tilde{D}^{*\prime} = Q^*$ line must pass through the point V at which the $\tilde{T}' = 0$ line intersects the relevant $\tilde{E}^* = Q^*$ line. This is so because when $\tilde{T} = 0$, the equilibrium level of Q^* is determined by the condition $\tilde{E}^* = Q^*$.

surplus.[12] Because H has a deficit, the demand for its output is lower than it would be under flexible exchange rates and, hence, its output is lower. Because F has a trade surplus, the demand for its output is higher than it would be under flexible exchange rates and, hence, its output is higher than under flexible exchange rates.

A reduction in M^* has the same effects on Q and Q^* as a reduction in g^*. This is so because the direct effect of a reduction in M^* is to increase the foreign interest rate and thereby reduce the amount that foreigners wish to spend at any given level of Q^*. The magnitude of the reduction in M^* can be specified so that this direct effect on desired expenditure in F is exactly the same as the direct effect of the reduction in g^*. It then follows that the effects of these two disturbances on Q, Q^*, T and t will be the same. Their effects on the interest rate in H, i, will also be the same; i falls because the reduction in Q reduces the demand for money in H. The two disturbances differ only in their effects on the foreign interest rate, i^*. The reduction in g^* reduces i^* and probably to a greater extent than it reduces i, since Q^* falls relatively more than Q. The reduction in M^* increases i^*, because an increase in i^* is required to restore equilibrium between money demand and money supply in F.

As a further example of the use of the Meade model, it is instructive to consider the effects of an increase in e, that is, a devaluation by the home country (or a revaluation by the foreign country). As illustrated in Figure 2, the effect of an increase in e is to rotate the $\tilde{T} = 0$ line in a clockwise direction from its initial position passing through the point A to the dashed line passing through the points U and V. This rotation occurs because at the initial equilibrium point A, an increase in e means an increase in the relative price of F's output in terms of H's output. This relative price change discourages imports by H (but increases the cost of imports) and encourages imports by F. To correct this trade imbalance, either Q must rise (encouraging imports by H) or Q^* must fall (discouraging imports by F). Therefore, the new $\tilde{T} = 0$ line must lie below and to the right of the point A. Further, since the increase in e affects the trade balance, it also affects the demands for both domestic and foreign output. Specifically, at the point A, $\tilde{D}$ now exceeds Q because H has a trade-balance surplus, and $\tilde{D}^*$ is now less than Q^* because F has a trade-balance deficit. To restore equilibrium between $\tilde{D}$ and Q, either Q must rise or Q^* must fall, indicating that the $\tilde{D} = Q$ line shifts down and to the right, to the dashed line passing through the point U. To restore equilibrium between $\tilde{D}^*$ and Q^*, either Q^* must fall or Q must rise, indicating that the $\tilde{D}^* = Q^*$ line shifts down and to the right, to the dashed line passing through the point V. The new equilibrium after the increase in e is at the point J in Figure 2, where the

---

[12] The point J necessarily lies to the right of the $\tilde{T}' = 0$ line, and points to the right of this line are points at which the home country has a trade deficit and the foreign country has a trade surplus.

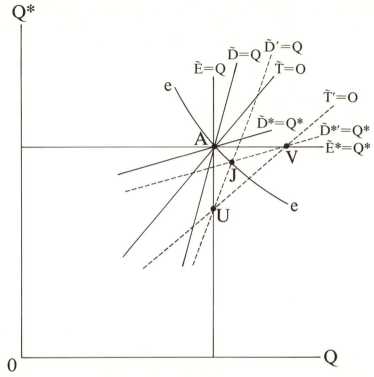

Fig. 2.   The Effects of an Increase in e.

new $\tilde{D} = Q$ line intersects the new $\tilde{D}^* = Q^*$ line. At J, Q is higher than it was at A, Q^* is lower than it was at A, and the home country's trade balance, T, is in surplus.[13] Because the increase in Q increases the demand for money in H, i must be higher at J than it was at A. Similarly, because the reduction in Q^* reduces the demand for money in F, i^* is lower than it was at A.

Finally, it is worthwhile noting that this analysis carries over in a natural way to the "full-employment" version of the model of Section II. In this

[13] Viewed from the perspective of the "elasticities approach," the trade balance improves because the import demands are sufficiently price elastic and the relative price of the home country's import increases as a result of devaluation; see, for instance, Jones (1961). Viewed from the perspective of the "absorption approach," the trade balance improves because expenditure in the home country rises by less than income, while income in the foreign country falls by more than expenditure; see, for instance, Alexander (1959). Viewed from the perspective of the "monetary approach," the balance of payments of the home country goes into surplus because the increase in Q increases money demand in H, which increases interest rates and depresses expenditure relative to income, while the decrease in Q^* reduces money demand in F, which reduces interest rates and stimulates expenditure relative to income; see, for instance, Dornbusch (1973b) and Mussa (1973).

version of the model, wages are assumed to be flexible, and the level of output in each country is always the full-employment level of output. Fluctuations in aggregate demand are absorbed completely by changes in prices. To deal with the full-employment case, all that is necessary is to replace Q with P and Q^* with P^*, both in the equations that define the conditions of equilibrium and along the axes of Figures 1 and 2. The various lines and curves in these diagrams retain the shapes that they have in the case where output is adjustable. They shift in the same manner under the impact of reductions in g^* or M^* or increases in e. The only significant difference is that the effect of these disturbances is on the prices of national outputs rather than on both the prices and levels of national outputs.

IV. CAPITAL MOBILITY AND THE TRANSMISSION OF DISTURBANCES

The importance of capital mobility for the appropriate conduct of monetary and fiscal policy in open economies and, by implication, for the international transmission of macroeconomic disturbances is a dominant theme in the work of Robert Mundell (1968). This section summarizes the principal implications of international capital mobility, utilizing the Mundellian assumption of perfect capital mobility, namely, that interest rates on bonds must be the same at home and abroad.[14] The analysis proceeds under the other simplifying assumptions adopted in Section III: wages are assumed fixed, and no inflation is anticipated.

A. Flexible exchange rates

Under flexible exchange rates, with capital internationally mobile, the equilibrium levels of Q and Q^* must jointly satisfy the conditions:

(24) $\tilde{D}(Q, Q^*, e) = Q:$

(25) $\tilde{D}^*(Q^*, Q, e) = Q^*.$

These conditions are the same as the equilibrium conditions (22) and (23), which determine equilibrium values of Q and Q^* under fixed rates, without capital mobility. The only difference is that now the exchange rate, e, is not fixed by central banks, but is free to be determined by market forces. For each value of e, the conditions (24) and (25) jointly determine a unique combination of Q and Q^* in precisely the manner indicated by the determination of point J in Figure 2. The locus of all such points, determined by considering all possible values of e, is the solid ee curve in Figures 2 and 3.

[14] An older approach is to assume that capital flows in response to the differential between home and foreign interest rates. For an exposition of this approach, see Metzler (1968), Swoboda and Dornbusch (1973), and Allen and Kenen (1976). A more sophisticated approach is the portfolio-balance approach exposited by McKinnon (1969), Branson (1972, 1976), and Frenkel and Rodriguez (1975).

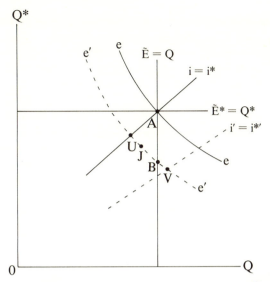

Fig. 3. *The Effects of a Reduction in g* and an Increase in* M* *with International Capital Mobility.*

To determine the equilibrium point for the world economy along the *ee* curve, it is essential to specify an additional equilibrium condition. This condition is given by the requirement that under conditions of perfect capital mobility, the interest rate in *H* must equal the interest rate in *F*:

(26) $\tilde{\imath}(Q) = \tilde{\imath}^*(Q^*)$.

The combinations of Q and Q^* that are consistent with this equilibrium condition are shown in the solid $i = i^*$ line in Figure 3. This line is positively sloped because an increase in Q increases the demand for money in *H*, requiring an increase in i. To maintain equality between i and i^*, there must be an increase in Q^* to increase money demand in *F* and stimulate a higher interest rate in that country.

Equilibrium occurs at the intersection of the *ee* curve and the $i = i^*$ line. At this point, the values of Q, Q^* and e are jointly consistent with the three equilibrium conditions (24), (25), and (26). The value of e is not shown explicitly in the diagram, but is determined implicitly by the value of e that is consistent with the position of the equilibrium point along the *ee* curve. For convenience, this equilibrium point is assumed to be the same point A that was the initial equilibrium point of the economy in the preceding section. At A, the trade balance is assumed to be zero, though, in general, trade imbalances are possible, since they can be financed by flows of internationally mobile capital. For simplicity, it is also assumed that at this initial equilibrium each country holds the stock of bonds that it has issued and, hence, that national income is equal to national output.

To understand the importance of capital mobility for the international transmission of disturbances under flexible exchange rates, it is useful to consider the same disturbances that were analyzed in the preceding section. A reduction in g^* does not affect the position of the $i = i^*$ line in Figure 3, because it does not directly affect either the demand for money or the supply of money in either country. A reduction in g^* does, however, shift the *ee* curve toward the origin to the dashed *ee* curve shown in Figure 3. The extent of this shift may be determined by asking what would happen if the exchange rate remained unchanged at the same value as it initially has at *A*. The answer is given by the analysis of Section IIIB: the equilibrium point would shift to the point *J* in Figure 1, which is also the point *J* in Figure 3. Since the equilibrium conditions (24) and (25) that define the *ee* curve are the same as the equilibrium conditions (22) and (23) that underlie the analysis of the shift from *A* to *J* in Figure 1, it follows that the new *ee* curve in Figure 2 must pass through the point *J*. The new equilibrium point in Figure 2, however, is not the point *J*, but rather the point *U* determined by the intersection of the new *ee* curve with the original $i = i^*$ line.

From the geometry of Figure 3, it is apparent that a reduction in g^* leads to a decline in both Q and Q^*. The economic rationale for this result is that the reduction in g^* reduces *F*'s demand both for its own goods and for *H*'s goods. The decline in *F*'s demand for imports implies that at the point *A*, *H* now has a trade-balance deficit. Without capital mobility, the exchange rate would adjust to eliminate this deficit and thereby insulate Q from the effects of the reduction in g^*. However, when capital is internationally mobile, the exchange rate does not have to adjust to achieve trade-balance equilibrium. Trade imbalances can be financed by a flow of securities. This is precisely what is happening at the new equilibrium point *U*. *H* has a trade deficit and *F* has a trade surplus, and there is a corresponding flow of bonds from *H* to *F*. Thus, the effect of the reduction in g^* is transmitted through the trade balance to affect Q, and the effect of the disturbance on Q^* is moderated (relative to the case of capital immobility).

The effects of a reduction in M^* are also shown in Figure 3. Like the reduction in g^*, the reduction in M^* shifts the *ee* curve toward the origin to the dashed *ee* curve passing through the point *J*. This is so because when the exchange rate is fixed, the reduction in M^* has the same effects on Q and Q^* as the reduction in g^*. In contrast to the effect of a reduction in g^*, a reduction in M^* does shift the position of the $i = i^*$ line, rotating it in a clockwise direction past the point *B* of the dashed $i = i^*$ line in Figure 3. This rotation occurs because the reduction in M^* drives up the interest rate in *F*. In particular, at the point *B*, which would be reached under flexible rates without capital mobility, *i* is the same as at the point *A* (since Q is the same), but i^* must be higher than at *A* (since otherwise there would be no reason for Q^* to be lower). It follows that to reach the new $i = i^*$ line from the point B we must increase Q and reduce Q^*. Further, it is noteworthy that the new *ee* curve passes through the point B and that at this point the trade balance is zero. Since the new equilibrium point is determined by the intersection, V, of the new $i = i^*$ line and the new *ee* curve, it is apparent that this point lies below and to the right of B. Thus, the effect of the reduction in M^* is to reduce Q^* by *more* than would occur if F were a closed economy, to *increase* Q, and to induce a trade balance *surplus* for H.[15]

The dramatic difference between the effects of a reduction in g^* and a reduction in M^* is due to the difference between these two distrubances in their incipient effects on interest rates. The reduction in g^* has no direct effect on either i or i^*. As Q and Q^* fall under the impact of declining demand, the demand for money in both countries declines, reducing both i and i^*. Only minor adjustments of the exchange rate are required to insure that Q and Q^* decline in the right relationship to maintain interest rate equality. In contrast, the reduction in M^* has the direct effect of increasing i^* at the initial equilibrium point A, while the value of i at A is unchanged. Under conditions of perfect capital mobility, this interest differential motivates a massive incipient flow of capital from H to F. The effect of this incipient capital flow is to appreciate the value of F's money (increase e). This appreciation stimulates the demand for H's output and reduces the demand for F's output. The result is that Q is forced to rise and Q^* is forced to fall, until the condition of interest rate equality is reestablished. This need to reestablish interest rate equality dominates the direct effect of the reduction in M^* on the trade balance, because under conditions of perfect capital mobility, even tiny divergences from interest rate equality imply massive capital flows.

A comparison of the present results with those obtained for the case of fixed exchange rates without capital mobility yields further insights into the transmission mechanism for macroeconomic disturbances. The effects of the reduction in g^* are similar in both cases. In both cases, the critical fact is that the reduction in g^* generates an incipient trade balance deficit for H at the initial equilibrium point, A. It makes little difference whether this deficit is financed by a flow of official reserves or by a flow of private capital. The effects of the reduction in M^* are markedly different in the two cases. This is because the behavior of interest rates matters when capital is mobile and does not matter when capital is immobile. Under flexible rates with capital mobility, H ends up with a trade-balance surplus as a result of the reduction in M^*, because this is the result that is required by the necessity of equating interest rates at home and abroad.

---

[15] These results were initially derived by Mundell (1964). In fact, the entire analysis of this section draws heavily on this article.

B. Fixed rates

When capital is internationally mobile and exchange rates are fixed, the supplies of individual national monies may not be treated as fixed, even in the short run. This is because private asset holders can always make good on their decisions to hold greater or lesser money balances by selling or buying bonds on the world capital market. The monetary aggregate that is fixed in the short run is the total world supply of money, $\bar{M} = M + e \cdot M^*$; the division of this aggergate between M and M^* is determined by the preferences of private-asset holders.

The effects of any disturbance under fixed rates with capital mobility may be decomposed into two parts: the effect of the disturbance under fixed rates without capital mobility and the effects of the redistribution of money and bonds induced by the disturbance. Since the effects of disturbances under fixed rates without capital mobility were analyzed in Section IIIB, it is convenient to consider simply the modifications of this analysis that are dictated by capital mobility. It has been assumed that at the initial equilibrium point A, interest rates in H and F are equal. If at the equilibrium position after the disturbance, under fixed rates without capital mobility, the interest rate in F is above (below) the interest rate in H, then, when capital is mobile, there will be a redistribution of the world money stock toward (away from) F and away from (toward) H, and a reverse redistribution in the outstanding stock of bonds. As a result of the asset stock redistribution, the interest rate in F will fall (rise) and the interest rate in H will rise (fall), until interest rates are equalized. These changes in interest rates imply that desired expenditure in F will rise (fall), while desired expenditure in H falls (rises). The likely net outcome of these changes in desired expenditure is that the equilibrium level of output in F will rise (fall), while the equilibrium level of output in H falls (rises).

Specifically, consider the effect of a reduction in g^*. As shown in Figure 1, under fixed rates without capital mobility, this disturbance shifts the equilibrium point from A to J. At J, it is probable that i exceeds i^*. This means that in the asset stock redistribution induced by the disturbance, M will rise, while M^* declines. The new equilibrium point, therefore, will lie below and to the right of the point J in Figure 1. Thus, the effect of capital mobility, under fixed exchange rates, is to focus more of the effect of a disturbance to desired expenditure on the country in which that disturbance originates.

Under fixed rates, without capital mobility, a reduction in M^* also shifts the equilibrium point in Figure 1 from A to J. However, for this disturbance, i^* will exceed i at the point J. Hence, in the asset stock redistribution induced by the disturbance, M^* will rise and M will decline, moving the new equilibrium point above and to the left of the point J. Thus, the effect of capital mobility, under fixed rates, is to increase the extent to which a monetary disturbance in one country is transmitted to the rest of the world. Indeed, the effects of a monetary disturbance are essentially independent of the place where the disturbance occurs. A reduction in M has virtually the same effect on Q and Q^* as a reduction in M^*, for what is critical is that there has been a reduction in the world supply of money. Through the mobility of capital, the effects of this reduction in the world money supply are distributed more or less equally around the world.

Finally, consider the implications of capital mobility for the effects of an exchange rate change (under fixed rates). As shown in Figure 2, when capital is immobile, an increase in e moves the equilibrium point downward and to the right along the ee curve, away from the initial equilibrium point, A. This movement is associated with an increase in i and a reduction in i^*. When capital is mobile, therefore, an increase in e induces an increase in M and a reduction in M^*. This money stock redistribution moves the equilibrium point further downward and to the right. Thus, the effect of capital mobility is to amplify the effects that exchange rate changes have under conditions of capital immobility.[16]

It is noteworthy that the effect of capital mobility on the transmission of disturbances under fixed rates is the opposite of what it is under flexible rates. Under fixed rates, capital mobility focuses the effects of disturbances to desired expenditure more directly on the economy in which they originate. In contrast, under flexible rates, capital mobility permits the transmission of expenditure disturbances from one economy to another. Under fixed rates, capital mobility facilitates the spread of a monetary disturbance from one economy to the whole world. Under flexible rates, however, capital mobility magnifies the effect of a monetary disturbance on the economy in which it originates and results in negative transmission to the rest of the world. These results indicate that great care is essential in interpreting the notion that a flexible exchange rate helps to insulate an economy from disturbances originating in the rest of the world. This notion is basically correct when private capital is not free to flow between countries, but is not generally valid when there is perfect mobility of capital.

C. Policy implications

The preceding discussion has been concerned with the effects of "disturbances" to desired expenditure, to national money stocks, and to the exchange rate. It is apparent that the source of these disturbances could be deliberate policy actions of governments. Indeed, a principal motivation for the analysis developed above has been the determination of the consequences of policy actions on internal balance (full employment and price stability) and on external balance (balance of payments or balance of trade equilibrium). Since the literature on this subject has been well surveyed by Whitman (1970), it suffices to summarize its major conclusions.

[16] This result is derived by Mundell (1964) and is emphasized in Frenkel and Rodriguez (1975).

First, the essential conditions for the successful use of macroeconomic policy are satisfied in the analytical framework set forth above. Specifically, monetary policy (changes in M or M^*), fiscal policy (changes in g or g^*), and exchange rate policy (changes in e) do, in general, have determinate and persistent effects on levels of national outputs and on the balance of payments (or the trade balance). This implies that the policy instruments may be used in a consistent and predictable manner to achieve the policy objectives.

Second, in order to simultaneously achieve all of the objectives of policy, it is necessary to have as many independent policy instruments as there are independent policy objectives. In particular, under fixed exchange rates, without capital mobility, monetary and fiscal policy do not suffice to maintain both external and internal balance. This is so because monetary and fiscal policy have precisely the same effects on both output and the balance of payments. Hence, the use of some additional policy instrument, such as the exchange rate, is essential to maintaining both external and internal balance.[17]

Third, the relative usefulness of different policy instruments in achieving external and internal balance depends on the exchange rate regime, on the extent of capital mobility, and on the size of the country. For a small country, under fixed exchange rates, with perfect capital mobility, monetary policy has a powerful effect on the balance of payments, but is impotent with respect to national output.[18] Fiscal policy is an effective tool for attaining internal balance.[19] In contrast, for the same country, under flexible exchange rates, monetary policy is effective for internal balance, but fiscal policy is not. These results suggest that monetary policy should be assigned to the objective of external balance and fiscal policy should be assigned to the objective of internal balance, under a fixed exchange rate, but that the reverse assignment should be made under a flexible exchange rate.[20]

Fourth, when countries are of comparable size, the design of policy must take account of the effects that the policy actions of one government have

[17] The general analysis of targets and instruments is due to Tinbergen (1952). The application of this general analysis to issues in open-economy macroeconomics owes much to the work of Mundell (1968).

[18] Monetary policy may have some power if there are domestic assets that are nontraded or if domestic assets are sufficiently distinct in the portfolio demands of asset holders. For discussion of these issues, see Branson (1976), Dornbusch (1975), and Girton and Henderson (1976).

[19] Fiscal policy will not be effective if it is directed toward goods whose prices are fixed in world markets and are beyond the influence of actions of the domestic government. Conversely, under a flexible exchange rate, fiscal policy may have some power to affect domestic output if it can be directed toward nontradables.

[20] In accord with the principle of effective market classification as developed by Mundell (1968, chap. 11), a policy instrument should be assigned to the policy objective for which it has the greatest relative effectiveness.

on the objectives of the other government. Failure of policy coordination may lead to a situation in which all governments cannot simultaneously achieve their policy objectives or may reduce the speed with which these objectives are attained.[21]

V. FURTHER DEVELOPMENTS

The analysis in preceding sections reflects the state of open-economy macroeconomics in the late 1960s. Since then, attention has focused on three issues, dealing primarily with dynamic considerations that are neglected in the preceding analysis. First, there are the consequences of changes in asset stock that are implied by flows of official reserves and flows of private capital. This is a principal area of concern in the literature on the monetary approach to balance-of-payments analysis.[22] Second, there is the issue of the endogeneity of the aggregate supply function and of the shifts of this function over time. This issue is dealt with in the extensive literature on the Phillips curve.[23] Third, there is the question of what determines expectations of future values of the exchange rate, and what effects such expectations have on the current exchange rate and on other macroeconomic variables. This issue is dealt with in the recent literature on the asset market view of the exchange rate.

A. The adjustment of asset stocks

Under fixed exchange rates, when capital is immobile, trade imbalances are financed by flows of official foreign exchange reserves. Since foreign exchange reserves are not infinite, monetary authorities cannot sterilize indefinitely the effects of foreign exchange flows on the national money stock. Ultimately, they must either allow the exchange rate to adjust to eliminate the trade imbalance or allow the national money stock to absorb the consequences of flows of foreign exchange. In either case, the longer-run consequences of a disturbance that affects the trade balance cannot be those that were described in Section IIIA. In particular, if the monetary authorities are seriously committed to the maintenance of a fixed exchange rate, it becomes relevant to consider what happens as national money stocks respond to flows of foreign exchange reserves.[24]

Specifically, consider the reduction in g^* and the reduction in M^*, each of which shifts the equilibrium point in Figure 1 from the point A to the point J. At J, the home country has a trade-balance deficit and the foreign

[21] See Cooper (1969) and also Roper (1973).

[22] See the papers in Frenkel and Johnson (1976) and the literature cited therein.

[23] This literature is surveyed in Laidler and Parkin (1975).

[24] Concern with the endogenous adjustment of national money stocks dates back to Hume's analysis of the price specie flow mechanism. For a review of the literature on this subject, see Frenkel (1976a).

country has a trade-balance surplus. This implies that official reserves will flow from the home country to the foreign country, increasing M^* and reducing M. As a result of this adjustment in national money stocks, i^* will fall, while i rises, implying that E^* will rise, while E falls. These changes in expenditure imply that output in F will rise, while output in H declines. Thus, the effect of the money stock readjustment induced by the flow of official reserves is to increase the extent to which a disturbance to desired expenditure or to the money supply is transmitted to the rest of the world and, correspondingly, to diminish the effect of such a disturbance on the economy in which it originates.

Under flexible exchange rates, with capital mobility, there are no flows of official reserves that affect national money stocks, but there are flows of privately held bonds that affect national income, desired expenditure, and the demand for money. Specifically, consider a reduction in g^*. As discussed in Section IVA, this disturbance results in a new equilibrium at a point above and to the left of the point B in Figure 3. At this new equilibrium, the home country is running a balance-of-trade deficit, financed by an outflow of bonds. Over time, as marketable wealth in the foreign country rises and that in the home country declines, desired expenditure is likely to shift in the direction of the foreign country's output. This means that the effect of the asset flows that take place over time will be to diminish the effect of the disturbance on the foreign economy and transmit more of its effect to the home economy. In contrast, a reduction in M^* results in a new equilibrium (below and to the right of the point B) at which the home country runs a trade-balance surplus. Over time, the asset flows associated with this surplus further reduce output in F, while increasing output in H.

Under fixed rates with capital mobility, the process of adjustment of asset stocks generally involves simultaneous redistribution of the world money supply and the world stock of bonds. At the equilibrium established following a reduction in g^*, the home country will be running a balance-of-trade deficit, financed in part by an outflow of official reserves and in part by an outflow of bonds. Over time, the accumulation of money and bonds by foreigners and the corresponding decumulation by home residents will increase E^* and reduce E, redistributing total world expenditure in the direction of foreign output. As a result, Q^* will rise, while Q declines. Thus, the effect of asset stock redistribution is to increase the extent to which the effects of the disturbance are transmitted to the home country and, correspondingly, to reduce the extent to which they are borne by the economy in which the disturbance originates. A similar conclusion holds for the disturbance created by a reduction in M^*.[25]

---

[25] For a discussion of the dynamics of adjustment of asset stocks under fixed rates, with capital mobility, see Frenkel and Rodriguez (1975) and Rodriguez (1976).

The policy implications of flows of official reserves and private capital are of particular importance in connection with the objective of maintaining external balance, especially under a system of fixed exchange rates. In this regard, there are three points of central importance. First, the adjustment of national money stocks through flows of official reserves provides an automatic mechanism through which balance-of-payments equilibrium will ultimately be restored. For this reason, it is not necessary for a country to have an explicit balance-of-payments policy, other than the policy of not completely offsetting the effect of foreign exchange flows on the national money stock. Second, a government cannot independently determine the nominal size of the national money stock and the exchange rate between domestic money and foreign money.[26] If a government tries to maintain too high (low) a level of its national money stock, it will be faced with persistent outflow (inflow) of foreign exchange. Ultimately, that government will either have to give up its commitment to the exchange rate or allow its national money stock to find its equilibrium level. This implies a significant constraint on the use of monetary policy for purposes of achieving internal balance. Given a commitment to a fixed exchange rate, monetary policy can only be used for short-run stabilization. Further, the short-run use of monetary policy will be limited by the government's willingness and ability to accumulate or decumulate foreign exchange and by the magnitude of the foreign exchange flow that is generated by a divergence of the money stock from its long-run equilibrium level. Third, the long-run, cumulative effect of any policy on a country's foreign exchange reserves depends on the effects of the policy on the long-run equilibrium level of the national money stock.[27] In particular, a devaluation induces a cumulative balance-of-payments surplus because, and to the extent that, it increases the equilibrium size of the nominal money stock.[28] Similarly, a tariff is likely to induce a cumulative balance-of-payments surplus because it increases the equilibrium size of the nominal money stock, not because it makes imports more expensive.[29]

B. The endogeneity of the aggregate supply function

The analysis of Sections III and IV assumes that the shape and position of the aggregate supply curve may be taken as given. One of the important implications of this assumption is that government policy can induce predictable and persistent changes in levels of national output and employment.

[26] This point is brought out in a number of papers by Robert Mundell, in particular, Mundell (1971).

[27] One of the essential features of the monetary approach to balance-of-payments analysis is its focus on the demand for money as the determinant of the long-run equilibrium size of the money stock; see Johnson (1973), Mussa (1974), and Swoboda (1976).

[28] See Dornbusch (1973b).

[29] See Mussa (1976a).

The experience of the postwar period, particularly the experience of the last decade, casts considerable doubt on the usefulness and validity of any analytical framework with this implication. Recent developments in macroeconomic theory also call into question both the assumption that the position of the aggregate supply curve may be treated as fixed (for the time period relevant for policy analysis), and the assumption that the form of the aggregate supply function is invariant to the policies pursued by governments for purposes of economic stabilization.

To illustrate the potential importance of shifts in the aggregate supply curve, it is instructive to consider the consequences of an increase in W^*. Such a disturbance could result either from an exogeneous push for higher wages by foreign workers or from the operation of some endogeneous wage-adjustment mechanism. An increase in W^* means an increase in the cost of producing foreign output and, therefore, a reduction in the amount of such output that will be supplied at any given level of P^*, or, equivalently, an increase in the value of P^* that is consistent with any given value of Q^*. In a closed economy, the effect of an increase in W^* would be to increase P^*, increase i^*, and reduce Q^*. The increase in P^* is the direct result of the increase in W^* at the original equilibrium value of Q^*. This increase in P^* increases the demand for money that drives up i^*. The increase in i^* reduces desired expenditure which, in turn, reduces Q^*.

In a two-country world, with flexible exchange rates and capital immobility, an increase in W^* has essentially the same effects as in a closed economy. As illustrated in Figure 4, the effect of an increase in W^* is to shift the $\tilde{E}^* = Q^*$ line downward from the line passing through A to the line passing through B. Since the increase in W^* has no effect on any of the variables entering into the equilibrium condition $\tilde{E}(Q; g, M, b, \tilde{b}, W, \pi) = Q$, it follows that the vertical $\tilde{E} = Q$ line in Figure 4 does not shift. Hence, the effect of the increase in W^* is to shift the equilibrium position from A to B. Foreign output falls by the same amount as it would if F had a closed economy. The home country's output is completely insulated from the effects of the increase in W^*, because the exchange rate adjusts to maintain trade-balance equilibrium, cutting off any transmission of the disturbance to the home economy. In particular, at B the relative price of F's output has risen, shifting demand in both countries away from F's output and toward H's output. This is the direct effect of the increase in P^*, at a given value of the exchange rate e. The exchange rate must adjust either up or down by enough to insure that the total effect of the relative price change just cancels the effect of the reduction in Q^* on F's demand for H's output. At B, the interest rate in F must be higher than it was at A, because the increase in i^* is the channel through which the increase in W^* affects desired expenditure in F. This increase in i^* does not lead to any flow of capital because, by assumption, capital is not mobile internationally.

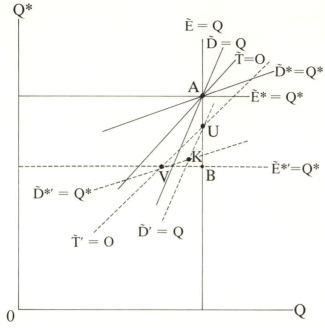

Fig. 4. The Effects of an Increase in W*.

Under fixed exchange rates, without capital mobility, an increase in W^* does affect the home economy. At the initial equilibrium point A, the increase in W^* increases P^*. This implies an increase in the demand for money in F and, hence, an increase in i^*. It also implies an increase in the relative price, $t = e \cdot P^*/P$, of F's output. The increase in i^* and the increase in t both imply a reduction in the demand for F's output, implying that the $\tilde{D}^* = Q^*$ line must shift downward and to the right from the solid line to the dashed line in Figure 4. The increase in i^* and the increase in t have conflicting effects on the trade balance and on the demand for H's output. The increase in i^* reduces F's demand for H's output (because it reduces desired expenditure in F); the increase in t shifts both domestic and foreign expenditure away from F's output and toward H's output. If the increase in t is dominant (but not too dominant), then the $\tilde{T} = 0$ line and the $\tilde{D} = Q$ line will shift downward and to the right, to the dashed lines in Figure 4.[30] The new equilibrium is at the point K, where the new $\tilde{D} = Q$ line intersects the new $\tilde{D}^* = Q^*$ line. At this point both Q and Q^* are lower than they were at A, with Q^* falling relatively more than Q. At K the home country has a trade-balance deficit, and it is this deficit that transmits part of the effect of the increase in W^* into a reduction in

---

[30] "Not too dominant" means that these lines do not shift past the point B in Fig. 4.

Q. If the increase in t is strongly dominant, then the trade-balance equilibrium line may rotate past the point B. In this case, the relative price effect of the increase in W^* will be so strong that H's output will actually rise, and F's output will decline by more than if F had a closed economy. On the other hand, if the increase in i^* dominates the increase in t, the new trade-balance equilibrium schedule will lie to the left of the original equilibrium point A. In this case, the contractionary effect of the increase in W^* will be more evenly split between a decline in Q^* and a decline in Q.

This analysis of the effects of an increase in W^* is easily extended to the case in which capital assets are internationally mobile. In particular, under flexible exchange rates, with capital mobility, it is apparent that an increase in W^* implies a new equilibrium point below and to the right of the point B in Figure 4. This is because at the point B the interest rate in F is higher than it was at A (when it was equal to the interest rate in H). This higher interest rate implies an incipient flood of capital from H to F. This forces the exchange rate to rise above its value at B, reducing Q^* and increasing Q.

Changes in W and W^* may occur not only as wholly exogeneous disturbances but also as the induced consequences of other disturbances. For instance, consider a devaluation by the foreign country; that is, a reduction in e under a fixed exchange rate regime. Holding W and W^* constant, this devaluation by F will induce an increase in output in F and a reduction in output in H. However, in countries that experience devaluations, particularly countries with a long history of devaluations, it is frequently observed that wage rates and other "fixed" prices do not remain constant in the face of a devaluation, but are adjusted very quickly to take account of the exchange rate change.[31] Specifically, suppose that a reduction in e were immediately followed by an equal proportionate increase in W^*. The combined effect of the increase in W^* and the reduction in e would leave the relative price of F's output, $t = e \cdot h^*(Q^*; W^*)/h(Q; W)$, unchanged at given values of Q and Q^*. Hence, the reduction in e would not stimulate the demand for F's output by reducing its relative price. At the initial level of Q^*, the devaluation by F would simply result in an equiproportionate increase in prices and wages. With a fixed money supply, this would force an increase in interest rates that would contract desired expenditure.[32] This would lead to a reduction in F's output, rather than an expansion. Moreover, this type of induced response of wage rates is not limited to devaluations; it may occur in

---

[31] For an empirical analysis of the effect of devaluation on wage rates in the United Kingdom, see Goldstein (1974).

[32] When capital is internationally mobile, the general level of world interest rates will be raised, and this will have a contractionary effect on desired expenditure in both countries.

response to other disturbances, both domestic and foreign. Whenever it does occur, it is likely to alter the total effect of whatever is the initiating disturbance.

In some cases, endogeneous wage rate responses may provide an additional channel for the international transmission of economic disturbances. This is particularly likely if domestic wage rates respond directly to disturbances originating in foreign economies, for instance, if labor unions attempt to emulate wage gains achieved in neighboring countries. Another possibility is that suggested by some versions of the "Scandinavian model."[33] Domestic wage rates may be linked to the prices of traded goods (the exposed sector). With fixed or controlled exchange rates, world inflation will force up the domestic money prices of traded goods. This leads to an increase in wage rates that increases costs and prices of nontraded goods (the sheltered sector). In this scenario, the response of wage rates to traded goods prices plays an important role in the transmission of inflationary impulses to the domestic economy.

Of course, wage adjustments may occur in response to a general wage adjustment mechanism, rather than in response to specific disturbances. This approach is suggested by closed-economy macroeconomic models in which wage behavior is governed by a mechanism such as the expectations-augmented Phillips curve;[34] specifically,

(27) $\quad \dot{W}/W = \pi + \alpha \cdot (Q - \bar{Q}), \alpha > 0;$

(28) $\quad \dot{W}^*/W^* = \pi^* + \alpha^* \cdot (Q^* - \bar{Q}^*), \alpha^* > 0.$

The expected rates of inflation, π and π^*, appear in these wage adjustment equations in order to deal with economies that are experiencing continuing inflation. They insure that the upward movement of wage rates will keep pace with the expected upward movement of prices. The second terms in the wage adjustment equations drive the economic system toward its long-run equilibrium ($Q = \bar{Q}$ and $Q^* = \bar{Q}^*$), when it is not already there. Since the analysis up to this point has not dealt with situations of continuing inflation, it suffices to focus on the second terms of the wage adjustment equations and continue with the assumption that both π and π^* are zero.

The implications of the wage adjustment equations may be illustrated by considering the consequences of a permanent reduction in M^*. Suppose that at the initial equilibrium point A, $Q = \bar{Q}$ and $Q^* = \bar{Q}^*$. Under flexible exchange rates without capital mobility, with W and W^* fixed, a reduction in M^* results in a reduction in Q^* and leaves Q unchanged. In earlier discussion, the reduction in Q^* was regarded as permanent. Now, with the wage adjustment equations in operation, the reduction in Q^* is not per-

---

[33] See Edgren, Flaxen, and Odner (1968), Lundberg (1972), and Kierzkowski (1974).

[34] The literature dealing with the development of this form of wage adjustment equation is discussed in Laidler and Parkin (1975).

manent. Since Q^* is below $\bar{Q}^*$, W^* will start to fall. The effects of this decline in W^* are just the reverse of the effects of the increase in W^*. Gradually, the level of output in F will rise, while output in H remains at $\bar{Q}$. This process will continue until Q^* reaches $\bar{Q}^*$ and the upward movement of W^* ceases. Moreover, the adjustment of W^* also changes the relationship between P^* and Q^*. As W^* falls, $P^* = h^*(Q^*; W^*)$ declines for any given value of Q^*. Ultimately, when the full equilibrium is reestablished, P^* will have fallen by the same proportionate amount as W^*, which, in turn, will have fallen by the same proportionate amount as M^*. Thus, the only long-run consequence of a reduction in M^* is an equal proportionate reduction in all nominal prices in F, with no effects on any real variable.[35] The rapidity with which these long-run results are achieved clearly depends on the speed with which wages respond to disequilibrium. It is apparent that if wages respond rapidly, monetary disturbances (including changes in monetary policy) will have only very short-run effects on real variables, such as output and employment. For this reason, the speed of adjustment of wage rates is a critical determinant of the potential usefulness of monetary (and fiscal) policy for purposes of stabilizing output and employment.

C. Exchange rate expectations

In the analysis of Sections III and IV, expectations of the future exchange rate played no role. This is appropriate when residents of one country are debarred from holding either money or bonds denominated in the money of the other country. However, when asset holders can take positions in such foreign assets, expectations of future exchange rates do play a vital role in determining the current exchange rate and other macroeconomic variables. An asset holder who has choice about the currency denomination of his assets will not hold his assets in a currency that he expects to depreciate, unless he is compensated by a nominal interest rate differential in favor of such assets.

This concern with the role of exchange rate expectations in determining current exchange rates is a central theme in the asset market view of the exchange rate.[36] To build this concern into the analytical framework used as the basis for the discussion in Section IVA, it is essential to modify the interest rate equilization condition (26) to the interest parity condition

$$(29) \quad \bar{\imath}(Q) = \bar{\imath}^*(Q^*) + f,$$

[35] It is generally recognized that the long-run effects of disturbances such as money supply changes and exchange rate changes differ from the short-run effects of such disturbances, because prices that are rigid in the short run are flexible in the long run. This issue is frequently dealt with by distinguishing different concepts of equilibrium; see, for instance, Swoboda (1972).

[36] See Black (1973), Bilson (1978), Dornbusch (1976a, 1976b), Frenkel (1976b), Genberg and Kierzkowski (1975), Kouri (1976), and Mussa (1976b, 1977).

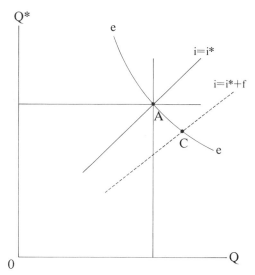

Fig. 5.   The Effects of an Increase in f.

where f is the forward discount on H's money in terms of F's money, stated as an annual percentage rate. Given the interest parity condition, we may examine the effects of changes in f on the values of Q and Q^*. Then we can consider how the value of f is linked to expectations of future values of the exchange rate.

When f is zero, equilibrium occurs at the point A in Figure 5, where the ee curve intersects the $i = i^*$ line.[37] When f is zero, the $i = i^*$ line is the interest parity line; it describes the combinations of Q and Q^* that are consistent with (29). An increase in f to some positive value rotates the interest parity line in a clockwise direction to the dashed line labeled $i = i^* + f$. This shift occurs because the maintenance of interest parity requires that $\bar{i}^*(Q^*)$ decline for any fixed value of $\bar{i}(Q)$. For any given value of Q, this can only be accomplished by a reduction in Q^*. The new equilibrium following the increase in f is at the point C, where the dashed interest parity line intersects the ee curve. It follows that the increase in f results in an increase in Q, a reduction in Q^*, and an increase in e. These results follow from the fact that at the initial equilibrium point A, the increase in f makes the holding of F's assets more attractive than the holding of H's assets. With perfect capital mobility, this induces a massive incipient flow of capital from H to F. This incipient capital flow forces up the value of F's money relative to H's money. This, in turn, shifts demand away from F's output and toward H's output, leading to an expansion of Q and a reduction of Q^*.

[37] This diagram appears in Dornbusch and Krugman (1976).

The forward discount on domestic money f is usually assumed to reflect asset holders' expectations of the future behavior of the spot exchange rate; specifically, it is frequently assumed that[38]

(30) $f = (\dot{e}/e)^x$,

where $(\dot{e}/e)^x$ denotes the expected rate of change of the spot exchange rate. From this assumption and the results of the preceding paragraph, it follows that the expectation of a rising exchange rate leads to an immediate increase in the exchange rate and causes Q to rise and Q^* to fall. This establishes that changes in the expected rate of change of the exchange rate are a potentially important source of disturbance to the world economy and a potentially important channel through which other disturbances may be transmitted from one economy to another.

In order to be more specific about how the effects of disturbances may be transmitted through their impact on $(\dot{e}/e)^x$, it is necessary to have a theory of expectations formation. One approach is to postulate some expectations-formation mechanism, concerning either the level or the rate of change of the exchange rate. Given such a mechanism, it is possible to analyze the effects that any primitive disturbance will have on $(\dot{e}/e)^x$ and, through this channel, on Q, Q^*, and e. Specifically, suppose that people have definite expectations about the "full equilibrium exchange rate," $\bar{e}$, that is, about what the exchange rate would be if the world economy were currently in a state of full equilibrium. Suppose that expectations concerning the full equilibrium exchange rate are adjusted in accord with an adaptive mechanism;

(31) $\dot{\bar{e}} = a \cdot (e - \bar{e}), a > 0$.

Further, suppose that the current exchange rate is expected to converge to its full equilibrium value at some positive rate;

(32) $(\dot{e}/e)^x = b \cdot ((\bar{e} - e)/\bar{e}), b > 0$.

Given these assumptions, consider the effects of a reduction in M^*, starting from full equilibrium. As discussed in Section IIIA, holding $f = 0$, the effect of a reduction in M^* is to shift the equilibrium point in Figure 3 from the initial equilibrium point A to the point U. At U, e is above its value at A. Since $\bar{e}$ is not immediately affected by the change in e, it follows that at U, $f = (\dot{e}/e)^x$ must be negative. But if f is negative, the relevant interest parity line is not the dashed $i = i^*$ line through U, but a line that

---

[38] As a theoretical matter, the forward discount may diverge from expected rate of depreciation, but as an empirical matter such divergences do not appear to be important; see Stockman (1977).

is rotated in a counterclockwise direction. Hence, taking account of the induced effect of a change in M^* on $(\dot{e}/e)^x$, the new equilibrium point cannot be U, but must lie somewhere along the dashed ee curve above and to the left of U. Thus, the implication of the expectations mechanism (31) and (32), relative to the naive assumption that $f = 0$, is that the effects of a monetary disturbance are less heavily focused on the economy in which the disturbance originates and may, as under fixed exchange rates, be transmitted positively to the rest of the world.

This conclusion, however, is sensitive to the assumed form of the expectations mechanism. For instance, (31) might be replaced by the assumption that people extrapolate observed changes in e over some finite horizon, T, in forming their views concerning the full equilibrium exchange rate; say,

$$(33) \quad \bar{e}(t) = e(t) + \int_{t-T}^{t} de(s).$$

Under the impact of a reduction in M^*, this assumption leads to the result that $\bar{e}(t)$ will increase by twice the observed increase in $e(t)$, implying that $f = (\dot{e}/e)^x = b \cdot ((\bar{e} - e)/\bar{e})$ will be positive at the point U in Figure 3. This, in turn, implies that the new equilibrium must lie below and to the right of the point U along the dashed ee curve. Thus, relative to the naive assumption that $f = 0$, the new expectations mechanism implies that the effects of a monetary disturbance are more heavily focused on the economy in which the disturbance originates and more negatively transmitted to the rest of the world.

To provide an analytical basis for the determination of the appropriate form of expectations mechanism, and to shed light on other interesting questions, much recent work has adopted the assumption of "rational expectations." Expectations are "rational" when they reflect all of the information available to economic agents, including information concerning the basic structure of the economic system and the stochastic processes generating the behavior of the exogenous variables. One implication of rational expectations, applied to the specific issue of exchange rate expectations, is that the expected speed of convergence of the exchange rate to its full equilibrium level is not an arbitrary parameter; its value reflects the speed of convergence inherent in the dynamics of the economic system.[39] Further, the assumption of rational expectations implies that the expected rate of change of the exchange rate should reflect the expected rate of

---

[39] In Dornbusch (1976b) and Mussa (1977) the speed of convergence to full equilibrium is determined by the speed of adjustment of prices to their equilibrium level. In Kouri (1976), the speed of adjustment is determined by the rate of accumulation of asset stocks. In Musa (1976), the speed of adjustment is infinite; the economic system is always in full equilibrium.

change of the full equilibrium exchange rate, $(\check{e}/\bar{e})^x$, as well as the expected speed of convergence of the exchange rate to its full equilibrium level;[40]

$$(34) \quad (\dot{e}/e)^x = (\check{e}/\bar{e})^x + a \cdot ((\bar{e} - e)/\bar{e}).$$

Finally, and perhaps most importantly, rational expectations imply that the level and expected rate of change of $\bar{e}$ should reflect peoples' expectations concerning the entire future time paths of the exogeneous variables that are relevant to determining the value of the exchange rate.

The importance of this last point may be illustrated by considering the effects of a reduction in M^*, under different assumptions concerning the effect of this disturbance on peoples' expectations concerning the future behavior of M^*. First, suppose that the reduction in M^* is interpreted by every economic agent as a permanent, once-and-for-all occurrence, with no other ramifications. In full equilibrium, e will rise proportionately with the reduction in M^*; P^*, and W^* will fall proportionately with the reduction in M^*; and Q^*, Q, P, and W, will be unchanged. In the short run, with W and W^* fixed, however, the reduction in M^* will have real effects of the sort analyzed in Figure 3. In particular, if the exchange rate at the point U corresponds to the new full equilibrium exchange rate, then the new short-run equilibrium will be at U. If the exchange rate at U is below (above) the new value of $\bar{e}$, the new short-run equilibrium point will be along the dashed ee curve above and to the left (below and to the right) of the point U. In other words, the relationship between the results obtained under the naive assumption that $f = 0$ and the sophisticated assumption of rational expectations depends exclusively on the relationship between the exchange rate at the naive equilibrium point U and the new full equilibrium exchange rate.

Second, suppose that the reduction in M^* is interpreted as the start of a trend toward even lower values of M^* in the future. This implies that the current value of $\bar{e}$ will rise more than proportionately with the reduction in M^*, since the expectation of deflation in the foreign country will increase the real demand for money. It also implies that $(\dot{e}/\bar{e})$ will become positive. Both of these forces operate in the direction of making $f = (\dot{e}/e)^x$ positive. Thus, in the short run, they increase the extent to which Q^* falls in response to the reduction in M^* and increase the extent to which Q rises in response to the reduction in M^*; they tend to magnify the effects of the disturbance.

Third, suppose that the reduction in M^* is interpreted as temporary. In this case $\bar{e}$ will fall by little, and $(\check{e}/\bar{e})^x$ will become positive. These forces operate to diminish the reduction in Q^* and increase the extent to which

---

[40] The term $(\check{e}/\bar{e})^x$ belongs on the right-hand side of (34) for essentially the same reason that the expected rate of inflation belongs in the wage adjustment equation. This term insures that if expectations are correct, then once equilibrium is achieved it will be maintained.

the contractionary effect of the disturbance is transmitted to the home country, rather than borne by the foreign country.

Finally, suppose that the reduction in M^* is not a sudden, unanticipated event, but rather an event that has been fully anticipated for a long time. In this case, the lower value of M^* will already be built into the exchange rate and into prices, and the actual event of the reduction in M^* will have no effect on the exchange rate or on the levels of foreign and domestic output. This accords with the general principle that when economic agents have rational expectations, only unanticipated changes in money supplies have any real effect.

VI. ANALYTICAL ISSUES AND POLICY IMPLICATIONS

Traditionally, the literature on open-economy macroeconomics has been oriented toward the analysis of questions of public policy. Three analytical issues that have come to the fore in recent years now appear to be of crucial importance to the further development of the literature in this direction. The purpose of this section is to discuss these analytical issues and indicate their importance to the theory and conduct of macroeconomic policy in open economies.

A. Mobility and substitutability of goods and assets

It is widely recognized that in a small and very open economy, macroeconomic policies will have virtually no capacity to affect the level of domestic output and employment. By definition, a small open economy is one that takes the world prices of virtually all goods and services and the real rates of return on virtually all securities as given. In such an economy, fiscal policy cannot affect output, because the demand for domestic output is infinitely elastic at given world relative prices. Similarly, monetary policy cannot affect output, because it cannot affect the real rates of return on assets, and, even if it could, the effect of any increase in desired expenditure stimulated by lower interest rates would have only a negligible effect on domestic output. Changes in exchange rates are also likely to be ineffective, because in a small open economy people will not be deceived that an exchange rate change is anything more than a change in an accounting unit. Prices and wages, measured in terms of domestic money, will adjust proportionately with any change in the exchange rate, and domestic output will remain unchanged.

The image of an impotent government in a small open economy is not satisfactory for those who would like to use open-economy macroeconomic models to make policy prescriptions. In recent years, considerable effort has gone into elaborating the circumstances in which this image is not wholly appropriate and in which there is at least some latitude for the effective use of policy to stimulate domestic output and employment. Of course, for a country that is of significant size relative to the world economy, policy actions can have effects because they can affect the values of world aggregates. However, since most national economies are not of sufficient size to make this consideration important, much attention has been focused on two special circumstances that allow domestic stabilization policies to be effective even in relatively small economies: immobility of some goods and assets between national economies; and imperfect substitutability between goods and assets of different national economies.

The importance and implications of immobility of some commodities is dealt with in the extensive literature on nontraded goods.[41] The general point is that if there are nontraded goods, then macroeconomic policies can be effective by influencing the demand for such goods. The effects of changes in demand for nontraded goods are not dissipated on the world economy as a whole. A similar point applies for assets that are not traded.[42] Open-market operations in nontraded assets can affect the real rates of return on such assets and, through this channel, affect domestic aggregate demand.

Imperfect substitutability is another assumption that provides some latitude for effective stabilization policy. This assumption has been explored extensively for assets in the literature on portfolio-balance models.[43] If German bonds are not perfect substitutes for U.S. bonds, then open-market operations in German bonds by the Bundesbank can affect the rate of return on such bonds, because the German government is a relatively large participant in the market for such bonds. The capacity to affect the rate of return on German bonds provides leverage for monetary policy to affect real economic variables. The assumption of imperfect substitutability can also be applied to goods. Automobiles are traded goods, but a Volkswagen is not a perfect substitute for a Chevrolet. At least in the short-run, the relative price of Volkswagens and Chevrolets can vary without demand shifting entirely from one automobile to the other. This suggests that the prices of some internationally traded goods may not be fixed, particularly in the short run, even for rather small national economies. This flexibility of relative prices provides a channel through which domestic stabilization policies can have an effect. It also suggests that exchange rate changes can have real effects through their impact on the relative prices of similar traded commodities that are produced by different countries. The extent and duration of such relative price effects has been a controversial issue in recent discussions of the effects of exchange rate changes.[44]

[41] See Dornbusch (1973a, 1973b), Flood (1977), Genberg and Kierzkowski (1975), Komiya (1967), Salter (1959), and Swan (1960).

[42] See Branson (1976) and Dornbusch (1975).

[43] See Brunner (1976), Branson (1972, 1976), and McKinnon (1969).

[44] Many theoretical models make the simplifying assumption that purchasing power parity is continuously maintained, implying that exchange rate changes have no relative price effects. Frenkel (1976) and (1977) has found that this is a reasonable empirical assumption for the case of Germany during the hyperinflation that followed World War I. Many other studies, however, have found that exchange rate changes do have relative price effects, at least in the short run; see, for instance, Clark (1977), and Dornbusch and Krugman (1976).

Immobility of some goods and assets and imperfect substitutability among goods and assets that are mobile provide some latitude for the successful use of stabilization policies by national governments. There is little doubt, however, that for most national governments, the latitude for successful policy manipulation is severely limited by the openness of the economy.[45] To increase the latitude for successful policy manipulation, some governments have sought to limit the openness of their national economy. This is the macroeconomic rationale for protectionist policies that have been advocated with increasing vigor in many countries as a means of limiting the openness of an economy to trade in goods.[46] Is it also the rationale for systems of dual exchange rates and other limitations on free international flow of capital?[47] In general, academic economists have been highly critical of such efforts to restrict the free international movement of goods and assets. However, the general question of what is the optimal degree of openness of a national economy in a world of stochastic shocks has not been resolved.[48] Nor has the important question of the optimal rules of the game for the international economic system been successfully addressed.[49]

B. Relative speeds of adjustment

A second issue of theoretical and practical importance concerns the relative speeds of adjustment of prices and quantities in the markets for goods and assets. A distinctive feature of most macroeconomic models is that they assume that in some markets prices adjust very rapidly to maintain equilibrium, whereas in other markets prices are "sticky" and short-run adjustment is achieved through variations in quantities.[50] In particular, in the "Keynesian" models analyzed in Sections III and IV, the nominal wage rate was assumed to be fixed. This crucial assumption led to the implication that disturbances to aggregate demand would affect levels of national output and employment in a consistent and predictable fashion,

[45] The latitude for successful policy manipulation has been the subject of a number of studies; see, for instance, Fair (1977a, 1977b), Helliwell and McRae (1977), and Kouri and Porter (1974).

[46] The "new Cambridge school" has attempted (without notable success) to provide a logical rationale for protectionist policies as a means of stimulating employment.

[47] For an analysis of duel exchange rate regimes, see Argy and Porter (1972), Dornbusch (1975), Fleming (1974), Flood (1977), and Swoboda (1974).

[48] One aspect of this general question that has received some attention is the appropriate choice of an exchange rate regime. See Fischer (1977) for a stochastic model in which the choice of regime depends on the nature of the shocks impinging on the system.

[49] There is a substantial literature on the subject of policy coordination and policy conflict. But, in most of this literature, it is assumed that disturbances can be responded to on an individual basis, with complete information on the nature of the disturbance.

[50] If all prices responded correctly and instantaneously to changes in economic conditions, we would not observe the fluctuations of output and employment that are the central concerns of macroeconomic theory and policy. This is one of the important messages of the "new microeconomics of inflation and unemployment theory"; see Phelps et al. (1970).

and that such disturbances could be offset by policy actions that had a countervailing effect on aggregate demand.

In recent years, the assumption of rigid wages has become empirically untenable. But this has not led to the complete abandonment of "Keynesian" models. The crucial assumption is not that wages are absolutely rigid, but only that they do not adjust instantaneously to preserve full employment. If wage adjustment is governed by a Phillips curve mechanism, disturbances to aggregate demand will have persistent and predictable effects on output and employment that can be offset by suitable policy actions. If wage adjustments are influenced by expectations of future inflation (with a unitary coefficient), macroeconomic policy will lose its capacity to permanently influence the levels of output and employment. But policy will retain some effectiveness in limiting fluctuations of output and employment around their "natural" levels. How much effectiveness depends critically on how rapidly prices and wages adjust to their equilibrium levels. If adjustment is rapid, policy will be of limited use both because natural equilibration forces are strong and because lags in the implementation or effect of policy may cause it to be destabilizing. If adjustment is not too rapid, then the broad outline of the results derived using traditional "Keynesian" models should remain valid, with suitable modifications to take account of the long-run inflationary consequences of some macroeconomic policies.[51] Another modification of potential importance concerns the spill-over effects from disequilibrium in one market to other markets. This has been the subject of much discussion in closed-economy models and promises to be an important area of development in open-economy models.[52]

Relative adjustment speeds of prices and quantities in different markets are of vital importance in understanding fluctuations in exchange rates and relative prices, as well as fluctuations in output and employment. In the asset market approach to exchange rate theory, it is asserted that the exchange rate is a relative asset price that is determined primarily by the conditions of equilibrium in the markets for asset stocks. What this means is that the exchange rate is a price that behaves like the prices of assets (stocks, bonds, commodities, options) that are traded on organized exchanges. The prices of such assets respond essentially instantaneously to

[51] There remains some controversy over whether the long-run Phillips curve is vertical; see, for instance, Friedman (1968) and Tobin (1972). But, the more important issue is "how long is the long run?" If the long run is a year, then macroeconomic policy (with its lags and uncertainties) cannot be very useful. If the long run is a decade, then it may be useful to think in terms of a policy trade-off between inflation and unemployment.

[52] The theory of disequilibrium macroeconomics is outlined in Clower (1965) and Barro and Grossman (1976). The International Monetary Research Programme at the London School of Economics has done a substantial amount of work in applying disequilibrium models to issues in open-economy macroeconomics; see especially Bergstrom and Wymer (1974) and Jonson (1976).

changes in economic conditions, in particular, to new information that is received by market participants. Of course, exchange rates are also related to general price levels in different countries through purchasing power parity. But, if price levels adjust relatively slowly in comparison with exchange rates, then changes in purchasing power parity should not be regarded as the proximate determinants of exchange rate changes. Purchasing power parity is a longer-run equilibrium condition that must ultimately be satisfied, either through the adjustment of the exchange rate (determined in the asset markets) to given national price levels, or through the adjustment of national price levels to the exchange rate.[53]

This view of the exchange rate as a rapidly adjusting asset price has important implications for the difference between a fixed exchange rate regime and a floating exchange rate regime. Under the Bretton Woods system, the "fixed" exchange rate was supposed to be a policy tool that was to be used in circumstances of "fundamental disequilibrium." In practice, exchange rate changes occurred only after (frequently long after) the nature and direction of the disequilibrium became apparent. Under "fixed" rates, disalignment of national price levels preceded the parity changes that were used to correct these disalignments. Under flexible exchange rates, however, exchange rate movements should frequently anticipate, rather than follow, movements in national price levels. Further, if anticipations of future price level movements are not correct, then variations in exchange rates, due to anticipatory adjustment in asset markets, may be a (temporary) cause of price disalignments.[54]

C. The role of information

The major challenge to the neo-Keynesian approach to macroeconomic analysis comes from the "rational-expectations" approach, developed expecially by Robert Lucas (1972, 1973, and 1975). In the neo-Keynesian approach, fluctuations in output and employment occur because of some short-run rigidity in wages and prices that prevents them from responding instantaneously to changes in economic conditions. In the rational-expectations approach, there is no short-run rigidity of wages or prices. Fluctuations in output and employment occur because economic agents lack complete information on the nature of the disturbances impinging on the economic system. As emphasized by Barro (1975) and Sargent and Wallace

[53] Virtually all theoretical models assume that purchasing power parity rules in the long run, subject to changes in real economic conditions. Some models assume that this relationship is maintained on an essentially continuous basis; see, for instance, Frenkel (1976), Kouri (1976), Mussa (1976*b*), and Stockman (1978). Other models assume that because of "sticky" prices, purchasing power parity is not continuously maintained; see especially Dornbusch (1976*a*, 1976*b*) and, also, Mussa (1977).

[54] Dornbusch (1976*b*) argues that such disalignments can also result from "overshooting" of the exchange rate, which will occur in a world in which prices are "sticky."

(1975, 1976), the rational-expectations approach has profound implications for the usefulness of macroeconomic policy in a closed economy. Feedback policy rules, in which policy actions are based on information available to the private sector as well as the government, can accomplish very little in terms of stabilizing national output and employment. Only if the government can make use of information not available to the private sector can macroeconomic policy do anything positive.[55]

The implications of the rational-expectations approach have not been fully worked out for multicountry models.[56] But, the broad outline of results in three important areas is already apparent. First, the rational-expectations approach vitiates the analytical basis for traditional discussion of policies to achieve internal balance. If the rational-expectations approach is substantially correct, policy actions will have little capacity to affect levels of output and employment in a systematic and predictable fashion. Policy actions that are anticipated by the private sector will not be effective. Only unanticipated policy actions, which of necessity cannot be systematic and predictable, will have any significant effect. Second, the rational-expectations approach suggests that new information must play a dominant role in explaining the large unanticipated movements in exchange rates that have been a major concern of policy-makers in recent years. In accord with the asset market view of exchange rate determination, current exchange rates reflect not only current economic conditions but also current expectations of future conditions. If expectations are "rational" then they must reflect all current information that is relevant to predicting future economic conditions. This implies that any divergence of actual exchange rate behavior from previously anticipated behavior must reflect the receipt of fundamentally new information.[57] Third, the rational-expectations approach suggests a fundamentally different view of the nature of macroeconomic policy. The effect of any policy action depends on the degree to which this action was previously anticipated and on the extent to which it conveys new information to economic agents concerning future policy actions. The degree of anticipation and the extent of new information, in turn, depend on what economic agents understand to be the general framework of economic policy, as influenced by past observations of policy actions.[58] This dynamic interrelationship between policy actions suggests that the traditional approach to policy analysis is not valid. Policy actions cannot be selected on an individual basis to meet particular needs

[55] This circumstance may arise if the private sector is locked into long-term nominal contracts that reflected information available at the time of negotiation but not all current information; see Fischer (1977) and Phelps and Taylor (1977).

[56] Much work is presently being done on this subject; see Bilson (1978), Saidi (1977), and Stockman (1978).

[57] This point is emphasized in Mussa (1977).

[58] The importance of this very general point for the analysis of all types of macroeconomic policy actions has been emphasized by Lucas (1976).

at particular moments of time. Rather, it is necessary to design a general framework for economic policy that will serve broad social objectives in the long run.

REFERENCES

Alexander, S. 1959. "The Effects of Devaluation: A Simplified Synthesis of the Elasticities and Absorption Approaches." *American Economic Review* 49 (2).

Allen, Polly R., and Kenen, Peter B. 1976. "Portfolio Adjustment in Open Economies: A Comparison of Alternative Specifications." *Weltwirtschaftliches Archiv* 112 (1): 33–72.

Argy, Victor, and Porter, Michael. 1972. "The Forward Exchange Market and the Effects of Domestic and External Disturbances under Alternative Exchange Rate Systems." *International Monetary Fund Staff Papers* 19 (3): 503–32.

Barro, R. 1976. "Rational Expectations and the Role of Monetary Policy." *Journal of Monetary Economics* 2.

———, and Grossman, Herschel. 1976. *Money, Employment and Inflation.* Cambridge: Cambridge University Press.

Bergstrom, A. R., and Wymer, C. R. 1974. "A Model of Disequilibrium Neoclassical Growth and Its Application to the United Kingdom." Discussion paper, International Monetary Research Programme, London School of Economics.

Bilson, J. 1978. "Rational Expectations and Exchange Rates." In *The Economics of Exchange Rates: Selected Studies*, edited by J. Frenkel and H. G. Johnson. Reading, Mass.: Addison-Wesley.

Black, S. 1973. "International Money Markets and Flexible Exchange Rates." Princeton Studies in International Finance, no. 32, Princeton University.

Boyer, Russell. 1975. "Commodity Markets and Bond Markets in a Small Fixed Exchange Rate Economy." *Canadian Journal of Economics* 7 (1): 1–22.

Branson, W. 1972. "Macroeconomic Equilibrium with Portfolio Balance in Open Economies." Working paper, Institute for International Affairs, Stockholm.

———. 1976. "Portfolio Equilibrium and Monetary Policy with Foreign and Non-traded Assets." In *Recent Issues in International Economics*, edited by E. Claassen and P. Salin. Amsterdam: North-Holland.

Brunner, Karl. 1976. "The Money Supply Process in Open Economies with Interdependent Security Markets: The Case of Imperfect Substitutability." In *Bank Credit, Money and Inflation in Open Economies*, edited by Michele Fratianni, pp. 19–75. Berlin: Duncker and Humblot.

Brunner, K., and Meltzer, A. 1972. "Money, Debt, and Economic Activity." *Journal of Political Economy* 80 (5).

———. 1976. "Monetary and Fiscal Policy in Open, Interdependent Economies with Fixed Exchange Rates." In *Recent Issues in International Economics*, edited by E. Claassen and P. Salin. Amsterdam: North-Holland.

Clark, Peter B. 1977. "The Effects of Recent Exchange Rate Changes on the

200 *Michael Mussa*

U.S. Trade Balance." In *The Effects of Exchange Rate Adjustments*, edited by Peter B. Clark et al. Washington, D.C.: Government Printing Office.

Clower, Robert. 1965. "The Keynesian Counter Revolution: A Theoretical Appraisal." In *The Theory of Interest Rates*, edited by F. H. Hahn and F. P. R. Brechling. London: Macmillan & Co.

Cooper, R. N. 1969. "Macroeconomic Policy Adjustment in Interdependent Economies." *Quarterly Journal of Economics* 83 (1).

———. 1976. "Monetary Theory and Policy in an Open Economy." *Scandinavian Journal of Economics* 78 (2): 146–63.

Corden, W. M. 1960. "The Geometric Representation of Policies to Attain Internal and External Balance." *Review of Economic Studies* 28 (1).

Dornbusch, R. 1973a. "Real and Monetary Aspects of the Effects of Exchange Rate Changes." In *National Monetary Policies and the International Financial System*, edited by R. Z. Aliber. Chicago: University of Chicago Press.

———. 1973b. "Currency Depreciation, Hoarding, and Relative Prices." *Journal of Political Economy* 81 (4).

———. 1975. "A Portfolio Balance Model of the Open Economy." *Journal of Monetary Economics* 1 (1).

———. 1976a. "The Theory of Flexible Exchange Rate Regimes and Macroeconomic Policy." *Scandinavian Journal of Economics* 78 (2).

———. 1976b. "Exchange Rate Dynamics." *Journal of Political Economy* 84 (6).

Dornbusch, R., and Krugman, Paul. 1976. "Flexible Exchange Rates in the Short Run." *Brookings Papers on Economic Activity* 3: 577–84.

Edgren, G., Flaxen, K., and Odner, C. 1968. "Wages, Growth and the Distribution of Income." *Swedish Journal of Economics* (September).

Fair, Ray C. 1977. "A Model of the Balance of Payments." Cowles Foundation Discussion Paper No. 451.

———. 1977. "On Economic Linkages among Countries." Cowles Foundation Discussion Paper No. 451.

Fischer, S. 1977. "Stability and the Exchange Rate Regime in a Monetarist Model of the Balance of Payments." In *The Political Economy of Monetary Reform*, edited by R. Z. Aliber. Montclair, N.J.: Allanheld, Osmun & Co.

———. 1977. "Long-Term Contracts, Rational Expectations, and the Optimal Money Supply Rule." *Journal of Political Economy* 85 (1).

Fleming, J. M. 1962. "Domestic Financial Policies under Fixed and under Floating Exchange Rates." *International Monetary Fund Staff Papers* 9.

———. 1974. "Dual Exchange Rates and Other Remedies for Disruptive Capital Flows." *International Monetary Fund Staff Papers* 21 (1): 1–28.

Flood, Robert P. 1977. "Essays on a Monetary Approach to Real and Financial Aspects of Various Exchange Rate Systems." Ph.D. dissertation, University of Rochester.

Floyd, J. E. 1969. "Monetary and Fiscal Policy in a World of Capital Mobility." *Review of Economic Studies* 36 (3).

Frenkel, J. 1976a. "Adjustment Mechanisms and the Monetary Approach to the Balance of Payments: A Doctrinal Perspective." In *Recent Issues in*

International Monetary Economics, edited by E. Claassen and P. Salin. Amsterdam: North-Holland.

————. 1976*b*. "A Monetary Approach to the Exchange Rate: Doctrinal Aspects and Empirical Evidence." *Scandinavian Journal of Economics* 78 (2).

————. 1977. "The Forward Exchange Rate, Expectations, and the Demand for Money." *American Economic Review* 67 (4): 653–70.

Frenkel, J., and Johnson, H. G. 1976. *The Monetary Approach to the Balance of Payments*. London: George Allen & Unwin.

Frenkel, J., and Rodriguez, C. 1975. "Portfolio Equilibrium and the Balance of Payments: A Monetary Approach." *American Economic Review* 65 (4).

Friedman, M. 1976. *Price Theory*. Chicago, Aldine.

Genberg, H., and Kierzkowski, H. 1975. "Short Run, Long Run and Dynamics of Adjustment under Flexible Exchange Rates." Discussion paper, Graduate Institute of International Studies, Geneva.

Girton, Lance, and Henderson, Dale W. 1976. "Financial Capital Movements and Central Bank Behavior in a Two-Country Short-Run Portfolio Balance Model." *Journal of Monetary Economics* 2 (1): 33–61.

Goldstein, Morris. 1974. "The Effect of Exchange Rate Changes on Wages and Prices in the United Kingdom: An Empirical Study." *International Monetary Fund Staff Papers* 21: 694–739.

Harberger, A. C. 1950. "Currency Depreciation, Income, and the Balance of Payments." *Journal of Political Economy* 58 (1).

Helliwell, John F., and McRae, Robert. 1977. "Interdependence of Monetary Debt and Fiscal Policies in an International Setting." In *The Political Economy of Monetary Reform*, edited by R. Z. Aliber. London: Macmillan & Co.

Johnson, H. G. 1958. "The Transfer Problem and Exchange Stability." In *International Trade and Economic Growth*. London: Allen & Unwin.

————. 1973. "The Monetary Approach to Balance of Payments Theory." In *International Trade and Money*, edited by M. Connolly and A. Swoboda. London: George Allen & Unwin.

Jones, R. W. 1961. "Stability Conditions in International Trade: A General Equilibrium Analysis." *International Economic Review* 2 (2).

————. 1968. "Monetary and Fiscal Policies for an Economy with Fixed Exchange Rates." *Journal of Political Economy* 76, part I: 921–43.

Jonson, Peter. 1976. "Money and Economic Activity in an Open Economy: The United Kingdom, 1880–1970." *Journal of Political Economy* 84: 979–1012.

Kemp, Murray C. 1966. "Monetary and Fiscal Policy under Alternative Assumptions about Capital Mobility." *Economic Record* 42: 598–605.

Kierzkowski, Henryk. 1974. "Theoretical Foundations of the Scandinavian Model of Inflation." Working paper, International Monetary Research Programme, London School of Economics.

Komiya, R. 1967. "Non-traded Goods and the Pure Theory of International Trade." *International Economic Review* 8 (2).

Kouri, P. 1976. "The Exchange Rate and the Balance of Payments in the Short Run and in the Long Run." *Scandinavian Journal of Economics* 78 (2).

Kouri, P., and Porter, Michael. 1974. "International Capital Flows and Portfolio Equilibrium." *Journal of Political Economy* 82 (3): 443–68.

Krueger, Anne O. 1965. "The Impact of Alternative Government Policies under Varying Exchange Rate Regimes." *Quarterly Journal of Economics* 79: 195–208.

Laidler, D., and Parkin, J. M. 1975. "Inflation—A Survey." *Economic Journal* 85.

Laursen, S., and Metzler, L. 1950. "Flexible Exchange Rates and the Theory of Employment." *Review of Economics & Statistics* 18.

Lucas, R. E. 1972. "Expectations and the Neutrality of Money." *Journal of Economic Theory* 4 (2).

———. 1973. "Some International Evidence on Output-Inflation Trade-offs." *American Economic Review* 63 (3).

———. 1975. "An Equilibrium Model of the Business Cycle." *Journal of Political Economy* 83 (6).

———. 1976. "Econometric Policy Evaluations: A Critique." In *The Phillips Curve and Labor Markets*, edited by K. Brunner and A. Meltzer. Carnegie-Rochester Conference Series on Public Policy, I. Amsterdam: North-Holland.

Lucas, R. E., and Rapping, L. A. 1969. "Price Expectations and the Phillips Curve." *American Economic Review* 59 (3).

Lundberg, Eric. 1972. "Productivity and Structural Change—A Policy Issue in Sweden." *Economic Journal* 82.

Machlup, F. 1955. "The Analysis of Devaluation." *American Economic Review* 45 (3).

McKinnon, R. I. 1969. "Portfolio Balance and International Payments Adjustment." In *Monetary Problems of the International Economy*, edited by R. Mundell and A. Swoboda. Chicago: University of Chicago Press.

McKinnon, R. I., and Oates, W. R. 1966. "The Implications of International Economic Integration for Monetary, Fiscal, and Exchange Rate Policy." Princeton Studies in International Finance, No. 16, Princeton University.

Meade, J. E. 1951. *The Theory of International Economic Policy.* Vol. I: *The Balance of Payments.* London: Oxford University Press.

Metzler, L. A. 1960. "The Process of International Adjustment under Conditions of Full Employment: A Keynesian View." In *Readings in International Economics*, edited by R. Caves and H. G. Johnson. Homewood, Ill.: Irwin.

Mundell, R. A. 1964. "A Reply, Capital Mobility and Size." *Canadian Journal of Economics & Political Science* 30. Reprinted as the Appendix to chap. 18 in Mundell (1968).

———. 1968. *International Economics.* New York: Macmillan.

———. 1971. "The International Distribution of Money in a Growing World Economy." In *Monetary Theory*. Pacific Palisades, California: Goodyear. Reprinted in Frenkel and Johnson, 1976.

Mussa, M. 1974. "Monetary Approach to Balance of Payments Analysis." *Journal of Money, Credit and Banking* 6 (3).

———. 1976a. "Tariffs and the Balance of Payments." In *The Monetary Approach to the Balance of Payments*, edited by J. Frenkel and H. G. Johnson. London: George Allen & Unwin.

———. 1976b. "The Exchange Rate, the Balance of Payments, and Monetary and Fiscal Policy under a Regime of Controlled Floating." *Scandinavian Journal of Economics* 78 (2).

————. 1977. "Real and Monetary Factors in a Dynamic Theory of Foreign Exchange." In *Proceedings* of the 1976 meeting of the Association of University Teachers of Economics, edited by R. Nobay and M. Artis.

Niehans, Jürg. 1975. "Some Doubts about the Efficacy of Monetary and Fiscal Policy under Flexible Exchange Rates." *Journal of International Economics* 5: 275–81.

————. 1968. "Monetary and Fiscal Policies in Open Economies: An Optimizing Approach." *Journal of Political Economy* 76, Part II: 893–920.

Pearce, I. F. 1961. "The Problem of the Balance of Payments." *International Economic Review* 2 (1).

Phelps, Edmund S. et al. 1970. *Microeconomic Foundations of Employment and Inflation Theory*. New York: Norton.

Phelps, E. S., and Taylor, J. B. 1977. "Stabilizing Powers of Monetary Policy under Rational Expectations." *Journal of Political Economy* 85 (1).

Raasche, R. 1973. "A Comparative Statics Analysis of Some Monetarist Propositions." St. Louis Federal Reserve Bank *Monthly Review* 55 (12).

Robinson, R. 1952. "A Graphical Analysis of the Foreign Trade Multiplier." *Economic Journal* 62: 546–64.

Rodriguez, C. 1976. "Money and Wealth in an Open Economy Income-Expenditure Model." In *The Monetary Approach to the Balance of Payments*, edited by J. Frenkel and H. G. Johnson. London: George Allen & Unwin.

Roper, Don E. 1971. "Macroeconomic Policies and the Distribution of the World Money Supply." *Quarterly Journal of Economics* 81: 119–46.

Saidi, Nasser. 1977. "Rational Expectations, Purchasing Power Parity and the Business Cycle." Processed September 1977.

Salter, W. E. 1959. "Internal and External Balance: The Role of Price and Expenditure Effects." *Economic Record* 35.

Sargent, T., and Wallace, N. 1975. "Rational Expectations, the Optimal Monetary Instrument, and the Optimal Money Supply Rule." *Journal of Political Economy* 83 (2).

————. 1976. "Rational Expectations and the Theory of Economic Policy." *Journal of Monetary Economics* 2 (2).

Stockman, Alan. 1977. "Relative Prices and Exchange Rate Determination in a Dynamic Model with Uncertainty." Processed January 1977.

————. 1978. "Risk, Information, and Forward Exchange Rates." In *The Economics of Exchange Rates: Selected Studies*, edited by J. Frenkel and H. G. Johnson. Reading, Mass.: Addison-Wesley.

Swan, T. 1960. "Economic Control in a Dependent Economy." *Economic Record* 36.

Swoboda, A. 1972. "Equilibrium, Quasi-equilibrium, and Macroeconomic Policy under Fixed Rates." *Quarterly Journal of Economics* 86 (1).

————. 1973. "Monetary Policy under Fixed Exchange Rates: Effectiveness, the Speed of Adjustment, and Proper Use." *Economica* (May).

————. 1974. "The Dual Exchange Rate System and Monetary Independence."

In *National Monetary Policies and the International Financial System*, edited by R. Z. Aliber. Chicago: University of Chicago Press.

————. 1976. "Monetary Approaches to Balance of Payments Theory." In *Recent Issues in International Monetary Economics*, edited by E. Claassen and P. Salin. Amsterdam: North-Holland.

Swoboda, A., and Dornbusch, R. 1973. "Adjustment, Policy, and Monetary Equilibrium in a Two-Country Model." In *International Trade and Money*, edited by M. Connolly and A. Swoboda. London: George Allen & Unwin.

Tinbergen, J. 1952. *On the Theory of Economic Policy*. Amsterdam: North-Holland.

Tobin, J. 1972. "Inflation and Unemployment." *American Economic Review* 62 (1).

Tsiang, S. C. 1961. "The Role of Money in Trade Balance Stability." *American Economic Review* 51 (5).

Whitman, M. 1970. "Policies for Internal and External Balance." Special Papers in International Economics, No. 9, Princeton University.

Comment

ALEXANDER K. SWOBODA

Michael Mussa's excellent survey of analytical models of macroeconomic interdependence provides us with a clear, useful, and synthetic overview of the state of the art as it has developed from Meade to Mundell et al. and of where its practitioners thought it was going in the middle 1970s. After a brief introduction, three sections analyze the comparative statics of the response of output and other variables to a number of disturbances (especially autonomous changes in either the supply of money or in aggregate real expenditure) within a useful synthetic two-country model under various permutations of assumptions concerning the exchange rate regime (fixed or flexible) and the degree of capital mobility (perfectly mobile or perfectly immobile). The penultimate section takes up some recent developments that enable one to introduce dynamic elements into the up-to-that-point (comparative) static analysis. These concern: the adjustment of asset stocks, a crucial element both for linking the short to the long run and for analyzing the evolution of the structure of the balance of payments through time; the adjustment of output to its long-run or "normal" value through the expectations-augmented Phillips curve; and the adjustment of the exchange rate to its long-run value through various forms of expectations mechanisms. In the concluding section, Mussa takes up three issues of importance for the design of macroeconomic policy in the open economy: the extent of independence is seen to depend in good part on lack of mobility and/or substitutability of goods and assets; the specific dynamics of adjustment and, hence, the appropriate policy are shown to hinge on relative speeds of adjustment in various markets; and the scope for systematic policy is contingent on the way in which information is spread and incorporated into decision-making—the rational expectations "revolution" extended to open economies.

Table 1 below summarizes the results of the Mundellian analysis of the transmission of monetary and fiscal disturbances that Mussa presents and extends in Sections II, III, and IV of his survey (especially by incorporating an explicit aggregate supply function, treating all cases in a two-country framework, and considering also autonomous changes in wages and in the exchange rate, i.e., devaluations).

The results in Table 1 differ in two minor respects from those noted by Mussa. First, they recognize (as Mundell does) that, under fixed rates and capital mobility, the redistribution of money and bonds toward a country that engages in the fiscal expansion that Mussa emphasizes, *may* be so large as to result in a decrease of income in the home country, hence (dQ/dg^*) $\geqq 0$ rather than > 0. Second, with capital mobility and flexible rates, transmission may be negative; this is to reflect the possibility of the Laursen–Metzler effect.

The table brings out one conclusion that is somewhat surprising, namely, that under flexible exchange rates, transmission tends to be negative—booms abroad tend to create depressions at home—except in the case of autonomous variations in real aggregate demand (fiscal policy) under capital mobility. This conclusion, though easily explained within the confines of the Meade–Mundell–Fleming variety of models, seems at variance with both intuition and casual empirical evidence. Inquiring why helps bring out both the limitations of our current knowledge as summarized by Mussa and the required directions for future research, both analytical and empirical.

On an intuitive level, suppose Rhode Island separated from the United States, created its own currency, central bank, and fiscal authority, and let the exchange rate float. Suppose now that there was a severe depression in

Table 1

	Fixed exchange rate	Flexible exchange rate
Capital immobility	$\dfrac{dQ}{dg^*} > 0$	$\dfrac{dQ}{dg^*} \leq 0$
	$\dfrac{dQ}{dM^*} > 0$	$\dfrac{dQ}{dM^*} \leq 0$
Capital mobility	$\dfrac{dQ}{dg^*} \geqq 0$	$\dfrac{dQ}{dg^*} > 0$
	$\dfrac{dQ}{dM^*} > 0$	$\dfrac{dQ}{dM^*} < 0$

the United States, would one expect that Rhode Island's floating rate would insulate it from the depression, or even help create a boom in the local economy? The answer must be no, but it immediately raises the question: What is the missing link in the transmission mechanism?

Mussa does list a number of possibilities in Section IIIA of his chapter. Of these, two would tend to make for positive transmissions: the rise in the price level that accompanies depreciation of the home currency may create a squeeze on real cash balances; and the rise in import prices may raise the price of, and hence lower the output of, exportables directly through the supply function. Presumably, however, both these transmission effects could be offset by appropriate macroeconomic policy. I suspect one should look elsewhere for a direct link in transmission—including some of the dynamic effects Mussa mentions. First, the degree of money illusion in a small open economy is likely to be quite limited: this makes for a vertical aggregate supply curve (or rapid convergence to such a curve) and little direct effect of price-level variations on aggregate output. Second, a fall in the volume of exports[1] is compensated for, in the model, by increased home consumption of exportables and decreased consumption of imports (or importables). In any event, neither the volume nor the composition of production changes.

There are at least three reasons why one may expect home production to fall as a result of a fall in foreign output and demand. First, suppose the home country produces both importables and exportables and the fall in foreign demand results in a worsening of the home country's terms of trade; to maintain full employment the production of importables must increase at the expense of that of exportables. This is likely to cause unemployment, at least in the short run. Second, suppose, alternatively, that the home country produces and consumes a composite traded good and nontraded goods; the fall in foreign demand then creates an excess supply of traded goods and a fall in their price relative to nontraded goods. Maintenance of full employment would again require a shift in the composition of production, this time towards nontraded goods. Third, in both these cases real wages must fall in terms of either importables or nontraded goods, as well as in terms of exportables. To the extent that the fall in real wages is resisted, unemployment results and transmission of disturbances is direct.

One can think of several further channels of direct transmission of real

---

[1] In terms of comparative statics, exports may either fall or rise as a result of a fall in foreign income. They will rise if the elasticity of demand for imports is sufficiently low to call for a large enough depreciation of the home currency. Algebraically, the change in home export volume due to a change in g^* is, under the assumption of perfectly price-elastic supplies of national output,

$$\frac{dX}{dg^*} = \frac{1}{1 + \dfrac{\eta_x}{\eta_m - 1}} \cdot \left(\frac{m^*}{m^* + s^*}\right).$$

business cycles under flexible rates. For instance, a downturn in economic activity in one important country due to falling *expected* rates of return on investment, or to increased uncertainty about these returns, may well have similar effects on expectations abroad and on investment there. Furthermore, a development that affects the prospective profitability of a large industrial sector in one part of the world is likely to affect competing industries abroad in the same direction. That is, for some purposes, the relevant unit for analysis may well be a particular industrial sector, wherever located, rather than the individual national economy.

Belaboring the above points would not be worthwhile were it not for the fact that empirical evidence seems to point to some direct transmission of real disturbances under flexible rates, and that the solution of a number of important current policy problems requires an understanding of the channels of transmission.

Empirical evidence on the channels and direction of transmission under flexible exchange rates is scant, partly because increased flexibility of rates is a quite recent development. One study of the postwar Canadian experience, however, does indicate that, though flexible rates do allow for divergent trends in the price level, the degree of synchronization of real economic activity between Canada and the United States was not significantly affected by the exchange rate regime.[2] More recent experience also suggests a number of direct transmission effects: the 1973–74 upturn and the 1974–76 recession were shared by most industrial countries; experience seems more diverse in the upturn of the past two years. One may, of course, wonder whether the upturn of 1973–74 was not the lagged consequence of common policies under fixed rates and the subsequent recession the common reaction to the common "outside" oil shock.

The answer to these questions does bear on the proper conduct of macroeconomic policy, both national and international. If real national economic activity were insulated from foreign real disturbances by flexible rates, one would be at pains to understand the "locomotive" country controversy or the call for coordinated economic expansion in the OECD countries.[3] If monetary disturbances give rise to negative transmission under flexible rates and capital mobility, the United States should urge Germany to adopt a restrictive monetary policy to sustain U.S. expansion—and European complaints about U.S. expansion being of a beggar-thy-neighbor character would not be entirely unfounded. Furthermore, the current situation would call for coordinated fiscal and not monetary expansion.

These considerations suggest that there is ample room for further research, both empirical and theoretical, in the field so aptly surveyed by

[2] See Bonomo and Tanner (1972).

[3] Of course, the model's home country suffers a loss of real income if its terms of trade worsen in the process of insulation, even if output and employment do not fall. It would therefore still prefer to see a booming rather than slumping world economy.

Mussa. Though the foundations are likely to remain, one can hope that future surveyors of the subject will be able to report substantial progress on issues that are of such obvious policy import.

REFERENCE

Bonomo, Vittorio, and Tanner, J. Ernest. 1972. "Canadian Sensitivity to Economic Cycles in the United States." *Review of Economics and Statistics* 54: 1–8.

CHAPTER SIX

On Modeling the Economic
Linkages among Countries

RAY C. FAIR

I. INTRODUCTION

This chapter is concerned with modeling the economic linkages among countries. Although there are by now a number of multicountry macro-econometric models in existence, it seems safe to say with respect to the treatment of capital flows and exchange rates that econometric work has not kept pace with theoretical developments. Since Mundell's pioneering theoretical work (1968) in the 1960s, the potential empirical importance of capital flows among countries has been known, and yet in most multi-country econometric models capital flows are either ignored completely or else taken to be exogenous. This usually means that exchange rates are also taken to be exogenous, which in the present regime of floating exchange rates is clearly an important limitation. Econometric model-builders are not, of course, unaware of these limitations. For a number of reasons, econometric work in this area is difficult, and these difficulties have undoubtedly impeded progress. One difficulty is the lack of good data for a number of countries. Another is the sheer size of the task of linking a number of single-country models together. Dealing with hundreds or thousands of equations is painstaking, and there is a natural tendency in this type of work to be less concerned with theoretical purity than with the practical issue of getting the model running.

Theoretical work in this area has, on the other hand, ignored a number of important economic linkages among countries that are accounted for in multicountry econometric models. The two-country theoretical models ·of the type surveyed by Myhrman (1976) and Mussa (1978), for example,

The research described in this paper was financed by grant SOC77–03274 from the National Science Foundation. I am indebted to Rudiger Dornbusch for many useful suggestions regarding this paper. I would also like to thank Franco Modigliani and David Richardson for helpful comments.

are too small to incorporate all the main features and links in the international economy, particularly with respect to price and wage behavior. There is thus currently a fairly wide gap in international economics between theoretical and econometric work, the former emphasizing capital flows and exchange rates at the expense of other features of the economy, and the latter emphasizing some of the other features of the economy at the expense of capital flows and exchange rates.

This chapter has three main purposes. The first is to present a comparison of the quantitative properties of seven multicountry econometric models; the second is to discuss briefly a quasiempirical model of the author's that has the detail of large-scale econometric models and yet also accounts for all capital flows and allows for the endogenous determination of the exchange rate; and the third is to suggest an approach for the future construction of multicountry econometric models.

The comparison of the quantitative properties of the seven models is presented in Section II. The evidence presented in this section should give one a general idea of the current range of estimated effects of U.S. actions on the economies of other countries. Given the diversity of the seven models, their quantitative properties are actually closer than one might have expected, although there are still some very large differences. With one exception, however, the results from the models are based on the assumption of exogenous capital flows and exchange rates, and this should be kept in mind in interpreting the results.

The quasiempirical model is discussed in Section III. This model, which will be called Model A, is a 180-equation two-country model. It was constructed by linking the 84-equation econometric model of the U.S. economy in Fair (1976) to itself. Model A is "quasiempirical" in that half of it is an actual empirical model of the United States and half is completely made up. This model accounts for all flows of funds between the two countries and allows for the endogenous determination of the exchange rate. It also has, of course, much more detail and many more links between the two countries than do the standard two-country theoretical models in the literature. Model A is an attempt to bridge, in part, the gap between theoretical and econometric work mentioned above. As will be seen, the properties of this model are quite sensitive to the treatment of capital flows and the exchange rate. This evidence, along with what is already known from the theoretical literature, rather strongly indicates that further work on making capital flows and exchange rates endogenous in multicountry econometric models is needed before much confidence can be placed in their properties.

The suggested approach for the future construction of multicountry econometric models is presented in Section IV. At the risk of some oversimplification, it will be useful to distinguish between two approaches to making capital flows and exchange rates endogenous in a multicountry econometric model—a "large" approach and a "small" approach. The large approach is to take a model like LINK and modify the single-country models in it to account for all flows of funds among the domestic and foreign sectors.[1] The problem with this approach is, again, the size of the task. It is a tedious job to account for all flows of funds in a large single-country model,[2] and the amount of effort involved in doing this for all the single-country models in LINK, some of which currently have fairly weak monetary sectors, is enormous.

The small approach, which is the approach discussed in Section IV of this chapter, is to specify and estimate a relatively small, highly aggregated multicountry model, but a model in which all flows of funds among the countries are accounted for. The emphasis in this approach is on the determination of the key aggregate macroeconomic variables in the system (e.g., prices, interest rates, and exchange rates), and on accounting for all the aggregate flows of funds and goods among the countries. The aim of this approach is to end up with an econometric model that, within its aggregate framework, accounts for all the adding-up constraints and is relatively easy to estimate and analyze. The aim is also to end up with a model that can, if desired, be fairly easily disaggregated later without changing its basic structure. In short, then, the small approach is to start with a small model that accounts for all the aggregate flows of funds and get larger later, rather than, as with the large approach, to start with a large model that does not account for all the flows of funds and work later on accounting for them.[3]

II. A COMPARISON OF THE QUANTITATIVE PROPERTIES OF SEVEN MULTICOUNTRY MODELS

There is by now a considerable amount of evidence on the quantitative properties of various multicountry models. The purpose of this section is not, however, to review this evidence in detail, since a fairly extensive review is already contained in Deardorff and Stern (1977). The purpose is rather to take from this evidence results for a common experiment for each model and compare these results across models. The common experiment is

---

[1] Hickman (1974), p. 203, has stated that work is currently in progress on making capital movements endogenous in the LINK model.

[2] See the 84-equation model in Fair (1976) for an example of a single-country model in which all flows of funds are accounted for. See, in particular, Section 1.3 for a description of the linking (by sector) of the U.S. national income accounts with the flow-of-funds accounts.

[3] The approach of Berner et al. (1976), who are concerned with the specification and estimation of a five-country model, is perhaps somewhere in between the small and large approaches. There is an attempt in this approach to account for capital flows, although the proposed treatment of exchange-rate determination as described in Berner et al. (1976) is suspect. Their proposed single-country models are also much larger than the proposed single-country models in Section IV of this chapter.

Table 1. Percentage Income Change of Country Induced by a Sustained One Percent Autonomous Increase in U.S. Income

Model	Time Period (years)	Country					
		U.S.	Canada	Austria	Belgium	France	Germany
MM	1	1.56	.27				
LINK	1	1.18	.31	.05	.05	.02	.04
DS	1	2.00	.72	.13	.39	.13	.19
METEOR	1	2.42	.65		.23	.12	.19
LINK	2	1.87	.56	.11	.09	.04	.08
METEOR	2	2.86	1.29		.46	.30	.43
RDX2–MPS[a]	2	2.11	.10				
RDX2–MPS[b]	2	2.11	.10				
RDX2–MPS[c]	2	2.12	.19				
RDX2–MPS[d]	2	2.11	.21				
MM	Long Run	4.11	.93				
LINK	3	2.58	.86	.24	.15	.06	.14
METEOR	5	8.33	4.19		1.66	1.49	1.81
OECD	Long Run	2.00	.70				.50
RDX2–MPS[a]	6	1.65	.14				
RDX2–MPS[b]	6	2.02	−.21				
RDX2–MPS[c]	6	1.66	.01				
RDX2–MPS[d]	6	1.99	.09				
RDX2–MPS[a]	8	−.83	−.29				
RDX2–MPS[b]	8	−.95	−1.06				
RDX2–MPS[c]	8	−.85	−.83				
RDX2–MPS[d]	8	−.92	−.80				

[a] Migration and all capital flows suppressed; fixed exchange rate.
[b] Migration and all capital flows suppressed; flexible exchange rate.

an autonomous increase in U.S. income of one percent. Some adjustment of the results for some models had to be made in order to make them comparable and, even given these adjustments, it should be stressed that the results are only approximately comparable.[4] The present comparison should give one a general idea of the different properties of the models, but it is by no means a rigorous evaluation of the differences.

The seven models are: (1) the Morishima–Murata (MM) trade-multiplier model (1972), (2) the LINK model (Ball 1973), (3) the OECD model (Samuelson 1973), (4) one of the multiplier models in De Rosa and Smeal (DS) (1976), (5) the METEOR model of the Netherlands Central Planning Bureau (1975), (6) the price-linkage model Kwack (KWACK) (1975), and (7) the RDX2–MPS model of Canada and the United States

[4] For example, the properties of nonlinear models are different for different starting points, and the starting points were not all the same for the results presented in this section. The results also may be sensitive to what is assumed about monetary policy, although most of the models considered here have either no or a weak monetary sector. Finally, the properties of nonlinear models are different in absolute value for positive and negative changes, and for some of the results presented in this section the U.S. policy change was negative rather than positive. For present purposes, the signs of the effects were merely reversed when the U.S. policy change was negative.

Table 1 (Continued)

Model	Time Period (years)	Country					
		Italy	Sweden	U.K.	Japan	Australia	Nether-lands
MM	1			.14	.19		
LINK	1	.08	.10	.08	.13	.03	
DS	1	.15	.19	.19	.17	.12	.33
METEOR	1	.15		.19	.22		.17
LINK	2	.17	.19	.21	.27	.09	
METEOR	2	.34		.45	.45		.36
RDX2–MPS[a]	2						
RDX2–MPS[b]	2						
RDX2–MPS[c]	2						
RDX2–MPS[d]	2						
MM	Long Run			.14	.87		
LINK	3	.31	.33	.35	.40	.24	
METEOR	5	1.38		1.83	1.79		1.38
OECD	Long Run				.35		
RDX2–MPS[a]	6						
RDX2–MPS[b]	6						
RDX2–MPS[c]	6						
RDX2–MPS[d]	6						
RDX2–MPS[a]	8						
RDX2–MPS[b]	8						
RDX2–MPS[c]	8						
RDX2–MPS[d]	8						

[c] Full transmission; fixed exchange rate.
[d] Full transmission; flexible exchange rate.

(Helliwell 1974). The results presented in this section are taken from the following seven sources: Morishima and Murata (1972) for the MM model, Hickman (1974) for the LINK model, OECD (1975) for the OECD model, De Rosa and Smeal (1976) for the DS model, Deardorff and Stern (1977) for the METEOR model, Kwack (1975) for the KWACK model, and Helliwell (1974) for the RDX2–MPS model. The income effects from the autonomous increase in U.S. income are presented in Table 1, and the price effects are presented in Table 2. Table 3 contains a description of how the numbers in Tables 1 and 2 were obtained. The results in the two tables are fairly self-explanatory, and so only a brief discussion of them will be presented here.

Except for some of the results for RDX2–MPS, the income effects in Table 1 are all positive. For the one-year results, the DS effects are larger than the LINK effects, which is due in large part to the use in the DS model of larger expenditure multipliers than exist in the LINK model. The METEOR effects are also larger than the LINK effects, and except for Canada, the MM effects are slightly larger than the LINK effects. For the

Table 2. Percentage Price Change of Country Induced by a Sustained One Percent Autonomous Increase in U.S. Income

Model	Time Period (years)	Country					
		U.S.	Canada	Austria	Belgium	France	Germany
LINK	1	.310	.000	.010	.000	.010	.050
METEOR	1	−.084	−.029		.005	.006	−.000
KWACK	1	−.013	−.003	.000	.000		.000
LINK	2	.290	.170	.010	−.010	.000	.110
METEOR	2	.152	.040		.053	.035	.031
RDX2–MPS[a]	2	.210	−.060				
RDX2–MPS[b]	2	.210	−.050				
RDX2–MPS[c]	2	.210	−.020				
RDX2–MPS[d]	2	.210	−.010				
LINK	3	.690	.640	.040	−.010	.020	.230
METEOR	5	1.050	.916		.627	.453	.480
KWACK	6	.373	.267	.003	.027		.027
RDX2–MPS[a]	6	2.770	.450				
RDX2–MPS[b]	6	2.910	.220				
RDX2–MPS[c]	6	2.780	.440				
RDX2–MPS[d]	6	2.880	.540				
RDX2–MPS[a]	8	5.090	1.000				
RDX2–MPS[b]	8	5.640	.060				
RDX2–MPS[c]	8	5.110	1.140				
RDX2–MPS[d]	8	5.550	1.140				

Model		Country					
		Italy	Sweden	U.K.	Japan	Australia	Netherlands
LINK	1	−.010		.000	−.020	−.010	
METEOR	1	.009		.008	.003		.018
KWACK	1	.000	.000	.000	−.003	.000	.000
LINK	2	−.020		−.060	−.030	−.030	
METEOR	2	.053		.058	.041		.076
RDX2–MPS[a]	2						
RDX2–MPS[b]	2						
RDX2–MPS[c]	2						
RDX2–MPS[d]	2						
LINK	3	.010		.000	−.030	−.100	
METEOR	5	.565		.629	.509		.647
KWACK	6	.030	.023	.020	.107	.107	.047
RDX2–MPS[a]	6						
RDX2–MPS[b]	6						
RDX2–MPS[c]	6						
RDX2–MPS[d]	6						
RDX2–MPS[a]	8						
RDX2–MPS[b]	8						
RDX2–MPS[c]	8						
RDX2–MPS[d]	8						

[a] Migration and all capital flows suppressed; fixed exchange rate.
[b] Migration and all capital flows suppressed; flexible exchange rate.
[c] Full transmission; fixed exchange rate.
[d] Full transmission; flexible exchange rate.

Table 3. Sources for the Results in Tables 1 and 2

Each number in Table 1 is $\Delta Y_j/Y_j \div \Delta A_i/Y_i$, and each number in Table 2 is $\Delta P_j/P_j \div \Delta A_i/Y_i$, where

ΔA_i = autonomous change in U.S. real income,
ΔY_j = induced change in the real income of country j,
Y_j = level of real income of country j,
ΔP_j = induced change in the price level of country j,
P_j = price level of country j.
(country j may be the U.S.)

Model	Source	Discussion
MM	Morishima–Murata (1972)	One-year values of $\Delta Y_j/\Delta A_i$ taken from Table 5 (p. 325); long-run values of $\Delta Y_j/\Delta A_i$ taken from Table 6 (p. 325); and values of Y_j taken from Table 8 (p. 328). Model is linear, so starting point does not matter. Values of Y_j are for 1964.
LINK	Hickman (1974)	Numbers in Table 1 taken directly from Tables 2–4 (pp. 211–13), and numbers in Table 2 taken directly from Tables 6–8 (pp. 218–20). Starting point was 1973.
DS	DeRosa–Smeal (1976)	The numbers in Table 1 are the numbers in Table 9 (p. 10*a*) multiplied by 2.0, the U.S. expenditure multiplier. The results are based on the following assumptions: use of Houthakker–Magee (1969) estimated income elasticities of the demand for imports in each country; use of a U.S. expenditure multiplier of 2.0; and use of an expenditure multiplier for each of the other countries of 1.5. The year was 1974.
METEOR	Deardorff–Stern (1977)	Numbers in Table 1 taken directly from Table 28 (p. 96), and numbers in Table 2 taken directly from Table 29 (p. 97).
OECD	(1975)	Numbers in Table 1 taken directly from Table 8B (p. 34). The effects are assumed here to be long-run, although no time period is given in OECD (1975).
RDX2–MPS	Helliwell (1974)	Full transmission numbers in Tables 1 and 2 taken directly from Table 1-A (p. 259), with signs reversed, and numbers in Tables 1 and 2, when migration and all capital flows are suppressed, taken directly from Table 5-A (p. 273), with signs reversed. Starting point was 1963.
KWACK	Kwack (1975)	The numbers in Table 2 are the numbers in Table 9 (p. 27) divided by -3.0. The effects in Table 9 are for a one percentage point increase in the unemployment rate; and from the Okun's Law equation for the United States in Table 6 (p. 20), a one percentage point increase in the unemployment rate corresponds roughly to a three percent decrease in real output. Starting point was 1968.

two-year results, the METEOR effects are again larger than the LINK effects. For Canada, the RDX2–MPS effects are considerably smaller than both the LINK and METEOR effects. For the three-year or more results, the METEOR effects are quite large relative to the others. The MM, LINK, and OECD effects for Canada are fairly close, as are the LINK and OECD effects for Japan. The RDX2–MPS effects for Canada are small for the six-year period, but fairly large and negative for the eight-year period. In general, the results for the RDX2–MPS model show evidence of a considerable amount of cycling.

For the one-year results in Table 2, the price effects are all fairly small, except perhaps for the LINK effect for the United States. This is also true for the two-year results. For the three-year or more results, on the other hand, the METEOR and RDX2–MPS effects are fairly large, as are the LINK effects for the United States and Canada. The KWACK effects are still small, and the three-year LINK effects for Belgium, Japan, and Australia are still negative.

To conclude, it is partly a matter of judgment whether one feels that the differences in Tables 1 and 2 are large or small. Clearly, however, the five-year METEOR results are quite different from the others, as are the RDX2–MPS results for Canada in Table 1. On the other hand, the MM and LINK differences in Table 1 seem fairly small, and many of the differences for the one-year results in Table 1 are also small.

With respect to the possible sensitivity of a model's properties to the treatment of capital flows and exchange rates, it should be noted that for the RDX2–MPS model the two- and six-year results in Tables 1 and 2 are not very sensitive to the treatment of capital flows and the exchange rate, but the eight-year results are. For the case in which migration and capital flows are suppressed, the eight-year income effect for Canada is -0.29 in the fixed-exchange-rate case and -1.06 in the flexible-exchange-rate case. The corresponding price effects are 1.000 and 0.060. For the case in which migration and capital flows are not suppressed, the eight-year effects are not sensitive to the treatment of the exchange rate. The income effect is 1.140 in both the fixed- and flexible-exchange-rate cases, and the price effect is -0.83 in the fixed-exchange-rate case and -0.80 in the flexible-exchange-rate case. The overall results for the RDX2–MPS model are thus somewhat mixed with respect to the sensitivity question.

III. A QUASIEMPIRICAL TWO-COUNTRY MODEL

As mentioned in the Introduction, the model discussed in this section (Model A) is an attempt to bridge in part the current gap between theoretical and econometric work in international economics. The fact that the properties of Model A turn out to be quite sensitive to the treatment of capital flows and the exchange rate casts some doubt on the reliability of the results presented in Section II. The properties of Model A also cast some doubt on the reliability of the results from the standard two-country theoretical models in the literature. In particular, the price links among countries that these standard models ignore appear to be important, at least as reflected in Model A.

Model A is a special case of a more general theoretical model of the balance of payments that is presented and discussed in Fair (1978*b*). Since Model A was constructed by linking the 84-equation U.S. econometric model in Fair (1976) to itself, the United States is half of the world in the model. Space limitations prevent a detailed description of Model A here. It is also discussed in Fair (1978*b*), and an appendix to this paper is available that contains a complete list of the 180 equations. The following is a brief discussion of some of its key features.

There are four sectors for each of the two countries in the model: household, firm, bank, and government. All flows of funds among the eight sectors are accounted for. This means that any financial saving or dissaving of a sector in a period results in the change in at least one of its assets or liabilities, that any financial asset of one sector is a corresponding liability of some other sector, and that the government budget constraints of the two countries are accounted for. The model is one in which stock and flow effects are completely integrated. The exchange rate, for example, has an effect on both stock and flow variables, and in the flexible-exchange-rate case it is simultaneously determined along with the other endogenous variables. As discussed in Fair (1978*b*), this integration of stock and flow effects is not true of other approaches to the balance of payments and is one of the main distinctions between Model A and other models.

Each country specializes in the production of one good, and the goods are traded. In addition to the obvious links between the two countries with respect to capital and goods flows, there are important price links between the two countries: in each country the price of the imported good has an effect on the price of the home-produced good. In other words, a price change in one country has a direct effect on the price change in the other country and vice versa. Wages are also endogenous in the model, and prices affect wages as well as vice versa.

One important feature of the model with respect to prices is that prices have, other things being equal, a negative effect on demand. One would expect, for the usual microeconomic reasons, the demand for a good to be a negative function of its price, and this is in fact the case in the U.S. econometric model upon which Model A is based. Although this may seem to be an obvious characteristic for a model to have, in most macroeconometric models consumption is not a direct function of prices, but only of income terms and the like. The consumption equations in Model A differ from the usual consumption equations in macroeconometric models in having explanatory variables that are consistent with microeconomic theory.[5]

In the more general theoretical model of the balance of payments in Fair (1978*b*), expectations of future exchange rates have an effect on the decisions of the private sector in each country. In the special case of Model A, however, this is not true because exchange-rate expectations were not explicitly taken into account in the 84-equation U.S. econometric model upon which Model A is based. This is clearly an important limitation of Model A, and it should be kept in mind in interpreting the following results. The treatment of exchange-rate expectations in multicountry models is discussed in the next section.

In Fair (1978*b*) the properties of Model A were analyzed in four different regimes: the regimes of (1) zero capital mobility and a fixed exchange rate, (2) zero capital mobility and a flexible exchange rate, (3) perfect capital mobility and a fixed exchange rate, and (4) perfect capital mobility and a flexible exchange rate. For the perfect mobility regimes it was necessary to make some assumption about exchange-rate expectations in order to link together the interest rates in the two countries, and for this purpose exchange-rate expectations were assumed to be static. This means that the interest rates in the two countries are always the same in the perfect mobility regimes in Model A.

A summary of the results from the analysis of Model A's properties is presented in Table 4. Two basic experiments were performed for these results: a monetary policy experiment and a fiscal policy experiment. For the monetary policy experiment, the amount of government securities outstanding of country 1 was decreased, a standard expansionary open-market operation on the part of the monetary authorities of country 1.[6] For the fiscal policy experiment, the value of goods purchased by the government of country 1 was increased. For this latter experiment, no change in the amount of government securities outstanding was made, which means that any government deficit that results from the increase in purchases is financed by an increase in nonborrowed reserves (high-powered

---

[5] See Section 1.1 in Fair (1976) for a discussion of the differences between the consumption equations in the 84-equation U.S. econometric model (and thus in Model A) and the consumption equations in other macroeconometric models. One of the three main features of the theoretical model in Fair (1974), upon which the econometric model in Fair (1976) is based, is the derivation of the decisions of the individual agents in the economy from the assumption of maximizing behavior. The other two main features of this model are an explicit treatment of possible disequilibrium effects and the accounting of all flows of funds in the system.

[6] The experiment in Fair (1978*b*) was actually one in which the amount of government securities outstanding was increased (a contractionary action) rather than decreased. All the results in this earlier paper are in fact for contractionary monetary and fiscal actions. Given the results in Section II of this chapter, it seemed best in the present section to talk about expansionary rather than contractionary actions, and so for purposes of the discussion in this section all the signs in Fair (1978*b*) have been reversed.

Table 4. Results for Model A: Effects after Three-Quarters

I. Monetary Policy Experiment (Decrease in government securities outstanding of country 1 of 1.25.)

Changes are *not* in percentage terms.

		Price Lags in Import Equations			No Price Lags in Import Equations	
Country 2	Country 1	Real Output Change Exchange Rate:			Real Output Change	
		Fixed	Flexible		Fixed	Flexible
Capital Mobility:	Zero	0.94 / 0.20	1.39 / −0.18	Zero	0.86 / 0.25	0.63 / 0.41
	Perfect	0.62 / 0.59	−0.41 / 1.68	Perfect	0.63 / 0.59	0.51 / 0.74

	Price Level Change			Price Level Change	
	Fixed	Flexible		Fixed	Flexible
Zero	−0.001 / −0.016	−0.159 / 0.173	Zero	0.016 / −0.026	0.117 / −0.165
Perfect	−0.015 / −0.014	0.867 / −0.904	Perfect	−0.015 / −0.014	0.158 / −0.185

II. Fiscal Policy Experiment (Money-financed increase in government purchases of goods of country 1 of 1.25.) These results are comparable to those in Tables 1 and 2.

Changes are in percentage terms.

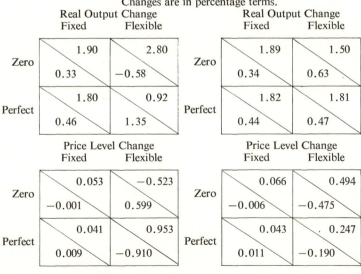

	Real Output Change			Real Output Change	
	Fixed	Flexible		Fixed	Flexible
Zero	1.90 / 0.33	2.80 / −0.58	Zero	1.89 / 0.34	1.50 / 0.63
Perfect	1.80 / 0.46	0.92 / 1.35	Perfect	1.82 / 0.44	1.81 / 0.47

	Price Level Change			Price Level Change	
	Fixed	Flexible		Fixed	Flexible
Zero	0.053 / −0.001	−0.523 / 0.599	Zero	0.066 / −0.006	0.494 / −0.475
Perfect	0.041 / 0.009	0.953 / −0.910	Perfect	0.043 / 0.011	0.247 / −0.190

(*Table 4   Notes*)

Notes:

    1. The monetary policy results are taken from Fair (1978*b*), and the fiscal policy results are taken from an earlier version of the paper: "A Model of the World Economy," Cowles Foundation Discussion Paper No. 430, April 27, 1976.

    2. The results for the monetary policy experiment have not been adjusted except for the change in sign discussed in footnote 6 and for multiplication of the price level changes by 100. The numbers are merely the total induced changes in real income after three quarters and the total induced changes in the price level after three quarters (ΔY_j and ΔP_j in the notation in Table 3).

    3. The results for the fiscal policy experiment have been adjusted and are as in Tables 1 and 2. The real output changes are $\Delta Y_j / Y_j \div \Delta A_i / Y_i$ and the price level changes are $\Delta P_j / P_j \div \Delta A_i / Y_i$, where the value of ΔA_i is -1.25. For these calculations the values for Y_i and Y_j were taken to be 169.4, the actual U.S. value in 1971IV, and the values for P_i and P_j were taken to be 1.26, also the actual U.S. value in 1971IV.

    4. The starting quarter for the experiments was 1971I, a quarter that is at or near the bottom of a contraction.

money). In other words, this latter experiment is a money-financed fiscal policy change. The effects of these two experiments after three quarters are presented in Table 4 for two variables for each country, real output and the domestic price level.

Results are also presented in Table 4 for two versions of the import-demand equations. The first version is the actual estimated equation for the demand for imports in the U.S. econometric model in Fair (1976). In this version there are price lags: prices affect the demand for imports with a lag of one or two quarters. In the second version these lags have been eliminated: imports respond in the current quarter to a change in prices.

The following is a brief discussion of some of the main features of the results in Table 4. Space limitations again prevent an extensive discussion here, and the reader is referred to Fair (1978*b*) for more detail. It should be stressed that the following discussion is somewhat loose. Reference is sometimes made to a change in one endogenous variable "causing," "leading to," or "resulting in" a change in another endogenous variable or variables. This discussion, while useful pedagogically, is loose because the model is simultaneous. Strictly speaking, each endogenous variable in the model affects and is affected by all the other endogenous variables. It should also be stressed that the effects in Table 4 are effects after only three quarters; they are of the nature of short-run effects. It is particularly important to keep this in mind when comparing the price-lag and no-price-lag cases. While the results for these two cases are sometimes quite different in Table 4, these differences are likely to lessen as the length of the period after the change increases.

Consider first in Table 4 the monetary policy experiment. In the fixed/perfect regime the monetary policy change has almost identical effects on the two countries. In this regime it makes no difference with respect to the aggregate effects in which country the open-market operation takes place. Therefore, since the two countries in the model are virtually the same, the effects on the two countries are virtually the same. In the fixed/zero regime, on the other hand, the effects on output in country 1 are greater than they are in country 2. This is because in this regime the monetary policy change lowers the interest rate more in country 1 than in country 2.

In the two fixed-exchange-rate regimes the results are not sensitive to whether or not there are price lags in the import equations. In these two regimes the changes in prices are not very large, and so the results are not very sensitive to what one assumes about the price responsiveness of imports.

In the flexible/perfect regime the expansionary monetary policy in country 1 actually has a negative effect on country 1's real output in the case in which there are price lags in the import equations. The reason for this is as follows. The expansionary monetary policy results in this case in a depreciation of country 1's currency (which is needed to keep the interest rates in the two countries the same[7]). This then results in a higher domestic price level in country 1 (since the price of country 1's imports is higher) and a lower domestic price level in country 2 (since the price of country 2's imports is lower). As mentioned above, a higher price level in a country has, other things being equal, a negative effect on demand. It turned out in this experiment that the negative effect on output from the increase in the price level in country 1 was large enough to offset the positive effects induced by the policy change, so that there was a net contraction in output in country 1. In country 2, on the other hand, the positive effect on output from the decrease in its price level and the other positive effects induced by the policy change resulted in an expansion in output.

Remember that the results just cited are for the case in which there are price lags in the import equations. Because of these lags, the depreciation of country 1's currency has no direct immediate effect on decreasing its demand for imports or on increasing country 2's demand for country 1's exports. In the no-price-lag case, on the other hand, this channel is open and, in this case, as can be seen in Table 4, there is no longer a contraction in country 1's output in the flexible/perfect regime. The output increase is, however, smaller in country 1 than in country 2, and this is again due to the negative effect (through the price level) of the devaluation of country 1's currency on country 1's output.

The flexible/zero regime is unusual and probably not very realistic. In the price-lag case in this regime the expansionary monetary policy in country 1 actually leads to a contraction in country 2's output. The reason for this

---

[7] Remember that exchange-rate expectations are assumed to be static for the experiments, and so the interest rates in the two countries are the same in the perfect capital mobility regimes.

result is as follows. In the flexible/zero regime the financial saving of country 1 (its balance of payments on current account) cannot change, since there is no capital mobility and no change in international reserve holdings. If imports do not respond to current price changes, as is true in the price-lag case, then the adjustment to the expansionary monetary policy must take place through a terms-of-trade effect. Country 1's currency must appreciate to turn the terms of trade in favor of country 1 to offset the decrease in its balance of payments on current account that would otherwise have taken place as a result of country 1's expansionary monetary policy. The depreciation of country 2's currency leads to an increase in its price level, which is, other things being equal, contractionary. This contractionary effect was strong enough in the present experiment so as to lead to a net contraction in country 2's output.

In the no-price-lag case in the flexible/zero regime, real output in country 2 expands rather than contracts. In this case country 1's currency depreciates rather than appreciates, which results, other things being equal, in a decrease in its imports and an increase in its exports. The offset to the decrease in country 1's balance of payments on current account that would otherwise have taken place as a result of its expansionary monetary policy occurs in the no-price-lag case through a change in imports and exports rather than through a change in the terms of trade. There is thus no depreciation of country 2's currency and so no contractionary effect on its output from this source.

One further point about the results for the monetary policy experiment in Table 4 should be noted, which is that in the fixed-exchange-rate regimes the expansionary monetary policy leads to a slight decrease in the price levels in both countries. This is explained by the fact that interest rates have, other things being equal, a positive effect on prices in the model.[8] An expansionary monetary policy leads to a decrease in interest rates and thus from this source to a decrease in prices. An expansionary monetary policy also has positive effects on prices through other sources, but the net effect on prices after three quarters is still negative for the results in Table 4.

The fiscal policy experiment reported in Table 4 is a combination of a direct increase in the sales of country 1's good and of an expansionary monetary policy. Since the monetary-policy effects have already been discussed, the further effects from the increase in sales will not be discussed here.[9]

---

[8] See footnote 1 in the Appendix for an explanation of this.

[9] The fiscal policy results in Table 4 are directly comparable in terms of units to the results in Tables 1 and 2. It should be kept in mind in comparing these results, however, that fiscal policy effects in Model A are sensitive to what one assumes about monetary policy (see Fair [1978a]). Quite different fiscal policy effects would have been obtained for the results in Table 4 had something different been assumed about monetary policy. This sensitivity is, of course, not necessarily true of the models considered in Section II, since, as mentioned in footnote 4, many of these models have either no monetary sector or a weak one.

This completes the discussion of the results in Table 4. It is clear that the properties of Model A are sensitive to the choice of regime, which, as mentioned in the Introduction, indicates the need to make capital flows and exchange rates endogenous in multicountry econometric models before much confidence can be placed in their properties.

The discussion of the results in Table 4 also shows the importance of price effects in the model in the flexible-exchange-rate regimes, something which is generally ignored or treated very lightly in small-scale theoretical models. In Model A import prices influence domestic prices, and prices in general influence demand. These price effects can be quantitatively quite important. To give one example where they are important, consider Model A versus Mundell's two-country model (1968, Appendix to Chapter 18) in the perfect/flexible regime. In Mundell's model in this regime an expansionary monetary policy has a positive effect on the output of the home country and a negative effect on the output of the other country. For Model A this result is either completely reversed (in the price-lag case) or else substantially modified (in the no-price-lag case). As discussed above, the depreciation of country 1's currency that the expansionary monetary policy causes in this case leads in Model A to a higher domestic price level in country 1, and then either an actual contraction in country 1's real output or else an expansion that is smaller than the expansion in country 2. It thus appears from the results in this section that Mundell's model and models of this type have omitted some potentially important price links between countries.

IV. A SUGGESTED WAY OF MODELING THE ECONOMIC LINKAGES AMONG COUNTRIES: A SMALL APPROACH

One possible way of constructing a multicountry macroeconometric model with endogenous capital flows and exchange rates would be to estimate for each country a model as in Fair (1976), in which all flows of funds among the sectors are accounted for, and then link these models together. The resulting overall model would be like Model A, only it would be completely empirical and for more than two countries. Since, as discussed in the Introduction, this is an enormous task, it may be better to start with a somewhat smaller approach. The purpose of this section is to propose such an approach. The model described in this section requires that only five or six equations be estimated per country, but it accounts for all the main economic links among the countries and allows for the endogenous determination of the exchange rates.

Although the model that is outlined in this section is for three countries, the generalization to more than three countries is straightforward. The model in this section is a simplified version of the three-country model in the Appendix, and the reader is assumed to have mastered the model in the Appendix before reading this section. The model in the Appendix is a three-country version of the two-country model of the balance of payments in Fair (1978*b*). The reason for separating the model in this section from the model in the Appendix is to make clear the simplifications that are being proposed in this section.

The six or seven equations to be estimated per country for the model in this section are equations explaining (1) the demand for imports, (2) the demand for foreign securities, (3) the demand for domestic money, (4) the price of domestic goods, (5) the demand for domestic goods, (6) the forward price of the country's currency (except for the *numéraire* country), and possibly (7) the domestic interest rate. The overall model consists of twenty-one equations per country. The notation used in this section is presented in Table 5. All domestic goods in each country are aggregated into one good X, and all domestic financial securities (except money) in each country are aggregated into one security B. (Liabilities correspond to negative values of B.) There is therefore only one domestic price and one domestic interest rate per country. Any possible effects on behavior of capital gains and losses on securities are ignored.

For those who would like to skip or skim the equations, a brief outline of them is as follows. Equations (1.1)–(1.5) and (1.7)–(1.11) are definitions: (1.1) and (1.2) define the financial savings of the private and government sectors; (1.3) and (1.4) define the budget constraints of the two sectors; (1.5) and (1.7)–(1.9) are adding-up constraints; and (1.10) and (1.11) define price and covered interest-rate indices. Equation (1.6) explains bank reserves, and equations (1.12)–(1.17) and (1.22)–(1.23) are the equations to be estimated. Finally, equations (1.18)–(1.21) determine the allocation of goods and securities among countries.

With respect to the equations, consider first for country 1 the aggregation of the household, firm, and bank sectors in the model in the Appendix into one private sector (denoted by a subscript p).[10] Adding the private saving equations, (13), (27), and (31), yields:

$$(1.1) \quad S_{1p} = P_1(X_{1f} - X^1{}_{1p}) - e_2 P_2 X^1{}_{2p} - e_3 P_3 X^1{}_{3p} + R_1 B^1{}_{1p} + e_2 R_2 B^1{}_{2p}$$
$$+ e_3 R_3 B^1{}_{3p} - V_{1p} - RD_1 BO_1. \text{ [saving of the private sector]}$$

The government saving equation, (33), remains unchanged except to note that $V_{1h} + V_{1f} = V_{1p}$.

$$(1.2) \quad S_{1g} = V_{1p} + RD_1 BO_1 - P_1 X^1{}_{1g} - e_2 P_2 X^1{}_{2g} - e_3 P_3 X^1{}_{3g} + R_1 B^1{}_{1g}$$
$$+ e_2 R_2 B^1{}_{2g} + e_3 R_3 B^1{}_{3g}. \text{ [saving of the government sector]}$$

---

[10] With the exception of X_{1f} and M_{1b}, all the h, f, and b subscripts in the Appendix have been changed in this section to p, even when a variable in the Appendix pertains to only one or two of the three individual sectors. As examples of the change of notation, $B^1{}_{1p} = B^1{}_{1h} + B^1{}_{1f} + B^1{}_{1b}$, $X^1{}_{1p} = X^1{}_{1h} + X^1{}_{1f}$, and $M^1{}_{1p} = M^1{}_{1h}$. Also, government purchase of labor (L_{ig}) has been dropped as an explicit variable in the model and has instead been taken to be part of the good of country i. In other words, $W_i L_{ig}$ has been taken to be part of $P_i X^i{}_{ig}$.

Table 5. Variables for the Model in Section III $(i, j = 1, 2, 3)$

Number of Variables		
Endogenous	**Exogenous**	
3^a $(i = j)$	6	B^i_{ig} = amount of country i's securities held by the government of country j in units of country i's currency (negative values are liabilities).
9		B^i_{ip} = amount of country i's securities held by the private sector of country j in units of country i's currency (negative values are liabilities).
3		B^i_{mp} = index of the total foreign security holdings of the private sector of country i.
	3	BO_i = bank borrowing from the government in country i.
3		BR_i = bank reserves in country i.
1^b		e_2 = price of country 2's currency in terms of country 1's currency.
1^b		e_3 = price of country 3's currency in terms of country 1's currency.
1		e^*_2 = forward price of country 2's currency in terms of country 1's currency.
1		e^*_3 = forward price of country 3's currency in terms of country 1's currency.
	9	M^i_{ig} = amount of country i's money held by the private sector of country j in units of country i's currency.
3 $(i = j)$	6	M^i_{ip} = amount of country i's money held by the private sector of country j in units of country i's currency.
3		M_{ib} = total money supply in country i (total deposits in the bank sector of country i).
3		P_i = price of the good of country i in units of country i's currency.
3		P^i_m = price index of the total imports of country i in units of country i's currency.
1	2^c	Q_i = amount of the international reserve held by country i (price = 1.0).
3		R_i = interest rate for country i's securities.
3		R^i_m = covered interest rate index for the total foreign security holdings of country i.
	3	RD_i = discount rate in country i.
	3	RR_i = reserve requirement ratio in country i.
3		S_{ig} = financial saving of the government of country i.
3		S_{ip} = financial saving of the private sector of country i.
	3	V_{ip} = taxes paid by the private sector of country i.
	9	X^i_{ig} = real value of the good of country i purchased by the government of country j.
9		X^i_{ip} = real value of the good of country i purchased by the private sector of country j.
3		X^i_{mp} = index of the total real value of imports of the private sector of country i.
3		X_{if} = total real value of sales of the good of country i.
62	44	

a Exogenous if no reaction functions of the monetary authorities are specified (equations [1.17], [1.17]′, [1.17]″).
b Exogenous in fixed-exchange-rate regime.
c Endogenous in fixed-exchange-rate regime.

Adding the private budget-constraint equations, (14), (28), and (32), yields:

(1.3) $O = S_{1p} + \Delta(M_{1b} - M^1_{1p}) - e_2\Delta M^1_{2p} - e_3\Delta M^1_{3p} - \Delta B^1_{1p} - e_2\Delta B^1_{2p}$

$- e_3\Delta B^1_{3p} - \Delta(BR_1 - BO_1)$. [private sector budget constraint]

The government budget-constraint equation, (34), remains unchanged:

(1.4) $O = S_{1g} + \Delta(BR_1 - BO_1) - \Delta M^1_{1g} - e_2\Delta M^1_{2g} - e_3\Delta M^1_{3g} - \Delta B^1_{1g}$

$- e_2\Delta B^1_{2g} - e_3\Delta B^1_{3g} - \Delta Q_1$. [government sector budget constraint]

Equation (35) also remains unchanged except for the replacement of h by p:

(1.5) $M_{1b} = M^1_{1p} + M^1_{1g} + M^2_{1p} + M^2_{1g} + M^3_{1p} + M^3_{1g}$. [total deposits

in the bank sector]

Equation (30) remains the same:

(1.6) $BR_1 = RR_1 M_{1b}$. [bank reserves]

Equation (36) in the new notation is

(1.7) $O = B^1_{1p} + B^1_{1g} + B^2_{1p} + B^2_{1g} + B^3_{1p} + B^3_{1g}$. [supply of the bond of

country 1 equals the demand for it]

Equation (109) remains unchanged:

(1.8) $O = \Delta Q_1 + \Delta Q_2 + \Delta Q_3$. [no change in total world reserves]

Equation (24) in the new notation is

(1.9) $X_{1f} = X^1_{1p} + X^1_{1g} + X^2_{1p} + X^2_{1g} + X^3_{1p} + X^3_{1g}$. [total sales of the

good of country 1]

Let X^1_{mp} denote an index of the total imports of country 1's private sector from countries 2 and 3, i.e., some weighted average of X^1_{2p} and X^1_{3p}; and let B^1_{mp} denote an index of the total foreign security holdings of country 1's private sector, i.e., some weighted average of B^1_{2p} and B^1_{3p}. Also, let P^1_m be a price index of the total imports of country 1 in the units of country 1's currency:

(1.10) $P^1_m = \alpha^1_1 e_2 P_2 + \alpha^1_2 e_3 P_3$, [price index of the total imports of

country 1]

where α^1_1 and α^1_2 are some appropriately chosen weights. Similarly, let R^1_m be a covered interest-rate index for the total foreign security holdings of country 1:

(1.11) $\quad R^1_m = \beta^1_1 \left[\dfrac{e_2}{e^*_2} (1 + R_2) - 1 \right] + \beta^1_2 \left[\dfrac{e_3}{e^*_3} (1 + R_3) - 1 \right],$

[covered interest-rate index for the total foreign security holdings

of country 1]

where the expressions in brackets are the covered interest rates on the securities of countries 2 and 3, respectively, and where β^1_1 and β^1_2 are also some appropriately chosen weights.

The stage is now set for explaining the equations to be estimated for country 1. In what follows, Z_1 denotes a vector of all the exogenous and lagged endogenous variables that help explain the LHS variable in the equation. The variables in Z_1 may, of course, differ for different equations. The following six equations are meant to be approximations to the equations that would be estimated were the complete model in the Appendix being estimated:

(1.12) $\quad X^1_{mp} = f_{12} (P_1, P^1_m, X_{1f}, Z_1)$, [demand for imports by the private

sector of country 1]

(1.13) $\quad B^1_{mp} = f_{13} (R_1, R^1_m, Z_1)$, [demand for foreign securities by the

private sector of country 1]

(1.14) $\quad M^1_{1p} = f_{14} (R_1, P_1, X_{1f}, Z_1)$, [demand for domestic money by the

private sector of country 1]

(1.15) $\quad P_1 = f_{15} (P^1_m, R_1, X_{1f}, Z_1)$, [price of the good of country 1]

(1.16) $\quad X^1_{1p} = f_{16} (P_1, P^1_m, X_{1f}, R_1, Z_1)$, [demand for the good of country 1

by the private sector of country 1]

(1.17) $\quad R_1 = f_{17} (R^1_m, P_1, X_{1f}, Z_1)$. [reaction function of the monetary

authorities of country 1]

The total level of sales of the good of country 1, X_{1f}, is used as the aggregate real income or activity variable of country 1 in equations (1.12) and (1.14)–(1.17). Equation (1.12) explains the demand for imports as a function of the two prices, real income, and other (nonendogenous) variables. This equation is an approximation to equations (3), (4), (18), and (19) in the Appendix. Equation (1.13) explains the demand for foreign securities as a function of the two interest rates and other variables. It is an approximation to equations (9) and (10) in the Appendix.

Equation (1.14) explains the demand for domestic money as a function of the interest rate, price level, real income, and other variables. It is an approximation to equation (5) in the Appendix. Equation (1.15) explains the price of domestic goods as a function of the import price index, the interest rate, aggregate real activity, and other variables. It is an approximation to equation (15) in the Appendix. The price of domestic goods is assumed to be set by the firm sector.[11] Equation (1.16) is a combination of the consumption and investment demands for domestic goods for country 1; it is an approximation to equations (2) and (17) in the Appendix. In this equation, the demand for the good of country 1 by country 1's private sector is a function of the two prices, real income, the interest rate, and other variables. Finally, equation (1.17) explains the interest rate of country 1; it is a reaction function of the monetary authorities of country 1. As discussed at the end of the Appendix, this is an optional equation. If it is specified, then B^1_{1g} is endogenous; if it is not, then B^1_{1g} is exogenous.

Equations (1.12)–(1.17) are the key behavioral equations of the model for country 1, and these are the equations where it is suggested that most of the estimation work be focused. Regarding equations (1.12) and (1.13), however, it is still necessary once X^1_{mp} and B^1_{mp} have been explained to explain the division of these variables into X^1_{2p}, X^1_{3p}, B^1_{2p}, and B^1_{3p}. This can be done by the following "share" equations:

(1.18) $\quad \dfrac{X^1_{2p}}{X^1_{mp}} = f_{18}\left(\dfrac{e_2 P_2}{e_3 P_3}, Z_1\right)$, [share of the imports of country 1's private sector from country 2]

(1.19) $\quad \dfrac{X^1_{3p}}{X^1_{mp}} = f_{19}\left(\dfrac{e_2 P_2}{e_3 P_3}, Z_1\right)$, [share of the imports of country 1's private sector from country 3]

(1.20) $\quad \dfrac{B^1_{2p}}{B^1_{mp}} = f_{20}\left(\left[\dfrac{e_2}{e^*_2}(1 + R_2) - 1\right] \middle/ \left[\dfrac{e_3}{e^*_3}(1 + R_3) - 1\right], Z_1\right)$,

[share of country 2's securities in the foreign security holdings of country 1's private sector]

(1.21) $\quad \dfrac{B^1_{3p}}{B^1_{mp}} = f_{21}\left(\left[\dfrac{e_2}{e^*_2}(1 + R_2) - 1\right] \middle/ \left[\dfrac{e_3}{e^*_3}(1 + R_3) - 1\right], Z_1\right)$.

[share of country 3's securities in the foreign security holdings of country 1's private sector]

The lagged value of the share in each equation is an obvious variable to include in Z_1. These share equations should probably be estimated directly, although with a large number of countries this is tedious, and one may

[11] Again, see footnote 1 in the Appendix for a discussion of the inclusion of the interest rate in the price equation.

instead want to assign parameter values to many of these equations without direct estimation.[12]

This completes the outline of the basic model for country 1. Equations (1.1)–(1.7) and (1.9)–(1.21) also hold for countries 2 and 3, with appropriate change of notation. Also, equations explaining the forward exchange rates are needed for countries 2 and 3:

(1.22) $e^*_2 = f_{22} (\cdots)$, [forward price of country 2's currency]

(1.23) $e^*_3 = f_{23} (\cdots)$, [forward price of country 3's currency]

As in the Appendix, the determinants of the forward prices can be left unspecified for present purposes.

Except for equations (1.22) and (1.23), let a single prime denote the equations for country 2, and let a double prime denote the equations for country 3. This then gives sixty-three equations in the model, one of which is redundant. As in the Appendix, it will be convenient to drop equation (1.8). The remaining equations for which there are no obvious LHS variables are (1.3), (1.4), (1.7), and the corresponding equations for countries 2 and 3. To equations (1.3), (1.3)', and (1.3)'' can be matched B^1_{1p}, B^2_{2p}, and B^3_{3p}. To the government budget-constraint equations, (1.4), (1.4)', and (1.4)'', can be matched either R_1, R_2, and R_3, if no reaction functions of the monetary authorities are specified, or B^1_{1g}, B^2_{2g}, and B^3_{3g}, if such functions are specified. Finally, to equation (1.7) can be matched Q_1, and to equations (1.7)' and (1.7)'' can be matched either e_2 and e_3 or Q_2 and Q_3, depending on whether there are flexible or fixed exchange rates.

To summarize, if a model like the one outlined in this section were estimated, it would account for the main economic linkages among countries. In addition to the obvious capital-flow and exchange-rate linkages, there are linkages through the price equations (1.10), (1.10)', (1.10)'', (1.15), (1.15)', (1.15)'', through the interest-rate equations (when reaction functions of the monetary authorities are specified) (1.11), (1.11)', (1.11)'', (1.17), (1.17)', (1.17)'', and through the total-sales equations (1.9), (1.9)', (1.9)''.

A few further points about this model should be noted. First, if for a given country a reaction function of the monetary authorities is not specified, then the interest rate for that country is implicitly determined. The solution value of the interest rate is, speaking loosely, the rate that makes equation (1.4), the government budget constraint, hold. If the interest rate is instead explained by a reaction function, then B^1_{1g}, the (negative of) the amount of government securities outstanding, is taken to

---

[12] There are clearly a number of ways in which one can model the allocations of goods and securities among countries. The present model is not restricted to one particular way. See Hickman (1973) for a discussion of the allocation of goods among the various countries in the LINK model.

be endogenous. In this case the solution value of B^1_{1g} is, again speaking loosely, the value that makes equation (1.4) hold.

Second, in the regime of flexible exchange rates, the exchange rates are also implicitly determined. In the above discussion, e_2 and e_3 were matched to equations (1.7)′ and (1.7)″, the equations that equate the supply of securities of countries 2 and 3 to the demand for them. In the regime of fixed exchange rates, the international reserve holdings of the countries are implicitly determined. In this case, Q_2 and Q_3 are the variables matched to equations (1.7)′ and (1.7)″. It is also possible, if desired, to add equations explaining e_2 and/or e_3 to the model and interpret these equations as reaction functions of some particular government authority or authorities. If this is done, then Q_2 and/or Q_3 must be taken to be endogenous. This procedure is analogous to the procedure of estimating equations explaining R_1, R_2, and R_3; interpreting these equations as reaction functions of the monetary authorities; and taking B^1_{1g}, B^2_{2g}, and B^3_{3g} to be endogenous.

Third, if the bonds of the three countries are perfect substitutes, then equations (1.13), (1.13)′, and (1.13)″ drop out of the model, and the above matching of variables and equations must be modified. This case is considered in detail in Fair (1978b) for the two-country model. It will not be discussed further here except to note that if the bonds are perfect substitutes, then it is not logically consistent to postulate reaction functions of the government authorities with respect to both a country's interest rate and its exchange rate.

Fourth, even though the present model is relatively small, it is not an easy task to collect the necessary data for it. The data first of all must satisfy equations (1.1)–(1.9), which requires for each country linking its national-income and flow-of-funds accounts. For the United States this is fairly straightforward to do, as described in Fair (1976), but for countries that have poorer data than does the United States, some data may have to be made up. Also, for most pairs of countries, data on B^j_{ig} and B^j_{ip} do not exist, although it is generally possible to get data on a country's total foreign security holdings. The same holds true for M^j_{ig} and M^j_{ip}. Much of the data on the allocation of a country's total holdings of foreign securities and foreign money among the individual foreign countries will thus have to be made up.

Finally, it should be noted that one important feature of the single-country model in Fair (1976) that is lost in the model in this section is an explicit treatment of disequilibrium effects. Disequilibrium effects are present in the model in this section in that the price of the good of each country is assumed to be set by its firm sector (equations [1.15], [1.15]′, and [1.15]″), rather than being such as to clear the goods markets each period. Also, the use of the aggregate activity variables, X_{1f}, X_{2f}, and X_{3f}, in equations (1.16), (1.16)′, and (1.16)″, respectively, can be assumed in part to be accounting for disequilibrium effects. Nevertheless, it should be clear from comparing the model in Fair (1976) to the model in this section that disequilibrium effects are only crudely accounted for here, and this is probably one of the first restrictions that should be relaxed if the model in this section is expanded. Within the present model one can include in the Z_1 vector variables that may pick up disequilibrium effects, but any variables so included must be taken to be exogenous.

It is, of course, a matter of judgment whether or not one wants to restrict the model in the Appendix in the ways proposed in this section, and, if desired, it is fairly straightforward to lessen some or all of these restrictions. It is clearly an open question whether an estimated version of the model in this section would be a more accurate representation of the economic linkages among countries than, say, some future version of the LINK model. Given, however, the enormous task of accounting for all the flows of funds in the LINK model or in a similar model, it does seem worthwhile to try the small approach suggested in this paper. After the model proposed in this section has been estimated and analyzed, one can then be concerned, within the context of this basic model, with further disaggregation.[13]

APPENDIX: A THREE-COUNTRY MODEL OF THE BALANCE OF PAYMENTS

The model presented in this Appendix is a three-country version of the two-country model of the balance of payments in Fair (1978*b*). Different versions of the two-country model were considered, and the one used for present purposes is the one in which there is a bank sector and in which the labor and goods markets are not always in equilibrium. The notation used here differs from the notation in Fair (1978*b*), because of the need to keep track of three countries rather than two. The countries are numbered 1, 2, and 3. A subscript number for a variable denotes that the variable pertains to the particular country, and a superscript number for a variable denotes that the variable is held or purchased by the particular country. There are four sectors per country: household, firm, bank, and government. Subscripts h, f, b, and g will be used to denote these sectors, respectively. Each country specializes in the production of one good (X). Labor (L) is homogeneous within a country, and there is no labor mobility among countries. Each country has its own money (M), which takes the form of demand deposits in the bank sector, and its own bond (B). The bonds are one-period securities. If a sector is a debtor with respect to a bond (i.e.,

---

[13] At this point, further disaggregation and expansion could include 1) disaggregation of goods by type; 2) disaggregation of securities by type and maturity; 3) accounting more explicitly for disequilibrium effects; 4) accounting for the effects of capital gains and losses on behavior; and 5) generally making more variables endogenous. Except for 1) and 2), Model A is expanded in this way.

a supplier of the bond), then the value of B for this sector is negative. The bank sector of each country holds bank reserves with its government (BR), some of which are borrowed (BO). The reserve-requirement ratio is RR, and the discount rate is RD. Prices, wage rates, and interest rates are denoted P, W, and R, respectively. e_2 is the price of country 2's currency in terms of country 1's currency, and e_3 is the price of country 3's currency in terms of country 1's currency. $e*_2$ is the (one-period) forward price of country 2's currency in terms of country 1's currency, and $e*_3$ is the forward price of country 3's currency in terms of country 1's currency. The government of each country holds a positive amount of the international reserve (Q), whose price is 1.0, and it taxes its citizens using a vector (T) of tax parameters.

Consider country 1. The household sector is assumed to determine jointly its labor supply and its demand for the three goods, the three monies, and the three bonds. It takes as given the wage rate, the three prices, the three interest rates, the tax parameters, the two exchange rates, the two forward rates, and all lagged values. The vector of all relevant lagged values will be denoted as Z_{1h}. These decisions are assumed to be derived from a multiperiod maximization problem. Expectations of various future values, which are needed for such problems, are assumed to be a function of current and lagged values. The equations representing the decisions for the current period will be written as:

(1) $L_{1h} = f_1(W_1, P_1, P_2, P_3, R_1, R_2, R_3, T_1, e_2, e_3, e*_2, e*_3, Z_{1h})$ [labor supply]

(2) $X^1{}_{1h} = f_2(W_1, P_1, P_2, P_3, R_1, R_2, R_3, T_1, e_2, e_3, e*_2, e*_3, Z_{1h})$ [demand for the good of country 1]

(3) $X^1{}_{2h} = f_3(W_1, P_1, P_2, P_3, R_1, R_2, R_3, T_1, e_2, e_3, e*_2, e*_3, Z_{1h})$ [demand for the good of country 2]

(4) $X^1{}_{3h} = f_4(W_1, P_1, P_2, P_3, R_1, R_2, R_3, T_1, e_2, e_3, e*_2, e*_3, Z_{1h})$ [demand for the good of country 3]

(5) $M^1{}_{1h} = f_5(W_1, P_1, P_2, P_3, R_1, R_2, R_3, T_1, e_2, e_3, e*_2, e*_3, Z_{1h})$ [demand for the money of country 1]

(6) $M^1{}_{2h} = f_6(W_1, P_1, P_2, P_3, R_1, R_2, R_3, T_1, e_2, e_3, e*_2, e*_3, Z_{1h})$ [demand for the money of country 2]

(7) $M^1{}_{3h} = f_7(W_1, P_1, P_2, P_3, R_1, R_2, R_3, T_1, e_2, e_3, e*_2, e*_3, Z_{1h})$ [demand for the money of country 3]

(8) $B^1{}_{1h} = f_8(W_1, P_1, P_2, P_3, R_1, R_2, R_3, T_1, e_2, e_3, e*_2, e*_3, Z_{1h})$ [supply of ($-$) or demand for the bond of country 1]

(9) $B^1_{2h} = f_9(W_1, P_1, P_2, P_3, R_1, R_2, R_3, T_1, e_2, e_3, e^*_2, e^*_3, Z_{1h})$ [demand

for the bond of country 2]

(10) $B^1_{3h} = f_{10}(W_1, P_1, P_2, P_3, R_1, R_2, R_3, T_1, e_2, e_3, e^*_2, e^*_3, Z_{1h})$. [demand

for the bond of country 3]

These ten equations are not independent, since they must satisfy a budget constraint. This constraint is as follows. First, the taxable income of the household sector (Y_{1h}) is assumed to be

(11) $Y_{1h} = W_1 L_{1h} + R_1 B^1_{1h} + e_2 R_2 B^1_{2h} + e_3 R_3 B^1_{3h}$, [taxable income]

where the first term on the RHS is wage income, the second term is interest income or interest payments on the domestic bond, and the third and fourth terms are interest income on foreign bonds. Second, net taxes paid by the household sector (V_{1h}) is assumed to be a function of Y_{1h} and T_1:

(12) $V_{1h} = f_{12}(Y_{1h}, T_1)$. [net taxes paid]

The financial saving of the household sector (S_{1h}) is then

(13) $S_{1h} = Y_{1h} - V_{1h} - P_1 X^1_{1h} - e_2 P_2 X^1_{2h} - e_3 P_3 X^1_{3h}$, [saving of the

household sector]

where the last three terms are expenditures on goods. Finally, the budget constraint is

(14) $O = S_{1h} - \Delta M^1_{1h} - e_2 \Delta M^1_{2h} - e_3 \Delta M^1_{3h} - \Delta B^1_{1h} - e_2 \Delta B^1_{2h} - e_3 \Delta B^1_{3h}$,

[household sector budget constraint]

which says that any nonzero level of saving of the household sector must result in the change in at least one of its assets or liabilities.

Before discussing the firm sector it will be useful to consider briefly the case in which the bonds of the three countries are perfect substitutes. From country 1's perspective the covered interest rate on the bond of country 2, say R^1_2, is $(e_2/e^*_2)(1 + R_2) - 1$. Similarly, the covered interest rate on the bond of country 3, say R^1_3, is $(e_3/e^*_3)(1 + R_3) - 1$. If for $R_1 = R^1_2 = R^1_3$ people are indifferent as to which bond they hold, then the bonds are defined to be perfect substitutes. In this case, equations (9) and (10) drop out of the model, and $R_1 = R^1_2 = R^1_3$ always. It is unnecessary for present purposes to consider this case in any detail. A complete discussion of the perfect-substitution case in the two-country model is contained in Fair (1978*b*). Note that the "perfect mobility" regimes for Model A in Section III of this paper are regimes in which the bonds in the two countries are perfect substitutes *and* in which the forward rate is always assumed to be equal to the spot rate. Note also that in the nonperfect-substitution case in this appendix the covered interest rates are implicit in equations (9) and (10), since R_2, R_3, e_2, e_3, e^*_2, and e^*_3 all enter as arguments in these equations.

For simplicity, the firm sector is assumed to hold no foreign bonds and no money. It is assumed to determine jointly its price (P_1), its production (X^*_{1f}), its demand for the three goods for investment purposes $(X^1_{1f}, X^1_{2f}, X^1_{3f})$, its wage rate (W_1), the maximum amount of labor that it will employ in the period (L_{1f}), and its supply of $(-)$ or demand for the bond of country 1 (B^1_{1f}). It takes as given R_1, T_1, P_2, P_3, e_2, e_3, and all lagged values (Z_{1f}). These decisions are also assumed to be derived from a multiperiod maximization problem, with the equations representing the decisions for the current period written as:[1]

(15) $P_1 = f_{15}(R_1, T_1, P_2, P_3, e_2, e_3, Z_{1f})$ [price of the good of country 1]

(16) $X^*_{1f} = f_{16}(R_1, T_1, P_2, P_3, e_2, e_3, Z_{1f})$ [production of the good of country 1]

(17) $X^1_{1f} = f_{17}(R_1, T_1, P_2, P_3, e_2, e_3, Z_{1f})$ [demand for the good of country 1]

(18) $X^1_{2f} = f_{18}(R_1, T_1, P_2, P_3, e_2, e_3, Z_{1f})$ [demand for the good of country 2]

(19) $X^1_{3f} = f_{19}(R_1, T_1, P_2, P_3, e_2, e_3, Z_{1f})$ [demand for the good of country 3]

(20) $W_1 = f_{20}(R_1, T_1, P_2, P_3, e_2, e_3, Z_{1f})$ [wage rate of country 1]

(21) $L_{1f} = f_{21}(R_1, T_1, P_2, P_3, e_2, e_3, Z_{1f})$ [maximum amount of labor that the firm sector will employ in the period]

(22) $B^1_{1f} = f_{22}(R_1, T_1, P_2, P_3, e_2, e_3, Z_{1f})$. [supply of $(-)$ or demand for the bond of country 1]

Disequilibrium in the labor market is handled as follows. First, note that $L_{1f} + L_{1g}$ is the maximum amount that the household sector can work in the period, where L_{1g} is the amount of labor employed by the government. (The bank sector is assumed to employ no labor.) It is assumed that the firm and government sectors make their decisions regarding L_{1f} and L_{1g}

---

[1] See Chapter 3 in Fair (1974) for a detailed discussion and analysis of this type of model of firm behavior. For present purposes, the production-function constraint on the firm sector should be assumed to be incorporated into the decision equations (15)–(22). For the model in Fair (1974), a production function was postulated explicitly, and the possibility that it may at times be optimal for a firm to hold excess labor and excess capital was considered.

It should also be noted that in the theoretical model in Fair (1974) the interest rate has a positive effect on the price that a firm sets, and so R_1 is included as an explanatory variable in equation (15). In the empirical work in Fair (1976) the bond rate did have a significant and positive effect on the price variable of the firm sector.

before the household sector makes its decisions, and that the household sector takes this possible labor constraint into account in making its decisions. Equations (1)–(10) are thus assumed to represent the household sector's decisions that incorporate this possible labor constraint, so that L_{1h} in (1) is always less than or equal to $L_{1f} + L_{1g}$.

Consider now the firm sector's adjustment to disequilibrium in the labor market. If L_{1h} is strictly less than $L_{1f} + L_{1g}$, then the firm sector is assumed to get only the amount $L_{1h} - L_{1g}$ of labor in the period. Call this amount L'_{1f}:

(23) $\quad L'_{1f} = L_{1h} - L_{1g}.$ [actual amount of labor employed by the firm

sector in the period. $L'_{1f} \leq L_{1f}.$]

In the case in which $L'_{1f} < L_{1f}$, the firm sector is assumed to change its production decision during the period, and so equation (16) should be interpreted as reflecting this fact.

With respect to the goods market, the total amount of sales of the firm sector (X_{1f}) is

(24) $\quad X_{1f} = X^1_{1h} + X^1_{1f} + X^1_{1g} + X^2_{1h} + X^2_{1f} + X^2_{1g} + X^3_{1h}$

$+ X^3_{1f} + X^3_{1g}.$ [total sales of the good of country 1]

The firm sector is assumed to hold inventories of the good (I_{1f}), so that any difference between production and sales in the period results in a change in inventories:

(25) $\quad \Delta I_{1f} = X^*_{1f} - X_{1f}.$ [change in inventories of the good of country 1]

The lagged value of inventories (I_{1f-1}) is one of the variables in Z_{1f} that affects the firm sector's current decisions.

The equations for the firm sector also must satisfy a budget constraint. The value of taxes paid by the firm sector (V_{1f}) is assumed to be a function of T_1 and of variables that determine profits:

(26) $\quad V_{1f} = f_{26}(T_1, P_1, X^*_{1f}, X^1_{1f}, X^1_{2f}, X^1_{3f}, W_1, B^1_{1f}, L'_{1f}, R_1, P_2, P_3, e_2,$

$e_3, Z_{1h}).$ [taxes paid]

The financial saving of the firm sector (S_{1f}) is

(27) $\quad S_{1f} = P_1 X_{1f} - P_1 X^1_{1f} - e_2 P_2 X^1_{2f} - e_3 P_3 X^1_{3f} - W_1 L'_{1f}$

$+ R_1 B^1_{1f} - V_{1f},$ [saving of the firm sector]

and its budget constraint is

(28) $\quad O = S_{1f} - \Delta B^1_{1f}.$ [firm sector budget constraint]

The main characteristic of the bank sector is that it takes in deposits (M_{1b}) and makes loans (B^1_{1b}). The bank sector is assumed for simplicity to employ no labor, buy no goods, pay no taxes, and hold no foreign bonds and monies. Its borrowing from the government is assumed to be a function of R_1 and the discount rate (RD_1):

(29) $BO_1 = f_{29}(R_1, RD_1)$. [bank-borrowing from the government]

The bank sector is assumed to hold no excess reserves, so that bank reserves are determined as

(30) $BR_1 = RR_1 M_{1b}$, [bank reserves]

where RR_1 is the reserve requirement ratio. The financial saving of the bank sector (S_{1b}) is

(31) $S_{1b} = R_1 B^1{}_{1b} - RD_1 BO_1$, [saving of the bank sector]

and its budget constraint is

(32) $O = S_{1b} - \Delta B^1{}_{1b} + \Delta M_{1b} - \Delta(BR_1 - BO_1)$. [bank sector budget

   constraint]

Equation (31) states that the saving of the bank sector equals the difference between the interest revenue on its loans and the interest payments to the government on its borrowing. Equation (32) states that the change in bank loans plus unborrowed reserves $(\Delta B^1{}_{1b} + \Delta(BR_1 - BO_1))$ equals saving plus the change in deposits $(S_{1b} + \Delta M_{1b})$.

The government is assumed to purchase labor from its own citizens (L_{1g}) and all three goods $(X^1{}_{1g}, X^1{}_{2g}, X^1{}_{3g})$. It also holds the three monies $(M^1{}_{1g}, M^1{}_{2g}, M^1{}_{3g})$ and the three bonds $(B^1{}_{1g}, B^1{}_{2g}, B^1{}_{3g})$, in addition to the international reserve (Q_1). Its financial saving (S_{1g}) is

(33) $S_{1g} = V_{1h} + V_{1f} - W_1 L_{1g} - P_1 X^1{}_{1g} - e_2 P_2 X^1{}_{2g} - e_3 P_3 X^1{}_{3g} + R_1 B^1{}_{1g}$

   $+ e_2 R_2 B^1{}_{2g} + e_3 R_3 B^1{}_{3g}$, [saving of the government sector]

and its budget constraint is

(34) $O = S_{1g} + \Delta(BR_1 - BO_1) - \Delta M^1{}_{1g} - e_2 \Delta M^1{}_{2g} - e_3 \Delta M^1{}_{3g} - \Delta B^1{}_{1g}$

   $- e_2 \Delta B^1{}_{2g} - e_3 \Delta B^1{}_{3g} - \Delta Q_1$. [government sector budget

   constraint]

The first two terms on the RHS of (33) are tax revenue, the next four terms are purchases of labor and goods, and the last three terms are interest income or payments. Equation (34) states that any nonzero value of government saving must result in the change in at least one of the government's assets or liabilities.

Two further equations complete the model for country 1. The total amount of deposits in the bank sector (M_{1b}) is:

(35) $M_{1b} = M^1_{1h} + M^1_{1g} + M^2_{1h} + M^2_{1g} + M^3_{1h} + M^3_{1g}$, [total deposits

in the bank sector]

and the supply of the bond of country 1 equals the demand for it:

(36) $O = B^1_{1h} + B^1_{1f} + B^1_{1b} + B^1_{1g} + B^2_{1h} + B^2_{1g} + B^3_{1h} + B^3_{1g}$. [supply

of the bond of country 1 equals the demand for it]

Equations (1)–(36) also hold for countries 2 and 3, with appropriate changes of numerical subscripts and superscripts and with appropriate modifications of e_2 and e_3. Call these equations (1)'–(36)' and (1)"–(36)". The overall model is then closed by the following three equations:

(109) $O = \Delta Q_1 + \Delta Q_2 + \Delta Q_3$, [no change in total world reserves]

(110) $e^*_2 = f_{110}(\cdots)$, [forward price of country 2's currency]

(111) $e^*_3 = f_{111}(\cdots)$. [forward price of country 3's currency]

For present purposes the determinants of the two forward prices can be left unspecified, although this is admittedly side stepping a difficult problem. Estimating equations (110) and (111) would clearly be an important and difficult part of any modeling effort.

Of the 111 equations, 7 are redundant. The redundant equations are: one from the household equations (1)–(14), one from the firm equations (15)–(28), the same for countries 2 and 3, and one because the savings of all sectors sum to zero: $S_{1h} + S_{1f} + S_{1b} + S_{1g} + e_2(S_{2h} + S_{2f} + S_{2b} + S_{2g}) + e_3(S_{3h} + S_{3f} + S_{3b} + S_{3g}) = 0$. It will be convenient to drop (8), (22), the same for countries 2 and 3, and (109). This leaves 104 equations. If all the government variables (i.e., all the variables with subscript g) except S_{1g}, S_{2g}, and S_{3g} are taken to be exogenous and if all lagged values are taken to be predetermined, then there are 106 variables left. Therefore, two further variables must be taken to be exogenous in order for the model to be determined. These variables are e_2 and e_3 in the fixed-exchange-rate regime and Q_2 and Q_3 in the flexible-exchange-rate regime.

It may be helpful to consider the matching of variables and equations to see that all variables are accounted for. The equations for which there are no obvious LHS variables are (14), (28), (32), (34), (36), and the corresponding equations for countries 2 and 3. To the three budget-constraint equations, (14), (28), and (32), can be matched B^1_{1h}, B^1_{1f}, and B^1_{1b}, and similarly for countries 2 and 3. To the three government-budget-constraint equations, (34), (34)', and (34)", can be matched R_1, R_2, and R_3. To (36) can be matched Q_1, which then leaves (36)' and (36)" to be matched to e_2 and e_3 or Q_2 and Q_3.

In the model as just outlined the interest rates are matched to the government budget constraints and therefore implicitly determined. Another possibility is to 1) assume that the monetary authority of each country behaves by controlling the domestic interest rate; 2) estimate a "reaction function" for each monetary authority with the domestic interest rate as the LHS variable; and 3) close the model by taking each government's holdings of domestic securities (B^1_{1g}, B^2_{2g}, and B^3_{3g}) to be endogenous. This was done in Fair (1978*a*) for the single-country model in Fair (1976), and the properties of this version of the model were compared to the properties of the version without the reaction function.

It should finally be noted that the above matching of variables and equations has to be changed in the case in which the bonds of the three countries are perfect substitutes. Again, see Fair (1978*b*) for a complete discussion of this case for the two-country model.

REFERENCES

Ball, R. J., ed. 1973. *The International Linkage of National Economic Models.* Amsterdam: North-Holland Publishing Co.

Berner, Richard, Clark, Peter, Howe, Howard, Kwack, Sung, and Stevens, Guy. 1976. "Modeling the International Influences on the U.S. Economy: A Multi-Country Approach." International Finance Discussion Paper No. 93, Board of Governors of the Federal Reserve System.

Centraal Planbureau. 1975. "Mini-METEOR: A Simple Multi-Country Simulation Model." The Hague, June 30, 1975.

Deardorff, Alan V., and Stern, Robert M. 1977. "International Economic Interdependence: Evidence from Econometric Models." Seminar Discussion Paper No. 71, Research Seminar in International Economics, University of Michigan.

DeRosa, Dean A., and Smeal, Gary L. 1976. "The Transmission of Economic Activity between the Major Industrial Countries." OASIA/Research, U.S. Treasury, January 5, 1976.

Fair, Ray C. 1974. *A Model of Macroeconomic Activity. Volume I: The Theoretical Model.* Cambridge: Ballinger Publishing Co.

———. 1976. *A Model of Macroeconomic Activity. Volume II: The Empirical Model.* Cambridge: Ballinger Publishing Co.

———. 1978*a*. "The Sensitivity of Fiscal-Policy Effects to Assumptions about the Behavior of the Federal Reserve." *Econometrica* (in press).

———. 1978*b*. "A Model of the Balance of Payments." *Journal of International Economics* (forthcoming).

Helliwell, John. 1974. "Trade, Capital Flows, and Migration as Channels for International Transmission of Stabilization Policies." In Albert Ando, Richard Herring, and Richard Martson (eds.), *International Aspects of Stabilization Policies*, Proceedings of a conference held in June 1974, Federal Reserve Bank of Boston, pp. 241–78.

Hickman, Bert G. 1973. "A General Linear Model of World Trade," Chapter 3 in R. J. Ball (ed.), *The International Linkage of National Economic Models*, pp. 21–43. Amsterdam: North-Holland Publishing Co., 1973.

————. 1974. "International Transmission of Economic Fluctuations and Inflation." In Albert Ando, Richard Herring, and Richard Martson (eds.), *International Aspects of Stabilization Policies*. Proceedings of a conference held in June 1974, Federal Reserve Bank of Boston, pp. 201–31.

Houthakker, H. S., and Magee, Stephen P. 1969. "Income and Price Elasticities in World Trade." *The Review of Economics and Statistics* 51: 111–25.

Kwack, Sung Y. 1975. "Price Linkage in an Interdependent World Economy: Price Responses to Exchange Rate and Activity Changes." Discussion Paper No. 56, Division of International Finance, Board of Governors of the Federal Reserve System.

Morishima, M., and Murata, Y. 1972. "An Estimation of the International Trade Multiplier, 1954–1965." In M. Morishima, Y. Murata, T. Nosse, and M. Saito, *The Working of Econometric Models*, pp. 301–29. Cambridge: Cambridge University Press.

Mundell, R. A. 1968. *International Economics*. New York: Macmillan & Company.

Mussa, Michael. 1978. "Macroeconomic Interdependence and the Exchange Rate." Chapter 5 in this book.

Myhrman, Johan. 1976. "Balance-of-Payments Adjustment and Portfolio Theory: A Survey." In E. Claassen and P. Salin (eds.), *Recent Developments in International Monetary Economics*, pp. 203–37. Amsterdam: North-Holland Publishing Co.

OECD Economic Outlook. December 1975.

Samuelson, Lee. "A New Model of World Trade," *OECD Economic Outlook— Occasional Studies*. December 1973.

Comment

FRANCO MODIGLIANI

One can hardly disagree with Fair's premise that the nature of linkages between countries is likely to be profoundly affected by exchange regimes and by the extent of mobility of capital across national boundaries, and that econometric analysis in this area has so far made limited progress. I also agree with his diagnosis that endeavors to secure empirical estimates of linkages so far have paid insufficient systematic attention to the exchange regime and financial aspects, while the empirical work focusing on the latter mechanisms has tended to rely on *ad hoc* models giving insufficient attention to other aspects of the economy. In his paper, Fair first endeavors to provide some "empirical" and "quasi empirical" evidence of the importance of capital flows and exchange regimes and then proposes a fresh attack on the problem.

Unfortunately, the "empirical" evidence, relying on a number of existing econometric models, is not very impressive. The only results that really bear on the issue are those relating to RDX2-MPS in Tables 1 and 2. It is apparent that for up to six years the differential impact is, on the whole,

rather puny, and anyone familiar with model simulations and their reliability cannot be much impressed by significant differences developing in
the seventh or eighth year after the shock!

On the other hand, the "quasi evidence" embodied in Table 4 is quite
valuable and fascinating, both because of the highly ingenious methodology
employed and because the results are in good part counterintuitive and inconsistent with currently prevailing paradigms. Fair's results seem to depend
crucially on three elements. (i) His model incorporates mechanisms that
have apparently been neglected, among them primarily the effect of devaluation on the real money supply and, hence, finally on real variables,
via prices. (ii) He assumes that exchange rate expectations are static. This
assumption greatly simplifies matters but is unwarranted, especially in a
model concerned with short-run adjustment paths and considering also that
the model itself implies that, in response to a shock, exchange rates keep
changing for quite a while. (iii) His model labeled "price lags" is characterized by a very strong J-effect: real imports do not respond at all to current
prices and hence to devaluation, and even the short-run elasticity for exports
is presumably small. Accordingly, in the initial periods the sum of the elasticities is distinctly below unity, i.e., the Marshall–Lerner conditions fail to
hold.

All of these elements are relevant in understanding the results, sometimes weird, reported in the left-hand block. Fair attributes these results
to some special feature of his model that recognizes "that prices have, other
things being equal, a negative effect on demand"; but, as far as I can see,
the results are really accounted for by the interaction of the above three
elements of which only the first is relatively new. Take, for instance, the
weirdest of his results—those for flexible exchanges and perfect capital
mobility. Because of assumption (ii), the interest rates must at all times
remain equal in the two countries; this is apparently achieved in large part
through a sizable devaluation of country 1's currency and mechanism (i):
the devaluation by raising prices, cushions the rise in real money supply
and hence the decline in interest rates; correspondingly, the revaluation of
country 2's currency, by lowering prices, leads to a lower interest rate.
Because of assumption (iii), the devaluation substantially worsens the
current account balance of country 1, with well-known deflationary effects
outweighing any possible short-run expansionary effect of lower interest
rates. Hence, the final result is a fall in real income. At the same time, in
country 2's currency, by lowering prices, leads to a lower interest rate.
both contribute to expanding income.

On the other hand, when capital is completely immobile, and thus
interest rates do not have to be equalized, the expansionary effect of a
lower interest rate in country 1 leads to an incipient deterioration in the
current balance, which, in view of the failure of the Marshall–Lerner conditions, can be offset only by an *appreciation* of the exchange. This further

boosts the income of 1 and reduces that of 2. One can only concur with Fair's judgment that this result is not very "realistic." But I would suggest that the same is true of the perfect mobility case, and, in both cases, not because of the extreme assumptions about capital mobility but primarily because of assumption (ii) interacting with (iii). Once we allow for exchange expectations and forward exchange markets, so that the equality of interest rates is replaced by interest parity, the path of adjustment in the presence of J-effects can be expected to look quite different.

The results for the case of a fiscal shock, reported in Part II of the table, strike me as less enlightening, since in Fair's experiment the increased expenditure is entirely financed by money—and in fact by high-powered money. As a consequence, his results appear to be swayed by the monetary effect—or at any rate, this is what I would infer from the table. In my view, it would be more enlightening to run the simulation with the money supply kept constant, because the government expenditure shock can be seen as a prototype of a large variety of demand shocks.

One can presumably obtain a rough approximation of the pure effect of a demand shock by subtracting from the entries of Part II the corresponding ones of Part I. If one relies on this somewhat perilous approach, one finds again some strange results. For instance, under flexible exchanges and perfect mobility, the shock appears to raise the income of country 1 by about 1.3, and to *lower* that of country 2 by some —.3. Both multipliers, and especially the second, are not in line with what one would expect from the received paradigms, and the reason appears to be, again, primarily in the failure of the Marshall–Lerner conditions: the appreciation of currency 1 due to the (incipient) higher interest rate *deteriorates* the balance of country 2, as well as raises its price level and interest rate with depressing effects on both accounts. I submit that these results again are not very "realistic"—though admittedly a good model of exchange market dynamics in the face of strong J-effects is still missing.

With this background I turn to a few comments on the programmatic Section IV. I find myself in full sympathy with the spirit of that program, and the critical remarks that follow are meant to contribute to it in a constructive spirit.

I have first a question of basic strategy: there clearly are advantages in moving away from the LINK format toward a stripped-down, standardized model for all countries. But how far should one go? That depends in part on the purpose of the exercise. If it is primarily to serve analytical purposes and each of the countries is but a prototype, then the case for standardization is strongest. But then one might ask why not push further Fair's earlier design of coupling the United States with many other United States, each multiplied by suitable scale factors and with judgmental variations in a few crucial parameters? Before doing so, the U.S. model might well be stripped down to the format of the "small approach."

If, on the other hand, one aims at actual forecasting for individual countries, be it unconditional or conditional on alternative policies, then one *must* take into account specific features of each economy and, especially, of its capital markets. As I have concluded elsewhere,[1] the working of the monetary mechanism is significantly affected by the composition of both firms' and households' balance sheets and the extent of rationing in the bank credit and bond markets. And this mechanism, in turn, will play an important role in the linkage through capital movements.

In the light of the above considerations, there seems to be little point in commenting on the individual equations of the "small" model proposed by Fair. I will limit myself to calling attention to two shortcomings, which in my view are so basic that they would have to be taken care of in order to obtain "realistic" results, independently of the specific countries to be "linked." The most serious one is the failure, noted earier, to model the forward exchange market and exchange rate expectations affecting the demand for foreign "bonds," and, probably, the related one of not distinguishing between long- and short-term markets and capital movements (including the possibility of short-term borrowing and lending abroad by firms). The other shortcoming is the failure to distinguish between real and nominal rates (or to allow appropriately for expectations of inflation). Both defects are, of course, remediable, though the first clearly presents a serious challenge.

Comment

J. DAVID RICHARDSON

I think that the first part of Ray Fair's paper documents very nicely the need for the second. Whether the quantitative predictions in Part I from the seven extant international linkage models are "closer than one might have expected" or notably divergent, explanations for any divergence at all are uncomfortably speculative. The large size of the seven models precludes definitive comparisons of behavior and structure (although, see, Deardorff and Stern 1977). Better for purposes of interpretation that a small, synthetic, and flexible model be constructed and employed—one that can be parametrically transformed to cover a large sample of alternative structures among several popular extremes. Part II does exactly that and pinpoints (reasonably to my mind) the extent of international capital mobility and of policy determination of exchange rates as the key reasons for divergent model predictions.

Many aspects of the Fair International Linkage Model (FILM?) deserve favorable mention, because macroeconometric work that follows should

[1] See Mattioli lectures, Milan, Italy, October 1977, forthcoming.

emulate them. One is the meticulous attention to stock-flow consistency, adding-up properties, and flow-of-funds precision (the analytical antecedent to Fair's econometric analysis is Mundell's [1963, 1964] meticulous and classic work). Another feature is the promising approach to disequilibrium dynamics proposed in the appendix, although regrettably not in the text (the analytical roots being the closed-economy work of Clower 1965, Patinkin 1965, Barro and Grossman 1976, Malinvaud 1977, and the econometric roots being presumably Fair and Jaffee 1972). A third feature is the restoration of supply-side macroeconometric influences through rational behavior of firms toward employment needs and inventory (also in the appendix but not in the text), and also through the impact of import prices, exchange rates, and interest rates on costs of production.

But other aspects of the work detract somewhat from its appeal. After outfitting his model in Mundell's (1963, 1964) familiar extreme regimes (rigidly fixed/cleanly floating exchange rates; no international capital mobility/perfect international capital mobility), Fair obscures the comparison of his quantitative results to Mundell's qualitative conclusions: Fair's fiscal expansion is financed by money creation; Mundell's by government borrowing. It would have been preferable to be able to observe more directly how much quantitative difference Mundell's categorizations really make.

Second, Fair's treatment of international linkages through capital movements would be measurably more compelling if he had included forward premia/discounts as one of the determinants of stock demands for bonds and cash balances. They are as important as interest rates in determining rates of return and borrowing costs. In excluding them by appeal (presumably) to stable exchange rate expectations (footnote 7 of the text and footnote 1 of the appendix), Fair has surrendered to the most convenient, tempting, inelastic, and nonrational of expectations mechanisms—that expected exchange rate changes remain exogenously stable, even in the face of endogenously flexible and variable exchange rates. Having turned frequently to this palliative myself, I do not want to sound too harsh. But I conjecture that important capital account linkages among nations would be revealed if exchange rate expectations were modeled rationally and endogenously, and if asset preference depended, as it should, on comparative *covered* rates of return. A closely related, and perhaps equally valuable, addition to asset preference would be the incorporation of exchange-rate-related capital gains and losses in stock-demand behavior.

Third, I wish that Fair had highlighted better the role that debt service may be playing in his model. He is to be commended for including it, but the inclusion sets up the possibility for J-curve responses of the combined capital and services account to rate-of-return changes, responses that generate many of the same counterintuitive predictions as J-curve responses of the merchandise trade account to exchange rate changes. A rise in domestic rates of return leads to temporarily increased capital inflows and permanently increased debt-service outflows (see, especially, Willett and Forte 1968). With zero capital mobility, in fact, debt service (on existing stocks) is all that remains, and a rise in domestic rates of return *weakens* domestic currency in the foreign exchange market, short run and long, *ceteris paribus*. With certain model structures and parameters, including debt service can furthermore imply unstable equilibria. Fair says little about the stability properties of his model. One place where they might have helped is in explaining why expansionary domestic monetary policy causes foreign recession under flexible exchange rates with zero capital mobility (p. 221). He twists and turns to arrive at an explanation that has no foundation in the microeconomic behavior of economic agents. I suspect, by contrast, a locally unstable equilibrium.

Attention to these quarrels notwithstanding, I have great respect and enthusiasm for this paper. It sets its feet firmly in theory, with precise attention to the consistency of its behavioral specification, and then carefully avoids building a body so intricate and obese that vision of the theory is obscured totally by clouds of equations. Since theory, by its nature, is designed to pose refutable generalizations (as Mundell [1964, pp. 421–22] impatiently reminded McLeod), empirical work that loses clear sight of theory is handicapped in its usefulness. Fair is to be commended, by contrast, for econometric work that illuminates theory and promises to interpret reality as well.

REFERENCES

Barro, Robert J., and Grossman, Herschel L. 1976. *Money, Employment, and Inflation.* London: Cambridge University Press.

Clower, R. W. 1965. "The Keynesian Counter-Revolution: A Theoretical Appraisal." In F. H. Hahn and F. Brechling (eds.), *The Theory of Interest Rates.* New York: Macmillan, for the International Economic Association; reprinted in R. W. Clower (ed.), *Monetary Theory: Selected Readings.* Baltimore: Penguin, 1969.

Deardorff, Alan V., and Stern, Robert M. 1977. *International Economic Interdependence: Evidence From Econometric Models.* Ann Arbor, Michigan; abbreviated as Research Seminar in International Economics Discussion Paper No. 71, University of Michigan.

Fair, Ray C., and Jaffee, Dwight M. 1972. "Methods of Estimation for Markets in Disequilibrium." *Econometrica* 40: 497–514.

Malinvaud, Edmond. 1977. *The Theory of Unemployment Reconsidered.* New York: John Wiley.

Mundell, Robert A. 1963. "Capital Mobility and Stabilization Policy Under Fixed and Flexible Exchange Rates." *Canadian Journal of Economics and Political Science* 29: 475–85; reprinted in Richard E. Caves and Harry G. Johnson (eds.), *Readings in International Economics.* Homewood, Illinois:

Richard D. Irwin. 1968. for the American Economic Association; and in adapted form as Chapter 18 of Mundell, *International Economics*, New York: Macmillan, 1968.

————. 1964. "A Reply: Capital Mobility and Size." *Canadian Journal of Economics and Political Science* 30: 421–31; reprinted in adapted form as the appendix to Chapter 18 of Mundell, *International Economics*, New York: Macmillan, 1968.

Patinkin, Don. 1965. *Money, Interest, and Prices: An Integration of Monetary and Value Theory*. New York: Harper and Row.

Willett, Thomas D., and Forte, Francesco. 1969. "Interest Rate Policy and External Balance," *Quarterly Journal of Economics* 83: 242–62.

CHAPTER SEVEN

On the Efficiency of Markets
for Foreign Exchange

RICHARD M. LEVICH

The major argument of this chapter is that a rigorous, and therefore convincing, test of the efficient-market hypothesis has not been completed for the foreign exchange market. Furthermore, until several economic and statistical issues are resolved, any meaningful test of market efficiency is unlikely.

The aim of this paper is first to outline the essential elements of the efficient-market hypothesis and to highlight the reasons why empirical tests of the hypothesis are difficult. Second, we review some of the recent empirical tests of foreign exchange market efficiency and argue that the interpretation of most of these tests is at best ambiguous. The critical economic and statistical issues that must be resolved are detailed in Section III and several suggestions are developed for how future research should proceed.

I. THE EFFICIENT MARKET HYPOTHESIS

The classic definition of an efficient market is a market where prices "fully reflect" available information.[1] When this condition is satisfied, it follows that investors cannot earn an unusual profit by exploiting available information. The macroeconomic importance of market efficiency is derived from the role of prices as aggregators of structural information. When asset and commodity markets are efficient (in the above sense of reflecting information), economic agents who make decisions on the basis of observed prices will insure an efficient allocation of resources.

But the previous definition is too general to be tested empirically. We

I am grateful to Ken Garbade, Ian Giddy, Christine Hekman, Steve Kohlhagen, and Clas Wihlborg for helpful suggestions.
[1] This section draws heavily on the discussion in Fama (1970, 1976).

must posit a precise meaning for the term "fully reflect." Typically, this has been accomplished by assuming that market equilibrium can be stated in terms of equilibrium prices or equilibrium expected returns. If we chose the latter, then the excess market return on asset j is given by

$$(1) \quad Z_{j,t+1} = r_{j,t+1} - E(\tilde{r}_{j,t+1} \mid \Phi_t),$$

where $r_{j,t+1}$ is the one-period percentage return and Φ_t represents the information set that is assumed to be fully reflected in the price at time t. When the excess return sequence $\{Z_{jt}\}$ is a "fair game" with respect to the information sequence $\{\Phi_t\}$, the market is efficient.[2]

The critical point of this discussion is that all tests of market efficiency are testing a joint hypothesis—first, the hypothesis on market equilibrium prices or expected returns, and second, the hypothesis that economic agents can efficiently set actual prices or returns to conform to their expected values.[3] For studies that reject this simultaneous test, it is impossible to determine whether an incorrect specification of equilibrium expected returns is responsible for the rejection or whether, in fact, investors were inefficient information processors. And for studies that cannot reject market efficiency, it can be argued that the wrong equilibrium expected-return process was assumed. Relative to the "correct" standard, the market is really inefficient and unusual profit opportunities are available.

To illustrate the importance of this result for empirical testing, consider Figures 1 and 2. In Figure 1 the equilibrium expected return is assumed to be constant at r_o. If actual returns vibrate randomly about r_o, the market is efficient. In this case, prices follow a random walk with drift parameter r_o.

A case where the equilibrium expected return is assumed to wander considerably is illustrated in Figure 2. If actual returns vibrate randomly about the equilibrium, the market is efficient. In this case, returns and prices are highly serially correlated about their mean values; prices do not follow a random walk. Still, the market is efficient.

Conditional on a constant equilibrium expected rate of return, random price movement suggests market efficiency. But random price movement per se is neither a necessary nor sufficient condition for market efficiency.

[2] If the sequence $\{Z_{jt}\}$ is a fair game, then $E(\tilde{Z}_{j,t+1} \mid \Phi_t) = 0$ and the Z_{jt} are serially uncorrelated. It follows that in an efficient market a few investors may occasionally make large gains or losses, but no group should make unusual gains or losses consistently.

[3] It is interesting that Fama organizes his 1970 survey according to the information set (Φ_t), which is being fully reflected. Information sets are classified as containing only historical prices (that test weak form efficiency), public information (that tests semistrong form efficiency), or all information including insider information (that tests strong form efficiency). However, Fama (1976) organizes the literature based on the underlying assumption for the equilibrium expected return. He considers four alternative equilibrium expected return processes—returns are positive, returns are constant, returns are generated by a market model, returns conform to a specific two-parameter model. The latter survey is more effective in highlighting the simultaneous nature of efficient market tests.

Fig. 1. Efficient Market Behavior with the Equilibrium Expected Return Constant.

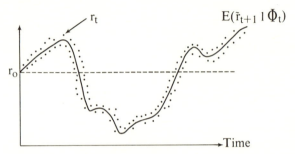

Fig. 2. Efficient Market Behavior Where the Equilibrium Expected Return Wanders Substantially.

If the expected equilibrium return varies considerably, market efficiency requires nonrandom walk price movements.

The early random walk studies in equity markets did not sufficiently recognize this point. However, in equity markets several equilibrium return processes could be assumed and tested. First, we could assume that expected returns on equities are positive in every period, based on the assumption that utility maximizing, risk-averse investors would not willingly accept nondiversifiable equity risk without expecting a positive return. Second, we could assume that expected returns on equities are constant. Fama (1970) suggests that this assumption is plausible for equities, since over the typical differencing interval (one month or less) variation in equilibrium expected returns is small relative to other sources of variation in returns. Third, we could assume that expected returns on equities are generated by a market model or a specific capital asset pricing model.[4] Since there is probably a considerable consensus across academics and financial practitioners that the equilibrium expected return is positive

---

[4] For a critical appraisal of empirical tests of asset-pricing models, see Roll (1977).

(and perhaps fairly constant), the empirical studies provided considerable evidence in favor of market efficiency.[5]

However, a convincing empirical test of efficiency in the foreign exchange market is made difficult because there is no general agreement on models for equilibrium pricing or equilibrium rates of return which is comparable to that for equity markets. Simply put, it is difficult to test whether investors efficiently set the actual spot exchange equal to its equilibrium value, unless there is some agreement on what the equilibrium value is. Similarly, it is difficult to test whether risk-bearing is efficiently compensated if there is no agreement on the fundamental nature of foreign exchange risk, an adequate measure of foreign exchange risk, and a model that determines the equilibrium fair return for bearing foreign exchange risk.

Equity markets and foreign exchange markets differ in another important respect. Equity markets in the United States are characterized by a large number of private market participants who trade at a central location. Securities and Exchange Commission (SEC) regulation encourages the production and distribution of information. Price movements are essentially unconstrained, except when a large shock prompts the SEC to halt trading.

In the foreign exchange market, a government agency is often interposed between the market and the investor. Under a pegged rate system or dirty floating, the government may enter the market in a nonprofit-maximizing and nonstationary manner. In this case, the presence of the government may alter the "normal" equilibrium pricing and return relationships in the market. Under pegged rates, changes in international reserves substitute for changes in the spot rate. Alternatively, the government may substitute capital controls or tariffs for exchange-rate changes. It would therefore seem that any model of equilibrium pricing of foreign exchange that omits the role of government would be misspecified.[6]

To summarize, the efficient market hypothesis requires a simultaneous test of two hypotheses. A number of plausible alternative models for equilibrium pricing or returns have been incorporated into efficient market tests for equities. However, in the case of foreign exchange there is no firm agreement on a model of equilibrium prices or returns, and still less agreement on the stationarity of any model over time, especially in the presence

[5] Professional investment managers have never completely adopted the view that the equity market is efficient. However, the trend away from active portfolio management and toward index funds suggests that professional managers are becoming less confident in their ability to outperform the market.

[6] It is important to note that government intervention per se does not imply exchange market inefficiency. To the extent that the intervention policy is known, it should be reflected in the price of foreign exchange and in other financial markets. To the extent that intervention is unpredictable, the increased uncertainty may reduce the willingness of traders to take positions. This increase in uncertainty may reduce the liquidity of markets and widen the bid-ask spread, but this is not a market inefficiency in the sense of Fama.

of erratic government intervention. We will expand on these issues again after a brief survey of the literature.

II. TESTS OF FOREIGN EXCHANGE MARKET EFFICIENCY

A. *Certainty and risk-free investment*

In the foreign exchange market, arbitrage is an elementary investment opportunity that promises a certain return with no increase in exposure to exchange risk.[7] The interest parity model illustrates a prime example of this type of investment. In an efficient market, prices of foreign exchange and interest-bearing assets should be set so that "unusual profits" from covered interest arbitrage are quickly eliminated. Since the arbitrage is essentially risk-free and can be completed in a matter of seconds, any profit in excess of transaction costs is unusual. In arbitrage, the equilibrium expected return is zero.

Two popular methods for testing interest parity theory have been the following.[8] The first method computes the deviations from interest parity

$$(2) \quad d = \frac{F - S}{S} - \frac{i - i^*}{1 + i^*}.$$

Interest parity holds when the null hypothesis, $d = 0$, cannot be rejected. A second method estimates the regression equation

$$(3) \quad \frac{F - S}{S} = a + b \frac{(i - i^*)}{(1 + i^*)}.$$

In this model, interest parity holds when the null hypothesis, $a = 0$ and $b = 1$, cannot be rejected. Since both tests are based on the average relationship between the forward premium and the interest differential, neither test is adequate for the purpose of testing market efficiency. A simple example illustrates this point.

Assume that deviations (d) from interest parity are $+2$ percent and -2 percent with equal probability. Neither test (2) nor (3) would reject interest parity theory. However, if the total cost of transacting were 1 per-

---

[7] The issue of whether exposure to political risk is increased will be considered shortly.

Two other types of arbitrage are important for an efficient foreign exchange market. First, spatial arbitrage of an individual currency reduces the dispersion of quotations across market makers. Some price dispersion is consistent with market efficiency, since there is a cost of searching for spatial arbitrage profits and some risk associated with exploiting them. For a detailed study of price dispersion in the U.S. Treasury Bill market, see Garbade and Silber (1976).

A second profit opportunity is available through triangular arbitrage—the process which keeps cross-exchange rates (DM/£) consistent with direct exchange rates ($/DM; $/£). This efficient market principle has been adapted to estimate transaction costs in foreign exchange markets. See Frenkel and Levich (1975, 1977) and McCormick (1977).

[8] For a survey of the interest parity literature, see Officer and Willett (1970).

cent, the data indicate that arbitragers failed to exploit pure profit opportunities in every period.

Returns in excess of the equilibrium expected rate were consistently available. The essence of market efficiency in this example relies on the ability of investors to police an arbitrage boundary condition in every single period and not in some average sense. A calculation of the percentage of times that covered arbitrage does not produce a profit allows us to make a direct inference about market efficiency. The higher this percentage, the greater the market efficiency.

Clendenning (1970) calculates the time series of deviations in covered arbitrage between Euro-dollar and Euro-sterling deposits for the period 1962–67. He concludes that a high percentage of the deviations are near (within 0.25 percent of) zero and therefore too small to exploit for profit. Frenkel and Levich (1975, 1977) develop a model of interest parity that explicitly introduces transaction costs. Transaction costs in securities and foreign exchange markets imply the existence of a neutral equilibrium band—around the interest parity line—within which no additional arbitrage is profitable. Using weekly data on external securities (Euro-dollars, Euro-deutsche marks, Euro-Canadian dollars) in three periods (1962–67, 1968–69, 1973–75), Frenkel and Levich calculate that a very high percentage of observations are within the neutral band. And therefore, the Euro-currency market is efficient in that there are few unexploited opportunities for risk-free profit through covered interest arbitrage.[9]

The results for covered arbitrage between domestic or onshore assets are ambiguous. Frenkel and Levich (1975, 1977) and Levich (1977) report that a much smaller fraction of observations are bounded within the neutral band when arbitrage is between treasury bills or commercial paper traded in different domestic markets (see Table 1). This apparent

Table 1. Percentage of Deviations from Interest Parity within ±0.25%

Country	Treasury Bills	External Deposit	Commercial Paper
Canada	71.86	93.43	82.71
United Kingdom	55.76	96.68	63.21
Belgium	36.95	78.25	—
France	29.73	82.85	—
Germany	44.21	98.82	—
Italy	11.07	65.78	—
Netherlands	56.37	97.40	—
Switzerland	27.27	78.59	—

Note: All assets are three-month maturity. Approximately 426 weekly observations from the period 1967–75. Source, Levich (1977).

[9] In private conversations, several traders have reported that they use the interest parity relation for setting prices. For example, one large New York bank computes the deposit rate for an external account denominated in SDR by adding the forward discount on SDR to the Euro-dollar deposit rate.

departure from market efficiency is more pronounced during turbulent periods on the foreign exchange market.

There are two general arguments for the failure of interest parity between onshore markets. The first is that onshore markets differ in terms of political risk (Aliber 1973), which represents the probability that the sovereign may interpose his authority between the investor and the market place.[10] If unanticipated capital controls are instituted, the investor's realized return will be less than his expected return. A second argument agrees that capital controls are more common in onshore (regulated) markets. However, once a control is in place it can be treated as a known cost (similar to a transaction cost or tax) rather than an unknown or risky factor.[11] Preliminary research reported by Dooley (1976) suggests that the price differential between onshore and offshore assets responds quickly and in the appropriate direction to reflect the differential regulation in place.

Overall, research on arbitrage between onshore assets is not satisfactory. If risk is a factor, it should be possible to document periods when unanticipated controls reduced the realized return from covered arbitrage below the expected return. If the risk is political, then the interest differential between onshore and offshore assets should be sensitive to political events. On the other hand, if the cost of capital controls in place can be quantified, then a neutral band analysis is possible to test the efficiency of covered arbitrage between onshore markets.

B. Uncertainty and risky investments

Introducing uncertainty into single period and multiperiod investment models adds a degree of complexity, as well as realism, to tests of foreign exchange market efficiency. When the future spot exchange rate is a random variable, the dollar value of assets denominated in a foreign currency is uncertain. In this case, an investor who holds a net (asset or liability) position in foreign currency is exposed to foreign exchange risk.[12] In an efficient market, prices (of spot and forward exchange, for example) should be set so that "unusual profits" from risky investment opportunities are quickly eliminated. Since a test of market efficiency tests a joint hypothesis, the specification of the expected equilibrium return for bearing foreign exchange

---

[10] Interest parity holds in a single offshore center because the assets are exposed to the same political risks. Political risk is a fundamental argument behind the elasticity explanation for deviations from interest parity. Presumably, if there were no risks in arbitrage, the arbitrage supply schedule would be perfectly elastic. An alternative explanation for less than perfectly elastic arbitrage supply is that institutional constraints restrict the ability of banks to supply a sufficient number of forward contracts.

[11] For an analysis of the impact of differential tax treatment of capital gains and ordinary income on the traditional interest parity model, see Levi (1977).

[12] Political risk was discussed in the previous section. Aliber (1973) argues that arbitragers bear political risk, while speculators bear exchange risk. For a model that considers default risk on forward contracts, see Adler and Dumas (1976).

risk is critical. We must have some standard to judge that profits from bearing foreign exchange risk are "unusual."

There are basically two techniques for bearing foreign exchange risk— spot speculation and forward speculation. In spot speculation, the investor borrows domestic currency (at interest rate, i), buys foreign exchange in the spot market (at the rate S_t) and invests in a foreign currency denominated asset (with expected return, i^*). A forward speculator can establish a similar long position by simply buying foreign exchange in the forward market (at the rate, F_t). In either case, the profit depends on the future spot exchange rate, $\tilde{S}_{t+1}$, which is uncertain. It is easily shown that when the interest rate parity theorem holds, spot and forward speculation are equivalent investments in that they lead to the same time series of expected profits.[13]

Spot market efficiency. One popular null hypothesis is that, under a regime of floating exchange rates, changes in spot exchange rates should be serially uncorrelated. Empirical tests of this hypothesis have been reported by Poole (1967) and Burt, Kaen and Booth (1977).[14] In general, this research concludes that there are significant departures from random behavior under floating exchange rates and therefore, the spot market is not efficient. However, as we suggested earlier, market efficiency requires a random behavior of returns only if the equilibrium expected return is constant. Therefore, only in the case where interest rates in the two countries differ by a constant and the equilibrium expected exchange rate follows a linear trend (equal to the constant) should we expect that exchange rates follow a random walk (with a drift factor equal to the constant). By contrast, if the fundamental determinants of exchange rates are serially correlated, then equilibrium exchange rates will be serially correlated also.[15] As Logue and Sweeney (1977) have noted, since serial correlation statistics implicitly assume that the equilibrium exchange rate follows a linear trend, they are not powerful as tests of market efficiency.

Another related test of market efficiency in spot speculation has relied on the profitability of simple filter rule trading strategies.[16] An x percent

---

[13] For a formal proof, see Tsiang (1959, pp. 86–92).

[14] Other authors have reported the time series properties of exchange rates for descriptive purposes (Frenkel and Levich 1977), for time series forecasting (Giddy and Dufey 1975, Bilson and Levich 1977), and in conjunction with a filter rule analysis (Dooley and Shafer 1976), without drawing a direct inference about market efficiency.

[15] Stein (1977) demonstrates that in response to a shock that changes the long-run equilibrium exchange rate, exchange rate changes may be serially correlated as the result of risk aversion.

[16] From the description of spot speculation, it is clear that profits are zero when $S_{t+1} = S_t (1 + i)/(1 + i^*)$. Levich (1978) analyzes this relationship as a forecasting model for the one-, three- and six-month horizons. Using weekly data on Euro-currency deposit rates for nine industrial countries in the period 1967–75, Levich shows that forecast errors are, on average, not significant; they are small relative to transaction costs and serially uncorrelated over time. Although filter rule trading strategies are not tested, the absence of serial correlation suggests that these strategies would not be profitable.

filter rule leads to the following trading strategy: "Buy a currency whenever it rises x percent above its most recent trough; sell the currency and take a short position whenever the currency falls x percent below its most recent peak." Poole (1967) reports filter rule profits for the Canadian dollar during the floating rate period, 1950–62, and for nine other series of flexible exchange rates in the post-World War I period. Poole finds evidence of statistically significant first-order serial correlation in exchange rate changes. As a result, filter rule strategies tend to make large profits relative to a buy-and-hold strategy. Profits are not adjusted for the interest expense of a short position, the interest income of a long position, or the cost of transacting. Because of the last factor, Poole believes his results do not conclusively reject market efficiency.

Two more comprehensive and rigorous studies of spot market efficiency were conducted by Dooley and Shafer (1976) and Logue, Sweeney, and Willett (1977). Dooley and Shafer report filter rule profits for nine countries (Belgium, Canada, France, Germany, Italy, Japan, Netherlands, Switzerland, and the United Kingdom) using daily spot rates over the period March 1973 to September 1975. The authors' calculations are adjusted to reflect the interest expense and income of short and long positions, and transaction costs are incorporated by using bid and asked foreign exchange quotations. Dooley and Shafer hypothesize that if the market is efficient, then filter rule profits, adjusted to reflect the above costs, should be a "fair game" (or martingale) process as in (1). Any gross profits from the filter rule strategies imply net, abnormal profits and therefore reject market efficiency.

Dooley and Shafer's results indicate that small filters ($x = 1$, 3 or 5 percent) would have been profitable for all currencies over the entire sample period. However, there appears to be some element of riskiness in these trading rules, since each filter would have generated losses in at least one currency during at least one subperiod. Furthermore, it is not clear that ex ante the size of the filter can be determined that optimizes or assures profits. During the first third of the sample period any small filter leads to profits in all currencies. However, the profits generally decline, sometimes becoming negative in the second and final third of the sample.

Logue, Sweeney, and Willett report filter rule profits for seven countries based on 692 trading days in the period April 1973 to January 1977. The authors' calculations are not adjusted for transaction costs or for interest income from long positions or interest expense from short positions. They do assume that profits are reinvested. Filter rule profits are compared to a buy-and-hold (the foreign currency) strategy based on the rationale that we must account for long-term trends in the currency. The authors argue that "the relevant alternative to the trading rule . . . is holding the foreign currency."

Logue, Sweeney and Willett's results are in many ways similar to Dooley and Shafer's. For the entire sample, small filters are generally more profitable than the buy-and-hold strategy. However, there is substantial variation across currencies and subperiods. For currencies that appreciated during the second (of three) subperiods (Netherlands guilder, French franc, Swiss franc), no filter rule is superior to buy-and-hold. Many small filter rules are profitable during the first subperiod, but for some currencies the amount of the profit appears highly sensitive to the size of the filter. On average, filter rule profits in the third subperiod are less than buy-and-hold profits which may indicate that foreign exchange traders are learning to exploit price trends more quickly.

What are the implications of these results for spot exchange market efficiency? The key question is whether "unusual" profit opportunities are available to spot speculators. In the context of a mean-variance model, an unusual return corresponds to a return/risk ratio that is greater than for the aggregate capital market[17] (see Fig. 3). To test market efficiency, we must measure the return and risk of spot speculation as well as the return and risk of alternative investments in the capital market.

A first problem is the measurement of speculative returns. Dooley and Shafer assume that the speculator starts from a zero asset position and borrows to commence his trading. As a purely technical matter, the rate of return is not defined in this case. Logue, Sweeney, and Willett avoid this problem by calculating the amount of profit rather than the rate of profit.

A more fundamental issue is whether the mean-variance model illustrated in Figure 3 is the appropriate model for pricing foreign exchange risk. And if it is appropriate, should it be implemented using an international portfolio of risky assets and an international risk-free rate, or

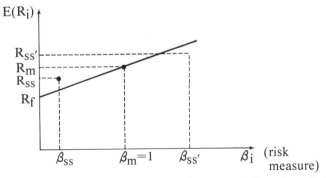

Fig. 3. A Test for Unusual Returns in Spot Speculation.

[17] For more on the measurement of investment performance, see Fama (1972).

should we compare spot speculation to the traditional domestic capital market line? The general issue is the choice of an appropriate model for foreign exchange risk pricing. More on this issue in Section III.

One way to avoid the above problem is to specify an alternative investment for comparison with spot speculation. For example, Dooley and Shafer assume that foreign currency investments are financed by borrowing local currency. Even if a bank does have a trading room with a positive asset position, the borrowing rate will underestimate the cost of funds. This is because filter rule trading alters the bank's cash flows relative to a do-nothing strategy. This is also true with the Logue, Sweeney, and Willett paper. The trading rule, with a variable currency position, is more risky than a buy-and-hold strategy, with a constant Euro-currency position.[18] Both the Dooley–Shafer and Logue–Sweeney–Willett procedures under-estimate the riskiness or the cost of capital for the trading rule. We, there-fore, expect the trading rule to outperform its alternatives, but by how much is not clear. This suggests that to know the cost of capital for the trading rule we need to know more than the alternative use of funds—we need to know the riskiness of the trading rule itself.

One procedure for estimating the riskiness of the trading rule would be to consider more subperiods. For example, we could calculate a weekly return based on five days of filter rule trading. Using the market model from portfolio theory, we could regress the weekly returns from spot speculation (R_{ss}) against the weekly returns on an aggregate market indicator (R_m) to estimate the covariance risk (β_{ss}) of spot speculation.

$$R_{ss} - R_f = \alpha + \beta_{ss}(R_m - R_f) + \epsilon$$

The realized return (R_{ss}) and the estimated risk $(\hat{\beta}_{ss})$ determine a point on Figure 3. If over time, the returns to spot speculation are significantly above the capital market line, then unusual profit opportunities are available, and the market is not efficient.

Another problem involves data considerations. Tests of market efficiency should be based on firm bid and offer prices that correspond to transaction prices. Even if this condition is satisfied, a finding of market inefficiency is still ambiguous. Market-maker quotations are typically valid only for a small and specified volume of contracts and for a limited time span. It is therefore possible that supply and demand elasticities are sufficiently small so that unusual profits in spot speculation would be eliminated quickly after a small volume of trading.

A final difficulty rests on the distinction between ex ante and ex post information. As Poole has noted, "It is obvious that for any particular series . . . one could always construct, ex post, some mechanical trading

---

[18] By maintaining a constant position, the buy-and-hold strategy captures a time diversification and reduces risk. See Black and Scholes (1974).

rule which would have provided excellent returns. A test of a mechanical trading rule requires that the rule be selected first and the series later."[19] Since filter rule profits are highly sensitive to the size of the filter, it follows that, ex ante, another element of risk is introduced. For the market to be inefficient it must be possible, ex ante, to select a filter that leads to unusual profits.

Forward market efficiency. Studies of the efficiency of the forward exchange market have focussed on the relationship between the current n-period forward rate $(F_{t,n})$ and the spot rate n-periods in the future $(S_{t,n})$.[20] Table 2 provides summary information on fourteen of these studies. Most of these studies have compared the *level* of the forward rate with the *level* of the future spot rate.

For example, regression analyses have tested the equation

(4) $S_{t+n} = a + b F_{t,n} + u_t$

against the null hypothesis that $a = 0$ *and* $b = 1$. If we cannot reject the result that $a = 0$ *and* $b = 1$, then we can conclude that the forward rate is an unbiased predictor. In many studies, this result is taken as an indication of market efficiency. Since movements in the spot rate are likely to be dominated by a trend, equation (4) is likely to produce a high R^2; that is, the *level* of the forward rate will explain a high percentage of the variation in the *level* of the future spot rate.

However, since *changes* in the spot rate about its trend are likely to be nearly random, an equation of the form

(5) $\dfrac{S_{t+n}}{S_t} = a + b \dfrac{F_{t,n}}{S_t} + e_t$

is likely to produce a low R^2. That is, the forward premium will explain a low percentage of the variation of *changes* in the spot rate series. However, if we cannot reject the result that $a = 0$ *and* $b = 1$, we can again conclude that the forward rate is an unbiased predictor. The low R^2 will simply mean that the forward premium is a poor predictor of *changes* in the spot rate, even though it is an unbiased predictor.

The empirical results generally confirm the above statements about regression testing. Kaserman (1973), Bilson (1976), Bilson and Levich (1977), Frenkel (1977, 1978), and Stockman (1978) have tested regres-

[19] Poole (1967, p. 477).

[20] An exception is Giddy (1977) who analyzes the term structure of forward rates. Under a pure expectations framework, long-term forward rates (the current twelve-month rate) should be unbiased predictors of future short-term forward rates (the three-month forward rate observed nine months from now). Giddy did not test this relationship directly. Instead he uses an error-learning model and concludes that short-term forecast errors are quickly incorporated by revisions in the long-term forward rate, a result that is consistent with the pure expectations theory.

Table 2. Empirical Research on the Forward Rate as a Predictor of the Future Spot Rate

Author	Currencies	Time Period	Horizon	Statistical Technique	Results
Porter (1971)	Canada	1953-60 N = 32 quarters	90 day	Regression	Forward rate is a poor predictor of *changes* in spot rate.
Kaserman (1973)	Canada	1955-61 N = 21 quarters	90 day	Regression and χ^2 tests	Regression coefficients indicate forward rate is unbiased.
Aliber (1974)	U.K., Belgium, France, Germany, Netherlands, Switzerland	1961-71 N = 43 quarters	90 day	Mean error. Mean absolute error. Runs test.	During pegged rate period, mean forecast errors are small and not significant.
Kohlhagen (1974)	Canada	1952-70 N = 227 months N = 874 weeks	90 day	Mean error	Over the 18 year period, the forward rate is an unbiased predictor.
Giddy & Dufey (1975)	Canada, France, U.K.	1973-74 N = 150 trading days	90 day	Mean square error	Forward rate is a poor forecaster, with higher MSE than other simple models.
Kohlhagen (1975)	Canada, Denmark, France, Germany, Switzerland, U.K.	1970-74 weekly data	90 day	Mean error. Mean absolute error	In most cases, and in the long run, forward rate is unbiased under floating rates.
Bilson (1976)	Germany (DM/£)	1971-76 N = 51 months	90 day	Regression	Regression coefficients indicate forward rate is unbiased.
Bilson & Levich (1977)	Germany, U.K.	1973-75 N = 142 weeks	1 month 3 month	Box–Jenkins time series analysis and regression	The forward rate is unbiased and reflects information in B–J forecast
Cornell (1977)	U.K., Canada, Germany, Switzerland, Netherlands, France, Japan	1973-77 N = 42 months	1 month	Mean error, regression techniques	Mean errors are not significant although there is some evidence of autocorrelation.

Study	Countries	Period	Maturity	Method	Results
Frenkel (1977)	Germany	1921–23, N = 23 months	1 month	Regression	Regression coefficients indicate a small bias that may be explained by transaction costs.
Giddy (1977)	Germany, U.K.	1967–76, N = 486 weeks	1, 2, 3, 6, and 12 month	Mean error	Mean errors are not significant. Forward rates do not seem to predict noticeably better than present spot rate.
Levich (1977)	Canada, U.K., Belgium, France, Germany, Italy, Netherlands, Switzerland, Japan	1967–75, N = 430 weeks	1, 3, and 6 month	Mean error. Mean squared error	Mean errors are small—either not significant or less than transaction costs. Mean errors are not correlated between time periods.
Frenkel (1978)	France, U.K.	1921–25, N = 51 months	1 month	Regression	Regression coefficients indicate forward rate is unbiased.
Stockman (1978)	U.K., Canada, Germany, Japan, Netherlands, Switzerland	1973–77, N = 222 weeks	30 day	Time series analysis and regression	Mean errors are not significant in the entire sample and in smaller subperiods.

sions similar to (4). With the exception of Frenkel (1977), no author can reject the hypothesis that the forward rate is an unbiased predictor. Frenkel reports a small (but statistically significant) bias. However, since he is testing the model during the extremely volatile German hyperinflation period, transaction costs probably exceed the magnitude of the bias.

Porter (1971) tested equation (5) on Canadian data and reported that the forward rate was unbiased, but explained only 1 percent of the variation in the spot exchange rate *changes*.

A second technique for analyzing forward bias has been to compute the forecast error $S_{t+n} - F_{t,n}$ and then to calculate the mean error, the mean absolute error, the mean squared error (MSE), or the number of errors bounded within a neutral band. Research along these lines has been reported by Aliber (1974), Kohlhagen (1974, 1975), Giddy and Dufey (1975), Cornell (1977), Giddy (1977), and Levich (1977). There are three important results to draw from this analysis.

First, over long periods and for most currencies, the mean errors are small. Many times the mean error is not significantly different from zero. When the mean error is significantly nonzero, it is likely smaller than transaction costs. Second, forecast errors in independent time periods are generally serially uncorrelated. Therefore, watching linear patterns in past forecast errors will not improve future forecasting performance. Third, the forward rate is not always the lowest MSE forecast that is publicly available. Giddy and Dufey (1975), Giddy (1977), and Levich (1977) report that forecasts based on relative Euro-currency interest rates or the lagged spot rate are often (marginally) superior to the forward prediction.

The important point regarding these studies is that unbiasedness is very often taken as the null hypothesis and then often equated with market efficiency. This approach is incorrect, since several theories of forward market equilibrium are consistent with a forward rate bias.[21] Therefore, the interpretation of these empirical studies is ambiguous. We are again confronted with the efficient market conundrum.

Another approach for testing forward market efficiency is based on the returns from forward speculation. The market is considered efficient if there are no unusual profits from forward speculation. An early study by Grubel (1966) calculated that over the period July 1955–May 1961 the average annual rate of return from sterling speculation was between 16 percent and 27 percent, assuming a 10 percent margin requirement. While Grubel indicated that these profits are large, he did not calculate a measure of risk, and so it is not clear that the profits are unusual in the sense we described earlier.

---

[21] One line of reasoning is that the bias represents a risk premium paid to speculators (Grubel 1966; Solnik 1973; Grauer, Litzenberger, and Stehle 1976). A second argument is that transaction costs contribute to bias (Kaserman 1973 and Levich 1977).

Levich (1977) reports speculative profits from a trading strategy that utilizes exchange rate forecasts based on time series analysis and interest rates. Levich develops a test for unusual profits that compares actual profits to "perfect information" profits, i.e., that level of profit that would be obtained if the speculator takes the correct position (short or long) in each period. Speculative profits were often significantly greater than zero, but small relative to the risk-free rate and to "perfect information" profits. This result is consistent with market efficiency, since the forecasts are based on publicly available information.

Filter rule tests, like the one tested in the spot market, have not been reported for the forward market.

The major problem with the above tests, as with tests of spot speculation, is that there is no adequate measure of risk to determine whether speculative profits are unusually high or low.

A final test of forward market efficiency is to test the forecasting accuracy of the forward rate against other models. A common null hypothesis is that the forward rate reflects exchange rate expectations and, therefore, the forward rate should be superior to any mechanically generated forecast. We have noted that Giddy and Dufey (1975) and Levich (1977) find that forecasts based on Euro-currency rates are often (marginally) superior to the forward rate. A recent study by Bilson and Levich (1977) tests the forecasting efficiency of the forward rate against (1) a Box–Jenkins time series forecast and (2) a composite forecast. On the basis of in-sample data, Bilson and Levich show that it is possible to construct a model that *fits* the data better than the forward rate. Bilson and Levich argue that this is not a proper test of forecasting efficiency, since the parameters of the constructed model are not known ex ante. Using post-sample data, the forward rate is generally a superior forecaster. Since two popular alternative models could not improve on the forward rate forecast, the authors conclude that there is no firm evidence against the forecasting efficiency hypothesis.

An additional topic, closely related to forward market efficiency, is the issue of stabilizing versus destabilizing speculation. The issue is relevant here because the methodology required to test both hypotheses is similar. A recent paper by Kohlhagen (1976) makes this point forcefully. Kohlhagen argues that tests for destabilizing speculation are testing a joint hypothesis. First, there is a hypothesis on the equilibrium exchange rate, based on fundamental variables but with the absence of speculators. Second, there is a hypothesis on how the presence of speculators or speculative expectations can be determined. Kohlhagen illustrates the approach by assuming (1) that the exchange rate is determined by monetary factors and (2) that the forward rate fully reflects speculative activity. The empirical results show evidence for both stabilizing and destabilizing behavior in the current floating period. In this case, the precise results seem less interesting than the methodology—evidence for speculative behavior is tested simultaneously with hypotheses (1) and (2).

III. MAJOR ISSUES FOR THE ANALYSIS OF FOREIGN EXCHANGE MARKET EFFICIENCY

The theoretical foundations of the efficient market hypothesis are well established, as summarized by Fama (1970). Initial tests of efficiency in equity markets benefitted (1) by the existence of several alternative and credible models for the equilibrium expected return associated with equity risk, and (2) by a long series of equity prices determined under fairly free market conditions. Related to the second point, corporate policies and the business cycle change slowly over time. Therefore, the process that determines equity prices is likely to be fairly stationary.

Early tests of foreign exchange market efficiency seemed to eschew theory in favor of ad hoc applications based on equity market tests. This was particularly unfortunate, since models of equilibrium pricing or returns were either poorly specified or subject to considerable debate. Furthermore, long series of firm transaction prices in freely floating foreign exchange markets were not available. The fundamental determinants of exchange rates (e.g., monetary policy, fiscal policy, and trade policy) were highly variable and government intervention unsteady, suggesting that the process determining foreign exchange rates was nonstationary.

Although the economics and environment of equity markets and exchange markets are dissimilar, the theory of efficient markets remains constant. The theory concludes that prices will adjust so that unusual profit opportunities are quickly eliminated. The following issues are critical for a rigorous test of foreign exchange market efficiency.

1. Weak form tests of market efficiency under uncertainty must specify an equilibrium model for exchange rates.[22] This model generates the time series of equilibrium expected prices (or equilibrium expected returns). Market efficiency is determined in relation to this standard. As illustrated in Figures 1 and 2, tests for serial correlation of spot rate changes (or forward rate changes) imply nothing about market efficiency without reference to some equilibrium model of the exchange rate.

2. Tests for unusual profits in spot and forward speculation must include a risk measure for the speculative activity. In all studies to date, risk measures have not been reported. This is legitimate in two cases: (1) Speculative profits are not correlated with the market and therefore returns in excess of the risk-free rate are unusual; or (2) speculative trading is equally risky as an alternative strategy (say, holding a constant Eurodollar position or buying and holding the foreign currency). However,

---

[22] For a recent survey of exchange rate models, see Isard (1977).

these conditions are typically not met. One solution, suggested earlier by equation (3), is to calculate speculative profits in many subperiods rather than aggregated over the entire sample, and then to compute a covariance measure of risk.

3. More general tests for unusual returns in currency speculation must be based on a foreign exchange risk pricing model, i.e., a model that relates the quantity of foreign exchange risk to the expected return for bearing this risk. Two single currency models (Tsiang 1959 and Feldstein 1968) assume that speculators are risk-averse and always require a risk premium. Other more general models (Solnik 1973, Grauer, Litzenberger, and Stehle 1976, and Levich 1976*a*) conclude that the risk premium can be positive, negative, or zero, but the relationship between exchange risk and return is positive and linear.[23]

The link between foreign exchange risk and return is a crucial, yet inadequately specified, part of many international financial models. Accordingly, this appears to be an important area for further research.

4. Tests for stabilizing or destabilizing speculation by private or official market participants or tests for insufficient speculation should follow a methodology similar to efficient market tests. An integral part of this methodology is to specify an equilibrium model of exchange rates in the absence of speculators.

5. Tests of the efficiency of arbitrage flows between offshore markets are fairly complete and convincing. Tests for efficiency of arbitrage flows between onshore markets or between onshore and offshore markets are inconclusive. In part, this is because the interest differential between onshore and offshore assets could result from two sources—(1) unknown political risks, or (2) known costs of differential taxes and exchange controls. The difference is important since (1) requires an uncertainty (return-risk) analysis and (2) requires a certainty (neutral-band) analysis. In either case, it will be difficult to document and quantify the necessary variables.

6. A final point involves statistical procedures for testing market efficiency. Under certainty, market efficiency requires that arbitrage boundary conditions are not violated. This suggests a neutral-band analysis rather than an analysis of mean values or regression equations. With uncertainty, tests for unusual returns must specify a risk measure or a similar alternative investment. In this regard, Cargill and Rausser (1975) have illustrated that filter rules may be an inappropriate technique for testing market efficiency. Since positive profits can be generated from a random price series, it is difficult to make a probabilistic statement about the profits achieved by any filter rule. A second statistical problem under uncertainty is the distinction between ex ante and ex post information.

---

[23] A test of the Solnik model appears in Roll and Solnik (1977). The models are reviewed in Levich (1976*b*).

The use of in-sample and post-sample data in Bilson and Levich (1977) is a useful procedure to continue in future tests.

In conclusion, the most simple tests—covered arbitrage between un-regulated, offshore markets—have provided adequate evidence that this segment of the market is efficient. Tests of other investment opportunities—covered arbitrage between onshore markets and speculative investments in spot and forward exchange—have not been adequately assessed. Several major obstacles remain before meaningful tests can be concluded. These obstacles include a model of exchange rate determination and a model of the relationship between speculative returns and exchange risk. This chapter has attempted to survey the important issues for testing exchange market efficiency in the hope that future research will resolve them.

There is no single definitive test for foreign exchange market efficiency. Future research will proceed in stages. Weak form tests will analyze whether trading rules based only on historical prices can lead to unusual profits. Semi-strong form tests will check that publicly available foreign exchange forecasts, balance-of-trade announcements, central bank inter-vention announcements, and other kinds of public information are quickly and fully reflected in market prices. Strong form tests will investigate whether professional foreign exchange traders or professional forecasting services possess inside information that is used to earn unusual profits. These tests are suggestive, not exhaustive. Several of them have been at-tempted and are described in this chapter. Empirical research that rec-ognizes the simultaneous nature of efficient market tests and explicitly specifies the underlying equilibrium model will make a useful contribution toward an assessment of foreign exchange market efficiency.

REFERENCES

Adler, Michael, and Dumas, Bernard. 1976. "Portfolio Choice and the Demand for Forward Exchange." *American Economic Review* 66 (2): 332–39.

Aliber, Robert Z. 1973. "The Interest Rate Parity Theorem: A Reinterpretation." *Journal of Political Economy* 81 (6): 1451–59.

———. 1974. "Attributes of National Monies and the Independence of National Monetary Policies." In *National Monetary Policies and the International System*, edited by R. Z. Aliber, pp. 111–26. Chicago: University of Chicago Press.

Bilson, John F. O. 1976. "A Monetary Approach to the Exchange Rate." Ph.D. dissertation, University of Chicago.

Bilson, John F. O., and Levich, Richard M. 1977. "A Test of the Efficiency of the Forward Exchange Market." New York University Working Paper No. 77–61.

Black, Fischer, and Scholes, Myron. 1974. "From Theory to a New Financial Product." *Journal of Finance* 29 (2): 399–412.

Burt, John, Kaen, Fred R., and Booth, G. Geoffrey. 1977. "Foreign Exchange

Market Efficiency under Flexible Exchange Rates." *Journal of Finance* 32 (4): 1325–30.

Cargill, Thomas E., and Rausser Gordon C. 1975. "Temporal Price Behavior in Commodity Futures Markets." *Journal of Finance* 30 (4): 1043–54.

Clendenning, E. Wayne. 1970. *The Euro-Dollar Market.* Oxford: Clarendon Press.

Cornell, Bradford. 1977. "Spot Rates, Forward Rates and Exchange Market Efficiency." *Journal of Financial Economics* 5: 55–65.

Dooley, Michael P. 1976. "Note on Interest Parity, Eurocurrencies and Capital Controls." International Finance Discussion Papers, No. 80. Washington, D.C.: Federal Reserve System.

Dooley, Michael P., and Shafer, Jeffrey R. 1976. "Analysis of Short-Run Exchange Rate Behavior: March 1973 to September 1975." International Finance Discussion Papers, No. 76. Washington, D.C.: Federal Reserve System.

Fama, Eugene F. 1970. "Efficient Capital Markets: A Review of Theory and Empirical Work." *Journal of Finance* 25 (2): 383–417.

––––––. 1972. "Components of Investment Performance." *Journal of Finance* 27 (3): 551–67.

––––––. 1976. *Foundations of Finance.* New York: Basic Books.

Feldstein, Martin S. 1968. "Uncertainty and Forward Speculation." *Review of Economics and Statistics* 50: 182–92.

Frenkel, Jacob A. 1977. "The Forward Exchange Rate, Expectations and the Demand for Money: The German Hyperinflation." *American Economic Review* 67 (4): 653–70.

––––––. 1978. "Purchasing Power Parity: Evidence from the 1920's." *Journal of International Economics* 8 (2): 161–91.

Frenkel, Jacob A., and Levich, Richard M. 1975. "Covered Interest Arbitrage: Unexploited Profits?" *Journal of Political Economy* 83 (2): 325–38.

––––––. 1977. "Transaction Costs and Interest Arbitrage: Tranquil Versus Turbulent Periods." *Journal of Political Economy* 85 (6): 1207–24.

Garbade, Kenneth D., and Silber, William L. 1976. "Price Dispersion in the Government Securities Market." *Journal of Political Economy* 84 (4): 721–40.

Giddy, Ian H. 1977. "Term Structure and Expectations in the Money and Foreign Exchange Markets." Columbia University Graduate School of Business Working Paper.

Giddy, Ian H., and Dufey, Gunter. 1975. "The Random Behavior of Flexible Exchange Rates." *Journal of International Business Studies* 6 (1): 1–32.

Grauer, F. Z. A., Litzenberger, R. H., and Stehle, R. E. 1976. "Sharing Rules and Equilibrium in an International Capital Market and Uncertainty." *Journal of Financial Economics* 3: 233–56.

Grubel, Herbert G. 1966. *Forward Exchange Speculation and the International Flow of Capital.* Stanford: Stanford University Press.

Isard, Peter. 1977. "The Process of Exchange Rate Determination: A Survey of Important Models and Major Issues." International Finance Discussion Papers, No. 101. Washington, D.C.: Federal Reserve System.

Kaserman, David L. 1973. "The Forward Rate: Its Determination and Behavior as a Predictor of the Future Spot Rate." Proceedings of the American Statistical Association, pp. 417–22.

Kohlhagen, Steven W. 1974. "The Forward Rate as an Unbiased Estimator of the Future Spot Rate." Mimeographed. University of California, Berkeley.

———. 1975. "The Performance of the Foreign Exchange Markets: 1971–1974." *Journal of International Business Studies* 6 (2).

———. 1977. "The Identification of Destabilizing Foreign Exchange Speculation." International Finance Discussion Papers, No. 100. Washington, D.C.: Federal Reserve System.

Levi, Maurice D. 1977. "Taxation and 'Abnormal' International Capital Flows." *Journal of Political Economy* 85 (3): 635–46.

Levich, Richard M. 1976a. "Pure Gambles and Portfolio Theory." Mimeographed, New York University.

———. 1976b. "The Rewards for Bearing Foreign Exchange Risk." Mimeographed. Federal Reserve System Board of Governors.

———. 1977. "The International Money Market: Tests of Forecasting Models and Market Efficiency." Ph.D. dissertation, University of Chicago.

———. 1978. "Tests of Forecasting Models and Market Efficiency in the International Money Market." In *The Economics of Exchange Rates: Selected Studies*, edited by J. A. Frenkel and H. G. Johnson. Boston: Addison–Wesley.

Logue, Dennis, and Sweeney, Richard. 1977. " 'White-Noise' in Imperfect Markets: The Case of the Franc/Dollar Exchange Rate." *Journal of Finance* 32 (3): 761–68.

Logue, Dennis, Sweeney, Richard, and Willett, Thomas D. 1977. "Speculative Behavior of Foreign Exchange Rates during the Current Float." Discussion Paper Series No. 77/2. Washington, D.C.: Office of the Assistant Secretary for International Affairs, U.S. Treasury.

McCormick, Frank. 1977. "Covered Interest Arbitrage: Unexploited Profits?: Comment." Mimeographed. Federal Reserve System Board of Governors.

Officer, Lawrence H., and Willet, Thomas D. 1970. "The Covered-Arbitrage Schedule: A Critical Survey of Recent Developments." *Journal of Money, Credit and Banking* 2 (2): 247–57.

Poole, William. 1967. "Speculative Prices on Random Walks: An Analysis of Ten Time Series of Flexible Exchange Rates." *Southern Economic Journal* 33 (4): 468–78.

Porter, Michael G. 1971. "A Theoretical and Empirical Framework for Analyzing the Term Structure of Exchange Rate Expectations." *Staff Papers* 18 (3): 613–45.

Roll, Richard. 1977. "A Critique of the Asset Pricing Theory's Tests." *Journal of Financial Economics* 4 (2): 129–76.

Roll, Richard, and Solnik, Bruno. 1977. "A Pure Foreign Exchange Asset Pricing Model," *Journal of International Economics* 7 (2): 161–79.

Solnik, Bruno H. 1973. *European Capital Markets*. Boston: D. C. Heath-Lexington.

Stein, Jerome L. 1977. "Assessing the Efficiency of Floating Exchange Markets." Brown University Working Paper No. 77–28.

Stockman, Alan C. 1978. "Risk, Information and Forward Exchange Rates." In *The Economics of Exchange Rates: Selected Studies*, edited by J. A. Frenkel and H. G. Johnson. Boston: Addison–Wesley.

Tsiang, S. C. 1959. "The Theory of Forward Exchange And the Effects of Government Intervention on the Forward Market." *Staff Papers* 7 (1): 75–106.

Comment

JOHN F. O. BILSON

Richard Levich argues forcefully that tests of market efficiency are hampered by the joint hypothesis problem. In response, I shall argue that, while the problem exists, it is more serious in domestic financial markets, and that existing empirical evidence provides sufficient grounds to warrant provisional acceptance of the hypothesis in international financial markets.

Levich follows Fama in defining an efficient market as one in which unusual profits cannot be made from the exploitation of available information. Because direct evidence on the profits made by foreign exchange market participants is lacking, empirical research typically attempts to make inferences about the efficiency of the market on the basis of observed market prices. For example, the equality of the covered yields on identical bonds denominated in different currencies leads to the inference that efficient covered interest arbitrage is taking place. The fundamental difficulty in this indirect approach to the efficiency question is that other factors—capital controls, transactions costs, differential risk, etc.—may cause the covered yields to diverge, even in the presence of efficient arbitrage. The joint hypothesis problem arises because it is necessary to make assumptions about these other factors in order to undertake the test of market efficiency. Obviously, the validity of the tests is directly related to the validity of these underlying assumptions.

In this respect, the international financial market provides a number of unique cases for undertaking tests of market efficiency. In the Eurocurrency market, deposits denominated in different currencies are offered in a market that is notably free from direct government intervention and control. Since these deposits are identical in all respects other than the currency denomination, efficient arbitrage should equate the covered yields on the different deposits, after due allowance is made for transactions costs. In particular, it is important to note that it is unnecessary to make any assumption about the equilibrium real rate of return in order to undertake the test of market efficiency, since this assumption appears to have been the main stumbling block in the path of domestic market tests of the hypothesis. Since, in the Eurocurrency markets, tests of the interest rate parity condition are reasonably effective tests of market efficiency, their results carry implications that lead far beyond the Eurocurrency markets themselves.

It is well known, for example, that tests of the interest rate parity condition between onshore assets—Treasury Bills in domestic markets, for example—are far more ambiguous than the generally positive findings of the studies based upon the Eurocurrency markets. In the absence of other evidence, it would be impossible to tell whether this ambiguity is due to the presence of 'other factors' or market inefficiency. However, the evidence from the Eurocurrency market surely suggests that the other factors should bear the bulk of the responsibility—there is no reason why the arbitragers who maintain the parity relationships between Eurocurrency rates should not also be at work in the onshore markets. Unfortunately, the investigation of these other factors is still in a preliminary stage, but Michael Dooley's work on capital controls does suggest that the discrepancies between onshore and offshore interest rates is not due to market inefficiency. In conclusion, the papers by Frenkel and Levich (1975, 1977) and McCormick (1977) support the view that the Eurocurrency market is efficiently arbitraged, and these studies therefore also offer circumstantial evidence in favor of the efficient market hypothesis in domestic markets.

There is, on the other hand, a distinct difference between covered interest arbitrage and forward exchange speculation. While the former is essentially riskless, the latter constitutes one of the hair-raising and heart-stopping activities available to the modern entrepreneur. Because of the unpredictable exchange rate movements that have occurred during the floating rate period, the actual and perceived risk from forward exchange speculation is large, and it is therefore difficult to envisage anyone accepting this risk without the expectation of a relatively large gain from the undertaking. Risk-averse speculators will demand a premium, represented by the differential between the forward rate and the speculators' expected future spot rate, in order to compensate for the risk of forward exchange speculation. There are consequently two difficulties in undertaking tests of market efficiency in speculative markets: adequately representing the speculator's expected future spot rate, and accounting for the risk premium. In particular, it is almost impossible to test market efficiency, using only data on spot and forward exchange rates. As I understand it, this is the point that is being made in Richard Levich's paper.

It is, however, possible to test the stronger hypothesis of forecasting efficiency, which requires both market efficiency and risk neutrality on the part of the dominant speculators. If the forward market is dominated by well-informed, risk-neutral, and profit-maximizing speculators with access to an infinitely elastic supply of funds, the forward rate should be equal to the best available forecast of the future spot rate. For many issues in international finance, forecasting efficiency is a more useful concept than market efficiency, and evidence that the market is forecasting efficient implies that it is also market efficient, in Fama's terminology. The available empirical evidence, as reviewed by Levich, suggests that the forecasting efficiency hypothesis cannot be rejected in most cases. This is consequently strong evidence in favor of market efficiency in the speculative markets.

For these reasons, I believe that a greater degree of optimism on the ability to test market efficiency is justified than is present in Richard Levich's paper. Tests that circumvent the joint hypothesis problem—like tests of interest rate parity in the Eurocurrency markets—are possible in international markets to a far greater extent than is possible in domestic financial markets. Second, where the joint hypothesis problem is unavoidable, as in the speculative markets, the available tests tend to support both hypotheses, so that the problem of distinguishing between them does not arise.

CHAPTER EIGHT

Stabilization and Stagflation in a Semi-Industrialized Economy

MICHAEL BRUNO

Economic policy issues cannot be discussed fruitfully without reference to particular economic structure and institutions. Models constructed for one set-up may be of little relevance in another. This is no less true for problems of short-term stabilization and macropolicies. In a single economy that is virtually closed, theories and policy debates might center on the inflation-unemployment trade-off to the exclusion of any influences of, or repercussions on, the outside world. In a very open economy, a model of the inflationary process must not only consider a major additional trade-off, and related policy tools, but might, in general, involve different prescriptions for domestic monetary and fiscal policy. Mundell (1962), Fleming (1962), and the growing and by now voluminous literature of recent years have contributed to the general acceptance of this distinction. Having agreed that we are in the open-economy game, however, there is room for making at least one other major typological distinction that has to do with the degree of development of particular markets within an economy and the class of external influences to which it would normally be confined.

There is growing empirical evidence, as well as limited theoretical discussion, centering on the characterization of short-term adjustment within a narrower subgroup of the LDCs which, for want of a better term, are usually called semi-industrialized economies.[1] This discussion would be of relatively little general interest were it not for the fact that it has brought up systematic evidence that runs counter to standard theories and macro-policy prescriptions. One major example is the possible contractionary or,

This chapter was written during a visit at Harvard University and at the Massachusetts Institute of Technology, with financial support by the Ford Foundation. I wish to thank R. Dornbusch for detailed and very helpful comments and discussions on an earlier draft. Helpful remarks by P. Aspe, R. I. McKinnon, P. A. Samuelson, and L. Taylor are also gratefully acknowledged.

[1] See Díaz-Alejandro (1963), Cooper (1971a,b), and Taylor (1974).

one might say, stagflationary effect of devaluations. Another aspect of stagflation that has received attention only very recently is the, possibly perverse, impact effect of contractionary monetary policy under credit rationing. The latter, to be discussed in some detail here, is of particular importance in the debate about the monetarist approach to stabilization and the balance of payments.

How would one define a semi-industrialized economy (SIE)? At the risk of oversimplification a few stylized facts and characteristics should be mentioned.

1. Typically, the country we are talking about would have a per capita income level somewhere between $300 and $1,000.

2. It is normally relatively small in economic size, is a price-taker in its import (and usually also export) markets, and is highly dependent on imports of machinery and some of its raw materials.

3. It would normally be past the early stage of industrialization, which is mainly characterized by import substitution of consumer goods. It would have a modest-sized industry that is usually heavily protected and quite oligopolistic in structure. Manufacturing exports would play a small but increasingly important role.

4. Its trade balance would be marked by substantial structural deficits and considerable publicly controlled flows of capital, mostly used to finance imports of capital goods, while endogenous private capital flows are relatively small.

5. Functional income shares are a major determinant of private consumption and saving behavior.

6. The country's fiscal base would typically consist of indirect rather than direct taxation and, within the latter, import duties often play a major role. Government deficit financing by money creation may be another important feature.

7. Finally, and for our purpose this may be the most important characteristic, its system of financial intermediation would be relatively underdeveloped.[2] The public holds money, but few primary securities. Investment is financed primarily from retained earnings and government loans. Short-term bank credit is rationed fairly centrally, with official interest rate ceilings. The unorganized financial 'curb' market plays a major role. It is a highly segmented and imperfect market and the marginal cost of borrowing involves a considerable risk factor. The money supply is fed by the government deficit or the private sector's trade balance. A change in the latter and in official credit will affect the system mainly through its impact on the cost of working capital and on the economy's aggregate supply schedule. Monetary restraint may thus have a direct cost-increasing

---

[2] Obviously there are considerable variations among countries, particularly in this respect, and such a stereotype description would accordingly have to be modified.

and output-reducing effect long before its more traditional demand-contracting role makes itself felt.

Our discussion here will be based on a macromodel for an open economy in which some of these stylized facts will be incorporated.[3] Section I discusses an aggregate price and output adjustment model for tradable and nontradable goods, in which both changes in costs and shifts in expectations and demand play a role. This is based on the microfoundations of firm behavior under monopolistic competition and credit rationing. In Sections II and III the model is closed with respect to domestic savings and expenditure, the real and monetary role of the balance of payments, and the government budget.

Section IV analyzes the role of devaluation (under fixed exchange rates) and demand management in terms of the impact effect and alternative secondary repercussions on wages, prices, and output along a dynamic path. The analysis emphasizes the differences in behavior compared with the more standard developed-economy case, with particular reference to the inflation-unemployment-incomes policy trade-offs and the limited role of monetary policy. The effects of alternative policy mixes involving import tariff changes, export subsidies, and fiscal policy are analyzed in Section V.

I. HOME-GOODS PRICE AND OUTPUT ADJUSTMENT UNDER MARKET IMPERFECTIONS

An important element in the understanding of short-term responses to macropolicy intervention is a characterization of the home-goods price and output adjustment process under alternative market structures. A convenient building block in the present context is the short-run maximizing behavior of a firm that can exercise some monopoly power over its product price (p) relative to the perceived general level (π) and takes shifts in demand and variable input prices as given. A detailed derivation of aggregate price and output adjustment relations from such microfoundations is given elsewhere (Bruno 1977). This model will here be modified to take into account an element that seems to be of key importance in many semi-industrialized economies, namely, the role of working capital and credit rationing.[4]

Consider a firm with a well-behaved separable production function:

$$(1) \quad x = f(k)F(\ell, n)^{1/\alpha},$$

[3] The basic framework is similar to that recently used for developed open economies, but there are some important differences. (See, for example, Turnovsky and Kaspura 1974, also Bruno 1978).

[4] This has been analyzed in the context of the finance of physical capital by McKinnon (1973) and Shaw (1973). Our approach here centers on the finance of variable inputs and has greatly benefited from a very interesting recent study by Cavallo (1977).

where $\alpha > 1$ and F is linearly homogeneous in ℓ and n; x is output, k is the capital stock, assumed to be fixed and exogenously given in the short-run; ℓ and n are variable inputs of labor and raw materials, respectively, commanding given prices w and p_n. Raw materials are assumed to be imported at the given world price (P_n). With given exchange rate e and *ad valorem* tariff rate t_n we have: $p_n = P_n(1 + t_n)e$.

Minimizing variable costs $c = w\ell + p_n n$ subject to given output (x) and capital stock (k) leads to a cost function of the following separable form:

$$(2) \quad c = x^\alpha f(k)^{-\alpha} v(w, p_n),$$

where $v(w, p_n)$ are minimized unit variable costs when $x/f = 1.$[5] v is linearly homogeneous in w and p_n, and its elasticities [to be denoted by λ and $(1 - \lambda)$] are the respective shares of the variable factors. Note that α turns out to be the constant elasticity of variable costs with respect to output. We have $MC = \alpha(AVC) = \alpha c/x$. The percentage rate of change of marginal costs ($\hat{MC} = \hat{c} - \hat{x}$) with capital held fixed is thus

$$(3) \quad \hat{MC} = (\alpha - 1)\hat{x} + \hat{v} = (\alpha - 1)\hat{x} + \lambda\hat{w} + (1 - \lambda)\hat{p}_n,$$

and $\hat{MC}$ is positively related to the rates of growth of output and input prices.

Since the purchase of variable inputs is assumed to take place some time (τ) prior to product sale, the costs of finance have to be taken into account. Let us assume that the firm can obtain only a limited amount of credit (c_0) from the organized financial market at a rate of interest r_0, which does not clear the market.[6] The amount allocated to it is determined by the monetary (or government) authorities independently of planned output or existing factor prices.[7] For the finance of the difference $(c - c_0)$, the firm has to go to a 'curb' market that is risky and highly segmented, so that the rate of interest facing it will be increasing with the amount of borrowing.

Maximizing profits with borrowing costs $\zeta[c(x)]$, the first-order condition gives $MR = c' + \zeta'c'$, or

$$(4) \quad MR = MC(1 + r),$$

where $r = \zeta' = $ marginal borrowing costs.

Suppose that the marginal borrowing cost is an increasing function of c/c_0 and takes the following constant-elasticity form:

$$(5) \quad (1 + r) = (1 + r_0)(c/c_0)^\eta = \rho_0 c^\eta,$$

---

[5] This can be obtained by writing $x' = (x/f)^\alpha = F(\ell, n)$ and minimizing c subject to given x'. This leads to $c/x' = v(w, p_n)$ as in (2).

[6] The rate of interest is measured per τ units of time.

[7] This assumption can be relaxed (see below).

where $\eta > 0$ for $c \geq c_0$, $\eta = 0$ otherwise, and $\rho_0 = (1 + r_0) c_0^{-\eta}$ is the interest factor for $c = 1$.

To complete the specification of firm behavior we introduce the following demand function

$$(6) \quad x^d = u(p/\pi)^{-\sigma},$$

where $\sigma > 1$. Here σ is assumed to be the fixed and known price elasticity, while π and u are the expected general price level and the expected level of demand, respectively. The parameter u will be related below to the income (or wealth) effect. All variables relate to a marketing period for which the producer is assumed to make his price and planned-output decisions.

From equation (6) we have

$$(6') \quad \widehat{MR} = \hat{p} = \hat{\pi} + \sigma^{-1} \hat{u} - \sigma^{-1} \hat{x}.$$

Using the latter and equations (2)–(5) in rate-of-growth form, one obtains, after suitable substitution,

$$(7) \quad \hat{p} = \beta \hat{\rho}_0 + \beta (1 + \eta) \hat{v} + (1 - \beta) \hat{\pi} + (1 - \beta) \sigma^{-1} \hat{u}$$

$$(8) \quad \hat{x} = \sigma \beta [-\hat{\rho}_0 - (1 + \eta) \hat{v} + \hat{\pi} + \sigma^{-1} \hat{u}],$$

where $\beta = \{1 + \sigma [\alpha(1 + \eta) - 1]\}^{-1} < 1$ and $\hat{v} = \lambda \hat{w} + (1 - \lambda) \hat{p}_m$,

$\hat{\rho}_0 = (1 + r_0)^{-1} r_0 \hat{r}_0 - \eta \hat{c}_0$, as before.

Equations (7) and (8) give the price and output adjustment relations in terms of four major factors: the exogenously imposed cost of finance, $(\hat{\rho}_0)$, the cost of variable factors $(\hat{v})$, price expectations $(\hat{\pi})$, and demand shifts $(\hat{u})$. The first two cost factors have a stagflationary influence over firm behavior, being price-increasing and output-reducing. Price expectations and demand shifts move both $\hat{p}$ and $\hat{x}$ upward, the relative price shift being $(1 - \beta)/\beta\sigma$ or $[\alpha(1 + \eta) - 1]$ times the output shift. This expression is the elasticity of the marginal (including financial) cost curve.

Second, we note that, unlike the case of a perfect financial market ($\eta = 0$), here the effect of the marginal financial constraint is to make the degree of homogeneity of $\hat{p}$ with respect to the three prices, $\hat{w}$, $\hat{p}_n$, and $\hat{\pi}$, greater than unity $(1 + \beta\eta \geq 1)$ and that of x negative [the sum of the respective coefficients in (8) is $\eta\sigma\beta \leq 0$]. Thus prices would increase by more and output might fall by more than they would otherwise do.

Third, let us note specifically the stagflationary bias of *nominal* credit rationing here. As we have seen a reduction in c_0 increases ρ_0, thus increasing price and reducing output. This would not necessarily be the case if we only had *real* credit rationing. Suppose, for example, that c_0 rises *pari passu* with the general price level (π). In that case we would have linear homogeneity of prices in (7) and zero homogeneity in (8), just as in the perfect financial market case.[8]

The latter point brings up another distinction that could be made between nominal and real variables. Should the marginal borrowing cost (r) be a nominal or a real interest rate concept? That depends on the assumptions underlying the model. As shown by Cavallo (1977), a case could be made for either assumption, depending on the role of working capital in the production process. We are implicitly regarding r as a *nominal* rate, and will continue to do so. Suppose, however, that the relevant procedure were to use a real concept in equation (4). In that case, we would have to divide $(1 + r)$ by π and subtract $\hat{\pi}$ from $\hat{p}_0$ in (7) and (8). In the special case in which the authorities see to it that $(1 + r_0)^{-1} r_0 \hat{r}_0 = \hat{p}$, this last interest factor will drop out altogether from our equations.

Finally, we note the implication of monopoly power in the commodity market facing the firm. The limiting case where the firm is in perfect competition (e.g., when producing tradable goods) can be obtained by letting $\sigma \to \infty$, in which case $\beta \to 0$, $\sigma\beta \to [\alpha(\eta + 1) - 1]^{-1}$ and we get $\hat{p} \to \hat{\pi}$, as expected, and the demand factor ($\hat{u}$) drops out of $\hat{x}$.

To get from individual firm behavior to aggregate price or output adjustment requires more detailed specification of the relationship between firm demand, industry demand, and aggregate demand, and a check on the internal consistency of price expectations, as well as a choice of a suitable index for aggregation purposes. A detailed discussion of these issues is given in Bruno (1977). We shall here assume the existence of a pair of aggregate adjustment equations:

$$(9) \quad \hat{P} = a_0\hat{\rho} + a_1\hat{w} + a_2\hat{p}_n + a_3\hat{\pi} + a_4\hat{U}$$

$$(10) \quad \hat{X} = -b_0\hat{\rho} - b_1\hat{w} - b_2\hat{p}_n + b_3\hat{\pi} + b_4\hat{U}.$$

Here P and X are aggregate price and output Divisia indexes for the home-goods sector, π is the expected aggregate price level, and U is an index of aggregate demand or the previous period's excess demand (see below); ρ is an aggregate index of the financial cost factors r_0 and c_0 for all firms; a_i and b_i ($i = 0, 1, 2, 3$) are weighted averages of the cost-and-demand elasticity parameters appearing in (7) and (8).

It is assumed here that the percentage changes in nominal wages and raw material costs are the same for all firms. For imported materials this would be so in the case of a devaluation or an equiproportionate rise in world prices. For wages this would be correct if the structure of relative wages can be assumed to stay the same (determined primarily by institutional considerations rather than market conditions). Another implicit assumption

[8] Note that (7) is in fact linearly homogeneous in the *four* variables $\hat{c}_0$, $\hat{w}$, $\hat{p}_n$, $\hat{\pi}$, the sum of coefficients being $-\beta\eta + \beta(1 + \eta) + (1 - \beta) = 1$. Similarly, we get zero homogeneity in (8).

is that even for a large group of firms the nominal wage can be assumed to be temporarily given, as is the case if there are binding wage contracts or a high degree of unionization in the wage-leading sector (industry). Wage adjustment will be discussed below.

Can planned output, in fact, always be realized? If there is sufficient slack in the labor market (which in a typical SIE would usually be the case), and sufficient foreign exchange reserves to finance unexpected increments of imports, there should be no problem in the short run.[9]

What if planned output falls short of, or surpasses, actual demand? Different mechanisms for market-clearing or expectation-revision are possible. Where inventory holdings exist, output can be assumed equal to planned output with inventories adjusting to any temporary discrepancies, or else consumers are rationed if there is a shortfall. Where inventories are not feasible (e.g., services) ex-post output might equal actual demand and firms could be assumed to adjust hours of work[10] and input of materials where required. The firm will adjust its expectation of u for the next period, taking into account the observed discrepancies between actual demand and planned supply, which is one way of bringing excess demand into the model.[11]

For simplicity, we shall assume here that actual output equals planned output (with inventories making up any difference), and expected $\hat{U}$ is determined as a function of the ratio of aggregate demand in the previous period (to be denoted by Q_{-1}) to output supplied (X_{-1}). Alternative assumptions about the formation of price expectations ($\hat{\pi}$) will be discussed in Section IV.

I. OUTPUT, INCOME SHARES, AND AGGREGATE DEMAND

For purposes of the subsequent macropolicy discussion, we shall divide the economy into two major groups of industries. A nontradable goods sector supplies goods for domestic consumption (C) and investment (I_x), and its price (P) and output (X) adjustment behavior are assumed to be described by the pair of equations (9)–(10). The other sector produces tradable goods for export (E).[12] We make the convenient assumption that E is given in net value-added terms (imports of raw materials for exports have been netted out) and that the economy is a small one, facing a given international export price P_e. The domestic price will be $p_e = e(1 + q_e)P_e$, where e is the exchange rate and q_e an export subsidy. In line with the

---

[9] If there is a rigid capacity (or full employment or import finance) limitation, then the aggregate supply relationship should be steeper than the average of the individual curves.

[10] This allows one to regard the *numbers* actually employed as a function of *planned* output, even if actual output turns out different.

[11] A more detailed argument is given in Bruno (1977).

[12] For the significance of the tradable/nontradable distinction for stabilization policy, see Dornbusch (1973) and Bruno (1978).

previous discussion,[13] we can write

(11) $\quad E = E(p_e/w)$.

Is this two-sector subdivision of the economy adequate? For present purposes it will be. One could add a sector producing tradable goods for domestic consumption. Formally, this would be very similar to the export sector. On the other hand, the import of goods for direct final consumption would complicate our model, without any real gain in insight. One could think of imported consumer goods as inputs to the aggregate nontradable goods sector (packaging and trade). For the bulk of final consumer goods in an economy of this kind, the assumption of nontradability is not very far from reality, at least in the short run.

To complete the aggregate-expenditure framework, we assume investment goods I_n (expressed in foreign exchange) to be imported and exogenously determined. Likewise, domestic investment (I_x) is part of the demand for nontradable goods. Public consumption will consist of direct wage payments wL_g where L_g are public sector employees.

Aggregate use of resources is given by $(PC + PI_x + wL_g + eI_n + p_eE)$ and GNP (V) is that minus total imports ($p_nN + eI_n$), i.e., $V = P(C + I_x) + wL_g + p_eE - p_nN$, where N stands for total current (noninvestment) imports.

If we leave out interest payments accruing to the financial system (these will be assumed to be transferred to the government budget), the rest of GNP on the income side will consist of wage payments $W = w(L_x + L_e + L_g)$ and profits $R = R_x + R_e$, where the subscript x refers to the X sector.[14]

Suppose there is an income tax rate t_w on wages and t_r on profits (with $t_r > t_w$), and, likewise, respective savings rates are $s_w < s_r < 1$. Denote the share of wages in total income by ϕ. Then real consumable net income can be written in the form $y(\delta_1 + \delta_2\phi)$. The variables are defined as follows: $y = Y/P = (W + R)/P = $ real income,[15] $\phi = W/Y, \delta_1 = (1 - s_r)(1 - t_r) > 0$ and $\delta_2 = (1 - s_w)(1 - t_w) - (1 - s_r)(1 - t_r) > 0$. Under any change in the system in which real income and employment remain more or less constant, but prices rise by more than nominal wages, the share of wages will fall and consumer demand will fall *pari passu*. The increase in profits may enhance investment and growth. This source of conflict between demand management, growth, and income-distribution considerations forms one of the problems often encountered by macropolicy in LDCs.[16]

---

[13] Strictly speaking, this might also be affected by the relevant marginal interest rate. We ignore this here, assuming that exports are always adequately financed by the authorities.

[14] Interest payments on the curb market are considered part of intra business-sector income flows and are therefore ignored.

[15] This is the same as V/P, except for interest payments.

[16] For a detailed model concentrating on this issue, see Taylor (1974).

For our subsequent discussion, we assume the following simple wage adjustment relation

(12) $\hat{w} = d_0 + d_1\hat{\pi}$,

where $d_1 \leq 1$, and $\hat{\pi}$ are price expectations. The parameter d_0 will here be considered fixed, but could alternatively incorporate a Phillips-type adjustment to excess demand conditions.

Even in an LDC with an undeveloped financial market, consumers may wish to hold money balances whose real cost of holding is the expected inflation rate ($\hat{\pi}$). Though there is unlikely to be much lending by what are primarily consuming households, there may be borrowing by households on the curb market for consumption purposes (or rather from the local grocer or supplier). Likewise, interest rates and price expectations might affect business holdings of inventories. To take care of these considerations, we can write the aggregate demand function Q in the form[17]

(13) $Q = Q[y(\delta_1 + \delta_2\phi), - \rho, \hat{\pi}; I_x]$.

Here, ρ is the financial cost variable, $\hat{\pi}$ are price expectations, and I_x is (exogenous) investment demand. The $\hat{U}$ function introduced in the previous section is considered to be positively related to $(Q/X)_{-1}$.

III. THE BALANCE OF PAYMENTS, GOVERNMENT BUDGET, AND THE MONEY SUPPLY

We next discuss the sources of money supply—the trade balance (in domestic currency) and the government deficit—as well as the implications for the financial constraint discussed earlier.

The trade balance

We first turn to the determinants of the current private-sector trade balance[18] $D = P_n N - P_e E$.

On an individual firm level the demand for imports can be expressed in terms of the relative price of imports and the output level. We can write the aggregate (for constant t_n and P_n) as $N = N(w/e, X)$. Similarly, we can write E as a negative function of w/e (for constant P_e), so we have

(14) $D = D(w/e, X)$.

The current trade deficit is a positive function of the relative wage in foreign exchange units and the output of the domestic sector [which is in turn determined by equation (10)].

---

[17] If we were to ignore household holdings of money and debt and inventories, we could simply write $Q = y(\delta_1 + \delta_2\phi) + I_x$.

[18] To make life simpler we leave I_n (imported equipment) out of the definition of D on the assumption that it is financed through external government debt (see below).

The deficit expressed in foreign currency is the important factor to look at for the external balance. The relevant measure from the point of view of domestic absorption, however, is the deficit expressed in terms of domestic prices

$$(15) \quad B = e[D + (t_n P_n N - q_e P_e E)].$$

For a nominal devaluation at a rate $\hat{e}$, the change in B (ΔB) is very likely to be positive, even though ΔD will be negative, provided the existing deficit is sufficiently large. We have (for small changes) :[19]

$$\Delta B = \hat{e}B + e\Delta D + e(t_n P_n \Delta N - q_e P_e \Delta E) \ iff$$

$$D + (t_n P_n N - q_e P_e E) > -(\Delta D + t_n P_n \Delta N - q_e P_e \Delta E)/\hat{e}.$$

A complete view of the balance of payments requires a look at the capital account. For a typical SIE, endogenous private capital inflows and outflows can be considered relatively small. As long as this is so, the analysis of the monetary effects of exchange rate changes assumes a very different form from what it would be in the perfect mobility case, since the economy will be insulated from the interest equalization effects that would otherwise take place.

We assume, for simplicity, that all of the external debt is handled by the public sector, which also services it and uses it for importing investment goods (I_n). The difference between the total trade deficit and the change in the external debt will show in a change in the country's foreign reserves. These are handled by the central bank, while the interest receipts accrue as part of central bank profits, which are transferred to the government.[20] Since the handling of the external debt will not affect the domestic money-creation process directly, we ignore it in the following discussion. The money-creating part of the balance of payments will thus be confined to the current private sector deficit, D.

The government budget and the money supply

Next consider the current government budget. Denoting the current account deficit by H we have

$$(16) \quad H = H_0 + H_n = \{wL_g - Y[t_r - \phi(t_r - t_w)]\}$$
$$+ \{e(q_e P_e E - t_n P_n N)\}.$$

Written in this form we can view the current government budget deficit (or surplus) as consisting of two major components. The domestic deficit (H_0) consists of expenditure (wL_g) minus taxes on wages and profits

---

[19] This distinction forms the focus of the discussion of devaluation effects in *LDCs*. See, especially, Cooper (1971*b*).

[20] For simplicity, assume that interest payments on current domestic credit extended by the financial system exactly offset its operating expenses.

(ϕ is the wage share W/Y as before). The deficit arising from the external account (H_n) consists of subsidies on exports minus import duties.

Assume that the deficit is financed by the Central Bank and that the money supply (M^s) is subject to a simple reserve ratio ($1/m$), whose base consists of the public debt and the private sector's foreign currency held by the Central Bank.

It follows that the change in money supply (for a fixed e) will be $\Delta M^s = m(H - eD)$ or, using (15)–(16) we have:

$$(17) \quad \Delta M^s = m(H_0 - B);$$

where $H_0 = wL_g - Y[t_r - \phi(t_r - t_w)]$, as in (16), and $m > 1$.

The sources of monetary expansion thus consist of the private balance-of-payments surplus in domestic prices and the government deficit on domestic transactions.[21] Given (17), the banking system is allowed an expansion (or contraction) of the amount $\Delta M^s (m - 1)/m = (m - 1)(H_0 - B)$ in its credit to the private sector. Assume all of it to consist of rationed credit (at rate of interest r_0). The analysis would not be substantially different if the banking system had to use only part of its resources for government-directed credit allocation and could lend the rest on a free market. This role is here taken up only by the curb market.

If m is held fixed by the monetary authorities, any factor that increases B or reduces H_0 will result in an appropriate multiplicative drop in the money supply (ΔM^s) and domestic credit-creation. As indicated, an increase in B may, for example, come about as a result of devaluation. If, as usually happens, it also results in a reduction in the wage share (ϕ) and an increase in nominal income Y, the domestic deficit H_0 may drop too.[22] The changes in B and H_0 will combine to cause a monetary contraction. The reduced availability of organized credit *ceteris paribus* drives producers (and possibly consumers) more into the curb market, with a resulting increase in the marginal borrowing costs and, thus, from (10), there is output reduction.

The financial mechanism

The substitute for the conventional monetary mechanism and money supply-demand equilibrium is here represented by the credit-demand model

---

[21] We have not specified the domestic role of the public external debt here. This can realistically be assumed to be used by the banking system, as a government agent, to lend to private business for the purchase of (imported) investment goods. If changes in the external debt correspond to changes in I_n, its monetary role can be ignored for the present purpose. It is obviously of great importance for both growth and distributional considerations, however. It may even have an important monetary role if the domestic lending terms are not the same as the external (foreign exchange indexed) terms. This too is ignored here.

[22] Assuming the adjustment in the nominal wage (w) is sluggish. See below.

of Section I, together with central determination of the official rate, r_0, and credit quotas, c_0. For the individual firm we have from (5) and (2) in rate-of-change terms:

(5') $\quad (1 + r)^{-1}r\hat{r} = \hat{p}_0 + \eta\hat{c} = (1 + r_0)^{-1}r_0\hat{r}_0 - \eta\hat{c}_0 + \eta(\hat{x} + \hat{v}).$

The marginal borrowing rate is a linear combination of three factors, positive with respect to changes in the official rate $(\hat{r}_0)$ and variable costs and negative with respect to changes in the credit quota $(\hat{c}_0)$. Suppose the individual quotas (c_0) move together with total bank credit available $[M(m - 1)/m]$. In that case, they would change at the rate $(m - 1)^{-1}\hat{m} + \hat{M}$. Remembering that $\hat{c}$ is a positive function of $\hat{x}$, $\hat{w}$, $\hat{p}_n$, we could write the adjustment equation for an aggregate index of marginal borrowing costs $(\bar{r})$ in the form

(18) $\quad \hat{\bar{r}} = \Psi\,\hat{r}_0 - \Psi_1[(m - 1)^{-1}\hat{m} + \hat{M}] + \Psi_2(\hat{x}, \hat{w}, \hat{p}_n)$

Equation (18) is very similar to what we would get from a conventional money-demand equation, but seems more consistent with the present approach.

Since the endogenous effect of rising costs [the Ψ_2 function in (18)] on the implied borrowing rate is already subsumed in the coefficients of our price and output adjustment equations (9)–(10), the completion of the system requires only that we express the aggregate financial cost index ρ appearing in those equations in terms of the monetary variables r_0, m, and M. Let us write it in the form [which is part of (18)]:

(19) $\quad \hat{\rho} = \Psi\hat{r}_0 - \Psi_1[(m - 1)^{-1}\hat{m} + \hat{M}].$

IV. WORKINGS OF THE MODEL: IMPACT AND DYNAMIC EFFECTS OF DEVALUATION

We start by recapitulating the complete model in summary form. Table 1 lists seven equations for seven endogenous variables: price adjustment (P) and output adjustment (X), aggregate demand (Q), wage rate (w), trade balance (D), the money supply (M) and the financial cost index (ρ).[23] It also defines the real income (y), the wage share (ϕ), and the domestic price of imports (p_n) and exports (p_e). Unless otherwise stated (by a minus sign), the functional relationship with respect to any stated variable is assumed to be positive.[24] There does not seem much point in working out the Jacobian for the system as it stands, since much depends on leads and

[23] By substituting equation (13) into (9) and (10), equation (17) into (19), and writing (14) separately, the only remaining key interlocking equations are (9), (10), (12), and (19), determining the adjustment of price, output, wages, and the interest rate. One could contract the system even further leaving only (9) and (10).

[24] We have left out exogenous investment and capital stock variables as well as the capital account of the balance of payments.

Table 1. The Model in Summary Form

Price adjustment

$$\hat{P} = a_0\hat{\rho} + a_1\hat{w} + a_2\hat{p}_n + a_3\hat{\pi} + a_4\hat{U}(Q/X)_{-1} \tag{9}$$

Output adjustment

$$\hat{X} = -b_0\hat{\rho} - b_1\hat{w} - b_2\hat{p}_n + b_3\hat{\pi} + b_4\hat{U}(Q/X)_{-1} \tag{10}$$

Wage adjustment

$$\hat{w} = d_0 + d_1\hat{\pi} \tag{12}$$

Aggregate demand

$$Q = Q[y(\delta_1 + \delta_2\phi), -\rho, \hat{\pi}; I_x] \tag{13}$$

Current trade deficit

$$D = P_nN(w/p_n, X) - P_eE(p_e/w) \tag{14}$$

The money supply

$$\hat{M} = M^{-1}m[-B(e, w, t_n, -q_e, X) + H_0(w, -yP, \phi)] \tag{17}$$

Aggregate financial costs

$$\hat{\rho} = \Psi_0\hat{r}_0 - \Psi_1[(m-1)^{-1}\hat{m} + \hat{M}] \tag{19}$$

Definitional equations

Real income: $y = X + \dfrac{e}{p}[P_eE(p_e/w) - P_nN(w/p_n, X)] + \dfrac{w}{p}L_g$

Wage share: $\phi = W/Y = (w/y)[L_x(p_n/w, X) + L_e(p_e/w) + L_g]$

Prices of imports and exports: $p_n = eP_n(1 + t_n), p_e = eP_e(1 + q_e)$

Policy parameters

Balance of payments $(e; t_n, q_e)$

Fiscal $(L_g; t_r, t_w)$

Monetary (m, r_0)

---

lags and the nature of expectation formation. Most of the qualitative changes, however, can be read off the equation system directly. We proceed now with the analysis of the impact of changes in policy parameters.

It is convenient to start off from the case in which price expectations take the simple adaptive form $\hat{\pi} = \theta\hat{P}_{-1} + (1 - \theta)\hat{\pi}_{-1}$, where $0 < \theta \leq 1$ is some constant. For the wage equation, this is similar to an assumption of partial indexation (which fits a number of SIE, especially in Latin America). Similar expectation formation is also implicit in the way we have written down the effect of aggregate demand on U. This allows one to analyze the impact of various policies as a two-stage adjustment process that may come close to the way the dynamic system may operate in the real world.

Suppose an improvement in the balance of payments is desired, and consider the effect of an unexpected devaluation starting from a position of price stability (or a steady fully anticipated rate of inflation).[25] Consider the impact effect of the change in e. This increase shows itself [equations (9) and (10)] in a cost-push (p_n) effect on prices (increase) and output (decrease). The initial effect on the external balance (14) is positive,[26] while the deficit in domestic market prices (B) may increase, for the reasons mentioned earlier. Since nominal income rises and the wage share almost certainly falls, the domestic government deficit, H_0, falls along with $-B$, causing a monetary contraction [see (17)], at a given reserve ratio $1/m$. The banking system may, of course, have difficulties in adjusting its outstanding credit downward instantaneously. In a system whose credit requirements are growing (due to cost increases), even keeping credit constant, however, will force more borrowers to the curb market, thus raising marginal borrowing costs everywhere. As equation (19) shows, monetary contraction leads to an increase in ρ, which in turn reinforces the cost-push stagflationary influence of the initial devaluation [see the sign of $\hat{p}$ in equations (9) and (10)].

This may be a suitable point to stop and underline the marked difference of behavior that seems to characterize this type of economy as compared with what is considered the standard case. First, with a well-functioning foreign capital market, an increase in domestic interest rates would be nullified by equilibrating capital flows into the economy, keeping the money stock from falling,[27] or even causing a net increase in M. Second, the existence of a segmented domestic money market implies that a monetary contraction could be expected to have a stagflationary impact effect coming from the *supply side*, quite independently of any subsequent demand effects. It is important to note that the role of financial costs in equations (9) and (10) derives from two separate but reinforcing sources. As shown in Section I, an increase in import costs accompanied by an endogenous increase in domestic finance will drive up marginal borrowing rates, unless

[25] This may be needed in order to repay debt or finance an expansion in investment I_n. It is easiest to think of the case in which initially I_n are financed by the external debt and current imports exceed exports.

[26] Even if the substitution effect on imports and exports is initially sluggish, the contractionary effect on X would cause a reduction through a drop in imports due to the income (output) effect.

[27] A partial phenomenon of this kind probably takes place even in an imperfect market if a devaluation is expected. Export proceeds may be held abroad in anticipation of a devaluation and then repatriated, or a speculative import 'bulge' may precede the devaluation. If this is a sizable factor, or if the country includes a large foreign enclave, equation (17) would have to be modified to take it into account, bringing the model closer to the standard case. Paradoxically, because of domestic financjal repression the authorities may sometimes allow certain firms to take expensive short-term commercial loans abroad, a factor that may weaken the monetary constraint in another costly manner.

official credit quotas increase.[28] The monetary contraction[29] reinforces this cost-push effect even more through an increase in ρ.

Consider now the second-round effects from a delayed adjustment due to aggregate demand (Q_{-1}), price expectations ($\hat{\pi}$), and wage-rate adjustment ($\hat{w}$).

Two factors contribute to a contraction in aggregate demand (Q). One is the fall in the wage share (ϕ), which, through the differential savings propensities, makes for a reduction in demand for consumer goods. This is the contractionary effect of a devaluation first stressed by Díaz-Alejandro (1963) and recently analyzed by Krugman and Taylor (1976) and others. The second may be a more traditional monetary contraction effect now working through the demand side [see equation (13)]. Both of these contribute to a downward pressure on prices as well as on output.[30] The timing and extent of the moderating influence on the previous cost push depends on parameters and lags that are specific to the circumstances. Empirical experience seems to point to a predominance of cost-push effects at least on prices. As far as output is concerned, both are in the same direction anyway.

What about the adjustment of $\hat{\pi}$ and $\hat{w}$? The immediate effect on prices is a strengthening of upward pressures [see the signs in equation (9)]. Since $b_1(1 - d_1) + b_2 > 0$, the effect on output, however, is now in a reverse upward direction. The second-round effects on the sources of money supply may also be expansionary. A rising wage in both the private and public sectors reverses the downward trend in the government deficit (H_0), while the effect on the balance-of-payments surplus ($-B$) is ambiguous. If the foreign exchange deficit continues to fall (which usually happens when there is a delayed substitution effect on imports and an initially sluggish export response), this would also show in a reduced B (i.e., increase in $-B$).[31] On both counts, the contraction in the money supply may thus be reversed, at least in part, with corresponding reverse pressures on prices and output. This pattern of endogenous perverse monetary behavior has led to the argument [Cooper 1971b] that under such circumstances a devaluation

---

[28] Sometimes credit quotas may be linked to nominal costs of production, in which case the financial constraint is mitigated. This explains why monetary policy often tends to be accommodating.

[29] This interest cost element, taken by itself, would also appear in a perfect market. However, the quantitative effect is likely to be relatively small. For example, if r_0 is a quarterly rate that increases from 2 percent to 3 percent (or from 8 percent to 12 percent in annual terms), the effect of a 50 percent increase in interest rates is to increase $(1 + r)MC$ only by about 1 percent and there will be no further repercussion on r from an increase in MC.

[30] The relative effect on output, however, is likely to be larger, since the magnitude of b_4/a_4 in equations (9) and (10) is of the order of the reciprocal elasticity of the MC curve (see Section I).

[31] Note that once the exchange rate (e) stays constant the direction of movement of D and B are the same.

should be coupled with an accommodating monetary *expansion* first, a contraction coming only afterward.

How much of the above argument rests on the sluggishness of expectation adjustment? If we let the process continue by itself without further intervention the system will finally come to an equilibrium at higher prices, wages, and money supply. In Section I we have seen the basic homogeneity properties of the price and output relations with respect to $\hat{c}_0$, $\hat{w}$, $\hat{p}_n$, and $\hat{\pi}$. If, in addition, there is no money illusion in wages,[32] the nominal system, having expanded at rate $\hat{e}$, would eventually end up with no real change having taken place in relative prices $(w/P$ and $e/P)$.[33]

What would be likely to happen eventually could also be gauged from making an alternative assumption on expectation formation, namely, that price expectations are rational, so that we have $\hat{P} = \hat{\pi} = \hat{w}$ everywhere. In that case, P will fully adjust with p_n, and there is no relative-price effect on output supply. Likewise, D would not have changed, nor would real aggregate demand, nor the real money supply. Obviously, if everything is fully and consistently anticipated and there is full information and no money illusion, even this economy would show no real response to a devaluation. However, the case of instantaneous adjustment cannot be considered more than a convenient reference point or a logical check on the model, as it is unlikely to be empirically relevant if one is interested in characterizing short-run adjustment processes out of equilibrium.[34] Anyway, before equilibrium is ever reached the economy would be subject to new shocks that would have to be analyzed in an analogous disequilibrium context.

The same framework could be used in order to work out the effect of an increase in international import prices (P_n). This has a cost-push effect on prices and output, which will lead to an increase in D and B and thus a contraction in the money supply. The terms-of-trade deterioration will, in general, also reduce the wage share, causing a further contractionary effect on demand and output. The attempt to fight the resulting domestic price increase by either monetary or fiscal means (working on Q) is likely to lead to a serious further contraction of output and employment.[35] Note that,

---

[32] Lack of money illusion implies either assuming $d_1 = 1$ or making d_0 in (12) itself depend on excess demand (Q/X), in a Phillips-curve fashion. The actual result in any particular *SIE* depends on unemployment conditions, the structure of labor markets, and the nature of labor contracts.

[33] But more asset accumulation may have taken place in the meantime, helping to satisfy the growth objective. For an analysis of convergence in a simpler but essentially similar dynamic system, see Bruno (1978).

[34] For example, in none of the twenty cases listed in Cooper's empirical study (1971a) did domestic prices and wages rise to the extent of the devaluation within twelve months.

[35] Note that this would emerge from the model even if the money market is perfect and expectations are rational, a point not without relevance to the role of monetary policy in a highly industrialized economy facing an increase in import prices (see Bruno 1978).

unlike in the case of a devaluation, the change in P_n, D, and B is a real change also in the long run, and the homogeneity property does not hold unless export prices (P_e) rise *pari passu* with the rise in P_n.

V. ALTERNATIVE BALANCE-OF-PAYMENTS AND STABILIZATION INSTRUMENTS

How does pure fiscal policy work in this model? Suppose government raises t_w and/or t_r, keeping M constant [by making compensating upward changes in m; see equation (17)]. This in itself only has a dampening effect on aggregate demand (Q) and through it on prices, unlike the inflationary impact effect of monetary policy. But there are other trade-offs involved. An increase in t_w may give an incentive to workers in the organized part of the labor market to push for higher wages.[36] On the other hand, an increase in t_r reduces profit rates and may reduce the incentive to increase investment, where profits are largely saved and invested. We have not incorporated this factor here, but it is familiar territory, and not specific to SIE.

Next, consider indirect taxes and subsidies of which only trade-related taxes are considered here. Using the tariff rate t_n as a fiscal and balance-of-payments measure has a cost-push effect of its own [working through p_n in (9) and (10)], even if monetary policy is made to accommodate the contractionary effect coming from $-B$ in (17). This leads to the possibility, sometimes advocated in practice, that a devaluation be coupled with a tariff *reduction*, so as to mitigate the cost-push effects on prices and wages as well as the contractionary impact effect on output.[37] This would be particularly appropriate in a situation in which imports are highly inelastic, while exports are responsive to a real devaluation.

In a world in which speculative private capital movements do not exist, or are to be avoided, the above combination of policies could be replaced by an alternative in the form of export subsidies (based on value added). Consider an increase in the subsidy rate q_e and a simultaneous increase in taxes on profits (t_r) that keeps aggregate demand (Q) from rising. At the same time, if needed, adjust m so as to make credit (and the money supply) accommodate the increased output of the E sector. If there is sufficient slack in the labor market,[38] this seems an almost ideal way of bringing about a simultaneous improvement in the balance of payments and employment, without a cost in terms of domestic inflation or changed income shares.

[36] Formally speaking, this would imply that in equation (14) d_0 includes a factor $(1 - t_w)^{-1} t_w \hat{t}_w$, on the assumption that workers negotiate for $(1 - t_w)w$, not for w.

[37] The case in which a devaluation is coupled with a relaxation of *quantitative* restrictions on imports should also be considered. Here the dampening price effect (and any positive efficiency effects on output) are not coupled with loss of revenue.

[38] In case of labor shortage, t_r and possibly t_w may have to be increased by more, so as to reduce aggregate demand.

Why do SIEs not normally resort to this method of adjustment, or else do so to only a very limited extent? Not so much because of possible distortions in the internal exchange rate system (after all, none of the alternatives is a first-best anyway). The main reason probably comes from restrictions usually imposed by international institutions (GATT [General Agreement on Tariffs and Trade], IMF [International Monetary Fund]) in their dealings with SIEs. For some reason the use of export subsidies is considered a more distortive or 'unfair' trade practice than other methods of export promotion that are less apparent to the outside and yet may in fact be much more distortive. Two examples come to mind—highly subsidized (unindexed) investment loans to export industries have harmful effects on factor-intensity choice and on the distribution of income. Similarly, allocating excessive doses of cheap credit to export industries may have similar very distortive effects internally and are no less 'unfair' a practice from the point of view of international competition. Yet IMF and GATT missions seem to mind the one but not the other.

VI. CONCLUDING REMARKS

There are a number of important policy tools that we have not touched upon and that could be analyzed within the same cost-push, demand-pull framework. One important example is the use of excise taxes and food subsidies. Usually, the analysis of indirect taxes and subsidies concentrates on their fiscal impact and possibly distorting allocational effects. In the context of an SIE, no less and sometimes more important are their effects on inflation and income distribution. A cut in food subsidies, for example, may be advocated on the conventional grounds, but might be objected to when the other considerations seem dominant.

Also left out of the analysis was the special role of agriculture in the inflationary process of many SIEs. Steep marginal costs in agriculture and a greater degree of competition as compared with manufacturing could make for an additional inflationary bias. This is the focus of an interesting recent study by Wachter (1976). By aggregating the home products into one sector, we have obviously ignored important differences within the domestic economy.

Our analysis has attempted to bring out the constraints imposed on various macroadjustment policies by their possible side-effects on inflation or unemployment. While some of these effects may also occur in a well-developed economy, they assume a particularly critical role in an SIE and greatly constrain the role of conventional stabilization tools. Of all the special constraining features that we have mentioned here, the most striking one is probably the limitation imposed on monetary management by the existence of a segmented credit market.

The need for monetary reform has been stressed by McKinnon (1973) and Shaw (1973). The building up of efficient economy-wide monetary intermediaries is of crucial importance if conventional macropolicy is to play a major role in the adjustment process of SIEs.[39] In the absence of such reform, extreme monetary restraint (or 'financial programming'), often advocated as the major component of stabilization policy, may defeat its purpose and do more harm than good. The process of reform and institution-building is slow and gradual, however, and in the meantime it is important to beware of hasty transfers of theories and policies from a developed institutional set-up to where they may be inappropriate.

REFERENCES

Bruno, Michael. 1977. *Price and Output Adjustment: Micro Foundations and Macro Theory*. Harvard Institute of Economic Research Discussion Paper No. 534. Cambridge, Mass.: Harvard University Press.

————. 1978. "Exchange Rates, Import Costs and Wage-Price Dynamics." *Journal of Political Economy* 86: 379–403.

Cavallo, D. F. 1977. "Stagflationary Effects of Monetarist Stabilization Policies." Ph.D. dissertation, Harvard University.

Cooper, Richard N. 1971a. "An Assessment of Currency Devaluation in Developing Countries." In *Government and Economic Development*, edited by Gustav Ranis, pp. 472–513. New Haven: Yale University Press.

————. 1971b. "Devaluation and Aggregate Demand in Aid-Receiving Countries." In *Trade, Balance of Payments and Growth: Papers in International Economics in Honor of Charles P. Kindleberger*, edited by Jagdish N. Bhagwati et al., pp. 355–76. Amsterdam and London: North-Holland; New York: American Elsevier.

Díaz-Alejandro, Carlos F. 1963. "A Note on the Impact of Devaluation and the Redistributive Effect." *Journal of Political Economy* 71: 577–80.

Dornbusch, Rudiger. 1973. "Devaluation, Money, and Nontraded Goods." *American Economic Review* 63: 871–80.

Fleming, John M. 1962. "Domestic Financial Policies under Fixed and under Floating Exchange Rates." *International Monetary Fund Staff Papers* 9: 369–79.

Krugman, P., and Taylor, L. 1976. *Contractionary Effects of Devaluation*. Department of Economics Working Paper No. 191. Cambridge, Mass.: Massachusetts Institute of Technology.

McKinnon, R. I. 1973. *Money and Capital in Economic Development*. Washington, D.C.: The Brookings Institution.

Mundell, Robert A. 1962. "The Appropriate Use of Monetary and Fiscal Policy for Internal and External Stability." *International Monetary Fund Staff Papers* 9: 70–77.

---

[39] In the present context, what may, among other changes, be involved is an increase in r_0 and a reduction in the *marginal* borrowing cost through a reduction in the η coefficient in equation (5).

Shaw, E. S. 1973. *Financial Deepening in Economic Development*. London: Oxford University Press.

Taylor, L. 1974. "Short-Term Policy in Open Semi-Industrialized Economies: The Narrow Limits of the Possible." *Journal of Development Economics* 1: 85–104.

Turnovsky, Stephen J., and Kaspura A., 1974. "Analysis of Imported Inflation in a Short-Run Macro-Economic Model." *Canadian Journal of Economics* 7: 350–80.

Wachter, S. M. 1976. *Latin American Inflation: The Structuralist-Monetarist Debate*. Lexington, Mass.: D. C. Heath.

Comment

RONALD I. McKINNON

For a typical semi-industrialized economy (SIE) that is also under-developed, Michael Bruno's main message is clear: conventional macroeconomic models of devaluation, inflation, and deflation can be very deceptive. For example, real output and employment may well respond quite differently to a devaluation from what either a pure Keynesian or a pure monetarist approach might predict. Unfortunately, both these traditional macroeconomic approaches deal with the determinants of aggregate demand (or aggregate absorption in open economies) under the assumption that, at least in the short run, the supply of real output will respond elastically to whatever policy determines demand to be.

In many semi-industrial economies, however, distortions exist on the supply side. For Keynesian macroeconomic models, the labor market presents no problems in SIEs: labor is in elastic supply because real wages are typically fixed above market clearing levels. But both Keynesian and monetarist approaches assume that the capital market is virtually perfect: private firms and the government compete in an integrated market for nonmonetary debt governed by a single representative rate of interest.

In practice, the capital market in SIEs is fragmented. No "organized" open markets exist for primary securities issued by government or the private sector because of experience with high and unpredictable inflation. The commercial banks are the principal financial intermediaries, but they are subject to interest ceilings on both deposits and loans. The trickle of loans to businesses typically leaves a large unsatisfied queue of private borrowers at the low or negative real rates of interest being charged. Government budgetary deficits are financed either by preemptively selling bonds to the deposit banks (thus directly reducing the availability of credit to firms), or by printing base money. Sometimes an informal curb market exists as a marginal and very high cost source of short-term finance to businesses. Elsewhere, these all too common policies that drive firms to rely mainly on self-finance have been analyzed under the sobriquet of "financial repression."[1]

In an overly complex model, the details of which take the first three-quarters of his paper to develop, Michael Bruno makes substantial progress in formalizing how a devaluation works itself out in a financially repressed economy. Within his model, devaluation reduces aggregate demand, causes an unintended liquidity squeeze on the supply of bank credit, and hence reduces real output and employment. As a preferred alternative policy, he suggests that a deficit in foreign payments might be better dealt with by introducing an export subsidy coupled with a tax on business profits. No loss in employment and output would ensue within his model. A devaluation leads to a net increase in government tax collections and is therefore deflationary, whereas the export subsidy *cum* tax avoids this deflationary bias in correcting the balance of payments.

My contention is that Bruno comes to this conclusion because his complex model is still incomplete regarding the way in which the public finances impinge on private investment in a financially repressed economy.

In practice, finance for private investment is limited to severely rationed credits from the commercial banks and to internal cash flow within enterprises. Moreover, as Bruno correctly models, this constraint falls heavily on private working capital for building up inventories and making advance payments to workers. Hence, there exists a supply constraint on output. During an economic stabilization program designed to improve the trade balance at minimum economic cost, output should rise even as absorption might have to fall. Therefore, stabilization policy should be oriented (in part) to relaxing the supply constraint associated with financial repression. And this important issue is not addressed by Bruno's model.

Because of fiscal deficits, the government typically preempts credits from the deposit banks by manipulating their required reserve ratio $1/m$, so that banks must hold government bonds in their portfolios. In addition, the government can levy the "inflation tax" by issuing base money directly. Hence, $1/m$ should be treated as a policy variable, instead of a fixed parameter, as Bruno does. A reduction in the fiscal deficit enables the monetary authority to reduce $1/m$ and directly increase the flow of real credit to the business sector, because the commercial banks can reduce their required purchases of low-yield government bonds. The supply constraint on output is relaxed. This fall in $1/m$ *is*, of course, equivalent to an increase in the base money multiplier. But its inflationary consequences can be controlled by reducing the amount of base money issued (or relying on the improvement in the balance of payments to reduce base money injected into the economy). Again, a reduced fiscal deficit or an

[1] See R. I. McKinnon, *Money and Capital in Economic Development* (Washington, D.C.: Brookings, 1973), Chapter 7.

actual surplus is devoutly to be wished in the course of an efficient economic stabilization program.

If a devaluation induces a reduced fiscal deficit, as it does in Bruno's model, this should be welcomed by the authorities, because it gives them a chance to reduce $1/m$, instead of keeping it fixed as under Bruno's specification. Similarly, the export subsidy financed by a tax on business profits that Bruno does advocate can be entirely inappropriate in a financially repressed economy. Business profits are a source of finance for investment in working capital—investment that is constrained to begin with. Hence, the export subsidy *cum* profits tax does not relieve the constraint on aggregate supply and might even aggravate it.

In short, the analytics of how to improve the trade balance efficiently in a financial repressed economy still remain to be fully worked out.

CHAPTER NINE

Macroeconomic Strategy and Coordination under Alternative Exchange Rates

KOICHI HAMADA

I. INTRODUCTION

During the postwar period, national economies have been integrated more and more closely through trade and capital movements; they have become increasingly interdependent. Thus the problems of policy conflicts and the need for international coordination have attracted a great deal of public interest.

However, the attention by economists to this problem is relatively new. Perhaps because of the influence of the wide use of the perfect-competition version of the general-equilibrium theory, economists are apt to conceive of an atomistic picture of the world economy, where the actions of each country taken individually have no influence on the other countries. However, the repeated process of international negotiation and continuing discussions on international rules of the game reveal the fact that this simplified picture neglects an important part of reality. At present, the mass that a major country like the United States or Germany occupies in the world economy is so great that it is hard to understand the world economy without considering mutual interdependence of macroeconomic policies among national economies. Naturally, aspects of policy coordination as well as policy conflicts among nations become crucially important.

The purpose of this essay is to assess existing literature and evidence concerning economic coordination and conflicts among national economies, and, at the same time, to provide a tentative theoretical framework to understand the current practice of managed floating.

The author is much indebted to Professors John Black, Ryutaro Komiya, Drs. Howard Petith, Takahito Mutoh, and the editors of this volume for their helpful comments and suggestions.

In the next section, the discussion starts from the nature of international interdependence and the reasons for the necessity of policy coordination. In Section III, various approaches such as direct cooperation, assignment, optimizing, and strategic approach are reviewed, and, in Section VI, some empirical evidence is discussed. These discussions are mostly confined to policy interactions under the fixed exchange rate system or its variants, like the adjustable-peg system. Then Section V reviews the interdependence and its strategic implications under the system of flexible exchange rates.

In order to evaluate the recent performance of the world economy, one needs a theoretical framework to analyze the mixture of these two exchange-rate systems, namely, the system of managed floating. In studying literature on policy coordination, one cannot help feeling that the analysis of managed floating is still very limited. Therefore, Sections VI and VII are devoted to an attempt to fill some of the gaps existing in the literature. I hope this attempt will serve as a step toward clarifying the nature of interdependence among monetary and exchange rate policies, and the strategic structure of the game under managed floating.

In place of a conclusion, the final section discusses the possibility of interdisciplinary studies in strategic interplays of economic policies and also in the process of agreeing on rules of the game.

II. THE NATURE OF INTERDEPENDENCE AND THE NECESSITY OF POLICY COORDINATION

Let us start by asking the question, what exactly is meant by a common-sense expression such as "economic interdependence" or "international interdependences." One must distinguish at least three elements involved in the general usage of these terms.

First, the world is closed so that the Walras law holds for the world as a whole. Similarly, the sum of balance of payments of all the countries should be equal to zero, or, if any, to the increase in outside international reserves. This element of interdependence exists for any situation in the world economy.

Second, when national economies are integrated, goods and assets in one country and those in another become closer substitutes. In some extreme cases, under fixed exchange rates only one price is set for the same commodity in any country (purchasing power parity relationship), or only one price for bonds with the same maturity (perfect capital mobility). In these circumstances, any price of a commodity or asset cannot be determined by a single country without considering repercussions through the rest of the world. In fact, under the fixed exchange rate system, national monies are almost perfect substitutes, and the adoption of the flexible exchange rate system implies cutting the chain of this close substitution.

The third element is the small number of influential countries. Even if the above two elements exist, economic analysis may proceed on the *ceteris paribus* assumption, provided that the number of countries is very large and that individual influence is negligible. It is the minority of influential countries that requires one's explicit attention to policy interactions. In the present world, one cannot talk realistically about the effect of economic policies by major countries without considering their interactions. In fact, the repercussion between policies is more acute where goods and assets are internationally close substitutes.

In summary, national economies are interdependent, by definition, due to the closeness of the world. But it is the small number of major countries that calls for explicit analysis of interdependence, the degree of which is intensified by increasing international mobility of goods and assets.

The recognition of this interdependence naturally leads to the recognition of the need for international coordination of economic policies. As early as the 1950s one can find, at least implicitly, substantial discussion about the consistency of national economic policies in a two-country model by Meade (1951, chap. 10). However, he is not so much concerned with international policy conflicts between two countries as with policy conflicts within each country. It is by Cooper (1968) in his book, *The Economics of Interdependence*, that the necessity of international cooperation is directly and most persuasively put forth.

Taking as an example the Atlantic Community, which was under the fixed exchange rate regime, he points out that increasing interdependence complicates the successful pursuit of national objectives by way of the following three factors.

First, increasing interdependence increases the number and magnitude of the disturbances to which each country's balance of payments are subjected, and this directs national policy instruments toward the restoration of external balances. Second, increasing interdependence slows down the process by which policy authorities are able to reach domestic objectives. Finally, greater integration may lead a community of nations to behave with counteracting motions that leave all countries worse off than they need be. Therefore, Cooper argues that it is necessary for the Atlantic Community to engage, at least partly, in the joint determination of economic objectives and policies.

Thus, the central problem of international economic cooperation is defined to answer the question "how to keep the manifold benefits of extensive international intercourse free of crippling restrictions, while at the same time preserving a maximum degree of freedom for each nation to pursue its legitimate economic objectives" (Cooper 1968, p. 15). According to him, as with marriage, the benefits of close relations can be enjoyed only at the expense of giving up a certain amount of independence or autonomy. Here the main theme in the analysis of economic cooperation is clearly presented. In particular, the third factor mentioned above, that the independent pursuit of individual national policies may not lead to a desirable situation for a community as a whole, is the crucial reason for the need of cooperation in a highly integrated world economy.

On the one hand, this argument traces back to the fallacy of composition that the sum of individual decisions may not be optimal for society as a whole, even though its members are acting individually on entirely national grounds—the fallacy that is so famous in association with the name of Keynes (1936).

On the other hand, this argument anticipates the analysis of economic cooperation from a game theoretic standpoint, in that the noncooperative solution is quite likely to be inferior to the cooperative (or contract-curve) solution, in a situation similar to the well known prisoner's dilemma[1] that is quite common in international economic confrontations.

In addition, the following points raised in his book are called to our attention. First, economic cooperation is not merely a technical or economic matter, it is also a political problem. There is a continual interaction between economic and political aspects. This political-economic nature of the problem will be taken up later in this essay.

Second, Cooper analyzes the dynamic as well as the static aspects of international cooperation. Even when all the national objectives are consistent and there are sufficient numbers of policy instruments to reach them, growing interdependence greatly slows down the process by which independently acting national authorities reach their economic objectives. In the discussion, he distinguishes policy coordination, where gains are achieved from better mutual timing, from policy harmonization, which is based on static efficiency grounds. In 1969, Cooper further developed this dynamic aspect of coordination. By using a Keynesian two-country model equipped with monetary and fiscal policies, he calculates the values of the characteristic roots of the dynamic system of adjustment equations, assuming different degrees of interdependence. He finds that increasing interdependence reduces the absolute value of the dominant (negative) characteristic root so that it slows down the speed of adjustment in the system.[2]

---

[1] The prisoner's dilemma is a game in which the pay-off structure corresponds to the following scenario. Suppose two prisoners in isolation are attempting by mutual cooperation to evade the punishment for the crime they committed. Cooperation would lead to a successful fullfilment of their objectives, but betrayal by one party would hurt the other party a great deal. Moreover, the pay-off to the betraying when the other is trying to cooperate is larger than that of the successful cooperation. Because of this difficulty, this situation is quite likely to end up with the noncooperative solution that gives low pay-offs to both parties (see, e.g., Luce and Raiffa [1957]).

[2] As is sketched in his footnote (Cooper 1968, fn. 15, pp. 158f), the negative real part of the dominant characteristic root of a system of linearized differential equations tends in most cases to decrease in its absolute value when an off-diagonal element increases.

The lack of coordination among policy-makers delays the achievement of national objectives, such as full employment and target rates of growth and, under fixed exchange rates, increases the need for international reserves. Most significantly, these delays in reaching the targets and their calls on reserves increase with the degree of economic interdependence among nations.

III. ALTERNATIVE APPROACHES TO POLICY COORDINATION AND REACTIONS

Given the problem of coordination as it is proposed here, one needs an analytical framework to analyze the policy interaction among national economies. A series of illuminating models for this purpose was supplied by Mundell (1962, 1963, and 1968). One of the common features of these varieties of models is that they are general-equilibrium models incorporating such monetary aspects as the stock of money and bonds. For the analysis of policy interdependence, two-country versions of these models are utilized.

There are several alternative approaches, not necessarily competing but complementing each other in many cases, to analyzing policy interactions, coordinations, and conflicts.

Needless to say, the first and most natural approach is to advocate direct cooperation or some joint actions among national policy authorities. Cooper's works are examples of what one might call the *direct coordination approach*. Later, when I examine economic cooperation under floating exchange rates, the proposal by McKinnon (1974) to create a tripartite agreement by major countries in the world will be taken as one of the pleas for direct consultation and cooperation among national monetary authorities.

The second approach is the celebrated *policy assignment approach*, skillfully applied to international economics by Mundell. This approach, which is based on the general theory of the economic policy by Tinbergen (1952), seeks to find the optimal combination between targets and instruments of economic policy. Here, Mundell advises that the achievement of desirable ends requires that each instrument be assigned to the market where it is relatively effective. Thus, this approach is also known as the principle of effective market classification.

In a generalized version of the two-country model, Swoboda and Dornbusch (1973) study the problem of global policy assignment and, in particular, that of reconciling national income targets in an interdependent world economy. They show that gearing monetary policies to the desired reserve distribution and fiscal policies to income targets constitutes a stable assignment of instruments to targets, while the reverse pairing leads to instability.

In fact, it is in the two- (or more) country case in an integrated world economy where the principle of effective market classification really comes into its own (cf., Niehans 1968), because in a national economy it is rather hard to find reasons why decentralized decision-making among various branches of the government is needed, except perhaps for the sake of some savings of immediate information in reacting to situations in the short run.

An international system is characterized by decentralized decision-making almost by definition. The instruments of each country are assigned to its own targets. Since each country's policies usually have a comparative advantage with respect to its own targets, this assignment usually satisfies the requirement of effective market classification.

However, there are exceptions, where the international division of policy assignment does not necessarily coincide with the above, "natural," assignment. As an example of the division of international policy assignments, Mundell (1971) advocates the following assignment of policies under the dollar standard: the United States adjusts its money supply to peg the price level for the world economy, and Europe (or the rest of the world) adjusts its money supply to keep balance-of-payments equilibrium.

In Figure 1, the rate of monetary expansion in country I, say, the United States, is measured along the horizontal axis, and that of country II, Europe, along the vertical axis. The downward sloping line *AA* indicates the rates of money growth in the two countries that would keep the international price level stable. The upward sloping line *OB* shows those rates of

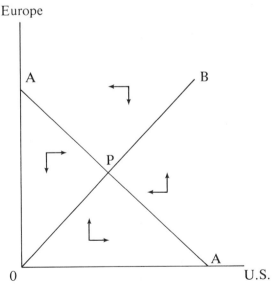

Fig. 1. International Assignment of Monetary Policies:
AA: *price stability;* OB: *balance-of-payments equilibrium.*

money growth that would keep the balance of payments in each country in equilibrium. The downward slope of AA reflects the proposition that the world price level depends on the weighted average of the monetary expansion of each country, while the positively sloped OB schedule follows from the balance of payments depending approximately on the difference between the money growth rates in the two countries (cf., Johnson 1972, Hamada 1974).

Above line AA, the world suffers from an inflationary pressure, below it from a deflationary pressure. On the right side of line OB, the balance of payments of the United States is in deficit, on the left it is in surplus. The policy assignment defined above, namely, the monetary policy of the United States to the price level target, that of Europe to the balance of payments, will yield a stable result as indicated by arrows, while the reverse assignment will lead to instability.

A collorary of this assignment approach is what is called the "redundancy" problem (Mundell 1968, Appendix to chap. 13). For the world as a whole, the sum of balances of payments is equal to zero, or more generally, equal to the increase of the outside money to the international system, i.e., gold or Special Drawing Rights (SDRs). This is a direct consequence of the first element of interdependence in our discussions in the previous section. If there are n countries, only $(n-1)$ of them can succeed in reaching their independent balance-of-payments targets; at least one of them must accept the position of acting as an international residual. In other words, interdependence creates another constraint on the national targets in order that they be consistent. Mundell argues that if each country has a distinct instrument to control its balance of payments, there is an additional degree of freedom. This redundant degree of freedom, according to him, should be used to control the international price level (see also, Cooper 1968 and Niehans 1968).

The strength of the assignment approach lies in its simplicity. One only needs to be concerned with the one-to-one correspondence between instruments and targets. The economy of information required for policy-makers when this prescription is followed is its advantage.

However, there are limitations in this' approach that need to be supplemented by alternative approaches. First, if one looks at the process of achieving economic targets, it will be clear that a one-to-one pairing of instrument and target is not enough, because an optimal mix of degree or strength of economic policies is needed in order to achieve an efficient realization of conflicting goals.

The need for another approach, which is called the *optimizing approach*, is developed by Niehans (1968). The first element is a social welfare function providing a ranking of the relevant bundles of target values. The second element is an efficient target frontier that specifies the maximum value of an objective that can be obtained for given values of the other objectives. The optimal combination of policy instruments is achieved when the social welfare function is maximized within the feasible region of target combination. Normally, this point is obtained at the point of tangency, where the efficient target frontier touches a social indifference curve.

The second limitation of the assignment approach, in particular when it is applied to the division of burdens in the international economy, is that it does not take into account the problems of whether there are sufficient incentives for national policy authorities to pursue economic objectives that should be assigned to them in order to achieve the best division of labor. In order that an international policy assignment be sustained by policy authorities, it is necessary that the policy assignment be "incentive compatible," in the sense that each country is induced to take necessary action if others are taking necessary action as well.

In the example of the dollar standard by Mundell, incentives exist to adopt contractionary policies in Europe (or the rest of the world other than the United States) when its balance of payments is in deficit. But it is not always true that there are incentives to adopt expansionary policies when the balance of payments in Europe is in surplus. Moreover, the United States is not necessarily induced to play the role of benevolent world leader to adjust its monetary or fiscal policy to keep the world price level constant.

Probably one of the reasons why the Bretton Woods regime collapsed is that the rest of the world did not play the game symmetrically and the United States had to be concerned with domestic policy objectives other than world price stability (see also, Niehans 1968, footnote 22).

This second limitation leads to the necessity of adopting a *strategic approach*, that is, an approach based on the joint reactions and counter-reactions of each participating country. This approach is most effectively carried out when one applies to the problem the theory of duopoly or oligopoly and some simple concepts of game theory.

As a matter of fact, further application of the optimizing approach to a two-country situation naturally opens the gate to the strategic approach. As is shown by Niehans (1968), once the optimizing approach is applied to a two-country model, each country's behavior depends on what it expects of the other's behavior. One can then draw a Stackelberg diagram, that is, the superposition of two sets of indifference curves in the same plane. If country I is acting independently, assuming that the other's policies are given, then it is acting on the reaction curve of country I. Similarly, one can draw the reaction curve of country II. This gives rise to a complete analogy to duopoly theory.

As emphasized by Niehans, it is worth noting that there are usually policy combinations that are superior to either of the noncooperative solutions for each country. It is only in the case of joint maximization (or contract) solutions that no alternative solution can be found that is superior

for each country. Ordinary rules of the game would not guarantee this
contract solution under decentralized decision-making, so that some conscious coordination of policies is necessary. In the absence of such rules, as
Niehaus (1968, p. 912) has noted, we might wind up in economic warfare
or monetary blackmail.

Figure 2 illustrates a typical example of the strategic approach. On the
horizontal axis, the rate of monetary expansion of country I is taken, and
on the vertical axis that of country II. Again *OB* indicates the combination
of monetary policies that would maintain equilibrium in the balance of
payments; *AA* indicates those combinations that yield price stability. Indifference curves of country I are drawn with solid curves and those of
country II with dotted curves. The reaction curve R_1 of country I is the
locus of welfare maximizing strategies for country I, given the rate of
monetary expansion of country II. R_1, therefore, represents the locus of
the points where the tangent of country I's indifference curve is horizontal.
Similarly, the reaction curve R_2 (for country II) can be written as the
locus of the points where the tangent to country II's indifference curve is
vertical.

The Cournot–Nash solution is given by the intersection of the two reaction curves. The leadership solution L_1, with country I as the leader, is

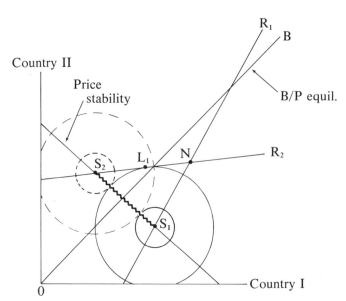

Fig. 2. *Stackelberg Diagram for Monetary Conflicts:*
AA: *price stability;* OB: *balance-of-payments equilibrium;* R_1:
reaction curve of country 1; R_2: *reaction curve of country 2;*
N: *Cournot–Nash solution;* L_1: *leadership solution with country 1 as leader;* S_1S_2:*contract curve.*

the best point for country I on the reaction curve of country II. Similarly, the leadership solution L_2 for country II can be defined. The Pareto efficient frontier, or the contract curve, is the locus of the points of tangency between the two sets of indifference curves and is drawn as the waved line segment between S_1 and S_2.

From Figure 2, one can note that neither the Cournot solution nor the leadership solution lies on the contract curve. Both of them lie on the inflationary side of the contract curve in this particular example, where both countries prefer some deficits in the balance of payments—this is indicated by the position of the most desired combinations S_1 and S_2.

It has been shown that in an *n*-country setting (Hamada 1976), the Cournot–Nash (noncooperative) solution does not in general lie on the Paretian contract surface, unless the aggregated national preferences concerning the desired balance of payments are matched by the creation of international (outside) reserves. If the injection of outside money into the international system falls short of the aggregate preferences concerning the balance of payments, monetary expansion takes on the nature of a public good, and the noncooperative actions of the constituent countries tend to lead to a more deflationary situation than implied by a cooperative choice. If the creation of international reserves exceeds the aggregate preferences concerning the balance of payments, monetary expansion takes on the nature of a public bad, and noncooperative actions tend to lead to a more inflationary situation than desired by the cooperative choice.

Moreover, one can analyze the effect of the number of the participating countries in the system, as well as the effect of the size of a particular countries. It can be shown that the increase in the number of participating country tends to work against the optimal supply (control) of public goods (bads)—a result congruent to findings in the theory of collective action (Olson 1965).

If mutual cooperation is attained without cost or difficulty, then the divergence of various solutions from the cooperative Paretian solution does not create serious troubles. If, however, there are insufficient incentives to induce voluntary cooperation, the achievement of mutual cooperation may not always be possible. In such a case, for a system to work successfully, it must be designed in such a way that the noncooperative result of individual national behavior will not be very far from the contract curve. Under fixed exchange rates, there are at least two ways of achieving this design. One way is to manipulate the rate of increase in (outside) international reserves to match the aggregated preferences by the monetary authorities for accumulating reserves. Another way is to devise a clearing system so that the preferences of monetary authorities for surpluses or deficits are kept at suitable values.

One of the problems concerning these strategic analyses is that they are obliged to appeal to economic models of rather simplified structure, because the study of interaction of two (or more) countries gives additional complications to the analysis. Therefore, either the Keynesian analysis, with given price levels, or the monetarist model, with given real income, is apt to be utilized (Hamada 1974).

However, in order to approach the current world situation with varying employment and inflation rates, more attempts should be made to analyze the situation with varying employment and price levels (see, e.g., Ethier 1976, Hamada and Sakurai 1978).

IV. EMPIRICAL EVIDENCE

It is hard to give a positive empirical analysis of the policy notions discussed above. Just as it is difficult to test a hypothesis in the duopoly or oligopoly theory incorporating conjectual variations on the behavior of others, it is difficult to test a hypothesis concerning the policy reaction functions in the world.

In fact, the existing empirical literature is at most a verification of some of the theoretical propositions by way of simulation in two-country models, which are either constructed as hypothetical numerical examples or estimated by actual data.

In his analysis of the speed of adjustment in an interdependent economy, Cooper (1969) calculates the dominant characteristic roots corresponding to numerical models with varying degrees of interdependence, and he also shows by way of simulations how income and reserve requirements vary with or without cooperation.

Using the linked American and Canadian econometric models, Helliwell and McRae (1977) study the effect of mutual responses of monetary policies reacting to an initial fiscal disturbance in one country. The results of their simulation, which assumes that the same type of monetary policies are used in both countries, suggest that the effect of the Canadian policy on the United States is larger and more cyclical if both countries use monetary policy of pegging interest rates than if they peg the money supply. In general, it is found that the nature of the transmission of economic disturbances takes different forms, depending on the *modus operandi* of monetary policies adopted in the two countries.[3]

A series of interesting studies on the role of sterilization policies was made by De Grauwe (1975) and (1977). By estimating the balance-of-payments equations for European countries and then experimenting with the system of these equations, he found that the systematic use of sterilization policies by two or more countries, in an attempt to offset the

[3] During their observation period, Canada experienced changes in the exchange rate regimes, flexible to fixed, and again to flexible. Their findings indicate, however, that there are no substantial differences between the two regimes.

monetary effects of the balance-of-payments disequilibrium, is most likely to lead to explosive reserve flows and therefore to the breakdown of the system. Even when those policies do not lead to unstable reserve flows, their effectiveness is extremely limited. According to him, because of the increased interdependence in the 1960s as compared to the 1950s, the use of sterilization policies would have created more acute policy conflicts during the second period.

Finally, in his study of the impact of monetary policy on world inflation and the balance of payments, Parkin (1977) shows that the main conclusion of the monetary approach to the balance of payments is approximately valid, and that the influence of productivity increase is also important. It should be noted in passing that a formula for monetary expansion is derived that is required for the attainment of the price stability in the world (or in a monetary union).

One cannot deny the impression that empirical analyses relating macroeconomic coordination are still sparse, especially concerning policy reaction behavior. The importance of those studies mentioned here, however, should not be undervalued, because, in that they clarify the nature of interdependence in the current world economy, they are the required steps to give solid foundations for the empirical analysis of strategic policy interplay. Moreover, some of them, e.g., those by De Grauwe and by Parkin, serve as a rationale for a new type of monetary cooperation suggested by McKinnon under the post-Smithsonian regime, which will be discussed in the next section.

V. MONETARY COORDINATION UNDER FLEXIBLE EXCHANGE RATES

Before the worldwide (on and off) adoption of flexible exchange rates or of managed floating dated from 1971, the interdependence and policy interactions were considered to be of secondary or minor importance as compared with the closely connected monetary link existing under fixed exchange rates. The actual performance of flexible exchange rates or managed float has revealed, however, that there still remain substantial policy conflicts and, accordingly, the need for coordination of economic policies, even if we leave the system of fixed exchange rate or an adjustable peg.

The nature of this interdependence under flexible exchange rates is neatly discussed in the companion essay by Mussa (1978), so that we shall confine our attention to a few notable channels of interdependence. First, in their celebrated article on a two-country model of unemployment, Laursen and Metzler (1951) demonstrate that the insulation effect can be more than a hundred percent in the presence of a nonproportional Keynesian consumption function. In the general argument of insulation, initial increase in effective demand by one country is considered not to be transmitted to another country, but is completely absorbed by exchange rate movements. Laursen and Metzler, however, show that an increase in effective demand in one country may exert a deflationary pressure on the level of employment in the other.

Second, in his discussion of capital mobility Mundell (1963) shows that, in the presence of capital mobility under flexible exchange rates, an expansionary monetary policy undertaken by one country may have a deflationary impact on the other. A monetary expansion leads to a lower domestic interest rate that, in turn, induces capital outflow from the country. In order to compensate for this capital account deficit, the exchange rate must depreciate to raise current account surplus, adversely affecting the other country. In other words, an expansionary monetary policy by one country exerts a contractionary impact, or beggar-my-neighbor effect, on the other.

This result, under capital mobility, was recently challenged by Tsiang (1975). According to him, if one considers the effect of interest payments on resulting increases in stock of foreign liabilities, then the above relationship may be reversed in the long run. Accordingly, the monetary impact will eventually turn out to be expansionary for the other country also. It does not seem very realistic, however, to trace the long-run effect of interest payments for a country faced with actual policy decisions. Thus we might, for the moment, neglect the debt service effects of capital movement.

According to these two views, by Laursen and Metzler and by Mundell, economic fluctuations in various countries under flexible exchange rates should be more desynchronized than under fixed exchange rates. If we look at the actual experience of a flexible exchange rate regime, however, we still see a high degree of synchronization in fluctuation in unemployment and price levels. Moreover, if these views explain a substantial part of interdependence under flexible rates, every country must be very eager to persuade other countries to pursue contractionary monetary and fiscal policies, instead of asking them to pursue expansionary policies. But a series of current monetary negotiations seems to indicate that every country wants others to expand simultaneously with its own expansion or, even in some cases, to expand without its own domestic expansion. In order to explain these synchronized economic performances as well as attitudes toward policy cooperation, the terms of trade effects should not be neglected. If one considers the link through the terms of trade, a fiscal policy-induced recession in one country is transmitted as stagflation to the other under floating exchange rates. A monetary expansion by one country is transmitted by output expansion, without much inflationary pressure, on the other (Hamada and Sakurai 1978). Therefore, if one considers the terms-of-trade effect, the strategic implication of interdependence becomes again the usually observed one that every country wants others to expand, in some cases without committing themselves very strongly to their own expansion.

In a more general analysis that incorporates relative prices, asset equilibrium, unemployment, expectations, and so forth, Dornbusch and Krugman (1977) show from theoretical arguments as well as from empirical evidence that the use of monetary policy by a single country under flexible exchange rates may have the following disadvantages. First, monetary expansion of a single country may exert the beggar-my-neighbor effect on the rest of the world along the line discussed by Mundell (1963) and Fleming (1962). Second, because of the *J*-curve effect through the sluggishness of responses in commodity flows, the depreciation of the currency does not improve current account in the short run. Finally, the Phillips curve trade-off becomes steeper under flexible exchange rates through the effect of import prices. Thus they recommend a cooperative fiscal expansion under worldwide recessions, combined with appropriate monetary adjustments by both countries to keep the exchange rate in a stable range.

Generally, the experience of actual flexible exchange rates has led a number of monetary economists to have quite critical views on proper functioning of the floating exchange rate regime, in striking contrast to earlier writers before the universal adoption of the system, who regarded flexible exchange rates as a kind of *deus ex machina* for international policy conflicts.

One of the reasons may be that economists are always unsatisfied, by profession, with the current state of affairs. But it is probably fair to say that when one looks at the new system more closely, then one can find more problems, even though the new system is, in principle, progressive. It may be just as a girl who looks very beautiful from a distance, may turn out to have freckles if one comes close. Whatever the reasons are, floating exchange rate regimes are not regarded to be functioning as was expected. The actual performance of floating exchange rates is just like the system of a limping dollar standard (Aliber 1973). In order to correct this situation and to restore the benefit of stable exchange rates, McKinnon (1974) suggests a practical cooperation scheme under floating exchange rates. This is indeed a scheme of gearing a flexible exchange rate regime to work as if it were a fixed exchange rate regime. Also this is rightly classified as one of the examples of what we call a *direct cooperation approach.*

McKinnon points out that the sale or purchase of foreign exchange for domestic currency is nothing but one technique for changing the domestic monetary base. Thus it is hard to distinguish exchange rate policy from monetary policy on purely theoretical grounds. Intervention to fix a nation's exchange rate is viable only if the domestic credit expansion by the monetary branch of government or the central bank does not offset what the exchange branch is doing.

On the basis of this equivalence of foreign exchange operations with monetary policy, McKinnon argues that the proper management of exchange rates can be done only by cooperation toward the consistent choice of changing the monetary base of major countries. Practically, he proposes a tripartite monetary agreement between the United States, Germany, and Japan. Once this consistency in national monetary policies is achieved, the remaining objective of international policy becomes the determination of the rate of monetary expansion by the union as a whole. Thus, the tripartite agreement would be concerned with the total size or growth of aggregate money supply of these countries and its distribution among them. The key to stabilizing the aggregate monetary base is to limit the rate of domestic credit expansion by each central bank.

By suitably restricting the freedom of monetary actions of the three major trading nations vis-à-vis each other, he argues, the world monetary system can be better stabilized. A theoretical justification for this tripartite scheme can be found in De Grauwe's argument that sterilizations of the balance of payments would be detrimental to the world monetary stability. At the same time, the political question of how to distribute the monetary base among three countries would present an interesting case for applications of the game theoretic or strategic approach. It is a question of what points on the contract curve the monetary agreement would lead to.

VI. MONETARY INTERDEPENDENCE UNDER MANAGED FLOATING

One of the reasons why the experience of flexible exchange rates has not been as successful as expected may be that the flexible exchange rate regime is not in fact operating in such a pure form as the logic of the system requires. Actually, the determination of the exchange rate is not left completely in the hands of market forces, but is influenced by government interventions. Thus we are living in a world of "managed" or "controlled" floating.

It is often claimed by monetary authorities that their interventions in exchange markets are only of a smoothing character, and not meant to influence trends in exchange rates. But from the fact that some countries have accumulated or decumulated a substantial amount of reserves even after the collapse of the Smithsonian agreement, one can deduce that interventions have been used not only to smooth movements of reserves but also to influence time trends in the balance of payments.

Under complete or "clean" floating, exchange rates are determined by market forces. Accordingly, the level or trend of exchange rates should not be included in the list of policy goals. Nor should the breakdown of the balance of payments into the current and capital accounts be a concern of policy authorities. In actual practice, however, there are lots of pressures, by the group of exporters and import competitors and others, for the government to list the current account and the levels of exchange rates as policy targets. (For rationales for these, see Krueger 1977.) This creates, as we shall see, interesting but difficult problems related to conflicting policy targets over exchange rates among national economies.

Mussa (1976) analyzes the issue of policy conflicts and policy co-ordination under managed floating. Policy conflicts arose in the 1930s, when everyone wanted to devalue relative to everyone else. He argues, however, that in a system of controlled floating, such policy conflicts are not inevitable, because the system has more freedom than a system of fixed exchange rates. While a conflict arises under fixed exchange rates whenever one government wants to expand and another government wants to contract, this conflict is easily resolved under controlled floating. Policy conflicts under controlled floating arise only when two countries want to expand output or reduce inflation simultaneously, and when each wants to use their mutual exchange rate in pursuing its objective.

Accordingly, the need for policy coordination arises in such a situation. Mussa then argues that, as is clearly indicated by the monetary approach to the balance of payments (Frenkel and Johnson 1976), the required type of coordination must be among monetary policies, similar to the monetary coordination suggested by McKinnon (1974).

Anyway, the analyses of managed or controlled floating are still new and sparse. In this and the next section, we shall attempt to present a simple framework to analyze the structure of conflicts under managed floating. (For the sake of economy of space, allow us to appeal to some algebraic treatment in the two sections.)

Let us consider a world where national economies are sufficiently integrated so that the price levels of these countries exhibit a relationship predicted by the purchasing power parity theory. In this section, we concentrate our attention on the long-run growth path of this world economy, assuming that real rates of growth of these countries are exogenously given.

Suppose there exist n countries in the world under the managed-float regime. Let us denote the money stock outstanding in i'th country by M_i. Let us take money of the first country, say dollars, as *numéraire*, and let R_i be reserves of i'th country, measured in terms of the money of the first country. Let the exchange rate of country i (the value of a dollar in terms of the home currency) be q_i. Naturally, $q_1 = 1$ by definition. Since an increase in money stock is either backed by an increase in international reserves R_i or an increase in domestic credit D_i, one may write

(1) $\dot{M}_i = q_i \dot{R}_i + \dot{D}_i,$

where "dot" indicates time derivatives.[4]

Define the total reserves in the world as R,

(2) $R = \sum_{i=1}^{n} R_i.$

R_i consists of gold, and the Special Drawing Rights (SDRs) and foreign exchanges. If country 1, say the United States, is the reserve-currency country, then R_i for country 2 to n may include liquid liabilities of the U.S. monetary system, so that R_1 may become negative. For the world as a whole, however, R consists of international reserves that are *outside* of the system, namely, gold and the SDRs. The purchasing power parity relationship requires

(3) $p_i = q_i p_1,$ $i = 1, 2, \ldots, n.$

The demand for real-money balances is simply assumed to be a function of real income Q_i. Thus we may write

(4) $M_i/p_i = L(Q_i),$ $i = 1, 2, \ldots, n.$

Of course, in the real world the demand for money may depend on the interest rate and other factors, but in order to focus our attention on the long-run behavior of the system, where the rate of interest can be regarded as constant, we have abstracted the model from various elements.

There are two alternative ways to formulate the monetary approach to balance of payments. One is to use a discrete-time model and allow lags into the process of the balance-of-payments adjustment (e.g., Dornbusch 1973, Komiya 1974). There, the balance of payments is defined as

---

[4] Apparently, the balance sheet of a monetary sector may seem to be

$$M_i = q_i R_i + D_i.$$

But this is false, because in the regime of managed float one must treat properly capital gains or losses due to depreciation or appreciation of currency. Rigorously, the balance sheet must be expressed as

$$K_i + M_i = q_i R_i + D_i,$$

where K_i is the net worth of a monetary sector. Taking the time derivative, one obtains

$$\dot{K}_i + \dot{M}_i = \dot{q}_i R_i + q_i \dot{R}_i + \dot{D}_i.$$

In most countries, however, capital gains (or losses) due to changes in exchange rates are credited (or debited) as the change in the net worth of the monetary sector. Therefore,

$$\dot{K}_i = \dot{q}_i R_i,$$

so that equation (1) in the text holds. In other words, capital gains or losses due to exchange rate fluctuations are not automatically reflected in an increase in money supply.

the difference between the demand and the supply of money. The other way is to appeal to a continuous-time model, and describe the dynamic process as a moving equilibrium (Johnson 1972a). Here, the demand and the supply for money is continuously adjusted to equilibrium by the flow of the balance of payments. In this chapter, where we are concerned with the dynamic changes in the rate of inflation, rather than with the comparative statics, we shall adopt the second approach and proceed in a continuous framework.

Denoting

$$\frac{dx}{dt} \text{ by } \dot{x}, \quad \frac{1}{x}\frac{dx}{dt} \text{ by } \hat{x},$$

and the income elasticity of the demand for money by η_i, logarithmic differentiation of (4) yields

$$\hat{M}_i - \hat{p}_i = \eta_i \hat{Q}_i$$

or, in view of (1),

$$(5) \qquad \frac{\dot{D}_i + q_i \dot{R}_i}{M_i} = \hat{p}_i + \eta_i \hat{Q}_i.$$

We see from this equation that the money supply can be increased either by pure domestic credit creation, $\dot{D}_i$, or by a surplus in the balance of payments, $q_i \dot{R}_i$.

The simplest way of interpreting this equation is to assume that the government does not sterilize the inflow or outflow of reserves. However, even when the government engages in sterilizing operations, equation (5) follows, if we define our policy variable, $\dot{D}_i$, to be inclusive of sterilizing operations.

Define the relative balance of payments normalized by the money supply as

$$z_i = \frac{\dot{R}_i}{(M_i/q_i)}.$$

Then equation (5) can be rewritten as

$$(6) \qquad \theta_i + z_i = \hat{p}_i,$$

where

$$\theta_i \equiv \frac{\dot{D}_i}{M_i} - \eta_i \hat{Q}_i.$$

From the purchasing power parity relationship (3), we obtain

$$(7) \qquad \hat{p}_i = \hat{q}_i + \hat{p}_1.$$

Thus we have the relationship between the excess money creation, the balance of payments, and the price level of country 1

(8) $\theta_i + z_i = \hat{p}_1 + \hat{q}_i.$

Define the relative magnitude of the amount of outstanding money as w_i, such that

$$w_i = \frac{M_i/q_i}{\sum\limits_{k=1}^{n} (M_k/q_k)}.$$

Thus we can equate the supply of money in equation (1) to the demand in equation (4). As θ_i is the rate of domestic credit creation in excess of the increase in money demand resulting from real economic growth, it can be regarded as a policy variable, excess money creation. After multiplying equation (8) by w_i, and then summing over $i = 1, \ldots, n$, we get

(9) $\sum\limits_{i=1}^{n} w_i\theta_i + \sum\limits_{i=1}^{n} w_i z_i = \sum\limits_{i=1}^{n} w_i\hat{q}_i + \hat{p}_1.$

However,

(10) $\sum\limits_{i=1}^{n} w_i z_i = \dfrac{\sum\limits_{i=1}^{n} \left(\dfrac{M_i}{q_i} \cdot \dfrac{q_i\dot{R}_i}{M_i} \right)}{\sum\limits_{i=1}^{n} \left(\dfrac{M_k}{q_k} \right)} = \dfrac{\sum\limits_{i=1}^{n} \dot{R}_i}{\sum\limits_{k=1}^{n} (M_k/q_k)} = \dfrac{\dot{R}}{\sum\limits_{k=1}^{n} (M_k/q_k)} = G_R.$

Thus the weighted sum of the normalized balance of payments is equal to the exogenous increase in total international reserves normalized by the total world money stock, in term of dollars. This normalized increase in the total international reserves is denoted by G_R.

Behind equation (5), the following mechanism is working. National policy authorities have two policy instruments, increase in domestic credit creation $\dot{D}_i$ and manipulation of the exchange rate $\hat{q}_i$, by intervening in the exchange market. Intervention in the exchange market may change the balance of payments, but it is assumed that governments either do not sterilize the effect of the balance of payments on the domestic monetary base, or that any attempt at sterilization is included in the definition of $\dot{D}_i$.

I shall treat from now on excess money creation θ_i $(i = 1, 2, \ldots, n)$ and the rate of change in exchange rate $\hat{q}_i$ $(i = 2, \ldots, n)$ as policy variables. To some readers, it may seem more natural to consider excess money creation θ_i and the (relative) amount of government intervention z_i as policy variables. Suppose for a moment θ_i's and z_i's are policy instruments.

Since

$$\sum_{i=1}^{n} w_i z_i = G_R$$

holds as an identity, only $(n - 1)$ of z_i's are independent. (This is an expression of the redundancy problem under the managed rate.) Therefore, one must treat one of z_i's as to be passively determined.

Suppose z_1 is passively determined in such a way,

$$z_1 = G_R - \sum_{i=2}^{n} (w_i/w_1) z_i.$$

Then, from equation (8)

$$\hat{q}_j = (\theta_j + z_j) - (\theta_1 + z_1)$$

$$= (\theta_j - \theta_1) + (1 - w_j/w_1) z_j - \sum_{i \neq 1, j} (w_i/w_1) z_i, \quad \text{for } j = 2, \ldots, n.$$

Thus, given θ_i's $(i \neq j)$ and z_i's $(i \neq 1, j)$, the j'th country can decide on its rate of depreciation. Therefore, one-to-one correspondence exists between the case where θ_i's $(i = 1, \ldots, n)$ and z_i's $(i = 2, \ldots, n)$ are strategies, and the case where θ_i's $(i = 1, \ldots, n)$ and $\hat{q}_i$'s $(i = 2, \ldots, n)$ are strategies. Since both cases are equivalent, we shall proceed to use the latter formulation where the rates of excess money creation and the changes in exchange rates are treated as policy instruments.

From (9) we obtain the equation for the determination of the price level of country 1

$$(11) \quad \hat{p}_1 = G_R + \sum_{i=1}^{n} w_i(\theta_i - \hat{q}_i),$$

and for j'th country

$$(12) \quad \hat{p}_j = G_R + \sum_{i=1}^{n} w_i(\theta_i - \hat{q}_i) + \hat{q}_j$$

These are essentially a generalization of the Johnson's formula (Johnson 1972a), though the expression is much simpler due to the changes in the definition of variables (cf., Hamada 1976). Now $\hat{q}_1$, the *numéraire*, has been set equal to one throughout; therefore, $\hat{q}_1 = 0$. Accordingly, the weighted average can be rewritten as

$$\sum_{i=1}^{n} w_i(\theta_i - \hat{q}_i) = w_1\theta_1 + \sum_{i=2}^{n} w_i(\theta_i - \hat{q}_i).$$

Thus, in the world where national economies are tied sufficiently enough to realize the relationship of purchasing power parity, the price level of the *numéraire* country is determined by the sum of the relative increase in the (outside) international money and the weighted average of excess money creation *minus* the rate of depreciation of exchange rate toward the *numéraire* currency. Equation (12) indicates that price changes in other countries are determined by the sum of the price inflation in the *numéraire* country and the rate of depreciation in their exchange rate.

The monetary structure of the managed-float system is expressed in equations (11) and (12). Under fixed exchange rates, one can speak of the world price level, which is determined by the weighted sum of excess money creation. Under flexible exchange rates, each country can choose its own price level, which is mainly determined by its own money supply. Under managed floating, each country is still able to choose its own price level, which, on one hand, is determined by the weighted average of rates of excess money creation minus rates of depreciation and, on the other hand, by its own rate of depreciation.

As is rightly pointed out by Johnson (1972*a*), devaluation is equivalent to a domestic credit contraction in its effect on the balance of payments. The same statement can be applied also to the price level of those countries in the rest of the world. With respect to the price level of its own country, however, devaluation has a positive effect that is similar to a domestic credit expansion mitigated by the factor $(1 - w_j)$, where w_j is the monetary weight of the j'th country.

Devaluation means a change in the relative value between domestic and foreign money. Accordingly, for other countries, devaluation exerts an effect that is equivalent to a decrease in the foreign money supply. For the home country, devaluation is equivalent to an increase in the amount of money stock in the rest of the world.

Under fixed rates, the effect of credit contraction of one country is diluted or leaked to the world through the balance-of-payments adjustment. Under managed floating, depreciation of exchange rates by one country negatively affects the rest of the world, while bringing about domestic expansion. Because of this asymmetry, manipulation of exchange rates is a very powerful policy instrument.

It is interesting to compute the average world price level weighted by the monetary weight w_i. Let us multiply (12) by w_j, for $j = 1, \ldots, n$, noting that (11) is interpreted as a special case of equation (12) with $\hat{q}_1 = 0$, and sum. Then we obtain the following simple relationship:

$$(13) \quad \sum_{j=1}^{n} w_j \hat{p}_j = G_R + \sum_{j=1}^{n} w_j \theta_j.$$

Thus we can state: Suppose the world price level is defined as the weighted average of national price levels, the weights being the relative monetary magnitudes. Then *the world price level is determined by the weighted average of excess money creation and the relative growth of the outside international reserves.* The attempt to manipulate exchange rates gives opposite influences in the home country and in the rest of the world, so that the total effect on the world price level is nil because opposite effects cancel each other.

VII. STRATEGIC INTERACTION OF EXCHANGE-RATE POLICIES UNDER MANAGED FLOAT

i) *The long-run conflicts*

So far, we have left unanswered the question of which country can decide on exchange rates. An exchange rate itself is the relative price between currencies. For example, q_j is the relative price of the *numéraire* currency in terms of the currency of j'th country. Because the change of an exchange rate is a powerful weapon, it matters greatly which country has control over a particular exchange rate.

In order to answer this question, we shall study more carefully the interdependent nature of monetary policies and the determination of exchange rates in a simplified model of the world economy consisting of two countries.

Suppose there are only two countries in the world, say, the United States and Europe. In addition, suppose that the supply of outside international money is held constant, so that

$$G_R = 0.$$

Then our basic relationship, equations (11) and (12), is reduced to

(14) $\quad w_1\theta_1 + w_2\theta_2 = \hat{p}_1 + w_2\hat{q}_2$

(15) $\quad w_1\theta_1 + w_2\theta_2 = \hat{p}_2 - w_1\hat{q}_2.$

The balance of payments of each country is expressed by

(16) $\quad z_1 = w_2\{-\theta_1 + (\theta_2 - \hat{q}_2)\}$

(17) $\quad z_2 = w_1\{\theta_1 - (\theta_2 - \hat{q}_2)\}.$

It is easy to verify the relationship

$$w_1z_1 + w_2z_2 \left[= G_R\right] = 0.$$

The structure of this interplay of monetary policy *cum* exchange rate policy is most clearly seen if we consider the system of equations (14) and (15) in a context of the policy assignment problem formulated by Mundell (1962).

Suppose a_1 is the most desired rate of inflation for country 1, and a_2 is that for country 2. To achieve these targets, there are three policy instruments

θ_1, θ_2 and $\hat{q}_2$. In order to achieve both targets at the same time, policy instruments must satisfy

(18) $w_1\theta_1 + w_2\theta_2 = a_1 + w_2\hat{q}_2$

(19) $w_1\theta_1 + w_2\theta_2 = a_2 - w_1\hat{q}_2$.

Even though two policy instruments θ_1 and θ_2 may seem to be sufficient to achieve both goals a_1 and a_2, given an arbitrary value of $\hat{q}_2$, it is not so. The simultaneous equation system is degenerate and has solutions if and only if $\hat{q}_2$ satisfies the following relationship:

$$a_1 + w_2\hat{q}_2 = a_2 - w_1\hat{q}_2,$$

that is,

(20) $\hat{q}_2 = a_2 - a_1$.

If condition (18) is satisfied, any combination of θ_1 and θ_2 with a varying parameter k, such that

(21) $\theta_1 = a_1 + w_2k$,

(22) $\theta_2 = a_2 - w_1k$,

will satisfy the system of equations (18) and (19).

With these preparations one can readily analyze the characteristics of alternative exchange rate regimes. Under flexible rates, q_2 moves so as to equate both z_1 and z_2 to zero in (16) and (17) so that $\hat{p}_1 = \theta_1$ and $\hat{p}_2 = \theta_2$. Therefore, there is no interdependence or conflict between monetary policies in the long run, because each country can set θ_i equal to a_i.

Under fixed exchange rates, $\hat{q}_2$ is set equal to zero by definition. Accordingly, equations (18) and (19) cannot be satisfied simultaneously, unless a_1 happens to equal a_2. If there is a discrepancy of preferences between the two countries on the desired rate of inflation and the desired level of the balance of payments, then a game-like situation will emerge.

Under managed floating, namely, under a mixture of the above two systems, price levels can be chosen independently, provided that $\hat{q}_2$ is chosen to be equal to the difference between the desired inflation rate of one country and that of the other. Then by coordinating monetary policies and manipulating exchange rate policies so as to satisfy equations (21) and (22), both countries will achieve the first best situation—a Paretian combination of price changes. This is satisfied if the balance of payments is in equilibrium, namely, when the system is operated as if it were a genuine float.

But this is not a necessary condition for the system to work. Even though θ_1 and θ_2 are set according to equations (21) and (22) with a nonvanishing k, the policy targets are satisfied so long as $\hat{q}_2 = a_2 - a_1$. In this case, international reserves of the country with a rate of monetary expansion smaller than the value of a_i will continue to accumulate all the time.

Suppose, however, that each country is not indifferent about the rate of depreciation $\hat{q}_2$. It is possible that a country wants a certain rate of currency depreciation for various reasons, for example, due to the lobbying of producers of exportables and import competitors.[5] Both countries are free to choose their own rates of monetary expansion, but if they do not agree with each other on the appropriate change in the exchange rate, then a conflict situation will emerge. First, if they differ on the desired rate of depreciation of country 2 (appreciation of country 1), then conflict will occur. Second, even though they agree on the desired value of $\hat{q}_2$, if it does not coincide with $a_2 - a_1$, it again creates problems.

The structure of possible conflict under managed floating can be illustrated by a Cournot diagram, because equation (18) and (19) can be interpreted respectively as the reaction curve of country 1 and that of country 2. In Figure 3, rates of excess money creation, which are strategies in this game, are depicted on the axes. Reaction curves by country 1 and country 2 are drawn as lines AA and BB. Let us assume, for simplicity, that $a_1 = a_2 = a > 0$, but that the desired rate of currency depreciation by

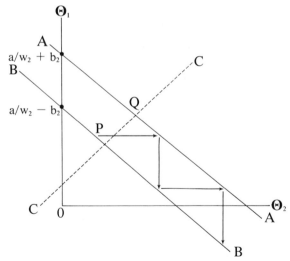

Fig. 3. Longrun Conflicts under Managed Float:
AA: reaction curve of country 1; BB: reaction curve of country 2; CC: balance-of-payments constraint on nonreserve country.

[5] Motives of choosing particular values of $\hat{q}_2$ are not endogenously derived from the model in the previous section. In the discussion of short-run effects below, such motives are more naturally justified (cf. also, Krueger 1977).

country 2 is $b_2 > 0$. Then, given rates of currency depreciation b_2, the reaction curve of country 1 is located above that of country 2. Since both lines are parallel, there is no equilibrium point. The path indicating the process of policy reactions is driven down as shown by arrows in the figure. Unless $\hat{q}_2$ is taken as the appropriate value ($= a_2 - a_1 =$ zero in this particular example) the process of policy retaliation may lead to the combination of accelerated monetary expansion by one country and accelerated contraction by the other.

Realistically, however, the current operation of the world monetary regime is not represented by unqualified choice of monetary policies and exchange rate changes. The reserve-currency country usually does not intervene in the exchange rate market, but nonreserve countries choose the combination of monetary and exchange rate policies under constraints on their balance of payments. In the two-country model, this can be formulated as follows: The right to determine $\hat{q}_2$ is left to monetary authorities of country 2, which is, in turn, restricted by the balance-of-payments constraint

$$(23) \quad z_2 = w_1[\theta_1 - (\theta_2 - \hat{q}_2)] \geqq 0.$$

Therefore, country 2 can only operate under the dotted line CC, which has a 45-degree angle. If the balance of payments needs to be in strict equilibrium, country 2 should on line CC. In other words, CC becomes the virtual reaction curve for country 2. Then Q is the only solution. But if both countries learn that $\hat{q}_2$ must be set to $(a_2 - a_1)$ for the simultaneous achievement of the price targets, they may agree on the value of $\hat{q}_2 = a_2 - a_1$ and return to the procedure of complete floating.

In reality, relationship (23) is not a strict equality, but allows inequality. Therefore, the whole region below the dotted curve CC is the feasible region for country 2, and, of course, for country 1. Therefore, in this more realistic picture, there is still danger of unstable policy interactions, so long as balance-of-payments surplus does not necessarily induce the nonreserve country to expand its money supply or appreciate its currency (cf. Henderson 1975).

The reader may notice that here reemerges the well-known redundancy problem in a new context. In the world of managed floating the redundancy problem takes the form, in general, that there are only $(n - 1)$ relative prices—exchange rates—to be determined, and there are n policy authorities. One solution is that the reserve-currency country, for example, country 1, does not intervene in the exchange market, and all other countries intervene in terms of dollars. That solves this redundancy problem but gives nonreserve countries an advantageous strategic position when there is a conflict about the proper rate of exchange rate depreciation (Cooper 1972).

On the other hand, if every country intervenes in exchange markets and tries to influence exchange rates, then the policy outcome will be indeterminate. For the attempt by one central bank to depreciate its own currency through buying other currencies will be counteracted by the attempt by other central banks to buy that particular currency. The structure of conflict in such a case would be a zero-sum game, and some international agreement is necessary for exchange rates to be settled to stable values.

Of course, if there is a *numéraire* different from a national currency, this redundancy problem formally vanishes. Suppose that the value of every currency is measured by a currency unit, say a SDR, and that any country can intervene in exchange markets by selling or buying SDRs. Then it is easy to see that every country can set the nominal value of its own currency in terms of SDRs. However, actual difficulties still remain, because it is not nominal value of a currency in terms of some *numéraire*, but relative values of a currency vis-à-vis other currencies that matter to policy authorities.

Needless to say, this analysis of interdependence depends on various simplifying assumptions. Relaxation of the purchasing power parity assumption, introduction of nontraded goods, and consideration of the rate of interest and capital movements would certainly modify the picture described above. We hope, however, that our analysis will serve as a first step to delineate the structure of conflicts under managed floating.

ii) *Transmission of short-run fluctuations*

So far the real side of the economy, in particular, real national income, is assumed to be exogenously given. However, the mere monetary effects are of little interest to economists unless they have some bearing on the real side of the economy. Now we shall consider the process of the transmission of business cycles under managed floating.

Consider a world consisting of two countries where a Phillips curve relationship generates output fluctuations in each. In this section, we abstract from secular growth factors in order to present a simplified picture of the transmission of short-run output fluctuations. In each country, the demand for real-money balance is assumed to be proportional to real permanent income. Real permanent income is again assumed constant.

Let the short-run Phillips relationships in the two countries be expressed as

$$(24) \quad \hat{W}_i = \psi(X_i) + \Pi_i, \psi(X_i) > 0, \qquad i = 1, 2,$$

where W_i, X_i and Π_i are, respectively, money wage, output, and expected rate of inflation in i'th country. Expected rate of inflation is formed by the adaptive scheme,

$$(25) \quad \dot{\Pi}_i = \gamma(\hat{p}_i - \Pi_i), \qquad i = 1, 2.$$

The demand for labor and output are determined by marginal productivity relationship and the production function $F(N)$.

(26) $W_i/p_i = F'(N_i)$, $X_i = F(N_i)$ $i = 1, 2$.

Since the demand for real-money balance is assumed to be proportional to a constant permanent income, we have

(27) $\hat{p}_i = \hat{M}_i$, $i = 1, 2$.

The purchasing power parity relationship requires

$$q_2 p_1 = p_2,$$

or

(28) $\hat{p}_1 + \hat{q}_2 = \hat{p}_2$.

Thus, we have from (27) and (28)

$$\hat{M}_1 + \hat{q}_2 = \hat{M}_2.$$

On the other hand, as explained in section 2,

$$w_1 \hat{M}_1 + w_2 \hat{M}_2 = G_R + w_1 \theta_1 + w_2 \theta_2,$$

where w_i is relative monetary weight of country i, and θ_i equals $\dot{D}_i/M_i$. Setting $G_R = 0$ for simplicity, we obtain

$$\hat{p}_1 = \hat{M}_1 = w_1 \theta_1 + w_2(\theta_2 - \hat{q}_2)$$

$$\hat{p}_2 = \hat{M}_2 = w_1(\theta_1 + \hat{q}_2) + w_2 \theta_2.$$

Thus, if we specify production functions of the Cobb–Douglas type with exponent β, i.e., $F(N) = N^\beta$, we can derive[6] the following pairs of differential equations:

$$\hat{X}_1 = \bar{\beta}\{w_1\theta_1 + w_1(\theta_2 - \hat{q}_2) - \psi(X_1) - \Pi_1\}$$

(29)

$$\dot{\Pi}_1 = \gamma\{w_1\theta_1 + w_2(\theta_2 - \hat{q}_2) - \Pi_1\}$$

$$\hat{X}_2 = \bar{\beta}\{w_1(\theta_1 + \hat{q}_2) + w_2\theta_2 - \psi(X_2) - \Pi_2\}$$

(30)

$$\dot{\Pi}_2 = \gamma\{w_1(\theta_1 + \hat{q}_2) + w_2\theta_2 - \Pi_2\},$$

where

$$\bar{\beta} = \beta/(1 - \beta).$$

The interdependence of the two economies can be illustrated by the phase diagrams in Figure 4. The solid curves in Figure 4 (a) and (b) indicate

---

[6] For the derivation and implication of these equations in a slightly different setting, see Hamada and Sakurai (1978).

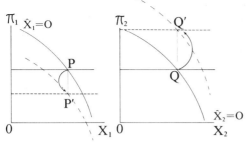

Fig. 4. Shortrun Transmission of Econon.ic Fluctuations under Managed Float: $QQ' = w_1 q_2$; $PP' = w_2 q_2$.

respectively the loci of $\hat{X}_1 = 0$ and $\dot{\Pi}_i = 0$. Locus $\hat{X}_2 = 0$ is drawn as an upside-down image of the Phillips curve; locus $\dot{\Pi}_i = 0$ is drawn as a horizontal line, the height of which can be defined as the monetary factor, namely,

$$w_1\theta_1 + w_2(\theta_2 - \hat{q}_2) \qquad \text{for country 1,}$$

$$w_1(\theta_1 + \hat{q}_2) + w_2\theta_2 \qquad \text{for country 2.}$$

Under flexible exchange rates, each country can choose its own money supply, so that only its rate of monetary expansion comes into the picture. In other words, there is a self-correcting mechanism in the exchange rate market to achieve $q_2 = \theta_2 - \theta_1$, so that always the above monetary factor equals θ_i for country i respectively. Therefore, each country can independently decide on the height of equilibrium P and Q. Suppose country 2 expands its money supply. Then equilibrium shifts from Q to Q', and under the assumption of adaptive expectations, country 2 can enjoy a short-term prosperity indicated by a counterclock-wise motion. This expansion is not transmitted to country 1 except for some terms-of-trade effect that is outside our single commodity formulation.[7]

On the other hand, $\hat{q}_2$ is always equal to zero under fixed exchange rates, so that each country cannot choose an independent economic policy. The two equilibrium points P and Q must always lie on the same horizontal level. Monetary expansion in one country is necessarily leaked to the other; a temporary boom in one country is transmitted as a boom in the other.

In the world of managed floating, which is our main concern, monetary factors can diverge from one another by the amount equal to $\hat{q}_2$. The salient feature of this regime is that, in spite of the interdependence between monetary factors, each country can choose different monetary factors by changing its own rate of monetary expansion and, if the country has initiatives in determining the exchange rate, by changing the rate of exchange

---

[7] See, for the effect of the terms of trade, Hamada and Sakurai (1978).

depreciation as well. The effect of exchange rate depreciation works in opposite directions in the two countries.

Suppose country 2 starts depreciating by intervening in the exchange market so that $\hat{q}_2$ becomes positive. The monetary factor for country 2 increases, while the monetary factor for country 1 decreases. The new equilibrium in country 2 shifts upward to Q', while that in country 1 shifts downward to P'. Thus the economy in country 2 experiences a prosperity depicted by a counterclock-wise motion from Q to Q', the economy in country 1 experiences a recession from P to P'. The horizontal gap PP' equals $w_2\hat{q}_2$ and the horizontal gap $Q'Q$ equals $w_1\hat{q}_2$. Therefore, both gaps add up to the value of $\hat{q}_2$. The smaller the scale w_2 of country 2 is, the larger is the relative weight of QQ' to PP'.

Depreciation of currency in country 2 may cause a chain of reaction due to the monetary interdependence between the two countries. If country 1 waits long enough, the economy will reach eventually to solution P that is less inflationary. But if country 1 is impatient, then it may appeal to expansionary monetary policy to push up P' slightly. Then this monetary policy will increase Q' a little further. The effect for the world as a whole will be more inflationary as compared with the initial situation.

By itself, depreciation of the currency of country 2 has no substantial effect on the average world price level, because inflationary effects in country 2 are offset by deflationary effects in country 1. If country 1 cannot endure the deflationary pressure by depreciation of currency 2, however, the induced monetary expansion by country 1 may leave some long-run effects on the average rate of world inflation. It is worth noting that this effect, due to interdependence, does not work when country 2 initially appeals to monetary policies rather than to a depreciation of its own currency.

Fluctuations in output in this model occur because the expected rate of inflation, which is formed adaptively, lags behind the actual rate of inflation in both countries. If the expectation is formed rationally, then the paths would be, on the average, vertical movements directly from Q to Q' and directly from P to P'. Again monetary factors loose their systematic influence on real phenomena. The picture of the world returns to those models discussed in previous sections. However, one must notice that the information requirement for rational expectations in a regime of managed floating is much stronger than in a closed model, or even stronger than in a regime of complete floating. Not only are individuals required to forecast correctly the rates of monetary expansion of both countries—this is in itself a rather strong assumption in the light of actual experiences of the world economy—but they are also required to forecast correctly future changes in exchange rates.

The above analysis reveals the short-run implications of the asymmetric nature of currency depreciation. Currency depreciation by one country affects that country in an equivalent fashion as a monetary expansion by the rest of the world, while it affects the rest of the world in a similar fashion as a monetary contraction by the home country.

VIII. THE POLITICAL ECONOMY OF INTERNATIONAL CONFRONTATIONS

The strategic approach to macroeconomic coordination naturally leads us to the interdisciplinary realm of politics and economics. The need for the political analysis of economic affairs as well as the need for economic treatment of political subjects in international relations is often advocated (e.g., Kindleberger 1970). There have been many attempts to integrate political approaches in a joint effort by political scientists and economists (e.g., Russett 1968, Bergsten and Krause 1975).

If we broaden our perspective to an area outside the monetary or macroeconomic conflicts, we find that works by Scitovsky (1942) and Johnson (1953) on tariffs and retaliation are pioneering analyses of the interdependence and strategic nature of trade conflicts. Mutual taxation of foreign investment incomes can also be formulated as a game, where the agreement to avoid double taxation helps the achievement of a contract curve situation (Hamada 1966). In the field of monetary relations, it is only recently that political or strategic aspects of confrontations in monetary policy and institution making are treated explicitly in a theoretical framework (Johnson 1972*b*, Cooper 1975, Aliber 1977*b*, Hamada 1977).

In earlier sections of this chapter we have argued that the structure of policy conflicts takes the form of the prisoner's dilemma. This structure of conflicts is also seen very frequently in the game of agreeing on the rule itself. Generally speaking, international monetary conflicts or confrontations can be regarded as a two-stage game: one is to agree on the rules of the game, and another is to play the policy based on one agreed rule of the game. Of course, these two stages are closely interrelated. The malfunctioning of the policy interplay based on a particular rule of the game may become incentives for the parties to change the rule itself. If one can change the benefit and cost structure of the policy game, then it may be possible to lead a noncooperative solution to be located near the contract curve. Or it may be possible and useful to change the structure of the pay-offs, so that countries are induced to agree on a better set of rules. In fact, this kind of approach is popular in peace research.

More than thirty years have passed since the publication of von Neumann's "Theory of Game and Economic Behaviour" (1944). Refinement in mathematical methodology of game theory has been made successfully, but useful applications to the actual economic problems seem to be less successful than was initially expected. It is in many problems on international economics, where the small number of participants and their interactions play a significant role, that strategic considerations seem to contribute more to the understanding of the nature of interdependence. Game theory may not help directly in solving actual conflicting situations or in prescribing an optimal strategy for each nation, but it certainly helps us to understand the structure of the benefit-cost relationships in conflicting situations and to design better rules of the game for the world as a whole. The more knowledge one obtains about the benefit and cost structure of international confrontations, the more and better ways one will find, we hope, to escape from the impasses of international confrontations.

REFERENCES

Aliber, R. Z. 1973. *National Preferences and the Scope for International Monetary Reform*, Essays in International Finance No. 101. International Financial Section, Princeton University. Princeton, New Jersey.

Aliber, R. Z., ed. 1974. *National Monetary Policies and the International Financial System*. Chicago: University of Chicago Press.

———. 1977*a*. *The Political Economy of Monetary Reform*. London: Macmillan & Co.

Aliber, R. Z. 1977*b*. "Monetary Rules and Monetary Reform." In Aliber (1977*a*).

Bergsten, C. F., and Krause, L. B., eds. 1975. *World Politics and International Economics*. Brookings Institution, Washington, D.C.

Cooper, R. N. 1968. *The Economics of Interdependence*. New York: McGraw–Hill.

———. 1969. "Macroeconomic Policy Adjustment in Interdependent Economies." *Quarterly Journal of Economics* 83 (1).

———. 1972. "Eurodollars, Reserve Dollars, and Asymmetrics in the International Monetary System." *Journal of International Economics* 2: 325–44.

———. 1975. "Prolegomena to the Choice of an International Monetary System." In Bergsten and Krause (1975).

De Grauwe, P. 1975. "The Interaction of Monetary Policies in a Group of European Countries." *Journal of International Economics* 5: 207–8.

———. 1977. "Monetary Interdependence among Major European Countries." In Aliber (1977*a*).

Dornbusch, R. 1973. "Devaluation, Money and Non-Traded Goods." *American Economic Review* 67 (5): 871–83.

Dornbusch, R., and Krugman, P. 1976. "Flexible Rates in the Short-Run." *Brookings Papers on Economic Activity* 3: 537–75.

Ethier, W. 1976. "Exchange Depreciation in the Adjustment Process." *The Economic Record* 52 (140): 443–61.

Fleming, J. M. 1962. "Domestic Financial Policies Under Fixed and Under Floating Exchange Rates." *International Monetary Fund Staff Papers* 9: 369–79.

Frenkel, J. A., and Johnson, H. G., eds. 1976. *The Monetary Approach to the Balance of Payments*. London: Allen & Unwin.

Hamada, K. 1966. "Strategic Aspects of the Taxation of Foreign Investment Income." *Quarterly Journal of Economics* 80 (3): 361–75.

———. 1974. "Alternative Exchange Rate Systems and the Interdependence of Monetary Policies." In Aliber (1974).

———. 1976. "A Strategic Analysis of Monetary Interdependence." *Journal of Political Economy* 84 (4).

———. 1977. "On the Political Economy of Monetary Integration: A Public Economics Approach." In Aliber (1977a).

Hamada, K., and Sakurai, M. 1978. "International Transmission of Stagflation Under Fixed and Flexible Exchange Rates." *Journal of Political Economy* (forthcoming).

Helliwell, J., and McRae, R. 1977. "The Interdependence of Monetary, Debt and Fiscal Policies in an International Setting." In Aliber (1977a).

Henderson, J. M. 1975. "Asymmetry in Quasi-Fixed Exchange-Rate System." *Journal of International Economics* 5 (2): 167–87.

Johnson, H. G. 1953. "Optimum Tariffs and Retaliation." *Review of Economic Studies* 21 (2), no. 55: 142–53. Reprinted in Johnson, H. G., *International Trade and Economic Growth*. London: Allen & Unwin, 1958.

———. 1972a. "The Monetary Approach to Balance of Payments Theory." Chap. 9 in Johnson, H. G., *Further Essays in Monetary Economics*. London: Allen & Unwin.

———. 1972b. "Political Economy Aspects of International Monetary Reform." *Journal of International Economics* 2.

Keynes, J. M. 1936. *The General Theory of Money, Interest and Employment*. London: Macmillan & Co.

Kindleberger, C. P. 1970. *Power and Money*. New York: Basic Books.

Komiya, R. 1974. "Economic Growth and the Balance of Payments: A Monetary Approach." *Journal of Political Economy* 82 (3): 443–68.

Krueger, A. O. 1977. "Current Account Targets and Managed Floating." Chap. 3 of Aliber (1977a).

Laursen, S., and Metzler, L. A. 1950. "Flexible Exchange Rates and the Theory of Employment." 32 (4): 281–99.

Lucas, R. E. 1972. "Expectations and the Neutrality of Money." *Journal of Economic Theory* 4.

Luce, D., and Raiffa, H. 1957. *Games and Decisions*. New York: John Wiley & Sons.

McKinnon, R. I. 1974. "A Tripartite Agreement or a Limping Dollar Standard?" In *Essays in International Finance*. Princeton, N.J.: International Financial Section, Princeton University Press.

Meade, J. E. 1951. *The Theory of International Economic Policy*. Vol. I: *The Balance of Payments*. London: Oxford University Press.

Mundell, R. A. 1962. "The Appropriate Use of Monetary and Fiscal Policy under Fixed Exchange Rates." *International Monetary Fund Staff Papers* 9: 70–79. Reprinted as chap. 16, in Mundell (1968).

———. 1963. "Capital Mobility and Stabilization Policy under Fixed and Flexible Exchange Rates." *Canadian Journal of Economics and Political Science* 29: 475–85.

————. 1968. *International Economics.* New York: Macmillan Co.

————. 1972. *Monetary Theory: Inflation, Interest, and Growth in the World Economy.* Pacific Palisades, Calif.: Goodyear.

Mussa, M. 1976. "The Exchange Rate, the Balance of Payments and Monetary and Fiscal Policy under a Regime of Controlled Floating." *The Scandinavian Journal of Economics* 17 (2): 229–48.

————. 1978. "Macroeconomic Interdependence and the Exchange Rate Regime." Chapter 5 in this book.

von Neumann, J., and Morgenstern, O. 1944. *Theory of Games and Economic Behaviour.* New Jersey: Princeton University Press.

Niehans, J. 1968. "Monetary and Fiscal Policies in Open Economies under Fixed Exchange Rates: An Optimizing Approach." *Journal of Political Economy* 76, no. 4, Pt. 2: 893–943.

Olson, M., Jr. 1965. *The Logic of Collective Action: Public Goods and Theory of Groups.* Harvard Economic Studies, Vol. 124. Cambridge, Mass.: Harvard University Press.

Parkin, M. 1977. "World Inflation, International Relative Prices and Monetary Equilibrium under Fixed Exchange Rates." In Aliber (1977*a*).

Russett, B. M. ed. 1968. *Economic Theory of International Politics.* Chicago: Markham.

Sargent, T. J., and Wallace, N. 1975. "Rational Expectations, the Optimal Monetary Instrument and the Optimal Money Supply Rule." *Journal of Political Economy* 83 (2).

Scitovsky, T. 1942. "A Reconsideration of the Theory of Tariffs." *Review of Economic Studies* 9 (2): 89–110; reprinted in American Economic Association *Readings in the Theory of International Trade.* Homewood, Illinois: Richard D. Irwin, 1950.

Swoboda, A. K., and Dornbusch, R. 1973. "Adjustment, Policy, and Monetary Equilibrium in a Two-Country Model." In Connolly, M. B. & Swoboda, A. K. eds., *International Trade and Money.* London: Allen & Unwin.

Tinbergen, J. 1952. *On the Theory of Economic Policy.* Amsterdam: North-Holland.

Tsiang, S. C. 1975. "The Dynamics of International Capital Flows and Internal and External Balance." *Quarterly Journal of Economics* 89 (2): 195–214.

CHAPTER TEN

Problems and Prospects for the World Economy: Round-Table

Discussants: RICHARD N. COOPER, RONALD I. McKINNON, FRANCO
MODIGLIANI, ROBERT A. MUNDELL, AND HENRY C. WALLICH

RICHARD N. COOPER: From the point of view of a policy-maker, there are
several characteristics of the world economy at the present time that stand
out. First, we are in the fourth year of a world recession. While it is true
that in this country things are on the rise again and unemployment is
declining, this is not the global condition; indeed, in Europe, general
unemployment is still rising, not falling. Second, there are extremely diverse
experiences around the world with respect to both inflation and growth.
Inflation rates range from a low of perhaps 2½ percent to highs of 80 to
90 percent, with a bunching around 10 percent and another bunching
between 20 and 30 percent. The third characteristic of the world economy
is that there are very large deficits in current accounts corresponding to the
large surpluses of the Persian Gulf countries. Moreover, the cumulation of
these deficits since 1974 has left a large burden of external debt.

One of the consequences of these diverse circumstances is that protectionist sentiments are gaining force. Another consequence is that, in many
semi-industrialized countries and in a number of the less-developed countries there is a degree of financial precariousness that is much more widespread than at any time since at least 1950. What happened was that a
number of countries took conscious and, I think, rational decisions to ride
out the recession. They chose not to experience it in 1974–75, but to
borrow abroad instead, to maintain growth and domestic demand, and
external debt rose accordingly. They took a gamble that I think was
rational and that, indeed, was very helpful from the point of view of the
world economy as a whole, because they helped to limit the extent of the
downturn. But it is a gamble that they essentially lost. The recession was
much sharper and much longer than was anticipated at the time, and now

these countries face serious decisions as to how much to retrench and how to accomplish it—partly through aggregate demand, partly through import constraints, partly in some cases through export schemes. While it is the countries that have had inadequate, inappropriate domestic economic policies that come to the fore as the identifiable problems, there are a number of countries right behind them who did not pursue inappropriate policies although, ex post, these policies have created problems.

What can be done? I'll mention here the kind of framework under which the U.S. government is operating. The first remedy is to pursue economic expansion. There is general agreement that it is desirable both domestically and internationally to have an expansionist policy, although one that is not so rapid that it triggers inflationary expectations. But there are substantial differences in judgment concerning how much expansion can be endured without triggering substantial increases in inflationary expectations. Germany and Japan are the other two countries that are in strong positions financially. They also happen to be, apart from the Soviet Union, the second and third largest economies in the world. Thus, the United States, Germany, and Japan together set the macroeconomic environment in which the other countries operate. It has been part of the U.S. strategy to bring this point to the attention of the German and Japanese governments. Second, the U.S. government supports the Witteveen proposal for a major increase in the International Monetary Fund's capacity for global financing. There are two problems here. First, the Witteveen facility is on such a small scale that official financing may still be inadequate, not only for direct financing but, more importantly, as the ultimate backstop for the continued private bank lending that will have to carry, in the end, 80 percent of the so-called recycling. The second problem concerns the conditions that the IMF will lay down for the use of its credit. Here the IMF should take more of a global point of view, since the corrective actions appropriate to each country individually do not necessarily lead to balance in the world economy.

In the area of trade, the industrial countries have pledged not to use trade restrictions under the present circumstances, and negotiations are taking place to reduce the existing trade barriers. It may seem paradoxical, in a period of rising protectionism, to set in motion negotiations for a major reduction in trade barriers. But it should be kept in mind that the lead time on internationally agreed changes in policy is long, similar to the long lead times on major investments in the private sector. We are now negotiating, not for the trade regime next year or the year after, but for the trade regime beyond 1985. By that time, presumably, the world will be back to full employment and protectionism will have abated. Moreover, to negotiate now, even while we are fending off protectionist pressures, serves to remind us all where our real long-term interests lie, namely, in a liberal world-trading system.

In the long run, the energy-induced imbalances in payments will be eliminated by growing import demand in the OPEC countries. Indeed, many OPEC countries are already spending their higher oil revenues fully. This long run will be very far off, however, if energy demands in the industrialized countries grow more rapidly than OPEC production is likely to, resulting in a continuing rise in oil prices. Once again, the lead times in adjusting our own behavior to changed economic circumstances, such as higher oil prices, is substantial. We, therefore, need to begin now to cut back on our energy consumption and to stimulate non-OPEC energy supplies. This will serve not only to reduce the vulnerability of the major industrialized countries to disruptions in oil supplies coming from the Persian Gulf, but will also serve to avoid major financial disruptions to the world economy in the next decade.

RONALD I. McKINNON: There are two major issues I would like to address. First, to what extent are we still on a dollar standard since the advent of floating exchange rates in 1973? Second, does the large Japanese trade surplus in 1976 and 1977 imply that the yen is undervalued so that official policies should be designed to force an appreciation?

Under fixed exchange rates in the 1950s and 1960s, the world was on a dollar standard in a strong form. Because each central bank pegged its currency to the U.S. dollar, national price levels for tradable goods were aligned with dollar prices in the United States and, concomitantly, were aligned with each other. Because this pegging was done through purchases and sales of domestic base money for dollars by each national monetary authority, the nominal money supplies in all countries but the United States were endogenously determined. In contrast, the influence of international payments on the U.S. monetary base was sterilized because foreign central banks quickly converted any monetary dollar assets (e.g., checking accounts with commercial banks or the Federal Reserve) into nonmonetary debt (U.S. Treasury bills and bonds). And, in war-torn Europe and Japan, from the Marshall Plan onward to the late 1960s, this monetary dependence was quite advantageous in maintaining domestic financial stability when such a crutch was needed.

Since 1973 these strong links among the domestic monetary systems of the major industrial economies have been severed. I shall argue, however, that the world is still on a dollar standard in a "weak" form. Moreover, preserving this weak form is essential if international trade in goods and services is to continue to be monetized and multilateral in nature, rather than bartered and bilateral. What then are the essentials of the current monetary order?

Among the 150 or so countries that trade, only about 15 or 20 currencies are used by merchants and manufacturers. Among capitalist and less-developed economies, these 15 or 20 currencies are used directly for invoicing and as a means of payment. Among the socialist economies of Eastern Europe and Asia, these few currencies serve as a *numéraire* to establish relative commodity values and so function as units of account. These are the convertible currencies of the major nonsocialist industrial countries of Western Europe, North America, and Japan. Although most countries in the world have inconvertible currencies, their trade depends heavily on using convertible currencies provided by others. Preserving free international convertibility among a few major national monies is a cornerstone of the present order.

But the U.S. dollar plays a singular additional role as interbank money, both for historical reasons and because American exchange controls on both trade and capital account are absent. This key interbank role has two facets. The U.S. dollar is the vehicle currency in spot and forward exchange transactions across any pair of other currencies, and this vehicle role shows up in the continued dominance of the dollar in Euro-currency transacting, which is mainly interbank. Second, central banks continue to intervene heavily in the foreign exchange markets mainly by buying or selling dollars in order to influence the values of their own currencies. Under floating rates, the U.S. dollar still functions as the principal intervention or "N^{th}" currency in the system. To avoid conflict among central banks in setting exchange rates, therefore, the U.S. government is still strongly advised to remain passive in the foreign exchange markets. If defense of the international value of the dollar seems warranted, internal adjustment in the rate of expansion of the American monetary base is the first best policy.

How does this principle of American passivity square with the recent imbroglio between the United States and Japan over the undervaluation of the Japanese yen? First, Germany and Japan are probably the only two trading countries sufficiently large for the United States to worry about whether their exchange rates are correctly specified. Even then, the American government should be extremely cautious in violating the passivity principle to give strongly worded advice. Second, some rough purchasing power parity calculation is a better indication of the correct alignment between the yen and the dollar than the state of trade balance between the two countries—which will fluctuate from one year to the next. Indeed, in this particular case, there is strong reason to believe that the large Japanese trade surplus does not arise from currency disalignment.

Consider instead an absorption approach to the Japanese balance of trade. In the postwar period, Japan has had the most remarkable internal savings capacity (as a proportion of GNP)—perhaps twice as high as its nearest industrial rival. But from the world recession of 1975, the increased price of energy, and increased environmentalist pressure, the long-sustained

Japanese investment boom came to an end and remained subdued in 1976 and 1977. The flow of internal savings continued, however, and now shows up as a means of finance for the large trade surplus. Uncomfortable although this surplus may be, it provides no evidence of currency disalignment. Indeed, a major appreciation of the yen could well depress private investment in Japan even further, and thus cause an even larger trade surplus.

On the other side of the coin, we have massive dissaving in the United States: a very large public sector deficit, even at an advanced stage of cyclical expansion. The appropriate adjustment is to reduce the fiscal deficit in the United States and to increase investment and/or government expenditures in Japan. But there is no justification for abandoning the passivity principle in the setting of exchange rates to force the Japanese to appreciate.

FRANCO MODIGLIANI: In reviewing the issues on international economic policies that loom most important at present, I feel that recent experience suggests cautiousness and humility. Since the late sixties we have been going through a sequence of crises, and great issues have come and gone with incredible rapidity. I would therefore not be surprised if those issues that right now seem to me of great and lasting importance will have disappeared or have been replaced by others yet more urgent before one can turn the page. Subject to these qualifications, I feel that the most pressing and momentous issue for international economic policy still centers on a cooperative approach to the financing of the oil deficits and the related problem of stagflation.

Some may hold that the financing of the oil deficits is not, and never was, a problem for economic policy, since it is, and should be, taken care of by private markets. There is no question that the private markets have done a good deal in financing unprecedented movements of capital, and what they have done is probably more and better than many have anticipated. Yet I agree with Cooper that they have not done, as they could hardly be expected to, an altogether adequate job. Indeed, in my view, the fact that after four years we are still contending with the problem of world-wide stagflation can be traced, at least in part, to the fact that the oil problem was not handled with adequate international cooperation, involving the coordination of domestic policies and international capital movements.

To justify this contention, let us first ask ourselves how the oil problem should have been handled. The quadrupling of the price of oil by shifting income to a group of countries having, as a whole, an exceptionally high propensity to save, had the effect of raising the propensity to save of the world as a whole. Such an increase, as we know, provides a valuable opportunity for increased capital formation. But we also know that except under conditions of complete price flexibility and a great rapidity of responses an increase in saving does not lead automatically to higher investment, without appropriate monetary and credit policies. And if it does not lead to higher investment, then it has the potential for serious deflationary effects. In the case of the oil episode, the problem was further complicated by the fact that the higher saving was largely concentrated in countries that were not in a position to increase investment promptly, so that translating the additional saving in some countries into additional investments in others required large capital movements. And, finally, the difficulties were compounded by the fact that the increase in saving was achieved by a redistribution of income, which was bound to create difficulties and inflationary pressures.

Basically, to turn the oil surpluses and incremental savings into incremental investment instead of an engine of deflation, the importing countries should have adopted policies permitting the loss of real income, due to the worsened terms of trade, to result in a reduction of consumption. The resources released thereby, which could not be used to produce more exports to pay for the larger value of imports, should then have been channeled toward increased investments. Since this policy would have left absorption unchanged, it would have left a deficit in the balance of trade to be financed. A coordinated management of the oil surpluses would have provided an incentive for countries to pursue the above policy by making credit readily available to them. Such an approach, in addition to increasing capital formation, would have facilitated the maintenance of income by largely eliminating the stigma attached to deficits, and accumulating foreign debts, both from the point of view of the lender and of the borrower. The rise in debt would in fact have been matched by a corresponding accumulation of physical capital, providing the means for servicing the debt.

Let me note in passing that one of the serious difficulties these policies might have encountered in these days of rampant monetarism is that they would have required a policy of low interest rates and corresponding monetary expansion. This consideration, I suggest, may explain in part the fact that most countries responded to the deflationary impact of the oil deficits by policies encouraging consumption and government expenditure, with the result that those incremental savings that were not wasted in lower output were absorbed into higher government deficits. It is indeed an irony of these times that conservatives-monetarists turn to fiscal policy to support income, while the nonmonetarists favor first the traditional remedy to depression, namely, an expansionary monetary policy.

As things developed, many countries with severe balance-of-payment problems deriving from oil have been under severe pressures to hold down income in order to contain trade deficits. This endeavor was motivated in part by a concern for mounting deficits seen as a burden on the future. In part, it reflected the fact that mounting debts frequently led to an impossibility of defending the exchange rate and thus to devaluation and resulting inflation—an important mechanism of stagflation. Finally, those countries that found it necessary or desirable to have recourse to the International Monetary Fund to secure part of their financing were generally required to reduce and eliminate their deficit as a condition of the loan. The pressure toward deflationary policy has, of course, also been reinforced by the fact that those countries that were best in a position to expand their output and take their share of unavoidable deficits, such as the United States, Germany, and Japan, have had in fact halting and sluggish recoveries accompanied by sizable surpluses—with the notable recent exception of the United States.

In my view, there is still a need for a coordinated approach to the allocation and financing of deficits. For even though the flow of the deficit is decreasing, the stocks are still mounting. Similarly, there is more than ever a need for a coordinated expansion of the stronger economies; and with the mounting deficit in the United States, the burden must fall primarily on Japan and Germany. This expansion is a necessary condition to enable many other countries to expand their own output and employment without fear that increased deficits would generate further devaluation and inflationary pressure, or without further deterioration in the terms of trade, which would also create difficult problems and again threaten inflationary effects. Unfortunately, there are in these three countries, and not only in these countries, powerful forces with little interest in a solid recovery out of concern for the lingering inflation, and I must confess that I am not very optimistic for the immediate outlook, neither in terms of cooperation nor in terms of performance.

ROBERT A. MUNDELL: There are ten major problems or issues that will have important effects on the world economy in the next few years. The first is the problem of the world currency—what the world currency will be and what role gold will play in the system. It is quite absurd the way the BIS (Bank for International Settlements) and IMF calculate international reserves. They count French gold reserves at a price of about $140 or $150 an ounce, while they count American gold reserves at a price of $42 an ounce, and other reserves at other prices, and then they add the group up and call that international reserves. They must find some means of cleaning up the accounting, because it is terribly misleading when one looks at international reserves. If the SDR (Special Drawing Right) is going to become a world currency, we need to shift it from a unit of account of foreign exchange into a reserve asset. If gold is going to be put back into the world monetary system, then its price must be stabilized in terms of the SDR, or the dollar, or something else.

The second issue is the issue of currency unions and the impact they are going to have. While the dollar is still predominant, there are growing up different currency areas—the Snake, the Gulf currency area, and different alliances and links between one country and another. How these areas emerge in the next five years is going to have an important political impact. The third issue is that of optimum currency areas. Number 4 is the issue of the monetary fiscal policy mix. How, in expanding, is the mix of growth and inflation affected by the mix of monetary and fiscal policies? One answer is that the mix can be changed toward more growth and less inflation by tax reduction with tight money. But more work needs to be done on this question, because it is fundamental now in managing the recovery over the next few years. Issue number 5 involves the international management of the recovery; that is, which country should push ahead first, what would be the impact of one country or another expanding ahead of the others, and which of the instruments—monetary, fiscal, or exchange rate policy—would be effective in pushing those countries ahead. We have the three instruments of monetary policy, fiscal policy, and exchange rate policy to be assigned to the three problems of unemployment, inflation, and the problem of the composition of the balance of payments. The sixth issue is that of controlling the world money supply and the relation of that money supply to the Eurodollar market. National monetary controls may not be sufficient for control over the world money supply and inflation. Some IMF management of the world money supply via reserves or via some policy rules or guidelines is of high priority here.

Problem 7 concerns the international allocation of deficits—in particular, the problem of allocating the deficit corresponding to OPEC's $50 billion surplus. This leads into the eighth problem, which is the problem of international indebtedness and, in particular, the growing indebtedness of the LDCs (less developed countries). Issue number 9 is the problem of scarcity and the way in which it is going to affect world trade, the terms of trade of different countries, and the patterns of world power over the next ten years. We must move toward global models that are comprehensive, looking at the major parts of the world economy. The final issue concerns the shifting pattern of power in the world economy, the growth of different nations' patterns of production, and the emergence of new countries as the big powers. By the 1980s or 1990s, the big powers will be quite different.

HENRY C. WALLICH: The contribution that I understand I am to make to this discussion is to deal with major policy issues in the international area and with research arising out of these issues. I shall focus principally on foreign exchange matters. In suggesting research topics, I realize that I may expose myself to the response that I have missed the definitive article on the subject written by somebody present in body or in spirit at this meeting.

My first focus will be on the broad features of the present exchange rate regime. In the last few years, some of us, myself included, have been dragged kicking and screaming into the promised land of floating exchange rates. Now that we are there, some of us, including some of its earlier proponents, do not seem to be very happy. Floating has produced important benefits, especially for the United States. It has also produced some unexpected difficulties.

For the United States, floating has brought relief from the bugaboo of gold convertibility. The long agony of the 1960s, the often antieconomic efforts to defend an increasingly overvalued dollar, are over. Over, too, should be the days of the *n*-th country role for the United States. Where under the regime of the gold-dollar standard other countries pegged to the dollar and thereby, in the aggregate, determined the exchange rate of the dollar, today floating permits the international value of the dollar to be determined by market forces. That does not mean that the United States can determine the international value of the dollar. But neither can other countries determine that value, so long as there is a reasonably clean float.

The benefits that the United States derives from a floating system depend, therefore, at least in part on the cleanliness of the float. To the extent that other countries manage their float, while the United States remains passive, we are moving back toward the old world in which the nonreserve currency countries in the aggregate determine the exchange value of the reserve currency. Before we talk glibly about "managed floating," we should bear this in mind.

Countries with strong currencies also have been comfortable under the floating system. Currency appreciation has reduced their domestic inflation, and reduced inflation, in turn, has made for further appreciation. Several countries have been the beneficiaries of this virtuous circle.

Countries with weak currencies have been less comfortable. Downward flexibility of their currencies has made for an immediate impact of exchange rate depreciation upon domestic inflation and a feedback from domestic inflation on the exchange rate. These countries have lost the temporary benefit that, under fixed rates, came from being able to postpone the effects of domestic inflation upon the exchange rate, and hence the feedback via the exchange rate upon inflation. As a result, some of these countries have been unable to take advantage of the freedom of monetary policy that floating is supposed to provide. The inflationary consequences of an expansionary policy are too quick, particularly once the exchange market begins to form its expectations with a minimal lag. These countries, therefore, have had to rely on export-led expansion in the presence of high unemployment.

Floating thus has tended to polarize countries. The strong have become stronger, the weak have become weaker. This has made it necessary for the strong to help the weak by financing them.

The answer, of course, is not to try to fix rates by intervention. The resources for that are not available. Monetary authorities frequently under-estimate the volume of reserves that is needed to make a lasting impact on the exchange rate, because they think in terms of flows rather than stocks. The reserves that they can put into the market day by day may be large relative to the flows of the day and will make some impact upon the exchange rate, but they are small relative to the total stocks that can move. A lasting impact, therefore, is not likely. It would be an interesting topic for research to look into the volume of resources that would be needed for that kind of an effect.

By the same token, it might be interesting to examine the nature of equilibrium exchange rates under these conditions. I say that not because I believe that it would be possible to fix those rates in the market, but interesting guidance, nevertheless, could be provided both to monetary authorities and to the private sector.

Next I would like to turn to the particular situation in which we find ourselves currently. It is characterized by the large surpluses and deficits generated mainly by the high price of oil. An aggregate deficit for the oil-importing countries is inevitable, although its present size could be signifi-cantly reduced by better conservation and production policies in the United States. For the allocation of these deficits, i.e., for the destination of the corresponding capital imports, two principles are conceivable. Capital could flow where it is most productive. Alternatively, capital could flow to those countries that represent the best credit risk. The two groups of countries unfortunately are not identical, although there should be overlaps. In all probability, capital is more productive at the margin in the developing countries. It would, nevertheless, be interesting to research this seemingly plausible hypothesis more closely. Given the possibility of a capital shortage in the United States, together with the need for large investments in the energy sector, it is at least conceivable that capital might show a higher marginal return in the United States and other developed countries than in developing countries.

As an empirical fact, capital so far has flowed principally, but by no means exclusively, to the LDCs. Unfortunately, it has served there not so much to increase capital formation as to finance consumption, mainly in the form of higher priced oil imports. Most LDCs have at best maintained their rate of capital formation. But the ability of the LDCs to add to their debt is slowing down. They may in future be limited to a growth rate of foreign debt that does not exceed the growth rate of their nominal GNP, or at best that of their exports. In that case, the burden of the deficits would have to be assumed increasingly by the developed countries. It seems peculiar to see the United States become a capital importer, but that may be the wave of the immediate future.

The present large current account deficit of the United States may be a reflection of this shift of deficits from LDCs to developed countries. But surely that is not the whole of the story. The U.S. deficit is at least in part a cyclical phenomenon. The United States is ahead of other industrial countries in cyclical phase. It would be interesting to examine to what extent that is the case, and I recommend it as a topic for research. One's views concerning the future of the dollar would be importantly influenced by a judgment on that point.

Today, discussion of the U.S. deficit and the value of the dollar suffers from a certain inconsistency. Some observers who are greatly concerned about the size of the deficit are likewise concerned about the threat to the dollar. Under a floating system, the answer to a structural deficit, of course, would have to be a decline in the value of the currency. If one is concerned about such a decline and its consequences, one had better go slow in claiming that the deficit is not sustainable, or else find an alternative way of dealing with it. There are two good approaches that immediately commend themselves: to economize on the use of oil, and to hold down inflation.

In order to evaluate the condition of the dollar, it is helpful to go back to the principles prevailing under the old Bretton Woods system. Under that system, a devaluation was permissible only in case of fundamental disequilibrium. A cyclical disequilibrium was to be ridden out, with the help of reserves, of borrowing from the International Monetary Fund and other sources, and of balance-of-payments adjustment measures, including fiscal and monetary policy. It seems most unlikely to me that, if the Bretton Woods system were still in effect, a fundamental disequilibrium of the dollar would be diagnosed today. Under the floating exchange rate system, we have one more degree of freedom—a temporary exchange rate movement. An increase in the supply of dollars to the rest of the world, which must somehow be held by private or official holders, puts downward pressure on the dollar rate. Willingness to hold these additional dollars can be created both by the prospect of future appreciation and by a rise in interest rates. In effect, both incentives have been offered to foreign dollar holders as the exchange rate declined while interest rates rose. The fact that oil-exporting countries must place their surpluses somewhere has the effect, of course, of increasing the demand for many currencies, including the dollar, and thus of minimizing the need for exchange rate or interest rate attractions.

We should be cautious in expecting too much from exchange rate movements as a means of adjusting current account imbalances. One must fear that our experience may parallel what we have learned about the effect of monetary policy actions. In the latter area, we have discovered that monetary policy effects are achieved with a considerable lag and that the effects, when they occur, may no longer be what currently is needed. Exchange rate changes achieve their effects on current account balances likewise with a long lag. Nobody can be sure whether one or two years hence, when the effects of exchange rate movements taking place today will have worked themselves out, these effects will still contribute to payments equilibrium.

At the same time, we should not underestimate the costs of exchange rate movements. Here, I suspect, our experience will parallel what we have learned in the domestic area about the problems of inflation. Most of us have come away from the position, fashionable years ago, that inflation did not matter because it was a monetary, not a real, phenomenon. We have seen that the real effects can be severe. Today there is a temptation to think that international imbalances can easily and painlessly be cured through exchange rate movements. I fear we shall learn, if we have not already done so, that these exchange rate movements are not costless. They create inflationary pressures in the depreciating country and protectionist pressure in the appreciating country. They contribute to uncertainty and then slow down investment. Once more, the answer is not a futile attempt to peg exchange rates. Rather, if we want to avoid costly and risky fluctuations in exchange rates, the answer is a steady and firm course of domestic fiscal and monetary policy that creates stable expectations and over time brings down inflation.

Index of Names

Library of Congress Cataloging in Publication Data

Main entry under title:
International economic policy.

"Prepared for the Wingspread III Conference on International Economic Policy: An Assessment of Theory and Evidence, Racine, Wisconsin, July 27–30, 1977, with subsequent revisions for publication."
Includes index.
1. International economic relations—Congresses. I. Dornbusch, Rudiger. II. Frenkel, Jacob A.

HF1411.151717   382.1   78–8423
ISBN 0–8018–2132–0   ISBN 0–8018–2133–9 pbk.